
25.	Азово-Черноморский край		2000	13000
26.	Дальне-Восточный край			00
27.	Западно-Сибирский край			00
28.	Красноярский край			50
29.	Орджоникидзевский край	1000	4000	5000
30.	Восточно-Сибирский край	1000	4000	5000
31.	Воронежская область	1000	3500	4500
32.	Горьковская область	1000	3500	4500
33.	Западная область	1000	5000	6000
34.	Ивановская область	750	2000	2750
35.	Калининская область	1000	3000	4000
36.	Курская область	1000	3000	4000
37.	Куйбышевская область	1000	4000	5000
38.	Кировская область	500	1500	2000
39.	Ленинградская область	4000	10000	14000
40.	Московская область	5000	30000	35000
41.	Омская область	1000	2500	3500
42.	Оренбургская область	1500	3000	4500
43.	Саратовская область	1000	2000	3000
44.	Сталинградская область	1000	3000	4000
45.	Свердловская область	4000	6000	10000
46.	Северная область	750	2000	2750
47.	Челябинская область	1500	4500	6000
48.	Ярославская область	750	1250	2000

УКРАИНСКАЯ ССР

1.	Харьковская область	1500	4000	5500
2.	Киевская область	2000	3500	5500
3.	Винницкая область	1000	3000	4000

D1539005

THE STATE
WITHIN A STATE

THE STATE
WITHIN A STATE

*The KGB and Its Hold on Russia—
Past, Present, and Future*

YEVGENIA ALBATS

Translated from the Russian by
CATHERINE A. FITZPATRICK

FARRAR · STRAUS · GIROUX
New York

Copyright © 1994 by Farrar, Straus and Giroux
ALL RIGHTS RESERVED
A version of this book was originally published in Russian
under the title *Mina zamedlennogo deystviya*
Russian edition copyright Yevgenia Albats, Moscow, 1992
Published simultaneously in Canada by HarperCollins*CanadaLtd*
Designed by Tere LoPrete
First edition, 1994

Library of Congress Cataloging-in-Publication Data
Al 'baīs, Evgeniīa.
[Mina zamedlennogo deīstviīa. English]
The state within a state : the KGB and its hold on Russia—past,
present, and future / Yevgenia Albats ; translated by Catherine
Fitzpatrick.—1st ed.
p.   cm.
Contains selected documents from archives of the KGB.
Includes bibliographical references and index.
1. Soviet Union.   Komitet gosudarstvennoĭ bezopasnosti—History.
2. Russia (Federation). Ministerstvo bezopasnosti—History.
3. Soviet Union—Politics and government—1985–1991. 4 Soviet
Union—Union—History—Attempted coup, 1991. I. Title.
JN6529.I6A4313   1994   94-10898   CIP
947—dc20

For permission to reprint the charts on pages 27–28 from *Intelligence and National Security*, the author would like to thank Frank Cass & Co. Ltd, Gainsborough House, London:

Desmond Ball and Robert Windren, "Soviet Signals Intelligence (Sigint): Organization and Management," *Intelligence and National Security*, vol. iv (1989), no. 4, and Gordievsky.

To Rika and Lev Razgon, who together spent a total of thirty-one years in Stalin's labor camps and exile.

Translator's Note

The English translation of *The State within a State* was prepared from the original Russian book by Yevgenia Albats entitled *Mina zamedlennogo deystviya: politicheskiy portret KGB SSSR* [Time Bomb: A Political Portrait of the USSR KGB] (Moscow: Russlit, 1992), as well as new chapters, revisions, and additions written by the author that constitute approximately a third of the present book. These include updates on the various recent reforms of the KGB and an exclusive interview with Russian security chief Nikolai Golushko shortly before he was forced to resign in 1994 after a confrontation with Yeltsin.

Since the August 1991 coup, the Soviet (then Russian) secret police organization has undergone a number of reforms. Throughout the book, the author uses the name "KGB" to refer to the secret police of the modern Soviet period as well as the post-coup Russian era, a usage reflecting current Russian idiom as well as the uncertainty of some of the reforms despite name changes. ("Cheka," the original name of the Bolshevik secret police still in use today, is interchangeable with "KGB.")

In the interests of making the text as readable as possible, the Russian transliteration system has been simplified. The soft and hard signs (often represented by an apostrophe) have been removed. Stressed "e" is rendered as "yo." To avoid the clutter of a transliteration like *zamedlyennogo*, "ye" is in most cases rendered as "e" except when needed to assist in pronunciation, e.g., stressed diphthongs in names such as Andr*ey*ev. "Yy" and "iy" are shortened to "y." The second name or patronymic has been eliminated except in direct speech or quotations. Lengthy terms like "the Politburo of the Central Committee of the Party" are shortened ("the Politburo," and so on).

The original Russian book contained an appendix of documents discovered by the author in recently opened KGB or Party archives, as well as materials obtained from relevant informed persons. Many of these documents are included in the text throughout the book, but regrettably, owing to space considerations, in some instances they had to be excerpted. Copies of the full text of the originals, including materials from the Politburo's top secret Special File, have been shown to the editors.

Because the author interviewed many security officials who are still on active duty, a number of sources could not be named. Further, documents obtained from these individuals or others outside the official archives could not be cited, although they are known by the author to be reliable.

Translator's explanations are contained in footnotes. All bracketed comments in the narrative or within the text of quoted documents are from the author, and italicized words are intended to indicate the author's emphasis.

Because of the complexity of the subject and the need for continuous updating of material from the turbulent Russian scene, the translation of *The State within a State* was very much a collaborative effort. I am grateful to Yevgenia Albats for her close reading of the translation and for her suggestions; to Sara Bershtel, senior editor at Farrar, Straus and Giroux, for her guidance and considerable care and patience in editing the book; to Ariel Kaminer for fine-honed attention to both content and style; and to Leslie Auerbach for her diligent and graceful revision of the translation. Finally, we are indebted to Roger Straus, president of Farrar, Straus and Giroux, for his forbearance.

Had Russia's upheavals and constant changes come to an end,

our labors would have been easier. But, given Russia's traumatic history and its current troubled climate, we can only welcome every revision of the age-old story of the secret police as a positive sign of continued liberty and transformation.

CATHERINE A. FITZPATRICK

Contents

THE STATE
WITHIN A STATE

To the Reader

I began this book in the spring of 1991. My article "Time Bomb: A Political Portrait of the KGB" had just appeared in the Soviet newspaper *Moscow News*, and had provoked a huge scandal and incredible fury in Party and KGB circles.

In the article, I argued what was to become the central theme of this book, although many people at the time found it impossible to believe: even as the Soviet regime was liberalizing and softening, even as cries of perestroika and glasnost filled the air, the KGB was transforming itself from an instrument of state power to a state power in its own right.

How could that be, my opponents objected. After all, they've stopped putting people in prison. The Iron Curtain has been lifted. They've started letting people travel abroad. There was a limited validity to these objections—but the truth was, they'd never stopped putting people in jail. Even more to the point, the KGB had seized the unique opportunity afforded by the political and economic chaos of the perestroika and glasnost years to acquire more power than it had possessed since the Stalin era. Time eventually would prove my analysis correct.

This book was to have ended with a rather unhappy prognosis: The Committee for State Security, the KGB,* would not remain

---

* The Russian acronym for *Komitet gosudarstvennoy bezopasnosti*, Committee for State Security—Trans.

behind the scenes forever. Inevitably, it would have to bid for the chief role in the drama unfolding in the USSR—and soon. (After all, the KGB had been a very active participant in developing the scenario.)

Then came the August 1991 coup, and suddenly, it seemed I was wrong. The KGB had made its bid for power, and had lost.

The first weeks after the bizarrely amateurish coup were filled with hope: perhaps, at last, the monster had been destroyed. As Mikhail Gorbachev stepped off the plane from Foros, the resort town on the Black Sea where he had been kept under house arrest, he declared: "There will no longer be a state within a state." Most certainly, the "state within a state" to which he referred was the KGB.

"The KGB Has Been Destroyed," "The KGB Is Dead," proclaimed headlines in our papers. The Western press was even more enthusiastic: perestroika, glasnost, and "new thought" apparently had lost their currency as hot topics, and it was time to create a new legend.

Meanwhile, the KGB weathered the general chaos and panic of the first months after the coup. It survived the collapse of the Soviet Union, the rise of people who declared themselves democrats, even the toppling of the enormous statue of its founder, Felix Dzerzhinsky, in Lubyanka Square. It survived; and it thrived.

Indeed, it gained strength. The KGB has managed to convince the current government that the new Russia cannot be built without the complicity of the old political police (whatever they choose to call themselves). Since August 1991, the KGB has changed its name no fewer than seven times. For a while, the "Ministry of Security (MB) of the Russian Republic" seemed likely to stick, but Yeltsin's December 21, 1993, announcement that he was again reforming (and renaming) state security has left matters up in the air. But while Western correspondents worry about keeping up with those changes, for the Russians the KGB is still the KGB. I have chosen for the most part to take the same approach, both to avoid unnecessary confusion and to emphasize the fact that the former political police haven't gone anywhere—they are still very much present.

The time bomb ticks on. Neither Yeltsin nor the democrats who surround him ever actually intended to mount a real minesweeping operation; they hadn't the nerve for it. Furthermore, in the months and years since the August 1991 coup, the situation has grown ever more explosive, as the secret government supports and manipulates the most reactionary political elements in our supposedly open society. Has history really taught us nothing?

I hope to God that I am mistaken. I hope to God.

Introduction

Shortly after my article appeared in *Moscow News*, where I was employed as a columnist, one of the chiefs of the KGB sent in a critical reply under the pseudonym Vyacheslav Artyomov. His real name was not one of the KGB's greater secrets: it was General Gurgenov, then deputy chief of KGB foreign intelligence.

The general's June 1991 article was not notable for originality or freshness. "You journalists all keep criticizing us, but we KGB officers have long since improved; we've gone through our own perestroika and have become decent, and, along with the country, we're moving from totalitarianism toward democracy." As for the organization's tragic past, which had cost the country tens of millions of innocent lives: Well, yes, the general admitted, the past was tragic.

"But what has that got to do with us? What are we supposed to repent of?" he asked in exasperation. The general had worked in the "organs"* for almost thirty years; and so, while it was true that he hadn't been present during the bloody purges of the thirties and forties, what about the thousands and thousands of lives crippled by the KGB in the 1960s, 1970s, and 1980s? It was as if General Petro Grigorenko—imprisoned for years in a psychiatric hospital for his dissident activities—had never existed; as if Yury

---

* Russians use the term "organs" to describe law enforcement agencies. The word is often used ironically, as a double entendre—Trans.

Galanskov, thirty-two-year-old poet and human rights activist, had not died in a labor camp in 1972, soon after writing: "Each of my days here is torment."[1] As if there had never been Anatoly Marchenko, who died in Chistopol Prison in 1986; or Andrei Sakharov, whose seven-year exile in Gorky was ended only in 1986 by Gorbachev's decree. As if poet and human rights activist Irina Ratushinskaya had not spent years incarcerated in labor camp No. ZhKh–385/3–4 (for "especially dangerous state criminals") or been stripped of her Soviet citizenship in 1987, years after perestroika supposedly had brought an end to such practices. As if the KGB's special Alpha Group had not, on the terrible night of January 12–13, 1991, killed fourteen citizens of Vilnius, crushed under tanks and caught in a hail of bullets.[2]

And yet, General Gurgenov's anger was directed at the journalists and political commentators who were, he wrote, falling all over each other to "tear the Chekists away from society, to force them to feel like outcasts, or, if you will, 'enemies of the people' in the era of perestroika."

I will come back to the subject of Chekists as outcasts. First, though, it's worth noting the general's casual invocation of the Cheka. The ancestor of the modern KGB, the Cheka—short for *Vse-Rossiyskaya chrezvychaynaya kommissiya*, All-Russian Extraordinary Commission—was founded in December 1917, and nearly drowned the fledgling Soviet republic in the blood of its people. Later, in 1934–41, the NKVD—*Narodnyy kommissariat vnutrennykh del*, the People's Commissariat for Internal Affairs—continued the tradition of genocide against its own citizens. In the interest of political legitimacy, the chiefs of the KGB, our general among them, take every opportunity to distance themselves from these organizations, insisting that the KGB is neither legal heir nor political successor to their brutal methods. Yet, as the general's article shows, he and his colleagues still refer to themselves with pride as "Chekists." Could we imagine today's German security agents publicly calling themselves "Gestapists"?

I know it's pointless to argue with "critics" from the KGB. As the saying goes, "We are people of different blood types." And I certainly wouldn't embroil myself in this right in the introduction to my book, were it not for a single sentence near the end of the general's article: "It sometimes seems to me that the appearance of all these articles and pamphlets about the KGB is the symptom of a persistent phobia, where the cause of fear is fear itself."

Are you saying, General, that *fear* motivates us journalists, and me in particular? Well, you're right, it is fear, you hit the nail on the head. And I can even tell you a thing or two about where that fear comes from.

When I first started interviewing current KGB employees and their predecessors from the days of Stalin (and you—that is, not you personally, General, but your colleagues—tried by every means possible to prevent my articles from being published), I experienced something like the fear children feel standing outside a dark, closed room. I knew I had to go in—my curiosity, my professional self-esteem pushed me forward—but I was frightened. What monsters were lurking in the dark corners behind the door?

To make a long story short, I braved the darkness and entered the room. I lit a match, brushed away the cobwebs, and carefully made my way through the millions of yellowing files that occupy its heart: the secret archives, the history that the organization has kept to itself through those many decades of secrecy. From the pages of those documents, the victims who by some miracle had survived the long years of Stalin's nightmare told me what the "valiant Chekists" of official propaganda had done to them. Next, I tracked down those valiant Chekists. As they joined me in that room, they assumed a variety of poses: some behaved with dignity, others obsequiously—what may I do for you, ma'am?—but they all talked and talked and talked. I listened, ceaselessly amazed at the regenerative capacity of the "organs of state security," their ability to adapt to new conditions, to double and multiply. I was amazed at their talent for turning anything, even the most pro- gressive changes in society, to their own advantage and to the disadvantage of everyone else. And in the presence of such virtuosity, I began to recognize, and see through, the masks the KGB wears today.

And after the Chekists? Then, those who had survived the Stalinist genocide came to my room. Do you know what I asked them, General? I asked them, How should I behave when they come to arrest me? What should I take with me? Should I have a little suitcase ready? What do women do to take care of themselves under prison conditions? How do I conquer my disgust? Thoroughly useful information, General, since fear of the unknown is always the worst. Which is why, as you know, surprise is the organs' favorite weapon.

Still later, some of today's KGB officers came to my room. They, too, had individual styles. Some of them looked around nervously for the tiny microphones they themselves so often had hidden in telephones or doorways or in the coats of people under surveillance. Are we being bugged? they asked. Others, Gen. Oleg Kalugin and Col. Vladimir Rubanov, for example, spoke frankly and gave me plenty of interesting background about KGB operations under Brezhnev, Andropov, Chernenko, and Gorbachev. But all of them, General, every single one of them, assured me that so long as the KGB continues to exist in this country, we can expect nothing good to happen.

And after I learned all that, General, I really did become afraid, and not just for myself—although I certainly do have an instinct for self-preservation. I was afraid for my little girl, afraid for her future, and for my relatives, friends, and colleagues. Forgive the pathos, but I was afraid for my long-suffering country, damned as it seems to be by all the gods.

That, General, is why I wrote this book. *Because I am afraid.*

The reader who expects from me a history of the Committee for State Security, or even a history of the KGB under perestroika, will be disappointed. As Western KGB watchers have noted, the true story can't be written until the KGB opens its archives, something it's in no hurry to do—it's scarcely about to embark on such a suicidal course of its own accord.

Still, here and there in various newspapers and magazines, some new data, a few facts, a few documents, have surfaced that do provide some opportunity for close analysis. In addition, over the past twenty years, some extremely interesting works about the KGB have appeared in the West. John Barron's *KGB*, Amy Knight's *The KGB: Police and Politics in the Soviet Union*, Christopher Andrew and Oleg Gordievsky's *KGB: The Inside Story*, and a number of other books provide considerable material for the interested reader, particularly on the KGB's activities outside the Soviet Union. They were a great help to me as well, and I am very grateful to the authors and their publishers.

My book, however, is not a scholarly work, nor is it written exclusively for Sovietologists or specialists on the KGB. This is a book for the general reader who is concerned about what is going on in a state that once occupied one-sixth of the planet, a book for people like myself, who are interested in the sad facts I was able to glean about my poor country.

I confess that I am obsessed with the subject. The general's article haunts me. I want readers to understand my obsession and thus, I hope, accept my somewhat, let us say, pointed and emotional style. For me, the KGB is not simply a fascinating research subject (although there's no question that it is that, hence the many extraordinary books devoted to it). For me, as for many of my fellow citizens, the KGB is a part of life—an inseparable part, alas, since I do not plan to leave the country (unless, of course, circumstances force me to do so).

And for me, the KGB means fear, and not just of telephones that periodically are tapped, or of patronizing warnings ("You'll go too far") passed along to me from above, or of anonymous letters containing threats.

For me, the KGB is also the fear felt by my grandfather before he put a gun to his head in the eleventh year of Soviet rule. And the fear felt by my great-uncle, who was shot at the peak of Stalinist terror, during the bloody year of 1937. And it is also the fear felt by my brave father, a Jew who in 1941 was working as a Soviet intelligence agent in Nazi-occupied territory. I recall the day during the Brezhnev era when he found me reading a *tamizdat** copy of Solzhenitsyn's *The First Circle*. "Don't bring any more of *that* home," my father begged. In those years, interest in such literature could easily have earned me a labor camp term.

"Genetic fear" was the term the KGB general used in his article. Yes, I'll admit it's genetic.

And for me, the KGB is also, and forever, the struggle against fear waged by Rika and Lev Razgonov, two people incredibly dear and close to me.

Now I must explain the dedication of my book.

·

Rika and Lev met each other in the northeast Russian city of Vozhael. It was the end of 1943, and Rika (or Revekka Efremovna Berg, according to her official dossier) was a senior clerk in the administrative office of the Ust-Vymlag Labor Camp complex, setting prisoners' work quotas. Lev—Lev Emmanuilovich Razgon—was a senior clerk at Ust-Vymlag Camp No. 1, thirty kilometers from Vozhael. The nearest civilization—Syktyvkar, the capital of the Komi Republic—was at least a hundred very rough kilometers away.

By 1943, both Rika and Lev were *volnyashki*, "freed people" whose labor camp sentences had come to an end. Rika, who had been arrested under Art. 58 (10–11), for "counterrevolutionary activity," was released in November 1942. Lev had been apprehended under Art. 58 (10–1), "counterrevolutionary agitation in peacetime." His "fiver" was to have been up in April 1943, but they tacked on another fiver while he was in labor camp. Then, by some miracle, they abolished the additional sentence, and at

---

* *Tamizdat*, literally, "published over there," the term used for books in the Russian language published abroad; as distinct from *samizdat*, "self-published," the term for works unofficially published within the Soviet Union—Trans.

the end of a dry, hot northern summer, he came out a free man.

This was "freedom" in the Soviet sense of the word, meaning that Rika and Lev were no longer confined to a labor camp or lined up for inspection every morning and escorted to work by guards. Now they walked to work themselves—although it was still the same work. That's essentially what being free meant: walking unescorted. They still didn't have regular identity papers (so-called internal passports), or the right to travel beyond the camp complex. In fact, they were *zeks* (*zek* is the Russian abbreviation for *zaklyuchyonuy*, prisoner) and yet not zeks; free, yet not free, something like perpetual exiles. The stamp in their papers, "detailed to the labor camp pending special orders," was what passed for "freedom."

Still, they were happy. Rika was unusually fortunate: the administration gave her her own little room—well, not quite a room, but a bit of space in a five-unit barracks on the bank of the Vislyana River. She had a pillow, a mattress cover, and something like a real outfit, a skirt and jacket that clever hands at the labor camp had made from the ski suit she'd been wearing on the November 1937 day when she was taken from her Moscow apartment on Krivoarbat Lane.

Every Saturday, Lev would walk the thirty kilometers from Labor Camp No. 1 to this damp, cold little dwelling. There, they celebrated their reunions, using their ration cards to get half a liter of rancid butter and some sour cabbage (there was almost as much hunger outside the camps as within). There, they enjoyed happiness and freedom—not the "freedom" the Soviet government allotted them, but the freedom that they, as young people, knew how to wrest from their crippled lives.

Lev Razgon himself chronicled his seventeen years in labor camp and exile in his book *Unimaginable*.[3] So let me say a bit more about Rika's life.

She was born in St. Petersburg in 1905, during the first Russian revolution, to the family of Efrem Berg, a Jewish machinist and professional revolutionary.

As one might expect, Berg had spent much of his life in exile and prison. So, when the monarchy fell in February 1917, Ida Savelyevna, Rika's mother, hoped the change would also bring an end to the crushing life of conspiracy and constant surveillance, the grueling years of sending food packages and making prison visits.

Unfortunately, Berg was not a Bolshevik; on the contrary, he was a top official of the right-wing Socialist Revolutionary Party, the Bolsheviks' main opposition. In June 1918, Berg's former comrades-at-arms from the fight against tsarism had him thrown in jail. It was a blow from which Rika's mother never recovered.

Rika, then fifteen, accompanied her mother, bringing warm clothing and food to her father as he awaited trial at the Gorokhovaya Street Prison. Thus began her acquaintance—at first mediated by her father, later all too direct—with the Soviet prison system. That acquaintance was to last right up to 1953, the year Stalin died, the year Rika turned forty-eight.

From the Gorokhovaya Street Prison in Petrograd (as St. Petersburg was then called) her father was sent to Butyrka in Moscow, and Rika was allowed to visit him every Sunday. Nineteen years later, when Rika herself was arrested and brought to Butyrka, she felt right at home. "I knew everything at Butyrka," she said.

Next, her father was moved to a prison in Suzdal, and Rika traveled there as well to visit him. Then came 1922, and the celebrated trial of right-wing Socialist Revolutionaries held in the Hall of Columns at the House of Trade Unions, with Pyatakov presiding and Krylenko, Lunacharsky, and Pokrovsky serving as attorneys for the prosecution. Relatives of the accused were seated close to the front. To the judge's question: "Do you admit you are guilty?" Efrem Berg replied, "I am guilty only of not opposing you fiercely enough. I will continue to fight in the future."

Berg was given five years. Two were spent in solitary confinement at Lubyanka, the rest in exile in Nagorny Dagestan, where Rika's mother died, and where Rika rounded out her political education by acquiring first-hand knowledge of exile life.

At this point, Berg's traces disappear. Apparently, he was moved from Dagestan, but where he was taken remains a secret, locked in the archives of the KGB. All that is known is that he was executed in September 1937. (Rika's efforts to obtain her father's files were fruitless; she never learned about his last days or where he was buried.)

By that time, Rika was herself already in Butyrka awaiting transfer to the labor camp at Mariisky. When they came for her, she wasn't afraid: she'd seen it coming ever since she'd resisted NKVD efforts to recruit her six months earlier. When they arrested her, she assumed that life as she'd known it was over. "*This* is forever," she thought; after all, she had her father's experience to go on.

But it was love I was going to write about—and what a love they shared, Rika and Lev. They broke all the rules just to see each other. When the authorities forbade Lev to go to Vozhael (depravity and debauchery were permissible, but love was a form of freedom, which could not be tolerated), Lev and Rika telephoned each other from their offices, talking and talking until the telephone operators grew tired of listening to their passionate outpourings.

The war ended in 1945. With considerable effort, Rika and Lev managed to obtain regular domestic passports—"emancipation from serfdom." But these bore a stamp forbidding them to reside in, or even travel to, Moscow, Leningrad, or some two hundred other cities in the Soviet Union.

They violated the regulations and made a visit to Moscow, which enabled Lev to get reacquainted with his daughter Natashka, who'd been only a year old when he was arrested. She lived with her grandmother, since Lev's first wife, Oksana, had died at the age of twenty-two in a transit prison without even reaching labor camp. No one was waiting for Rika in Moscow. Her sister, Anyechka, had died during the war, while being evacuated.

Shortly thereafter, Lev and Rika were permitted to leave labor camp for good. They settled in Moscow illegally, living with Lev's mother until a neighbor informed on them; after this, they made their way to Stavropol, a small town in the south of Russia. Life was difficult, and they often went hungry. Lev worked as a program officer in a cultural education office; Rika did typing. They had no money, but they made a fine life for themselves in a corner of a room that they rented from a nurse, sleeping behind a curtain on a narrow brown leatherette medical couch.

In March 1949, Rika was arrested again, this time as a "repeater" (she'd already had one prison sentence). The investigation was swift and simple. Soon enough, Rika was able to add a thing or two to her prison education. In 1937, for example, they'd allowed you to sit in your cell; by 1949, you could only sit down after lights out. In 1937, there'd been no stools; by 1949, some were provided, but they were screwed to the floor so you couldn't move them to lean against the wall or push them closer to the low prison table to keep your back from growing stiff as a board when you ate.

Of course, Rika's prison repertoire was already quite extensive. She knew they'd yank the elastic out of her underpants, but she also knew a way to roll them so that they wouldn't fall down. She knew they would take away her garters, but she knew how to keep her stockings up without them—and, indeed, how to get by without any underwear at all. (A sobbing woman, evidently from the upper classes, was brought in one day. "What's wrong?" asked Rika, turning toward her; the woman did not appear to have been beaten. "They took away my lingerie," the woman cried, her voice breaking. She pointed to her large breasts, now unsupported beneath her dress. "That's why you're crying?" laughed the hardened women in the cell. "Because they took away your lingerie? Here, they take away your life.")

Rika knew how to wash herself and her clothes in the prison baths, where there was only one tub of water for everyone. She knew how to use snow, when there was no water, to take care of—let's put it delicately—feminine hygiene. She always kept herself carefully groomed. She knew that any fish bones that landed in her soup should be saved, because they could serve as sewing needles, forbidden in prison. If there were no bones, she made needles out of matches, sharpening them on a chunk of sugar. She drew threads out of her own clothing. She knew how to choke down her disgust at drinking from the same mug as a woman with syphilis. She knew how to talk to the common criminals, and how to defend herself against the camp guards.

Lev faithfully waited on the long lines to bring her packages in prison. Letters were forbidden, but Lev outfoxed the prison guards, writing to her on the food itself. On the shell of a hard-boiled egg, he scratched the date of their labor camp wedding. To the guards, these were just numbers—people put all kinds of dates on eggs—but to Rika it was an eloquent memento of that day which said everything that people say to each other when they recall such moments.

On the bread rolls he used a nail to scratch a message—surely the guards wouldn't look at every roll? or at the comb?—for which Rika had an urgent need.

Rika couldn't even scratch such little messages to him; all she had was her signature on the package receipts. *Full name, patronymic, last name, date*, meant: Everything's fine; I received your little note: thank you, it made me so happy; I'm thinking of you, worrying about you; I miss you. On their anniversary, with no other way to send a message to Lev, she decided to quit smoking, and asked the guards to "tell him not to bring me any more cigarettes. Please tell him, I stopped smoking as of June 15; *since the fifteenth* I haven't smoked." One way or another, Rika and Lev made shift to survive.

In 1949, after six months in jail, Rika was sentenced to lifelong exile in Birilyusy, a little village in Krasnoyarsky Krai, Siberia. Rika wasn't surprised; she'd known from the day of her arrest that *this* was forever. It was Lev whose fate worried her.

Lev remained free for nearly a year. He even managed to travel to see Rika in Birilyusy and live for a month and a half in her tiny room "behind an enormous Russian stove" (as he described it in his book). In the evenings, they'd go out visiting; or they'd stay home, Rika would fry some fish, and they would savor one of their

"Birilyusy feasts." Together in their Siberian hideaway, they lived and loved and dreamed of their future life.

But before long, Lev was arrested. When, one Friday, the weekly telegram—Lev's confirmation that he was still free—did not arrive, Rika knew what to think. A few days later, she received a letter from Lev's landlady in Stavropol: "Lev's caught the same disease you had."

Rika's heart was heavy, but she'd always known that they would arrest Lev again sooner or later. She waited to hear where he would be exiled, and dreamed of how they might manage to be together there, how they might somehow persuade the "humane" Soviet government to give them permission to serve their sentences of eternal exile together.

But under Art. 58 (10), "counterrevolutionary agitation," Lev was sentenced to ten years of labor camp, not exile. When Rika learned of his sentence, she began to scream as she had never screamed in her life. She was certain that Lev could never survive another ten years in labor camp. And, given her sentence of eternal exile—even a brief absence was regarded as an attempt to escape, and punished by twenty-five years of hard labor—she knew she would never see her beloved again.

I cannot write this calmly. I try to fathom the agony of this woman who had fallen passionately in love amidst the nightmare of labor camp, who had managed to live happily and with dignity for almost six years despite inhuman surroundings, and now, at the age of forty-five, suddenly saw her life end yet again.

And how did Lev take it? During the interrogation, he shouted at his investigator: "I'll survive! I'll survive even labor camp, you can be sure of that! I'll read books, drink vodka, sleep with the hired nurses and doctors and even the wardens' wives! I'm forty-two years old, and when I get out I'll be fifty-two. I'll survive!" He went on shouting, but as a seasoned zek, he knew only too well what ten more years of labor camp would mean.

For five years, they wrote almost daily. Rika tore up all of Lev's letters after reading them—she didn't want them to be used as evidence at the next arrest or exile.

In 1953, Stalin died.

Rika returned to Moscow in 1954. Lev arrived a year later. They had nothing, no belongings at all, just thirty-one years of labor camp and exile between the two of them. When they registered their marriage, they didn't even have enough money for the *chetvertinka*, a quarter-liter bottle of vodka, to toast their formal union.

And then? Lev did some writing, Rika did some typing, and they raised Natashka. It was already too late for Rika to have her own children, although doctors had told her that God himself had created her for childbearing. (God was one thing, the Soviet government quite another.) They got a room, and then an apartment—twenty-eight square meters in all. Their everyday conversations were peppered with labor camp slang: "the rations," "the latrine." And wherever they were, they never left their key on the outside of the door, the memory of prisons and the wardens who locked them into their cells from outside was still too strong.

What else remained? Love, of course; and life—and then came perestroika, and Lev published *Unimaginable*, which for twenty years he had been writing "for the desk drawer." Suddenly Lev became famous. He and Rika went to Italy, England, France. Rika laughed: "I had to live to be eighty-three years old to make my first trip abroad."

In the summer of 1991, some film people putting together a documentary about Lev took him to his old cell in Butyrka. He returned home in tears. Much had changed in Butyrka, Lev reported: the cell now had water for washing, the crap bucket had been replaced by a civilized toilet bowl, and there were not seventy prisoners, as in Lev's day, but only forty. Still, when the *balander* (the person who served the *balanda*, the slops that passed for food) began to pour the stuff into the prisoners' bowls and pass it into the cell, Lev suddenly felt ill.

"I don't know how to explain it, but I felt as if I were one of them, the people in the cell. Yes, I know they're real criminals who've committed real crimes. But there in Butyrka, where the world is divided only into prison guards and *zeks* . . . how could I be on the side of the guards?"

I once asked Rika: "When you were released from exile, weren't you afraid they would get you a third time?"

"I'm still afraid," Rika replied.

I loved to watch them. After many broken bones, Rika walked with difficulty, but there was always something regal in her stance, in the turn of her head, her hands, her whole way of being.

She usually remained quiet and let Lev do the talking. I saw how, when she listened to him, a smile would start in the corners of her lips and eyes, and she would look at him lovingly and a little condescendingly, as if to say: "Don't puff yourself up like a peacock, now!" It wasn't the difference in ages—how much difference is there between eighty-six and eighty-three? It was just that there was still something quite boyish about Lev.

When they sat next to each other on a bench, Lev would place his hand between Rika's palms. And as they talked to a visitor or to each other, Rika would constantly pat and stroke Lev's hand. After all that, they were at peace together: yes, at peace.

My God, it was amazing: such a life behind them, and yet they were still like new lovers. "If there is love on earth . . . " goes the song. If there is love on earth, they were its chosen ones, Rika and Lev Razgon.

CHAPTER

1

A State within a State

In the summer of 1990, I had an opportunity to work at an American newspaper. Each morning, I would turn on my computer and read through the information coming in over the wire services. At that time, KGB General Oleg Kalugin was giving sensational interviews exposing the Soviet intelligence service, which returned the favor by stripping him of all his ranks, awards, and pension.

I noticed that these news agency reporters repeatedly characterized the KGB as "a combination of the CIA and FBI." Presumably, this would convey to readers that the KGB was engaged in foreign intelligence, like the CIA; and in counterintelligence—most likely in battling organized crime, the drug trade, and terrorism as well—just like the FBI.

Frankly, each time I read one of these descriptions, I wanted to go to the editor and say, "Couldn't you at least write something about how the KGB is still maintaining political surveillance over people and continuing to function as a secret police? Isn't that its real claim to fame?"

I'll confess, I never went to those editors. Countless conversations with American colleagues who'd never been in the USSR had taught me that as soon as I brought up the secret police, they would respond, "Look, the FBI's involved in political investigations, too. Don't you remember the 1950s and 1960s, the McCarthy era? What about Watergate?" And then I, in turn, would point

out that despite the considerable muscle of the FBI or the CIA—
or the SIS or Mossad, for that matter—the presence of democratic
institutions had prevented any of these secret services from turning
into an autonomous political force. The KGB, by contrast, was a
partisan body, a political institution operating in a complete legal
vacuum. The danger it posed to its own country (and not only its
own) was many times greater and more terrible than the threat
posed to America by an FBI circumscribed by many decades of
democratic tradition. After all, I would remind my colleagues, the
Bureau's own charter prohibits the FBI from investigating any
activity connected with "citizens' expression of their religious and
political views"; and the FBI *did* get its wrists slapped for Watergate. Neither the Soviet Union then, nor Russia now has ever had
anything like the 1966 Freedom of Information Act or the 1974
Privacy Act. (Of course, after all that, I would have to add that
when I asked the FBI for a copy of the dossier it kept on me, I
was told that none existed—hard to believe, given that the Chicago
FBI chief himself had acknowledged that his agency had been
taking an interest in me ever since my arrival.)

But I didn't go into any of this in my actual conversations with
my American friends. Was it that I simply couldn't bring myself
to defend any secret service, given my belief that they all—CIA,
FBI, SIS, or Mossad—pose a serious threat to democracy and civil
rights.

THE STATE WITHIN

Just what is the KGB, this "state within a state," as Nikita Khrushchev called it? What is this force that neither Gorbachev the
communist nor Yeltsin the democrat was able to topple, although
both promised to destroy it? (Weren't able? Or weren't willing—
didn't dare try?)

Perhaps the best place to begin is with statistics.

Western estimates place the number of KGB employees prior

to August 1991 at somewhere between 400,000 and 700,000 agents.[1] In October 1991, Vadim Bakatin, appointed KGB chairman after the August coup, put the staff at 488,000, including 220,000 Border Guards. I had serious doubts about this figure: either Bakatin was deliberately disinforming the public, or he himself had been the victim of disinformation. Interviewed, he'd told me that the KGB had about 180,000 officers.[2] The rule of thumb was four non-ranking KGB employees for every officer; this would give a total KGB staff of 720,000 people, which sounded about right. I was never able to get a more exact count—the total number of people it employs is the KGB's most closely guarded secret. And for good reason, since if they were to answer the question truthfully, they would immediately be faced with the far more challenging question: What exactly does this vast army of people *do*?

At the end of January 1992, Viktor Barannikov, Bakatin's successor as head of state security (the KGB had been renamed Ministry of Security, or MB), announced that the ministry's staff would be reduced by a factor of twelve. Cuts did begin, but they consisted mainly of foisting various service divisions like drivers and medical personnel onto the payrolls of other ministries and of pushing some of the old guard into early retirement. Of course, the old bosses were soon replaced by new ones, and the drivers were back in demand. Proportionate to the population it oversees, the institution has actually grown: the Soviet Union, with a population of 300 million, had approximately 700,000 political police agents; the new, "democratic" Russia, with a population of 150 million, has 500,000 Chekists. Where we once had one Chekist for every 428 Soviet citizens, we now have one for every 297 citizens of Russia. The KGB has also maintained a presence in all the former Soviet republics; and, with the exception of the Baltic states, these staffs have been enlarged rather than reduced.

Some specifics: According to former KGB col. Oleg Gordievsky, who was recruited by the British SIS, as of December 1991, there were 65,000 officers in the KGB's headquarters in Moscow alone.[3]

I was able to glean a more exact figure of 89,000 Chekists in the capital, including the various specialized KGB institutes and the Border Guards (the reason for deployment of border guards in Moscow remains unclear). For the sake of comparison, a total of 21,000 agents are employed at FBI headquarters. Former KGB Gen. Oleg Kalugin claims that more people worked in the Soviet KGB than in all the security agencies of Europe put together.[4] And even though current authorities have repeatedly claimed a reduction in numbers since August 1991, in fact the opposite is true.

Muscovites have had visual evidence of this surge in numbers. In the mid-1960s, under Khrushchev, the KGB's Moscow branch took up two buildings on Lubyanka Square. It now occupies eight, the most recent of which was "recalled" in the spring of 1993 from the Timber Ministry, to which it had been donated in the 1940s by Lavrenty Beria, Stalin's notorious secret police chief. Moscow's Chekists are running out of space and reclaiming territory—has their workload increased with the burgeoning of a wide spectrum of new political parties? Come to think of it, it's amazing how the Tsar's secret police, the *okhrana*, ever managed to keep up with all the opposition parties, the Bolsheviks, Mensheviks, Socialist Revolutionaries, etc., with a staff of only twenty-four officers.[5]

As for the KGB's own troops, its 220,000 Border Guards: if we can believe the official statistics, in the early 1930s, when the only socialist country in the world was (as it was customary to say) under "hostile encirclement," the Soviet government found the need for only one seventh as many border guards.[6]

Additional troops were available to the KGB for special assignments, including military construction engineers and government communications forces. In 1990, several army divisions were transfered to the KGB: the 103rd Vitebsk Guard Paratroopers Division; the seventy-fifth Nakhichevan Motorized Rifle Division, the forty-eighth Motorized Rifle Division, and the twenty-seventh Motorized Rifle Brigade, numbering a total of 23,767 officers, sergeants, and soldiers.[7] Army Gen. Filipp Bobkov, then first deputy to the KGB chairman, claimed in an interview that the special assignment divisions "were used only at the border."[8] But that was untrue; they have also been used (as their charter permitted) to suppress uprisings within the country.[9]

Furthermore, many branches of the KGB maintained their own special assignment groups (the so-called *spetsnaz*, from the Russian *spetsialnogo naznacheniya*, special assignment). For example, Group A-7 (known as the Alpha Group), run by the directorate in charge of surveillance, led the bloody suppression of Lithuanian nationalists in Vilnius on the night of January 12–13, 1991.[10] After the failure of the August 1991 coup, *spetsnaz* A-7 was rewarded for its loyalty to Yeltsin by being placed directly under presidential aegis (first Gorbachev, then Yeltsin).

The directorate in charge of foreign intelligence also had its own *spetsnaz*: Group B (a separate training division for KGB operatives); Thunder Group and Vympel Group, which seized the palace of Afghan president Hafizullah Amin in December 1979; and Zenith Group. The primary function of these groups was to carry out government-sanctioned acts of terrorism against foreign powers—but, should the domestic situation shift, there was nothing to stop them from moving against their own people. Nowadays, all these special assignment groups have to operate under the aegis of the Russian Security Service (yet another new security system).

No outsider knows just how many special divisions and groups the KGB had at its disposal: according to some sources, more than the entire U.S. Navy,[11] while others claim that the KGB *spetsnaz* numbered "only" about 60,000 to 70,000 members.[12] And no one knows the precise figure today. But whatever it may be, one still wonders: why does a country that is going around the world with outstretched hand, a country where three-quarters of the population lives below the poverty level, have such an enormous army of Chekists? What do they *do*? Can work be found for such a host of officers?

Indeed, it can. As Oleg Kalugin said: "There is no area of our lives—from religion to sports—where the Committee doesn't pursue some interest of its own."

The structure of this vast organization is as difficult to pin down as its size, especially in this time of transition and turmoil. Prior to August 1991, the KGB had four chief directorates: First (intelligence), Second (domestic security and counterintelligence), Eighth (communications and cryptography), and the unnumbered Border Guards directorate.*

Aside from these four *chief* directorates, there were at least nine other directorates: Third (military counterintelligence); Fourth (transport); Fifth (ideological counterintelligence and dissidents); Sixth (economic counterintelligence); Seventh (surveillance); Ninth (government security); Fifteenth (security of government installations); Sixteenth (communications interception and signal intelligence); and the unnumbered Military Construction directorate. Parallel, and sometimes subordinate, to these directorates were various departments and services, such as the Tenth Department (archives); the Investigation Department; the Government Communications Service; the KGB Academy; Sixth Department (interception and inspection of correspondence); and Twelfth Department (wiretapping).

After the August 1991 coup, a series of changes were made. The KGB was formally renamed—several times. Some KGB departments, such as intelligence, were spun off into a number of supposedly independent services. Others were merged to create new agencies, or were dismantled. Still others simply had their names changed. But despite the various reconfigurations, personnel shuffles, renamings, and department closings, the essential structure and function of state security remained unchanged: the same employees still sat in the same offices, doing the same jobs, sometimes even reporting to the same bosses. Indeed, by December 1993, even these minimal "reforms" had been undone. The agencies that had been created (if only on paper) were formally disbanded, and a new round of juggling begun, to give the impression of reform

---

* Note that the numbers do not run in sequence—see the chart on page 27 for clarification of the rather bewildering nomenclature.

THE ORGANIZATION OF THE KGB

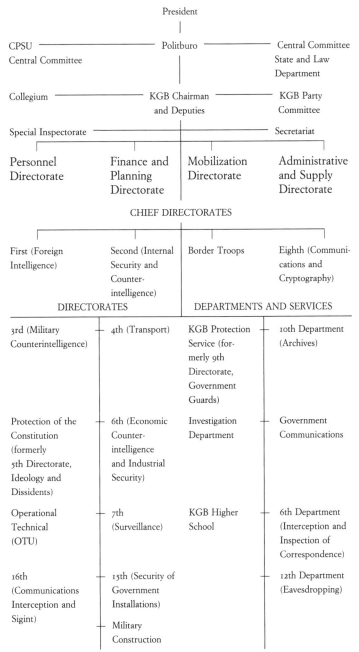

President

CPSU Central Committee ———— Politburo ———— Central Committee State and Law Department

Collegium ———— KGB Chairman and Deputies ———— KGB Party Committee

Special Inspectorate ———— Secretariat

| Personnel Directorate | Finance and Planning Directorate | Mobilization Directorate | Administrative and Supply Directorate |

CHIEF DIRECTORATES

| First (Foreign Intelligence) | Second (Internal Security and Counter-intelligence) | Border Troops | Eighth (Communications and Cryptography) |

DIRECTORATES   DEPARTMENTS AND SERVICES

3rd (Military Counterintelligence)	4th (Transport)	KGB Protection Service (formerly 9th Directorate, Government Guards)	10th Department (Archives)
Protection of the Constitution (formerly 5th Directorate, Ideology and Dissidents)	6th (Economic Counter-intelligence and Industrial Security)	Investigation Department	Government Communications
Operational Technical (OTU)	7th (Surveillance)	KGB Higher School	6th Department (Interception and Inspection of Correspondence)
16th (Communications Interception and Sigint)	15th (Security of Government Installations)		12th Department (Eavesdropping)
	Military Construction		

Source: Desmond Ball and Robert Windren, "Soviet Signals Intelligence (Sigint): Organization and Management," *Intelligence and National Security*, vol. iv (1989), no. 4, and Gordievsky.

THE ORGANIZATION OF THE KGB FIRST CHIEF DIRECTORATE
(FOREIGN INTELLIGENCE)

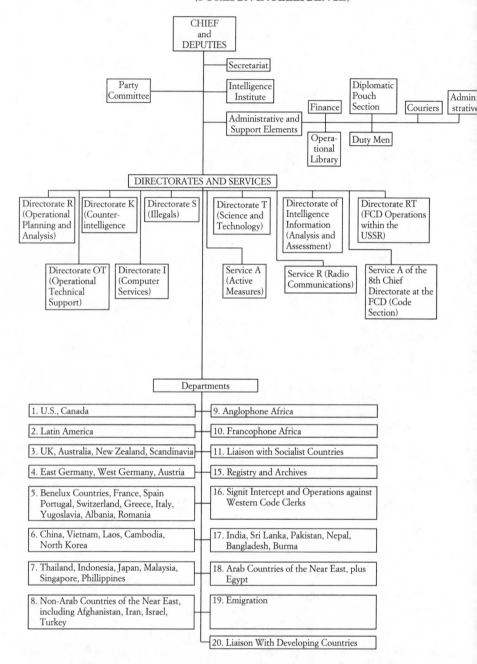

and housecleaning. Again, the names all changed; again, the cast remained the same.

The latter chapters of this book contain the saga of the endless cosmetic repairs the KGB has made in an effort to acquire a more civilized Western veneer. But what interests me more here is the manner in which this institution that has penetrated every sphere of life in Soviet (now Russian) society operates, and what this may mean for the future.

The FCD, whose jurisdiction included the many KGB agents engaged in gathering intelligence abroad, had always been considered the nerve center of the KGB. In the autumn of 1991, it was renamed the Central Intelligence Service, and then renamed several times over; it is now called the Foreign Intelligence Service (FIS) of Russia. On paper, at any rate, it has become independent, no longer part of the KGB. In fact, intelligence has always had its own separate existence, right down to location: the basic divisions of the KGB are on Lubyanka Square, but intelligence is in Yasenevo, a district in southwest Moscow. Its officers considered themselves an elite and bent over backward to disassociate themselves from "dirty KGB affairs." (Readers can judge for themselves just how "clean" intelligence's hands were.)

Estimates are that the FCD's staff was approximately 12,000 employees.[13] In the winter of 1992, in a flush of reformist zeal, the new intelligence chief, Yevgeny Primakov,* announced substantial personnel cuts. A number of intelligence old-timers accepted early retirement. Some turned up in the business world, others in various new government bodies, on the President's staff, in the Supreme Soviet and in Parliament; yet others in newspaper and magazine editorial offices. They swelled the ranks of officers who continued to toil away in the *rezidentury* (residencies) of the Russian embassies

---

* Yevgeny Primakov, member of the USSR Security Council under Gorbachev, formerly head of the Institute for International Relations and the World Economy and the Institute for Oriental Studies—Trans.

abroad under cover of the more respectable titles of diplomat, journalist, trade official, or tourist.[14] In the old days, the Soviet wire service APN [*Agenstvo pechati novosti*, News Press Agency] had about a hundred "journalists with shoulder boards"—foreign correspondents who held military-style ranks in the KGB. Primakov admitted unabashedly that intelligence agents would go on using civilian cover in the future—although the newcomers no doubt have become more deft in concealing the true nature of their work.

Intelligence is broken down into eighteen regional departments (Number 1, U.S. and Canada; Number 2, Latin America; and so on), plus departments of Emigration (Number 19) and Liaison with Developing Countries (Number 20). So-called functional directorates are identified with specific tasks or areas of interest: Directorate K is counterintelligence; RT handles territories formerly part of the USSR; S is the "illegals"; T deals with scientific and technical intelligence. There is also an Information Department, which analyzes the information gathered and prepares daily briefings for the country's leaders. In the past, these reports had to be cleared by the KGB chairman; now, the intelligence flows directly. Word has it that Primakov has been favored with weekly audiences with President Yeltsin; such access is available to only a few high-ranking Russian leaders.

In addition to information-gathering, intelligence spends its resources on manufacturing disinformation. This is the task of the "Active Measures" Service (Service A), now renamed the Facilitation Service ("facilitation" of *what?*). Service A often targeted dissidents, as can be seen in an October 10, 1975, memo (No. 2574-A) written by then–KGB chairman Andropov to the Central Committee of the Communist Party and headed "On Measures to Compromise the Decision of the Nobel Committee to Award the Peace Prize to A. D. Sakharov":

On October 9, the Nobel Committee passed a decision to award SAKHAROV the Peace Prize, clearly for provocative purposes, in order to support his anti-Soviet activity and on that basis consolidate hostile-minded elements within the country . . . the following actions are considered expedient:

—Assign the Central Committee's Department of Science and Academic Institutions and the Department of Propaganda, in cooperation with the Presidium of the USSR Academy of Sciences, to prepare on behalf of the Presidium of the USSR Academy of Sciences and prominent Soviet scientists an open letter condemning the action of the Nobel Committee in awarding the Peace Prize to a person who has embarked on the path of anticonstitutional, antisocial activity, which, to our great sorrow, unwittingly compromises the above-mentioned august body . . . to be published in *Izvestia*;

—The editorial board of the newspaper *Trud* [Labor] should publish a satirical article portraying the award of the Nobel Peace Prize to SAKHAROV for the sum of 122,000 dollars as a reward from the reactionary circles of the West for his continual slandering of the Soviet social and state order;

—Transmit via the state news service (APN) to the West materials that support the idea that awarding the Peace Prize to a man who has spoken against détente . . . contradicts the policy of the Soviet government and worldwide progressive forces, which is aimed at international détente and disarmament;

—Through the channels of the Committee for State Security, promote articles in the West showing the absurdity of the Nobel Committee's decision to award the Peace Prize to the inventor of a weapon of mass destruction;

—When petitioning begins to allow SAKHAROV to go abroad to receive the Nobel Laureate medal and the cash award, it appears necessary to refuse him permission as an individual in possession of critical state and military secrets. In the event that other options should arise, the matter should be resolved as the specific situation demands . . .

Service A was also notorious for its interest in peace movements abroad, which it was fairly successful in influencing, and for its significant role in disarmament campaigns. Disinformation was given special priority in Third World countries, where a number of false news stories were planted.

As a reporter, I had occasion to run across some such pieces of disinformation. One, in particular, stands out in my mind: a KGB-concocted story that the AIDS virus was a product of American experimentation with biological weapons. I recall vividly how this story was pushed in 1986–87 by Soviet newspapers testing the uncharted waters of glasnost. Some, such as *Literaturnaya gazeta*, fell for the story; others, like *Moscow News*, resisted it. At that time, *MN* was still an organ of APN, which was headed by Valentin Falin, a former Central Committee secretary and ambassador to Germany, and a highly educated member of the intelligentsia. And yet I witnessed how he pressured my editor-in-chief, Yegor Ya-kovlev, to print material describing this "unprecedented crime of the American military machine." Yakovlev stood his ground, backed by a prominent immunologist, Rem Petrov, who told me he considered the AIDS story a sick hoax.

But for journalists, the most fascinating intelligence department is Directorate S—*nyelegaly* ("illegals"), or covert agents. Spy novels aren't generally to my taste, but even I was intrigued to learn that the Eighth Department of this directorate had assumed the function of the infamous Department V, informally known (in a phrase familiar to readers of spy novels) as the "wet affairs" department, which planned and executed terrorist acts and assassinations, both home and abroad. In a top secret document from the late 1940s that until quite recently was kept in the Special File—the archives of the Politburo—the tasks of this department were defined as follows:

> To conduct subversive acts at important military and strategic facilities and communications facilities in the chief aggressor states—the U.S. and England—and also in the other capi-

talistic countries used by the main aggressors against the USSR. To acknowledge as expedient as well the execution of acts of terror against the most active and hostile enemies of the Soviet Union in capitalist countries, particularly dangerous foreign intelligence agents, chiefs of anti-Soviet emigré organizations and traitors to the Motherland [defectors].

A shockingly candid document lists these victims of the "wet affairs department" in 1946–47, a period of just eighteen months, within the USSR alone:

1) By order of Khrushchev, member of the Politburo of the Central Committee of the Communist Party and first secretary of the Central Committee, drafted by the Ministry of State Security of the Ukrainian SSR and approved by Khrushchev: in the city of Mukachevo, Romzha, head of the Greek Catholic Church, who had actively resisted the incorporation of the Greek Catholic Church into Russian Orthodoxy, was eliminated;

2) By order of Stalin, Polish citizen Samet, who, while working in the USSR as an engineer, had obtained top secret information about Soviet naval submarines and intended to leave the Soviet Union and sell this information to the Americans, was eliminated;

3) In Saratov, Shumsky, a well-known enemy of the Party (the founder of Shumskyism, a Ukrainian nationalist movement), was eliminated on orders from Abakumov, who cited instructions from Stalin and Kaganovich;

4) On orders from Stalin and Molotov, American citizen Oggins, who, while serving a sentence in labor camp during the war, had contacted the U.S. embassy in the USSR, leading the Americans to make repeated requests for his release and return to the U.S., was eliminated.

The author of this document, KGB General Pavel Sudoplatov, who headed the "wet affairs" department in the 1940s and early 1950s, was tried during the Khrushchev thaw years, and subsequently spent thirteen years in prison. I ran into Sudoplatov in the corridors of the Chief Military Procuracy—an angry-faced old man clutching a cane that he banged along the stairs. He'd come to seek rehabilitation, claiming that he had only murdered people on orders from above (and he'd murdered them with his own hands) and therefore that the charge of "hostile activity against the Soviet government" for which he had been jailed was false. Technically, he was correct: everything Sudoplatov did was done in the name of, and in the interests of, the Soviet state. Sudoplatov remains a hero among intelligence veterans. As recently as December 1993, during a gathering of the Association of Intelligence Veterans, Sudoplatov was hailed by his fellow spies and former colleagues with a thunderous ovation.

The use of "dirty" tactics fell in and out of favor, according to the political exigencies of the day. After the murder of Stepan Bandera (leader of the Ukrainian nationalists) in 1959, and the arrest of his murderer, security agent Stashinsky, the Politburo prohibited such actions except in special cases.

Bulgarian state security's "fraternal" request for help in knocking off the dissident writer Georgy Markov was probably just such a special case. Oleg Kalugin says that KGB Chairman Yury Andropov opposed Soviet security involvement in this operation, but was persuaded by FCD head Vladimir Kryuchkov to give the Bulgarian comrades a hand. The result of all this brotherly love was London's infamous "poisoned umbrella" stabbing of 1978, in which Markov was murdered.[15]

The next known special case was the 1979 murder of Hafizullah Amin, the leader of Afghanistan, which called upon the services of sixty-five KGB officers: five from intelligence, and the rest from *spetsnaz* units Thunder and Zenith. One of the agents told my *MN* colleague Natalya Gevorkyan: "When we left the palace, our boots sloshed in the blood-soaked rugs." Amin's eight-year-old son was killed in the crossfire, his infant daughter was wounded, and forty-six *spetsnaz* agents were wounded or killed. (Three Chekists were later given the state's highest award, the title of Hero of the Soviet Union, one posthumously.) The murder was only a prelude to further bloodshed; shortly thereafter, the eight-year-long Afghanistan war was unleashed. The cost to the Soviet Union was 13,833 people dead, 49,985 wounded, and untold psychological damage. For the Afghans, it was far worse yet: their death toll was in the millions.

I am not aware of any special cases during the perestroika era, although there have been several strange murders of Russian Orthodox priests in recent years—most notably that of Father Alexander Men, a popular priest and well-known writer of Jewish origin, who'd been subjected to long-term harassment by both secular and church authorities. The police investigation has come to a halt, and despite speculation, there is little reason to believe that Father Men's killer will be identified soon, if ever.

A former officer once told me that the KGB rarely uses its own operatives for domestic political murders. After all, the country had plenty of convicted criminals with nothing to lose, and everything to gain. Such a criminal could simply "disappear" for a time: during transfer, his rail car could be switched onto another line and a Chekist could show up with some pressing reason to take him off the train. A few hours later, a body would be discovered on some back road—but by then the murderer, returned to his rail car cell, would be heading off to rot in some godforsaken prison. An investigation would be mounted, but the killer would never be found. And no wonder: Directorate V (no relation to "wet affairs") of the KGB's Third Directorate, charged with overseeing the troops of the regular police as well as the military, would be receiving step-by-step reports from its numerous police informers.

I'm not sure how much of what my source told me was true, but one has to admit that it seems extremely plausible—and that it has extremely little to do with gathering intelligence.

One other division of the Foreign Intelligence Service deserves special mention. Referred to by the Chekists themselves as the "Department of Torture and Execution," it is charged with preventing Soviet intelligence agents from being recruited by Western special services. By all accounts, this division has not been doing its job very well of late: while between 1960 and 1980 only three KGB agents defected to the West, between 1980 to 1990 there were twenty-three—since which time dozens have crossed over.[16]

The KGB's Second Chief Directorate, known today as the Federal Counterintelligence Service, is in charge of domestic security and counterintelligence, although it shares this function with a number of other directorates. The Military Counterintelligence Directorate (formerly the Third Directorate), for example, fights espionage in the armed forces and the police. It also oversees the Defense Ministry, its General Staff, and the separate Chief Intelligence Directorate (*Glavnoye razvedyvatelnoye upravleniye*, the GRU) of the military, which is in charge of intelligence in the navy, ground forces, air force, and troops responsible for nuclear weapons. In addition, a special Customs Service (spun off from the Third) monitors all travel in and out of the country (these are the people who take such good care of us when we arrive at Sheremetovo International Airport).

Another secret sharer, the Directorate of Economic Security (formerly the Fourth and Sixth Directorates), is in charge of counterintelligence in public transportation and airlines, and maintains surveillance over the postal, telegraph, and telephone services. It also protects secrets involving defense installations, factories, offices, and scientific institutions that could be of some interest to foreign intelligence agencies. State secrets undoubtedly must be protected, but this directorate interprets its mandate so broadly that—as one of the KGB people I interviewed complained—the only places safe from economic security agents are candy and toy factories.

And yet, economic and trade secrets still mysteriously keep turning up abroad, and the press keeps on carrying stories of Russian technological innovations being patented and adapted by foreign countries. Where were our glorious Chekists when all this vital information was leaking across our borders?

At home, of course, right where they've been all along. Because despite the extravagant claims the KGB may make to justify its bloated ranks, its primary interest has always been our own populace. First and foremost, it is the citizen himself from whom the KGB is protecting the power elite, and its own hide. In his book *KGB*, John Barron writes that during the Brezhnev era, six out of the twelve departments of the Second Chief Directorate spent Soviet taxpayers' money on surveillance of foreign diplomats in order to prevent their contacts with Soviet citizens. The other six departments took care of tourists and foreign students.

While contacts with foreigners no longer are forbidden in the current era of travel and joint ventures, the KGB admits that it still maintains surveillance over all joint ventures.[17] According to Col. Valentin Korolev, a former agent of Second Chief, "agents' reports on citizens who have even one written contact with a foreigner are filed and preserved forever."[18] I find it hard to imagine that the KGB is capable of monitoring the ever-increasing number of citizens who have met a foreigner, or even the smaller number who have had foreign visitors in their homes. But I suppose that with so many hundreds of thousands of agents, the KGB has to give them *something* to do to earn their salary.

Heads of counterintelligence insist that their directorate has switched its primary focus to the war against organized crime. Well, fighting organized crime certainly is a worthy cause—the FBI allots about 60 percent of its resources to this front—but the KGB has a habit of turning all its battles into assaults on human rights.[19] At the height of perestroika, in the winter of 1990–91, the KGB announced that it was going after the mafia's* economic stranglehold, whereupon Gorbachev issued a decree granting KGB agents the right (already held by the police) to "unimpeded en-

---

* The term "mafia" is used by Russians for all criminally minded "gangs," not only organized crime on the Cosa Nostra model—Trans.

trance to the premises of businesses, offices, organizations . . . and production spaces used by citizens for enterprises of individual labor."[20] (Note that this is without a warrant.) Since many new businesses were being run from their owners' apartments, the presidential decree also effectively overturned the constitutional guarantee of privacy of the home.

And the results? Have the "saboteurs" been caught? Have the stores suddenly filled with food and goods? Of course not. But that's beside the point. The true aim of this campaign has been achieved: our citizens have been reminded that whatever they do, whatever work they take up, the Chekists will be watching them.

Gorbachev and the Soviet Union may both be long gone, but the ill-reputed decree, in a somewhat modified form, has found its way into new laws on economic security and criminal investigations. While Chekists now must obtain a procurator's warrant before entering a private establishment, it doesn't take much to get that piece of paper. Procurators have always been in the vest pocket of the KGB, and appeals are a waste of time; the courts in Russia have virtually ground to a halt. There's no point in even talking about parliamentary oversight. One alternative does exist —giving a bribe, a practice that has practically become legalized in today's Russia. The functionaries will help those who have the money; God help those who don't.

In truth, citizens' private lives have always been the KGB's main target. They were the special purview of ideological counterintelligence (the former Fifth Directorate). It was through the efforts of this directorate that Solzhenitsyn, Rostropovich, and many other members of the artistic community were harassed, forced into exile, or sentenced to the thin gruel of labor camps. And yet, its agents included a good many connoisseurs of the arts: for example, I recently learned that the high-ranking KGB official who forced the avant-garde painter Mikhail Shemyakin into exile was a great admirer who assiduously collected the artist's paintings after his subordinates broke up various underground exhibits and confiscated the artworks. Gen. Ivan Pavlovich Abramov, the former head of the directorate's First (intelligentsia and press) Department, who had been put at the helm of the whole directorate during the first years of perestroika, harbored a passion for high-quality art books—foreign ones, of course, not our home-grown sort. His fellow officers were delegated to collect these books for him as they "serviced" book fairs and exhibits.

The Fifth was the brainchild of Army General Filipp Bobkov, who for many years remained the guiding spirit of ideological counterintelligence. Bobkov is an especially revered figure in the KGB. He came to work for the organs in 1945, when Beria was still alive, yet survived Beria and eleven subsequent secret police chairmen. During the 1970s and '80s, Bobkov effectively became the KGB's real chairman, although officially he held the post of first deputy.

Bobkov has been out of office since the end of January 1991, when he left the KGB to take the honorary post of adviser to the USSR Ministry of Defense, and to join the so-called paradise group (senior officials near retirement). But, according to agents of the KGB, his presence continued to be felt at least until the August coup, and may well have done so after it.

In 1989, in the spirit of perestroika, the Fifth was renamed Directorate Z* (the Directorate to Protect the Constitutional Order). Its mission remained the same—combating dissent and dissidents—but the battle was now waged in the name of "protecting" the Constitution. Interestingly, Directorate Z seemed to be co-opting the work of the parliamentary committee established in 1988 to watch over the Constitution. Apparently, our constitution simply can't get along without the KGB, while the KGB can't bear to have a civilian institution encroach on what it considers *its* territory.

Many of us were naïve enough to believe the KGB in 1989 when

---

* The Z is the first letter of *zashchitit*, to protect—Trans.

it assured Soviet citizens that our thoughts, deeds (so long as they didn't violate the Constitution), political views, and beliefs were no longer of interest to the Committee. Now, the Federal Counterintelligence Service—the KGB's heir—is repeating those reassurances. Should we believe them, or take a wait-and-see attitude?

The transformation of Fifth into Directorate Z, and the granting to it of responsibility for our constitution's well-being, are too important and complicated to be dismissed with a skeptical shrug. So I hope the reader will indulge a few paragraphs of perhaps obsessive detail.

With the formation of Directorate Z, surveillance of the intelligentsia and media became the purview of the Department for Work with Anti-Soviet Organizations Abroad. Again, the functions of the pre-perestroika section (in this case, the former First Department) were not abolished, simply modified a bit in keeping with the spirit of reform. A new Third Department was created within Directorate Z (under Fifth Chief, the Third Department had been concerned with the activity of young people) to monitor "informal associations and organizations," that is, the new political parties and movements. "The reason we control the activity of emerging parties is so that they do not accidently threaten the state order and constitutional civil rights," explained Alexander Kichikhin, a KGB lieutenant colonel and then-officer of Directorate Z.[21]

Ideological counterintelligence continued to take a special interest in young people. Under perestroika, the youth section was changed from the Third Department to the Ninth, but its actual function was not altered. According to Kichikhin, "Virtually every single university or institute [was] serviced by the KGB."[22] For its own internal purposes, the KGB had divided the student body into separate spheres of influence. Intelligence (First Chief) and counterintelligence (Second Chief) had long been entrenched in MGIMO, the Moscow State Institute of Foreign Relations, and always took particular interest in the journalism department of Moscow State University. Bauman University was considered counterintelligence turf, while the Construction Engineering Institute, for some reason, was covered only at the level of the district KGB offices for Moscow and Moscow Region.

But this did not mean that ideological counterintelligence was sidelined in the struggle for Soviet youth. On the contrary, Directorate Z remained keenly interested in all of Moscow's major academic institutions. The "student section" was considered one of the directorate's elites, in part because it controlled admission to such prestigious academic programs as the philology department of Moscow State University. "The children of the nomenklatura —Party and state—go there," I was told by KGB officials. "Competition is fierce, and it's hard to get in. The nomenklatura comrades knew that the department was serviced by the KGB. They'd just pick up the *vertushka** and put in a call."

"You don't mean to tell me that Bobkov was spending time helping kids get into Moscow State University?" I asked in surprise.

"Not personally, of course; Bobkov wasn't about to stoop so low. He'd give an order to the head of the student section, who in turn would call in an agent who serviced the philology department, and that agent would go to the dean's assistant . . . We always had our people in the admissions office—agents or trusted people or contacts. The KGB would give a list of who should get in and who shouldn't," the officials told me.

Those who "shouldn't," needless to say, didn't. "During the initial review of the applications coming into the Institute of Literature, compromising material was received on some of the candidates. On the basis of such information, the applications of V. Romanchuk, O. Kasyanov, O. Aleshin, V. Chernobrovkin, and G. Osipova were rejected during the entrance examinations," one report stated in 1985.[23]

The same went on in the glorious years of perestroika, perhaps on a slightly reduced scale. "In short, July and August were the

---

* *Vertushka*, from the Russian word *vertet*, to dial—Trans.

hottest months for the guys from [Third] Department, but many of them made their careers; the papas and mamas were adept at showing their gratitude," one agent told me.

In the pre-perestroika era, another elite department, the Eleventh, covered sports. As Lt. Col. Alexander Kichikhin told me: "In any sports delegation we definitely had our man . . . and trips abroad always meant buying things and having hard currency and everything else. During the Olympics this department was the most corrupt." In 1983, for example, I. A. Maslova, captain of the Dinamo volleyball team, was taken off a delegation to East Germany because an undercover agent in Dinamo's sports medicine board learned of her intention to marry a foreigner. "Work is continuing on influencing Maslova in a direction favorable to us," the operative reported in December 1983.[24]

In the perestroika era, the former "sports" department was retrained to work on joint ventures of a humanitarian nature. (The "non-humanitarian" joint ventures were under the jurisdiction of other KGB departments.)

The workhorses of the KGB were the employees of Directorate Z's Fifth ("organized crime and mass disorders"), Sixth ("terror"), and Seventh ("anonymous letters") departments. Yes, it's true, there really was a special section exclusively for anonymous letters. It was thought that the efforts of these Chekists were aimed primarily at ferreting out the authors of terrorist threats, but as the komitetchiki themselves have said, anonymous letters of a political nature certainly were not thrown in the wastepaper basket—especially not of late. (Some advice for novice conspirators: using a special technique, texts that have been typed within the past several weeks can be read off the ribbon; to get rid of the evidence, the ribbon should be boiled.)

My sources at the Directorate also said that the analysts from Tenth Department were workaholics, as were the "nationals," those who worked in Second Department, the section on interethnic relations, toiling in the field (as the Committee leadership loved to put it) of "separatist movements." According to my information, despite some opposition from within the KGB, this section did quite a bit to maintain the tension between Russian-speaking and native populations in the Soviet republics, particularly in the Baltics.

The Directorate to Protect the Constitutional Order also kept up its "Israel line," the Eighth Department, which was the refuseniks' bane in the pre-Gorbachev era. ("Anti-Semitism is one of the trademarks of the KGB," I was told by a person from GRU, military intelligence, a traditional rival of the KGB.) In the glasnost years, the Eighth was renamed the "International Exchange Department." You can't fault the Committee directors for want of imagination . . .

The Fourth Department, which dealt with the Church, succeeded during perestoika in remaining part of ideological counterintelligence without changing its name or number. Indeed, it's hard to find another division in the KGB system (except perhaps for those covering the intelligentsia and the press) with such long and deep-rooted (and, sad to say, successful) traditions. The following excerpt from the minutes of a 1921 meeting of the Cheka's Secret Department is indicative of the KGB's continuity in this area:

> The question of informant agent work on the clergy is the most troublesome in the Cheka, both because performing such work is so difficult, and because, to this day, the Cheka has paid little attention to it. For a more rapid and certain implementation of this work, it is necessary at the outset to take the following measures:
>
> 1. Use the clergy themselves for our own purposes, especially those who occupy an important position in Church life, for example, bishops or metropolitans, forcing them under fear of severe consequences to publicize various instructions/orders that may be useful to us among the clergy: for example, to stop prohibited agitation against decrees to close monasteries, etc.

2. Study the characters of various bishops and vicars in order to play out various scenarios taking advantage of the trait of vanity, encouraging their desires and intentions.

3. Recruit informers among the clergy after familiarization with the clerical world and close analysis of the character of individual cult leaders. Materials may be obtained by various methods, chiefly through confiscation of correspondence during searches and personal acquaintance with the religious community.

Material incentive for a clerical informer is essential, and sometimes all that is needed to reach agreement with a priest, whereas he cannot be relied upon to have a positive attitude toward Soviet rule. Moreover, subsidies in cash or in kind will ensure that he becomes permanently enslaved to us through fear that his cooperation might be divulged.

Recruitment of informers must also proceed through threat of prison and labor camp for trivial offenses, such as selling on the black market, violating the orders of the authorities, etc., although this method may be useful only if the subject for recruitment is of weak character and complaisant.[25]

That was how it all began; and that is how it continued for more than seventy years.

The recruitment of clergy to perform "counterintelligence activities inside the country and abroad"—an effort reaffirmed by a KGB directive as late as July 1970[26]—served the secret police well, as a June 1987 memo from Col. V. Timoshevsky, chief of the Fourth Department, shows:

In order to forestall the actions of foreign mass media in transmitting the reports of a Moscow press conference by religious extremist Yakunin [Fr. Gleb Yakunin served a number of years as a prisoner of conscience in the Mordovian labor camps—Y.A.] and his fellow believers regarding their "appeal" to the authorities with "a demand to liberalize religious life in the USSR," a press conference was held by Metropolitans Yuvenaly and Filaret for Soviet and foreign correspondents, using the operative capabilities of Fifth Directorate and Second Chief Directorate of the KGB. The priests of the Russian Orthodox Church gave an objective account of the situation of the church and freedom of conscience in the USSR, critically reviewing the appeal of Yakunin and his fellows. Materials from the press conference were sent to the West via TASS, APN, and Gostelradio.[27]

They intimidated people with threats of prison and labor camp, even in the relatively "vegetarian" days (to use Anna Akhmatova's expression). In October 1982, Col. N. Romanov, deputy chief of the Fourth, reported:

At the present time, there are 229 church officials and sect members serving sentences for specific crimes. (In 1981, there were 220.) In addition, eighteen people are in exile. KGB officers have more than 2,500 cases of surveillance over hostile elements from this category of citizens.[28]

Using their agents, the KGB brought the noncompliant to heel. As one Comrade Zotov reported in 1983:

In December of last year a group of monks from the Pskov-Pechorsk Monastery expressed dissatisfaction with monastery procedures and sent a complaint to Patriarch Pimen concerning the head of the Pskov-Pechorsk Monastery. Through agents "Drozdov" and "Skala," educational work was conducted among the monks of Pskov-Pechorsk Monastery. As a result of the measures, the instigators (four people) were sent to parishes in the Pskov diocese, two remained in the monastery, and four were removed from the Pskov diocese. The situation today has been normalized.[29]

The KGB helped to promote their people to high offices in the Church. The archives reveal a number of such career moves. "Agent 'Pavel,' who is being sent to Irkutsk, is to be promoted to a leading office in the Russian Orthodox Church" (April 1980).[30] Six years later, agent "Pavel" became a metropolitan. "Five personal and work files have been reviewed for agents of the territorial offices who are recommended for promotion to leading positions in the Russian Orthodox Church" (October 1988).[31]

Following the old Cheka instructions, the character of individual bishops was also determined, and with the financial incentive of trips abroad, a number of clergymen were converted to simple informers. In March 1990, according to a KGB report, "Agents 'Abbat' and 'Markov' were sent to a meeting of VAAK (an international organization of Church journalists). Information has been received from them about the situation in VAAK and also regarding Hesler, a subject of our operative interest, which is of interest to the KGB organs."[32]

Agents were recruited from among Church leaders; Agent "Abbat" noted above is Metropolitan Pitirim, the former head of the Publishing Department of the Moscow Patriarchy. (I am disclosing only those names that have become public knowledge.) Agent "Drozdov," who brought the Pskov monks into line, is Aleksy II, currently the Patriarch of the Russian Orthodox Church, the religious leader who recently attempted to broker a reconciliation between the warring Russian parliament and President Yeltsin. A KGB document states that in 1988, "An order was drafted by the USSR KGB chairman to award an Honorary Citation to Agent Drozdov."[33] An award for pacifying monks? Or for his many years of service? According to Konstantin Kharchev, former chairman of the Council on Religious Affairs of the USSR Council of Ministers, "Not a single candidate for the office of bishop or any other high-ranking office, much less a member of the Holy Synod, went through without confirmation by the Central Committee of the CPSU and the KGB." And according to Fr. Yakunin, "contacts with the KGB—or worse, work for the KGB—was an inevitable condition for career growth in the Russian Orthodox Church; there were practically no exceptions."[34]

Informers were also recruited among ordinary local priests. "One out of every two clergymen is an overt or covert agent of the Committee for State Security," claims Fr. Georgy Edelshtein, himself the subject of KGB surveillance (he appears in their dossiers under the code name "Clerical") and harassment.[35] "I don't know of a single priest who hasn't had a talk with KGB agents." A KGB official in charge of religious affairs once shouted at Fr. Georgy: "There isn't a priest who hasn't broken. You will get down on your knees on this rug and kiss my hand!" A year later, dying of cancer in a hospital, the official begged that "Clerical" forgive him for his sins. (Nevertheless, Fr. Georgy was sent to the remote village parish of Kostroma, an area without roads, congregations, or means of survival.)[36]

The Russian Orthodox Church was not unique in the degree of its complicity: similar collaborations were achieved in other denominations, including Catholics, Muslims, Jews, Buddhists, and Seventh-Day Adventists.

A November 1984 report from the Tula KGB Directorate notes: "Through agents 'Vinogradov,' 'Grigoyev,' 'Sokolov,' and others working among the pastors at the Seventh Day Adventist Church in Tula, a new election was held for the senior church pastor for the Central Region. As a result, agent 'Svetlov' was promoted to this post."[37] "Practical assistance in organization of counterintelligence work through the Buddhist church and among so-called supernumerary lamas" is the subject of a June 1984 report on activities in the Buryat and Tuva autonomous republics. "Fourteen personal and work files from the agents' network were reviewed, as well as four files of the agent reporting on church and sect matters and reviews were conducted with nine agents."[38] Nor were Orthodox "schismatics" slighted. According to a June 1986 report, the KGB took an active interest in elections for the head of the Belokrinitsky sect: "A memo was sent to twenty offices of the KGB and KGB Directorate with a request to support the most acceptable candidate for us, Bishop Alimpiya, through the available opportunities."[39]

Well, you have to hand it to them; the agents of the Fourth Department were always hard workers. In 1982 alone, "1,809 meetings were held, 704 reports received, thirteen safe houses, and two clandestine hideouts were used to work with the agents' network."[40] But how many of them had to put on cassocks? Study Biblical texts? Graduate from seminary school?

Several years ago I obtained a transcript of a session of the military tribunal of the North Caucasus Military District, which was hearing the case of KGB Maj. A. M. Khvostikov. This document, more than any other I have seen, reveals the technique of the KGB's work among religious believers. I will cite a few paragraphs from the indictment:

> Interrogated in the case, the Director of Religious Affairs of the USSR Council of Ministers in Rostov oblast, Kolganov, V. N., testified to the court that the former registrar of the chapel of the Rostov Cathedral, Koshelyayeva, was dismissed from her job for fiscal misconduct and embezzlement of large sums of money . . . Shortly thereafter, with the knowledge of Khvostikov, Koshelyayeva was hired as a representative of the church council of the Alexandriisky Church, where she also began to embezzle large sums of money. Complaints began to come in from parishioners and other citizens requesting that she be fired from the job. However, Khvostikov did not allow her to be fired, making reference to the fact that she was a person necessary to the KGB.
>
> While conducting counterintelligence work in the Russian Orthodox Church from September 1972 to January 1984, Khvostikov repeatedly used extortion to obtain bribes from priests and clergy in the Rostov diocese . . . a total of 142,000 rubles. Abusing his office, Khvostikov demanded bribes in the amount of 400 rubles per month from F. V. Kharchenko, the chairman of the church council of the Pokrovsky Prayer

House in the city of Shakhty, and continued to receive these bribes from Kharchenko until [Khvostikov's] arrest, accumulating a total of about 50,000 rubles.

What were these bribes meant to secure? Nothing extravagant, only to protect the priests from being declared "anti-Soviet" in their preachings, a charge that could not only lose them their parish, but land them in prison.

I have devoted so much attention to the KGB's church operations because the Russian Orthodox Church as an institution has of late come to occupy the ideological niche filled until recently by the Communist Party. The plethora of KGB agents, informers, and officers in the various denominations is not only morally repugnant (after all, these people speak from the pulpits as spiritual leaders), but also a serious threat to society: increasingly, clergymen are standing before icons and making statements irreconcilable with Christian ideals of love for one's fellow man.

What else did Directorate Z do to defend the people's constitution from the people? My sources assure me that Directorate Z had its people everywhere, in every ministry, institute, university, and factory, and in the media—newspapers and journals, not to mention television and wire services—a subject to which I will return.

But enough about Directorate Z, although it certainly is intriguing—the stuff of fiction, albeit the kind that makes you feel rather grubby. In any case, it was technically abolished in the fall of 1991; there is no equivalent directorate in today's security service. But the overwhelming majority of the employees of Directorate Z remain at Lubyanka, many in the newly created Department to Combat Terrorism, or in the Directorate of Counterintelligence.

Of course, the boundaries among the various KGB directorates are quite arbitrary. Take, for example, the Directorate of Surveillance (the former Seventh). The job of these agents, known in Chekist jargon as *toptuny*,* was to watch over foreign "aliens" and Soviet citizens, either in person or electronically. This directorate is also responsible for communication with various state agencies that directly affect citizens' private lives, such as the housing offices on every block of every city, whose brief still includes (although less so than in the past) monitoring residents as well as their housing, and the offices where marriages, divorces, and deaths are registered, obvious sources of information of great interest to Counterintelligence as well as Surveillance. (In the Stalinist era, all public service workers, from the janitor to the gravedigger, were on the staff of the NKVD.)

The former Eighth Chief Directorate ("cryptography and communications"), now part of the Federal Agency of Government Communication and Information, ostensibly was separated from the KGB after the coup and made an independent office. According to my information, however, this vitally important directorate continues to work as it always did, with the same people at the same desks. "Communications" (whatever its official title) is responsible for devising codes and designing technical devices needed for the encrypting of secret information sent by telephone, fax, telegram, or computer, and for the monitoring and decoding of foreign signals; it is also in charge of communications security for important offices and government buildings, most of which have special rooms outfitted with surveillance equipment.

In short, all Russian coding services—those of the Foreign Ministry, of the government, and even of the President—are controlled by the KGB, which thereby controls all official correspondence. Although the encoders on the staff of the Foreign Ministry or President's administration technically are on the payroll of these respective organizations, their real bosses are at the KGB.

The KGB has an additional source of information on the leaders of the country through its control of ATS-1 and ATS-2 (the au-

---

* From the Russian verb *toptat*, to stamp. The *toptuny* were so named because they could frequently be seen loitering on the street, stamping their feet from the cold—Trans.

tomatic telephone stations), the special government lines known as the *vertushka*, the *kremlyovka*, and *VCh*,* and the Security Service (the former Ninth Directorate), which guards the President and other top leaders of the country.

Interestingly, the longtime head of the Ninth was the same General Plekhanov who placed Gorbachev under house arrest at his Black Sea dacha during the unforgettable days of August 1991. Plekhanov previously had been in charge of the KGB's Twelfth Department, the division whose thousands of employees (mostly women) were responsible for monitoring telephone conversations. At one time its offices even contained in a separate suite of rooms the highly sophisticated equipment used to bug the conversations of the country's top leaders. Ironically, the KGB also maintained (and still maintains) a section with the more public task of safeguarding government communications channels against any wiretapping or surveillance—any but their own, apparently. And because even KGB leaders are capable of the occasional indiscreet phone call or memo, the members of the Twelfth Department have always managed to maneuver their way into important positions, frequently becoming aides to the KGB chairman. (The Twelfth has now lost its autonomy and has been subsumed by the Operations and Technology Directorate.)

Scared by the events of August 1991, first Gorbachev, and then Yeltsin, ordered that communications and security be removed from Chekist control. Communications was put under the control of the Federal Agency of Government Communications and Information, security under the personal direction of the President. Either Yeltsin got over his fright quickly, or, more likely, he was persuaded that the Chekists who had been bad boys under "bad" Gorbachev would be obedient and quiet under "good" Yeltsin. In any event, these perturbations in the structure of the KGB never went any farther than the paper they were written on. In late 1993, we learned that telephones of such well-known political figures as

---

* *Kremlyovka*, from the Russian word for Kremlin; *VCh*, an acronym for *vyshsaya chastota*, high frequency—Trans.

the Speaker of Parliament, Ruslan Khasbulatov, and President Yeltsin himself, continue to be tapped. This information allows the KGB to maintain surveillance over top leaders and even to get advance knowledge of their actions. The Security Service, which follows the President's every step no matter where he is, passes on to the KGB information to which only they have access—the President's contacts, his personal life, and his weaknesses. Frankly, I was amazed that Gorbachev, knowing what he did about the KGB's role in Khrushchev's overthrow, apparently did not suspect that he, too, was the object of such unfriendly surveillance. And why isn't Yeltsin afraid of the same thing?

The reader is probably tired by now of all these "sevens" and "Zs" and "Chiefs." But before the list ends, we must mention the Operations and Technology Directorate of the KGB, which encompasses all the laboratories and scientific research centers where the marvelous surveillance technology is created, where the arts of bugging, shooting, taping, and the like are perfected. The most important of these sites are the Central Scientific Research Institute of Special Research (TsNIISI) and the Central Scientific Research Institute of Special Technology (TsNIIST). Here, the best scientific and engineering minds of the country have been gathered, unacknowledged geniuses whose monographs, dissertations, and articles are stamped "top secret" even as the country's deteriorating industry goes begging.

The infamous Laboratory No. 12, which concocted poisons and various psychotropic substances, was also under the aegis of the Operations and Technology Directorate. "Searching for means to utilize various poisons to commit clandestine murders, Beria ordered that a top secret laboratory be created in which the effect of poisons would be studied on persons sentenced to capital punishment," states the indictment in the case of Beria, Merkulov, and Kobulov, chiefs of the NKVD and Stalin's main henchmen.[41]

According to Oleg Kalugin, it was a chemical manufactured by this laboratory that poisoned the umbrella tip with which Georgy Markov, the Bulgarian dissident, was murdered. Kalugin also described other, even more cunning methods of killing people. For example, poison could be rubbed on the handle of someone's automobile. A couple of days later, the unsuspecting car owner would be taken to the hospital, where he would die, diagnosed with a "heart attack."

Oleg Gordievsky, another former colleague of Kalugin's and now an agent of British intelligence (SIS), claims that Operations and Technology includes "a remarkable system to forge documents and passports" that by 1971 was succeeding at the hardest counterfeiting challenge there is—faking U.S. passports, which are printed on a special paper that is almost impossible to reproduce.[42]

This directorate also deserves credit for the operation it conducted in East Germany. Two days before an angry crowd stormed the Stasi building, all the electronic files of the East German state security were removed and sent along to the Soviet Union, where they were kept safe and out of reach. Of course, this was hardly the KGB's first successful effort to influence the workings of Eastern Europe's secret police; on the contrary, they were long known to be de facto divisions of the KGB's Eleventh Department. (The chiefs of these "divisions" were all required to study at the KGB's academy, and a number of the agents also completed the academy's three- or five-year courses.)

An overview of the KGB's structure would be incomplete without the Tenth Department, now simply called the Archives Department. It is here that the authentic, tragic history of the Soviet state and its people is preserved. Most likely with the help of the Eleventh Department (which used to coordinate the security services of the former socialist countries), some of the archives of the Czechoslovak StB, the East German Stasi, and the Romanian Securitate found their way here, as well as some of the long-sought secret archives of Lithuania, which have been noted as missing since the former republic declared its independence.

KGB archives have only been opened a crack so far, and access to them is still being regulated and monitored by the KGB. I fear that our descendants will be disappointed when they gain full access to these files. Several sources claim that the files on Andrei Sakharov and Alexander Solzhenitsyn, for example, have already been destroyed.[43] According to Lt. Col. Kichikhin, "Directorate Z employees were given an oral command from the directors to clear out the documents in the safes so that no one would find out what we had been doing up till now."

But it's equally possible that these "reliable sources" are deliberately spreading disinformation to distract citizens from their desire to see what the archives contain. Others have told me that the Committee never destroyed anything of consequence, that the papers were merely transferred to diskettes and entered into the agency's vast network. Still, it would be very like the Soviet totalitarian state to destroy priceless archives even as they build bunkers to save the country's leaders in the event of a nuclear war. (The KGB actually has a special "bunker division"; Viktor Chebrikov, KGB chairman from 1982 to 1988, was even awarded the title Hero of Socialist Labor for building a special complex in Moscow for high-ranking national officials. According to some reports, the bunker division also oversees the construction of villas for the government elite and the training of domestic personnel (maids, for example) to service these dachas. I suspect that the notion of "training" here has a broader meaning than learning to dust furniture.)

Finally, I must say something about the Sixteenth Directorate. It, too, survived the coup, becoming the third (unnumbered) component of the Federal Agency of Communications and Information, along with the former Eighth Chief and Twelfth Department. But its job remains the same: to intercept and decode communications electronically. The finest mathematicians work in this division, which maintains a large computer complex in the center of Moscow, a research laboratory on the outskirts of town, and electronic intelligence stations at more than sixty former Soviet diplomatic and trade missions abroad. Of course, these agents work very closely with military intelligence (the GRU). But while the GRU concentrates on the interception and decoding of military information, the electronic ears of the Chekists are cocked primarily for signals containing coded economic and diplomatic information.

In sum, the KGB's vast domain comprises intelligence, counterintelligence, government communications, security, military counterintelligence, border troops, investigation divisions, as well as a separate army, a network of covert scientific research institutes, and an extensive array of organizations operating in the public arena. The names may have changed: where once we had "Chiefs" and "Directorates," we now have the Foreign Intelligence Service of Russia, the Federal Counterintelligence Service, the Federal Agency of Government Communications and Information, the Security Service, and so on. But the KGB, equipped with almost infinite human and material resources, continues to regulate (probably even more stringently) every aspect of civic and military life, and remains in every sense a "state" all its own.

Obviously, such a state needs myriad housekeeping, technical, and medical services (KGB agents certainly can't be treated in ordinary clinics). It also needs to keep refilling its ranks, and for this it has a network of one- and two-year schools scattered throughout the country, not to mention a powerful complex of academies, where 90 percent of those whom I interviewed had been educated. The training there is said to be among the best in the country, and, according to *Komsomolskaya pravda*, competition to get into particular departments is fierce, with six applicants for every place.

Needless to say, an empire this vast can be maintained only at a staggering cost to taxpayers. In the spring of 1991, swept along by the spirit of glasnost, the KGB published its budget: barely 4.9 billion rubles a year (then the equivalent of 7.4 billion dollars), including the cost of the border troops. For the sake of greater persuasiveness, it also cited the expenditures of the American intelligence community, which includes the CIA, the FBI, military intelligence, and other organizations: 32 billion dollars.[44]

There's no doubt that our KGB was thrifty. But when you

consider that the KGB combines in one body the functions of twenty-five different American intelligence, security, and law enforcement agencies, when you think of those sixty electronic surveillance stations installed abroad, you wonder . . .[45]

Not much in the habit of believing the KGB, I made some simple mathematical calculations of my own. I divided the alleged 4.9 billion ruble budget by the minimum number of employees of the KGB—400,000, according to various sources, not counting the 220,000 Border Guards. I was left with 12,250 rubles for each Chekist, a little more than 1,000 rubles per month. In October 1991, the new, post-coup KGB leadership quoted a slightly higher figure for its budget—6.5 billion rubles. Neither figure is remotely plausible.

True, this sum would take care of payroll and uniforms. But what would be left for the Operations and Technology Directorate, with the countless inventions it designs and manufactures? According to my sources, the budget of a single institute in this directorate is two million dollars—dollars, not Soviet "wooden" rubles! And what of the Department of Electronic Surveillance? Not to mention the Federal Agency for Government Communications, which designs extremely expensive decoding technology.

Has the KGB found some independent means of support? Has it gone into business? There's no point in speculating; neither journalists nor the parliamentarians charged with overseeing the Ministry of Security know just how much money is involved. After all, the formal structure of the "state within a state" is only the tip of the iceberg, underneath which is an invisible "shadow staff"—perhaps the most dangerous part of the KGB.

THE SHADOW STAFF

The KGB's shadow staff consists of three main groups: the "active reserve," the "reliable people," and the "secret helpers." The "active reserve" comprises KGB staff officers who work undercover,

either pretending to assume various jobs or using as cover professions in which they are actually trained. Examples of the former
include deputy directors of scientific research institutes and deans
responsible for foreigners in academic institutions. The latter include translators, doormen at hotels that serve foreigners, telephone engineers, and journalists. For their undercover jobs, they
receive the same salary as their civilian colleagues, but the KGB
makes up the difference between that (usually lower) pay and a
KGB salary, also kicking in bonuses for rank and years of service.

On December 27, 1991, Anatoly Oleynikov, then first deputy of
the Ministry of Security, stated in a letter to a commission of the
Russian Supreme Soviet: "In connection with the reorganization
of the organs of state security, the active reserve of the KGB has
been disbanded." It was true that the category had been dissolved,
but the officers continued to do the jobs they had always done—
only now they were referred to as being "on special assignment."

The second and probably largest group in the KGB's shadow
staff is curiously elusive. These are the "reliable people" who have
no financial ties or documented relationships with state security
and perform isolated assignments.

"Personnel directors are very reliable people—they provide the
necessary information and keep quiet," Lt. Gen. Viktor Ivanenko,
who began his career as an ordinary operative, told me.[46] According
to Lt. Col. Alexander Kichikhin, there were also many "reliable
people" among mass media executives, plant directors, deans of
academic institutions, Party officials, editors of publishing houses,
telephone operators, garment workshop employees, telegraph
workers, and housing office staff. Their function was to provide
information—for example, the attitudes of members of such
professional communities as the writers' and filmmakers' unions
or newspaper staffs. Their contacts with the *komitetchiki* were no
big deal, more like a friendly chat. Committee people usually took
care of writing up their reports: "A memo has been received from
reliable person 'SAG' containing information about the moods,
plans, and intentions of Academician D. S. Likhachev and reported

to the administration" (a prominent scholar).[47] When the "reliables" traveled abroad as heads of delegations, they might write a
description of their contacts, what their acquaintances had said
about the Soviet Union, and the degree of "political maturity"
displayed by members of their own delegation. The KGB did not
remunerate them directly for this, but the reliables acting as tourist
group leaders, for example, might have all expenses paid. In the
majority of cases, these people did no harm. I'm sure few of them
suspected that the KGB regarded them as "reliable people"—
writing reports was a normal activity, after all. Those who were
less disingenuous about Chekists' interest in their views most likely
justified their complicity as a prerequisite for professional advance.

The number one specialist in recruitment of reliables was Gen.
Filipp Bobkov, whose interlocutors include still-prominent figures
whose names I won't divulge here, since I haven't actually seen
the documents and don't entirely trust the memory (let's call it
that) of my sources at the KGB. Some sources say the KGB kept
special card files on all the reliables; others say, only on some of
them. I know that Bobkov, for example, helped make it possible
for some persons to travel abroad, and I doubt that his motives
were altruistic—after all, he was a professional.

The third and most dangerous category of the KGB's shadow
staff are the informers, or "secret helpers," as they are known in-
house. Outside, they're generally known as *stukachi* (from the verb
stukat, to knock . . . on a door, for example)—uttered in a tone
that makes it clear that the general public finds these "snitches"
anything but helpful.

Informing is one of the world's oldest professions, hardly a Soviet
invention, but it has played a particularly important role here.
"Helpers" were a vital element of the Tsar's secret police, and
figured prominently in the struggle against the Bolsheviks. After
the Bolsheviks came to power, they co-opted the tsarist system,
but on a scale vaster than the Tsar's secret police ever could have
imagined.

At a Central Committee meeting in 1920, the Bolsheviks approved a letter apprising all Party members working in the army of their obligation to become informers; the Committee also ruled that this assignment be "extended . . . to Communists working in transportation."[48]

In 1921, the Bolsheviks cast their net farther. A memo advised regional Cheka officers to take measures to establish a network of informers at "plants, factories, provincial centers, state farms, co-operatives, logging camps, penitentiaries, and villages." The officers were given instructions outlining how to recruit informers and gather intelligence, and were urged to proceed "with all possible care, observing all principles of conspiracy."[49]

The pretext for the memo was the need to correct a "funda-mental flaw" in the Cheka's operations: without an informers' network, the memo warned, the local secret police would not be able to maintain political control in their territories. The chief task of the Cheka was identified as the "struggle against anti-Soviet parties," in aid of which local Cheka officers were admonished:

1) Within three days of receiving this notice, draft a concrete plan to recruit and place secret informers deep within the political parties;

2) Disregarding any personal animosities or protocol, regroup regional Cheka agents according to their work so as to max-imize productivity;

3) Recruitment, placement, and management of informers should be conducted under the personal supervision of the chairman of the regional Cheka, the chief of the secret de-partment, and the agent for political organs;

4) Informers from the political parties should be recruited from the ranks of these same parties, and not from non–Party members or from the commissariats, since these can only be backup or tangential informers, not key informers;

5) Do not strive for quantity of informers, but for quality in informing. Two or three sensible informers from a party are enough to control its activities;

6) No informer will be accepted by any employee of the regional Cheka without sanction by the chairman of the Cheka and the chief of the secret department . . .

7) [missing]

8) All information from the informers must be carefully checked or verified against other data and immediately reported;

9) Any important files on political parties based on information from a reliable informant are not to be destroyed without sanction of the All-Union Cheka, except for cases that cannot accommodate delay;

10) After drafting the program within the three-day period, all regional Chekas must complete the organization and establishment of the secret informers' network among the political parties within three months, in accordance with this circular;

11) All chairmen of the regional Chekas and chiefs of the secret departments who do not establish a secret informers' network within the three-month period will be considered to have performed inadequately.[50]

Oh yes, we have a rich past!

There are various gradations of informers: "lookouts," "watchers," "consultants," "agents," "especially valuable agents," and "residents." The KGB kept two types of files on each secret employee, a personal dossier and a work file.

"Lookouts" watch and report on both their colleagues and the general situation at such strategic facilities as nuclear power stations. The "watchers" and the "consultants" have similar functions.

The "especially valuable agents," who comprise approximately 10 percent of the total number of secret KGB employees, have a different task. While their colleagues are paid for their observational talents, this group is valued for its more subtle powers of persuasion. One of Andrei Sakharov's personal physicians fell into this category; his job wasn't so much to keep track of his patient's movements, or even his health, as to try to talk Sakharov out of unwelcome actions, statements, and protest letters by invoking his long-term medical problems.[51]

The terms "agent" and "resident" are familiar from spy novels.

How are informers recruited? Regulations prohibit recruitment of young people under the age of eighteen and generally discourage active use of "helpers" over sixty, who are instead used to maintain apartments that double as meeting places.

Once likely candidates in the appropriate age range are identified, they are carefully checked to make sure they are not already in the employ of the KGB or Interior Ministry (police). Next, it is determined whether any *kompromat* is available on them at these agencies. Their backgrounds are thoroughly vetted, and police files are scanned for criminal records. Their correspondence, including any letters sent abroad, is monitored by the Sixth Department of the Operations and Technology Directorate, which opens and peruses mail.[52]

The next step is a chat with the possible "helper." I can relate from my own personal experience how this was done.

Thirteen years ago, at the very beginning of my journalistic career, I covered a conference organized by the USSR Academy of Sciences on missile and space technology. In the pre-perestroika era, I wrote exclusively on popular science, and space medicine was one of my favorite subjects. A certain Ivanov (his real name) approached me. A very nice man of about thirty-five, elegant and bearded, he was the "first department" officer of the Academy's Presidium, which meant he dealt with personnel and security at the Academy. He asked me about my work as a reporter, if I often went on business trips, and if I was interested in attending other scientific conferences, including ones abroad. Of course, I was interested—extremely so. "I'll help you," said Ivanov. "We'll send you on trips ourselves. The only thing that I'd ask you to do would be to make copies for us of your interviews with foreigners—you speak English, don't you? Well, that's great. Those copies would probably have to be a little more detailed than what you publish in the press. You would provide some details for us: what kind of conversations you had with your interviewee beyond the basic topic of the interview, what his interests are, what he said about our country. I don't have to tell you; you're a professional," Ivanov said, flattering a twenty-two-year-old reporter. I mumbled something in reply about how there was a lot of work at the office and I wasn't sure how the boss would like it. "Well, think about it, think about it," the nice Chekist said, without pushing me.

Another conference came along. Again, he approached me. This time, I was fairly sharp with him; and, I realized later, insufficiently cautious, saying that I was too busy to take on another profession.

For the next eight years, I was not allowed to travel abroad.

When I told Lt. Col. Kichikhin this story, he was quite indignant at my recruiter's behavior. (We had been talking about informers at the time, and Kichikhin was trying to convince me that practically any person could be recruited.) "What a fool; I wouldn't have tried that with you," he said. I'll admit I was flattered again.

"I always had enough candidates. But you have to find the right key to each one. With some you can get close to them on some interests; with others, you need other interests. For still others, you can't get near them with any 'interests'; you need something more heavy-duty—you have to threaten them, tell them they can't escape, tell them they have no choice but to work with us; that it's part of their job," he explained.

Some informers, of course, came to the *komitetchiki* on their own. "When I worked at a factory in Voronezh," Col. Rubanov told me, "I often literally had to turn away the volunteer 'helpers.' I would do a background check, and I'd be right: the person was angling to get his boss's job, and he was hoping that with my help, as a kind of payment for his services, he'd be able to do this faster."

This ambitious fellow may have been a bit too obvious for his own good, but in truth, the list of possible enticements is endless, given all the hardships in Russia. KGB officers could help someone find an apartment or a job. They could arrange for a trip abroad or a spot in a day care center. (In fact, they could promise the moon; but after the client was hooked, he'd find it hard to collect on those promises.)

"I had trouble finding an apartment, and couldn't locate a place for my daughter in day care. A KGB agent hinted that he could help me with the apartment" (V. Aleshchenko, Kiev).

"If I hadn't cooperated with them, I wouldn't have found a job with the Khana company, which was building a video player factory in Voronezh" (M. Yaroslavtsev, alias "Felix").

"Do you have any requests for us?" the *komitetchiki* asked B. Krivolatov, then a waiter from Novokuznetsk. "Yes, I'd like to work in the Novokuznetsky restaurant." That same day he was transferred to his new job.[53]

Officers also appealed to people with the "romance" and "adventure" of intelligence work (does this still work?) or with its supposed social utility, in the fight against governmental corruption, for example. Vladimir Lysov, a member of the Writers' Union, described a typical encounter in an interview with me. "How did it all begin? I remember exactly: it was on October 25, 1985. That day, I was summoned to see the head of the personnel department at the Leningrad Radio and Television Committee. I had just submitted my resignation from the radio's literary and theater editorial board; my first book had come out, I was forty-one years old, and I decided that I should take up writing serious literature. But, for old time's sake, I had agreed to keep doing some work for my old editorial office. When I walked in, the personnel director immediately left to take a walk. At his desk sat a young, athletic, and neatly dressed man, a major of the Leningrad City and Region KGB Directorate, Boris Ivanovich Tkachenko. He was the one who made the offer—who asked me to help them. Without much hesitation, I agreed. Why? I felt I was a new type of Chekist, responding to Gorbachev's call, so to speak."

In some fields, service for the KGB was built right into the normal work of the profession: you played along or risked losing your job. Virtually every Soviet journalist who worked abroad, as a foreign correspondent for example, was obliged to fill out and then send to a KGB officer at the Soviet embassy "first contact" and "second contact" cards after meeting citizens of the country in which he was stationed. These journalists were also expected to send notes of any conversations with local political figures, and some correspondents were forced to go to a *mokrukha** (Committee slang for a meeting that could be dangerous for an intelligence agent). "Could journalists refuse to get involved?" I asked my colleagues. I was told: "If you refused, you would be flying out of the country where you were assigned within twenty-four hours. Because in Moscow, at the Central Committee of the Party, you had signed a paper: 'I promise to observe the rules of behavior of a Soviet person abroad.' " Let us note: "knocking" is part of those rules.

"I worked at a magazine intended for foreigners," one journalist told me. "Practically everyone in the editorial office cooperated with the KGB. It was a requisite if you wanted to travel abroad. The department head was a career Chekist, a former intelligence officer. At first I thought intelligence work was romantic. But later I understood that I was stuck. And now? Sometimes they call and ask me to write an analysis of the situation in our country. I write approximately the same thing that I write in my magazine, and don't soften it a bit."

Mikhail Kazakov, another journalist, described a darker scenario. "They told me that if I refused to work with them they would ruin my brother's life—he worked in a defense institution. And they could ruin my wife's life, after I had spent so much effort finding her a job."

Viktor Orekhov, a renegade KGB captain who eventually was imprisoned for helping dissidents, identified four main motivations for working with the KGB: professional ambitions; the existence of *kompromat* in the hands of the KGB that could jeopardize one's future; fear of the organs; fear that the KGB will not take no for

---

* From the underworld slang for bloody murder, based on the Russian word *mokryy*, wet—Trans.

an answer and will keep up the pressure till the candidate acquiesces.

"In eight years of work," Orekhov recounted, referring to his time in ideological counterintelligence, "only one student refused to be recruited, though I intimidated him with unpleasant consequences. And my quota for recruitment each year was four to five people."[54]

The quota for recruitment in 1991 (before the coup) was two people per year for each KGB operative. (The current quota is unknown.) Some Chekists, according to Kichikhin, were particularly productive, and landed four or five new helpers. Such zeal might earn them bonuses—unless the bosses believed they hadn't realized their full potential. "He could have recruited five agents, but recruited only four; therefore, his bonus is reduced by 30 percent," a department head explained at a meeting in the winter of 1991. In the interests of filling their quotas, agents sometimes listed as helpers people with whom they'd had no more contact than a casual social encounter. According to Vadim Bakatin, merely talking with a KGB operative could be enough to get you on the Committee's card file. For example, an operative might report the successful recruitment of "an actress of the Sovremennik Theater, 'Yevgenia Ryumina,' and an art critic, an employee of the USSR Art Fund, 'Ponomaryov,'" although such people were unlikely candidates and might have done no more than exchange pleasantries with the operative.[55] The point is, even the most innocuous of interactions with a Chekist can have serious and far-reaching repercussions.

To formalize relationships with informers, the KGB used to require new helpers to sign a statement that read: "I, *Ivanov, Ivan Ivanovich*, voluntarily declare my wish to cooperate with the organs of state security [another version: to assist the organs of the KGB in their work]. I have been warned of the penalties for divulging the fact of cooperation. I will sign the material I submit with the pseudonym *Vesnin*." Date. Signature. The selection of a code name for an informer is a subtle matter; it cannot sound like his real name or the name of one of his relatives, but it must be easy to remember.

As soon as a person signed his name, an employee of ideological counterintelligence explained to me, he was immediately forced to write an agent's report: in Committee slang, a *shkurka*—a "little hide," as in the skin of an animal.

A *shkurka* was also necessary when a person refused to sign a statement of cooperation with the KGB. "There are some tough cases," my sources in the KGB complained to me. "We talk to them, we have a good chat, and the source gives some intelligence information. Finally, you say to him: 'You have to provide your signature.' He refuses. You explain: 'The signature is necessary so that the fact of cooperation will not be divulged.' And he won't budge. Then you suggest: 'Write down the names and the facts briefly, so that we won't be mistaken and punish anyone accidentally.' That often works. The agent's report is sufficient to start a file on him. The signature will come later."

And, despite the changes in the KGB's function, despite today's "liberal" climate, these personal statements continue to be crucial.

In May 1993, the Second International Conference on the KGB was held, a forum arranged by human rights advocates and democratic reformers in Russia to promote reform of state security. KGB officials were invited. At one of the sessions, a young man suddenly stood up in the auditorium. "I am an agent of the KGB, and now the MB. Let me go: I don't want to lead a double life anymore!" the fellow shouted. "Well, go," said a colonel of state security hesitantly, giving him permission to resign. The colonel had just read a paper. "But will you return my signed statement? Will you promise not to bother me anymore?" asked the young man. The colonel did not reply.

In recent years, the signature has ceased to be mandatory. Official meetings between Committee members and their helpers can take place anywhere, at any time. According to Lysov, his major would either come to his home or talk to him at a *yavochnaya* (a specially requisitioned rendezvous site). "That would be the apartment of some old lady. Usually, the major would already be waiting for me there. The old lady would give us tea and cookies, and would go away to the kitchen. What was the major interested in? What people were doing at the radio, what people were saying at the Writers' Union. Once, he asked me to get better acquainted with a certain writer, a Jew, who had relatives in New York, and asked me to find out their address."

For such work, informers are usually compensated, although not generously. Orekhov claims that it was customary among his colleagues to "write off" the petty cash allocated for informers and use it to go on a spree in a restaurant. True, if the "secret helper" had no job, the Chekists would display some charity and would write up a "special assignment" addressed to their superiors. "In connection with the fact that [last name, first name, and patronymic] has no job, payment is recommended in the sum of . . ." For the most part, however, the compensation for the "knock" was made as previously mentioned—promotion to a new job, intervention with a problematic boss, arrangements for a trip abroad, publication of a manuscript. There were many options; there still are.

Just how many shadow agents are there in the country in addition to the official KGB staff? No one knows; or, in any case, no one is telling. Vadim Bakatin promised me shortly after the August coup that the figure would be published. It never was. He later told me that Gorbachev had not approved his recommendation. And besides, Bakatin said, the figure prepared for him by his subordinates was too outlandish to publish. According to my sources, the number in question was 400,000—truly hilarious, given even a moment's reflection. "I was simply deceived, they foisted off old information on me," said Bakatin.

A look at some other former East Bloc countries yields a fairly consistent ratio: the number of informers seems to be about one percent of the country's population.[56] Based on this, in the Soviet

Union, a minimum of 2.9 million people must have worked for the KGB. Yaroslav Karpovich, a retired KGB colonel who spent his life working in ideological counterintelligence, believes this figure is far too low. Karpovich claims that approximately 30 percent of the adult population of the country has worked for the KGB in one way or another, either as "reliable persons" or "secret helpers."[57] Lt. Col. Kichikhin is even more pessimistic: "Sixty or 70 percent of the population maintained relations with the KGB."[58] Hard to believe? Not at all, if we remember that there are two KGB agents at each and every railroad district in our vast country (each route contains five such districts). According to Maj. Gen. Viktor Ivanenko, "Practically all the conductors and all—or almost all—the inspectors were agents, and their job consisted not only of keeping track of the state of the railroad but also of informing on their colleagues."[59]

And the changes of recent years have had almost no effect on this shadow world, except perhaps for the call from a few of the more radically minded Committee bosses to "conduct agent work in a new way." At a KGB conference in the summer of 1991, Maj. Gen. Ivanenko, at that time head of the Russian Federation's separate state security service, said: "A new resolution on the organization of work with secret helpers has been drafted, and methods have been identified to renew this important sphere of the KGB organs' activities. The agents' network henceforth will be formed according to new principles. Only those secret helpers who are involved in strategic tasks should be included in such a network. All the rest, the so-called lookouts, watchers, consultants, who make up more than 50 percent (or even in some places 80 percent) of the agent networks, should be transferred to another category that does not require keeping personal and work files or following other procedures. At the same time, all operatives should be given significant freedom of choice in determining their form of secret cooperation."[60]

They certainly jumped at that "freedom of choice"—and how!

"Try to understand, once and for all," Col. Vladimir Rubanov once said to me angrily, "the concept of 'KGB agents,' or as you love to call it, *stukachi*, does not reflect coercion on the part of the KGB, but rather the mentality of the society around it."[61] "Informer mentality"—talk about blaming the victim!

"One of the paradoxes of perestroika is that despite the country's substantial progress toward the creation of a more free, democratic system, the KGB has preserved its enormous significance in the Soviet Union," writes Amy Knight in her article "The Future of the KGB."

A paradox of perestroika, or its tragedy? For years, our nation has been breeding a special type of person, one capable of fulfilling the KGB's orders. For years, our people have been conditioned to tolerate the KGB. After all these years, all these decades, how could it turn out otherwise?

CHAPTER

2

Victims and Executioners

Sometimes, miracles happen—and that's what this was. I suppose you could say it was just reporter's luck; but luck like this, for a Russian journalist in 1987, really was a miracle.

This is how it happened.

In lieu of a telephone book or directory assistance, Moscow at that time had the street kiosks of its City Information Bureau. The kiosk near the Intourist Hotel, a five-minute walk from the Kremlin, was open, and there was no line. The person on duty, a fortyish woman with a gray, unhealthy complexion, thrust a form at me and barked: "Fill this out."

The first three blanks were easy—last name, first name, and patronymic. I wrote out "Khvat, Alexander Grigoryevich." I skipped line 4, "place of birth." Under "occupation," I wrote "NKVD investigator," although I knew it was hopeless to expect any information after putting down that job title and employer. By 1987, the NKVD—the People's Commissariat for Internal Affairs—had already twice hung out a new shingle, becoming the MGB (Ministry of State Security) in 1946, then the KGB (Committee for State Security) in 1954. The man I was looking for had probably long since retired, and maybe even from another job altogether. To fill in "age," I had to do some arithmetic. In 1940,

Khvat was a senior lieutenant of the NKVD,* which implied some seniority. Most likely, he'd been one of the many Komsomol members recruited to fill the NKVD's depleted ranks in 1938, after Stalin's purge of the organs and the ouster of People's Commissar Yezhov and his cadres left room for a new generation of "Beria's men." How old would Khvat have been then? Twenty-five? Thirty? I wrote down "1910" as the year of birth. The seventh, and final, line asked for the "probable district of residence"—precisely what I wanted to know. I handed the completed form back in through the window. Now all I could do was wait.

I'd been on the trail of NKVD Investigator Alexander Khvat for a long time, ever since I'd encountered his name in the course of researching an article on the renowned geneticist Nikolai Vavilov, who'd suddenly disappeared from the world scientific scene in 1940, arrested and charged with espionage and sabotage. Khvat had been in charge of the case. Vavilov spent a year on death row before Beria ordered his sentence commuted to twenty years of imprisonment, time Vavilov did not live to serve out. In January 1943, as he lay dying of dysentery starvation in Cell No. 56, Block 3, of Saratov Prison, Vavilov—prominent geneticist, botanist, biologist, geographer, former president of the Lenin Agricultural Sciences Academy and director of the world-famous Institute of Plant Cultivation, creator of whole families of new plants, including dozens of new varieties of cereal grains—begged the prison warden to give him just a little bit of rice. "It would be wrong to give rice to an enemy of the people," he was told.[1]

As I pored over hundreds of pages of archives, memoirs, and books published abroad in *tamizdat*, Khvat's name repeatedly struck my eyes.[2] The clerk at the KGB Press Center, at that time the only channel of communication with Lubyanka available to journalists, responded to my telephone inquiry with the statement

---

* The NKVD had military-style ranks including three lieutenant ranks, *mladshiy* [junior] *leytenant, leytenant,* and *starshiy* [senior] *leytenant*—Trans.

that Alexander Grigoryevich Khvat had died a long time ago. My intuition told me this was a lie.

Now, my only alternative was to use the same method that ordinary Soviet citizens use when they're trying to find other ordinary Soviet citizens—the street kiosks of the Moscow City Information Bureau. But Khvat was hardly an ordinary Soviet citizen, and probably would not be listed in the card files of the regular Moscow City Information Bureau. Still, perhaps the years had made him more ordinary?

The woman reappeared at the little window and beckoned to me. "That will be forty kopecks," she said, and handed back my form.

The year of birth had been changed from 1910 to 1907. An address was written in ballpoint pen: 41 Gorky Street, Apt. 88.

Here was my miracle. I stood stock-still on the sidewalk as people pushed past me in all directions, and, in a state of shock, reread the address a dozen times, trying to figure out what to do with my inexplicable good fortune.

That fall was a strange and uneasy time. People were lining up before dawn to buy *Moscow News*, but the newspaper and its editor-in-chief were coming under ruthless political attack from above. The era of glasnost had been proclaimed; in practice, however, it existed only intermittently. Censorship was still widespread and any sensitive materials had to be sent for "approval" to the Department of Propaganda of the CPSU Central Committee. The first articles about Stalin's repressions* were just beginning to appear; the press certainly hadn't carried anything like an interview with an NKVD investigator. Everyone was waiting to hear what Gorbachev would say in his speech on the seventieth anniversary of the Revolution. There had been a battle behind the scenes over the speech, especially regarding Stalin's purges—our Party bosses were still afraid to match the candor of Nikita Khrushchev's 1956 "secret speech" denouncing Stalinism. Gorbachev himself had

---

* The somewhat euphemistic term for Stalin's mass terror and persecution, which led to the deaths of millions—Trans.

praised Stalin's wartime services in a 1985 Kremlin address, to thunderous applause. Both editors and censors would take their cue from his speech: if it soft-pedaled Stalinism, our material would be censored out of shape. Who knew whether I'd be able to publish anything on Khvat, even if I managed to track him down?

But standing on the pavement outside the Information Bureau kiosk, shaking my head in disbelief as I studied the long-sought address, I had only one question in my mind: should I telephone Khvat and arrange a meeting? (Now that I had his address, it would be easier to get his number.) Or should I go straight to him? If I phoned, he might get frightened and ask some of his old KGB bosses for advice, and that would be that. But if I just showed up without phoning ahead, it would be awkward. He might slam the door in my face . . . Finally, I decided to go in person.

Fifteen minutes later, I was standing in front of a hulking relic of grim, Stalin-era architecture, complete with massive wooden doors and a marble entryway. I peered into the inner courtyard, where I could see some gray-haired old men sitting on a bench, chattering away peacefully. They were easily eighty years old or more, and evidently had come out to warm themselves and enjoy the late autumn sunshine. I was on the verge of going up to ask them where I could find the apartment I was looking for, when I stopped short. These nice old folks, I realized, probably had been Khvat's colleagues—for, as native Muscovites knew, this building had been constructed in the 1930s as a residence for NKVD employees. I wasn't afraid of them now, of course—why be frightened of a few old men? It was just that I, born five years after Stalin's death, four years after Beria's execution, never before had come face to face with the people who had ruined the lives of so many of my friends and relatives, who'd even brought death into my immediate family. No, until now, I had only read about them in books.

There, in that courtyard, a scene suddenly came to life, a scene from the past, from before I was born. I saw these nice old men as they had been forty or fifty years ago, rolling up to this building in black cars and stepping out in the predawn darkness—young and strong, in snug-fitting uniforms with crossed belts. Tired to the point of punchiness from constant lack of sleep, they still had the look of men who'd worked well and hard at that night's interrogations, these crack investigators coming home to rest for three or four hours before climbing back into the government limousine or streetcar and returning to conduct searches, write indictments, pass sentences ("corrective measure: execution"), and punch people in the kidneys.

I saw these investigators ride the elevators up to their apartments to be met by their sleepy wives—or no, they weren't met; they opened the door a crack, and quietly slipped off their shoes in the hall, so as not to make tracks, tiptoed to the bathroom to wash their work off their hands, then crept into the kitchen where a late dinner (or an early breakfast) was set waiting. Perhaps they'd peep into the children's room and gaze tenderly at their boys and girls sprawled in sleep—Khvat himself had four children. Finally, they'd go into the bedroom, and when their wives asked "Are you tired?" they'd say "Yes, it was a tough night." And they would lie down beside their wives and caress them with the same hands they'd used for torturing.

Did anyone ever give a different answer? Perhaps repent of his terrible crimes? Be shaken by a sudden, chill thought, What's to stop them from turning on me . . . they could trump up a case against me; they'd force me to confess: I know their methods.

Did anyone ever bite his lips until they bled as he agonized over the impossibility of going back to his job in the morning . . . and of the impossibility of not going back?

I went up to the third floor of the building and rang the bell. A middle-aged woman opened the door.

"Does Alexander Grigoryevich Khvat live here?"

"Papa," she called softly.

He emerged from the next room. Tall and broad-chested, bald

except for a fringe of closely cropped gray hair, he still looked younger than his eighty years, but his halting gait and hunched stance gave away his age. In fact, he was not so much hunched as bent: it was as if pressure from above had pushed him down into a strange arc, bowing closer and closer toward the ground. I realized then that he was bent less from old age than from fear.

With a practiced flick of the wrist, Khvat opened up my ID and studied it with a professional's eye, matching the photograph with my face.

"What do you want?" he asked.

"Let's go inside," I said, to forestall the possibility of being chased off.

"Please come in." He obligingly opened the door and allowed me to pass in front of him.

A large double bed stood in the room; judging from the crushed pillows, he had been lying down. There were two little cupboards for the bedclothes, a bureau, and a pair of chairs—nothing else.

Khvat placed a chair near the window, where the light would fall on my face. He sat down opposite me near the wall.

I took the bull by the horns.

"Did you work as an investigator for the NKVD?"

"Yes."

"Do you recall being in charge of the Vavilov case in 1940—the academician?"

"Of course, I remember."

Khvat's willingness to respond took me by surprise. I was suddenly tongue-tied; this was the last thing I expected. The aggressive offense I had prepared turned out to be unnecessary. Before me, sat an old man . . . old, tired, and, it seemed, ill.

He admitted to his former career, but some of the details were lost in the fog of age. I had to remind him that he had tortured Vavilov for eleven months, that he'd summoned him four hundred times to interrogations that often lasted for hours on end. According to eyewitnesses, Vavilov could not walk unaided after these sessions; the Butyrka Prison wardens would push and prod him

back to Cell No. 27 and dump him by the door; his cellmates
would help him get up on his bunk, and remove the boots from
his bruised, horribly swollen feet.[3] The professor had been subjected to the so-called stand-up, a form of torture in which a person
was forced to stand for ten or more hours (sometimes this would
be stretched to days, until the veins in the victim's legs would
burst). After six months of such investigation, Vavilov had been
turned from a strong, fit, even dandyish fifty-three-year-old into a
doddering old man.

Awkwardly, I forced the question out:

"Witnesses claim that you used—" I searched for a euphemism
"—harsh methods of investigation on Vavilov."

"I categorically deny it," he snapped back, as if by rote. "There
was another investigator, Albogachiev," he said, selling his colleague down the river without a second thought. "He was a *natsmen*, an ethnic," he added.

Natsmen—short for *natsionalnoye menshinstvo*, or national
minority—is Russians' somewhat pejorative term for people from
Central Asia or the Caucasus.

"Albogachiev wasn't a cultivated man; a *natsmen*, you know
. . . He didn't get along so well with, ah, *him*." (Khvat stubbornly
refused to give Vavilov a name.)

Playing one ethnic group against another was a Stalinist specialty
that continued to serve a very useful function throughout the Soviet
period, even as the government declared its internationalism and
proclaimed the "friendship of nations." Since Vavilov was a Russian, naturally it would have to be a *natsmen* who did the torturing.
After all, Khvat couldn't torture a fellow Russian—you couldn't
treat your own that way, could you?

Khvat searched my face for a sign that I understood his logic,
a sign I doubt he found.

"Tell me, did you believe Vavilov was a spy?" I asked.

"No, of course I didn't believe the espionage charge; there was
no evidence. The agent department—there was one in the NKVD's
Chief Economic Directorate [apparently the ancestor of the KGB's

Seventh Directorate, the so-called *toptuny*]—decided for some reason or other that he was a spy. The agent department worked him over, but they didn't pass any information on to us; they kept it to themselves. It was they who issued an arrest warrant, for unspecified reasons. But as for the sabotage—well, there was some problem related to his work in agricultural science. I put together an experts' commission, with an academician at its head, and went to see Trofim Lysenko.* They—that is, the academicians and professors—confirmed the sabotage.†

"Didn't you feel any compassion for Vavilov? After all, he was facing the death penalty. Didn't you feel any pity for him, as a human being?"

I was almost certain Khvat would say, "Yes, I did feel some regret; but, you know, those were the times." After all, Khvat was not made of stone; a mere five minutes before, he hadn't been able to hold back the tears as he told me how, under Khrushchev, his Party card had been taken away and his KGB pension withdrawn "for violation of socialist legality during the years of employment at the NKVD." Naïvely, I had expected the same compassion for a man whose life had been taken away.

Khvat laughed out loud. "What do you mean, compassion?" Those were his exact words. "It wasn't like he was the only one, or anything."

He was right about that. Not one, but millions of innocent people disappeared into the damp earth. Nikolai Vavilov may have been an extraordinarily gifted man—he even managed to write his *History of World Farming* in prison (the manuscript was confiscated)—but in the face of death and suffering, all victims are equal.

What do you mean, compassion? asked Khvat. This was not a

---

* Trofim Lysenko (1898–1976), agronomist, opponent of genetic theory of inheritance; president of Agricultural Academy, 1938–56, 1961–62—Trans.

† On August 20, 1955, Nikolai Vavilov was rehabilitated by a decision of the Military Collegium of the USSR Supreme Soviet "owing to lack of evidence"—Author. ("Rehabilitation" is the Russian term for political exoneration and/or annulment of criminal charges—Trans.)

callow youth speaking, or a senior lieutenant of the NKVD in his prime, but an eighty-year-old man nearing the end of his life.

The story would have been simple, barely worth writing about, if Khvat and his colleagues were sadists, executioners by nature, to the depths of their very souls. Of course, there were sadists, plenty of them, in the Cheka and the NKVD. But this was something else. Khvat was a thoroughly normal person. After *Moscow News* ran my story, his nephew, a physicist who lived in Leningrad, showed up unannounced—completely stunned, he said, by what he had read about his uncle.[4] "You have to understand," he told me, "Uncle Sasha was the kind genie of our family. He saved me and my family when we were dying of hunger during the German blockade of Leningrad, and I know he helped other people." There's no reason to doubt it; and to his daughter Natasha, who worked as a Party secretary at the Keldysh Institute of Applied Mechanics, as to his other three children, Khvat was the best and most beloved of fathers. Even after all the exposés, they continued to feel the same way—in my view, all to their credit.

But even as Uncle Sasha was saving people in the dying city of Leningrad, his colleague, Lieut. Nikolai Kruzhkov, was busy jailing and torturing scientists—whose work, let us note, had served to strengthen the nation's defense. And when the scientists "confessed" their guilt—when, exhausted from hunger and looking like skeletons, they signed the statements fabricated by Kruzhkov—their reward was a pitiful 125 grams of bread. And Kruzhkov's son, a scientist from Moscow University, also showed up and tried to prove to my colleague Yaroslav Golovanov that his father, too, was a kind and good man who had just been following orders.

So, they were just normal people; or—normal *Soviet* people: maybe that adjective is the key to this enigma.

Khvat, for example, grew up in a large peasant family, and as a young boy attended a church parish school, where he undoubtedly learned the basics of God's law. Then came the revolution, and Khvat was quick enough to learn that for this government, he was one of the chosen, a "blue blood." The others, those not of "our class"—the children of the nobility, merchants, and other "exploiters"—were the enemy, and as such were barred from schools, institutes, and universities, including the Soviet Party school where Khvat studied the founding fathers of Marxism-Leninism. Khvat went from the Party school directly to employment at the Komsomol's district Party committee. There, he worked his way up, writing denunciations of his colleagues.[5] As time went on, his career path became clear. He was promoted and then transferred to Moscow, where he was given a post at the Central Soviet of Osoaviakhim, a government enterprise in charge of crop dusting.

In 1938, when Lavrenty Beria became People's Commissar, Khvat was invited in for a chat with the NKVD and told that he had been selected for work in the organs. According to his version of the story, Khvat tried to refuse. "I have no higher education; I don't know a thing about the law." "No matter," he was told. "We'll help you, we'll teach you, everything will be alright." They hinted that if he refused, his Party card would be taken away; so he went to work for them. What did he have to offer? What did he know? As a matter of fact, he really was rather poorly educated, and he'd never developed the habit of reading—not that he had much time for it, anyway.

What he did know was the following:

As Lenin said: "Looked at soberly and categorically, which is better: to imprison several dozen or hundred troublemakers, *guilty or innocent*, deliberate or not deliberate, or to lose a thousand Red Army soldiers and workers? The first is better."[6]

As Stalin said: "The *Shakhtintsy* (enemies of the people and "wreckers"*) are sitting in all branches of our industry now.[7] Many of them have been caught, but far from all."[8]

As USSR Procurator General Vyshinsky said: "Many enemies

---

* The term used during the Stalin era for alleged saboteurs—Trans.

have penetrated into all Soviet institutions and organizations, disguised as Soviet office workers, laborers, and peasants, and they are waging brutal and cunning battle against the Soviet economy and the Soviet state."[9]

As Lazar Kaganovich, secretary of the Central Committee, said: "We reject the concept of the *rule of law*. If a person who claims the title of Marxist speaks seriously about a law-based state and, what is more, applies the concept of a law-based state to the Soviet state, that means he is departing from the Marxist-Leninist teaching about the state."[10]

This is the "education" Khvat got, the lessons he learned. These were Khvat's "universities."

From all the loudspeakers, from all the radios and newspapers, he could hear the chant: *enemies, enemies, enemies*. Children came home from school gossiping about "Ivanov's father, the spy"; wives returned from work with news that Petrova's husband was a saboteur; people standing in line for milk said, "Have you heard about Tukhachevsky? He's a spy. And the wives of Budyonny, Molotov, Kalinin? They're spies, too." And people really believed it, even though only a month before, the newspapers had celebrated "Our Red Marshal Tukhachevsky, Civil War hero."

Espionage became the country's leading occupation. According to the NKVD's statistics, thirty-five times as many people were arrested for espionage in 1937 as in 1934. Sixty times as many were "discovered" to be Trotskyites—even though Trotsky himself had been exiled in 1929—and five hundred times as many were arrested for participating in so-called bourgeois-nationalist groups.

On July 30, 1937, Nikolai Yezhov, then chief of the NKVD, issued Order No. 00447: "On the operation to repress former kulaks, criminals, and other anti-Soviet elements." It is a monstrous document, horrific evidence of the Bolshevik regime's decision to add to its planned economy the planned murder of its citizens. Under this order, the prospective victims—kulaks, criminals, and other "anti-Soviet elements"—would be divided into two categories. The "most hostile" would be placed in the first category and be subject to immediate arrest; review of their cases would be followed by summary execution. The remaining, "less active, but still hostile" elements would be placed in the second category, in which they would be subject to arrest and imprisonment in labor camp for a term of eight to ten years.

The document proceeded to numbers—numbers, not names— of people who, according to the plan, should be shot in each republic, territory, and province. For example, the Azerbaijan NKVD was ordered to put 1,500 people into the first category, to be shot, and to send 3,750 to labor camp. Western Siberian Territory was told to shoot 5,000 and arrest 12,000; Moscow Province to shoot 5,000 and put 30,000 in labor camp. Within the four months allotted for the operation, a total of 76,000 people were to be shot, and 1,915,000 to be sent to labor camp. The *names* to be placed on this list were left to the discretion of the local authorities. In a top secret resolution, the Council of People's Commissars (the Soviet government) allocated 75 million rubles "for operational expenses related to conducting the operation." The Politburo approved of the release of 10 million rubles from reserve funds "to organize labor camps and conduct preparatory work."

The order specified that the investigation was to be conducted "in an accelerated and simplified manner." Stalin personally issued instructions for the summary execution of those adjudged to be members of the first category (with the word "summary" stressed). Party and Chekist bosses complied eagerly, vying to demonstrate their zeal. Urgent telegrams were fired off to Moscow: "As of August 19 in Omsk Province, 5,111 persons arrested in first category . . . Request instruction *re*: increase of quota in first category to 8,000 persons." Omsk proposed to exceed the plan—the number of victims assigned it by Politburo and NKVD planners—eightfold. Appended to this telegram is an order written in Stalin's own hand: "Comrade Yezhov: Approve increase of quota to 8,000 persons. J. Stalin." There were dozens, even hundreds, of telegrams and authorizations to increase quotas: "Permit Orenburg Provincial Party Committee to place 3,500 persons in first category" (the planned quota had been 1,500); "Approve proposal by Dagestan Provincial Party Committee to increase number of repressed persons in first category to 1,200 persons" (from 500). In its first two months alone, the operation covered three or four times the number originally planned, some 250,000 victims. The NKVD jackals, their appetites whetted, demanded more blood, more corpses. In January 1938, a resolution was passed "to approve an additional number of those subject to repression"; and a new list of republics, territories, and provinces, each with its "plan" of one, two, six, eight thousand deaths, appeared.

These were lessons Khvat could not fail to heed. And as for the fact that this wave of suspicion touched everyone—friends, acquaintances, neighbors, and coworkers—well, as the saying in those days went, "when you chop wood, chips fly." Khvat even repeated it to me: eighty years old, and he'd still never stopped to think that these "chips" were people.

That was the educational background Khvat brought with him to the NKVD. And they made good on their promise to "help" and "teach" him. "NKVD investigations are to be conducted according to the Code of Criminal Procedures. But the basis for initiating a criminal case is *somewhat broader* than in the Code." And Khvat was further instructed: "Do not let the accused obtain an advantage over you . . . During the course of the investigation the accused must be kept in hand. Remember, this is a serious battle with an enemy; you must identify him and get him to confess." If the investigator didn't want to end up on a prison bunk, he was well advised to memorize the following: "Renunciation of truthful testimony [any confession the accused had given previously] can only be explained by the fact that the detainee has escaped the influence of the investigator and has fallen under alien influence, which is not permissible. It must be recalled that an arrestee who has confessed has not ceased to be an enemy and will not cease looking for a loophole to evade responsibility. When the suspect renounces his testimony, this illustrates that investigators have done a poor job of working with the detainees." These citations come from NKVD agents' handbooks written by investigators Vladimirsky, Ushakov, and Shvartsman on orders from People's Commissar Yezhov, and adopted under People's Commissar Beria sometime after Yezhov's execution by firing squad. It was a period of confusion and inconsistency—no wonder, after a year so bloody, that "1937" became synonymous in Russian with "the Terror." Matters reached the point that in November 1938, the Central Committee Plenum actually passed a special resolution condemning lawlessness in the NKVD organs, and a small percentage of those who had been arrested were declared victims of unjust procedure and released from prisons and labor camps (only to wind up in them again later). But there is abundant documentary evidence that the abuses went on even as the resolution was being passed, and continued thereafter.

So, what might the NKVD have taught Khvat about a good job well done?

Here's an exemplary case. Arkady Yemelyanov, former manager of the Chief Construction Administration of the USSR People's Commissariat for Food Industry, gave this testimony to Maj. Kozhura, the military procurator, after Yemelyanov was exonerated in 1955 for his 1937 arrest.

> "Do you know why you were arrested?" Lukhovitsky, the investigator who handled my case, asked me. "No, I don't," I replied. Lukhovitsky took a step backward, spat in my face, and swore at me. I lunged at him. He was expecting that, and kicked me in the solar plexus. I lost consciousness. When I came to, I was on the floor of the toilet across from the investigator's room, with a split lip and a broken nose. My clothing was wet with blood. Lukhovitsky was standing nearby with an orderly who gave me some medicine, felt my pulse, and said, "It's not so bad." I was taken back to the room and placed against the wall. Lukhovitsky warned me that he would make me stand on the "conveyer belt" [as the relay of torturers was called] until I signed the confession.

He tormented me until morning. Then another man of about twenty-three or twenty-five with curly, light hair came on shift to take his place. He was there until midday, trying to convince me to stop suffering and testify. Then a plainclothesman of about twenty to twenty-two came in. He was replaced late that night by Lukhovitsky. And so it went for three days straight. I had to stand the entire time. They didn't give me anything to eat. During Lukhovitsky's shift they didn't give me any water, nor did they allow me to smoke. On the fourth day of uninterrupted standing, the arteries in my swollen legs erupted, and my limbs turned into a formless, bloody mess. I began to hallucinate and fainted repeatedly. Each time I fell, I was lifted to my feet, and as Lukhovitsky expressed it, "given a little pick-me-up" with corks that had large pins and needles stuck into them. They pricked my back and legs with them. They also used other methods to give me a "pick-me-up"; as soon as I shut my eyes, they pulled out the hairs of my beard and mustache.

"Just write on this piece of paper the name of the person who recruited you. We won't write up a report." "Against whom, specifically, must I give testimony?" I asked. "Only you know that. But whoever it is should be someone well known, and definitely a member of the Party leadership." "Should he be a member of the Central Committee?" "Don't worry about that, he could even be a member of the Politburo; keep in mind that there are already members of the Politburo behind bars—Rudzutak, Kossior, Chubar, and Eikhe." "What sort of accusations would you be interested in?" I asked. "Here are the main ideas. You just have to develop them." Since I no longer had the strength to endure the "conveyer belt," I wrote the following: "I consider it pointless to resist the investigator any further. I admit that I was a member of such-and-such a group . . ." Several days later, I was again summoned for interrogation. "When are you finally going to give testimony?" "But I already did, what else do you need?" "That was nonsense. We need real testimony." I remained silent. "You'll be taken to Lefortovo Prison, there you'll write everything required, I'm sure of it."

Two or three days later, Lukhovitsky and two other investigators interrogated me at Lefortovo. They beat me for an hour with a rubber truncheon and a whip made of bare copper wire, then they stomped on me.

Then they brought in Temkin. [Aron Temkin was the head of the Supply Administration of the People's Food Industry Commissariat.] Temkin said, "I was a witness when the people's commissar of the food industry gave Yemelyanov the assignment to murder Mikoyan." Temkin was immediately taken away.

"Can you confirm what Temkin said?" they asked.

"Now I understand."

"Temkin's testimony means a guaranteed death penalty for you. Your fate is in your own hands," they said. I refused to sign the fabricated report. Once again, they beat me and forced me to stand. They stepped on my toes with their boot heels and tore out my fingernails. A month later, in October, I signed the paper without even reading it.[11]

Arkady Yemelyanov signed eighty-two pages of testimony "in his own hand"—in fact, dictated to him by the investigator. He was sentenced to fifteen years of labor camp.

The files on Yemelyanov also contain the story of Aron Temkin.

Brandishing his truncheons and the wire whips, Lukhovitsky asked me if I knew where I was. He demanded my confession. "What exactly am I accused of?" I asked. "That question is an attempt to provoke the Soviet investigator." And he immediately began to beat me. Other people came into the office, and they beat me, too. During the breaks, Lukhovitsky would sit at the desk, going through the drawers of torture implements, selecting what he needed and singing a song with the words, "My eyes can't get enough of you." He kept laughing. When I fell unconscious on the floor, he threw cold water over me.

The next morning, I came to in my cell when I felt the prick of a hypodermic needle. (It was camphor.) The doctor expressed sympathy, saying I had apparently injured myself falling down the stairs. I was so bruised and swollen that I could not get my underwear on. I gave the most fantastic testimonies. Lukhovitsky tore them into pieces without reading them, and began to beat me with his belt, trying to make the buckle land on my wounds. He spat in my face. It turned out they expected no fewer than one hundred and twenty pages of testimony from me.

Aron Temkin signed one hundred and twenty pages of testimony "in his own hand," and received twenty years of labor camp. Lukhovitsky continued to serve in the organs until 1951, and retired with the rank of colonel.

I once asked an officer at the Chief Military Procuracy whether Lukhovitsky was mentally ill. "He was saner than you or I," I was told.

After reading dozens of such documents, I stopped asking such questions, just as I ceased to be amazed that people gave such unlikely testimony against themselves and their colleagues, friends, relatives, husbands or wives, all "in their own hand." The sheer quantity of denunciations seemed fantastic even to people who were serving the system. As Nikolai Gusalov, a Stalin-era prisoner who until his arrest was chairman of the State Planning Commission of Northern Ossetia, testified: "Ivan Gatsoyev, head of the Organization Department of the Provincial Party Committee, fingered six hundred people [as being involved in counterrevolutionary activity against the Soviet government] and Kokov named five hundred people. What was this all about? *They could have at least given them some kind of limit.*"

"They had a special torture for each and every individual," Lev Razgon explained to me. Razgon, too, signed anything they put before him. He wasn't beaten; he was simply informed that if he didn't sign, his wife Oksana, who had a severe form of diabetes, would have her insulin taken away.

"Naturally, I agreed; if they took Oksana's insulin away, it would kill her," Razgon told me. But they took Oksana's insulin away anyway, and she died in transit on the way to the labor camp, twenty-two years old.

To reiterate, what Lukhovitsky did was standard procedure, the practice of psychologically healthy, normal, *Soviet* investigators. And it was officially sanctioned from above, by the one person whom all Chekists, from the People's Commissar to the lowest operative, regarded with mortal fear, and whom they obeyed without question: Joseph Stalin.

On January 10, 1939 (a year after the Central Committee Plenum at which NKVD abuse was condemned), Stalin sent a coded telegram to the secretaries of all local Party offices, the central committees of the Communist Party in the Soviet republics, the people's commissars of internal affairs in all the republics, and the chiefs of the NKVD:

> The Central Committee hereby affirms that the use of physical persuasion in NKVD practice was allowed by permission of the Central Committee in 1937 . . . It is well known that all bourgeois intelligence agencies use physical persuasion against representatives of the socialist proletariat and, more-over, employ the most monstrous kinds. We may well ask why socialist intelligence should be more humane in treating inveterate agents of the bourgeoisie, sworn enemies of the working class and collective farm workers. The Party considers that physical persuasion must continue to be used in exceptional cases against clear and unrelenting enemies of the people, that it is then a perfectly appropriate and expedient method.[12]

After such a clear directive, it's not surprising that investigators who permitted themselves, shall we say, courtesy in their dealings with arrested people (that is, who didn't beat them) would attract suspicion, and would be accused of sympathizing with the enemy.

Perhaps it was in order to uproot this softness that the new MGB handbook of 1950, written under the supervision of Nikolai Leonov, chief of the MGB investigative unit, and approved by MGB Minister Viktor Abakumov, contained a demand to "step up the intensity of interrogations of detainees."[13]

So what of such "trivia" as arresting people without obtaining procurator's warrants (especially given that from 1932 to 1954, the secret police had their own institutionalized procuracy), jailing people for several months or even years without making formal charges, or keeping people in prison or even executing them after they had been found innocent by the court: what of it? That was the order: "step up the intensity." Khvat was guided by it, and nothing else.

But what of the law? *Were* there any laws? Of course, there were. For example, on January 2, 1928, the Seventeenth Plenum of the USSR Supreme Court passed a resolution "On Direct and Indirect Intent in Counterrevolutionary Crime," meant to clarify the definition of counterrevolutionary activities for judges. Point *b* explains "indirect intent" as occurring "when a perpetrator, even though he *did not directly have* counterrevolutionary aims, nevertheless deliberately allowed such [counterrevolutionary] actions to happen or *should have foreseen* the socially dangerous nature of the consequences of his actions."[14]

Over the next quarter-century, in part thanks to this "clarification," millions of people were sent to the camps by investigators who were better able to "foresee" socially dangerous consequences and to punish for them suspects who might not themselves be blessed with such keen imaginations. The active commission of a crime did not have to be proved.

But perhaps a discussion of laws is beside the point, since Khvat, like the majority of his colleagues, never received any instruction in the laws of the state and how they applied to his work. "To the extent that I understood, I conducted the cases," Khvat explained. To the extent, indeed.

Yet, in many situations, investigators were empowered to administer the law, to act as judge. If a case was sent to a "special conference," the surrogate court created in 1934,[15] the investigator not only argued for the prosecution, but proposed the sentence, which could be anything at all, up to execution by firing squad.[16] The special conference usually accepted the recommendation without comment.

But even if Khvat *had* known the law, there was nothing in his environment to indicate that laws were binding or permanent. "There are periods, moments in the life of society and in our own lives in particular, when laws become outmoded and must be set aside." These unforgettable words were spoken not by some faceless Party bureaucrat, but by the Chief Procurator of the Stalin era, Andrei Vyshinsky, the country's top law enforcement officer.[17] So it's no surprise that laws were treated as indulgences, and were set aside when they became inconvenient. When "sufficient evidence" became an undue burden on the prosecutor, there were the special conferences, specifically designed to adjudicate cases "for which *there was insufficient documented evidence*" without juries, without witnesses, without a procurator's statement, without the right to defense, and, quite often, without the defendant himself present.[18]

Those convicted of taking part "in a terrorist act or a terrorist organization" were denied the right to appeal their sentence or to petition for clemency. The sentence of capital punishment—that is, to death by firing squad—was carried out immediately.[19] Thus, Marshal Tukhachevsky and his "codefendants," other major ranking Red Army officers, were sentenced on June 11, 1937, and all shot on June 12.

And if the special conferences were too cumbersome, there were always the *dvoikas* and *troikas* (two- and three-man tribunals, respectively). On a single day—October 18, 1937—one dvoika alone, made up of NKVD People's Commissar Nikolai Yezhov and USSR Procurator Andrei Vyshinsky, "reviewed" the cases against 551 people and sentenced all the accused to execution.[20]

In fairness, it should be said that these kangaroo courts were not a revolutionary invention. The Bolsheviks drew heavily on the practice of the tsarist government they had overthrown in 1917, in whose prisons they had languished. In fact, they essentially copied the "Rules for the Procedure of Officials of the Gendarmes Corps to Investigate the Crimes of May 19, 1871" and the "Addenda of August 14, 1881," passed under Tsar Alexander III, which gave gendarmes "the right to arrest any person without any evidence of guilt at all for an act not recognized by law as a crime, based on information not subject to verification."[21]

During tsarist rule, however, such lawlessness at least could be criticized and condemned. At the so-called Trial of the Forty-four, an attack on the precursor of the Bolshevik Party, defense attorney V. N. Novikov said:

> Your honors! It is not a new fact that the gendarme's interrogation, although performed in accordance with the Rules of Criminal Investigation, is not reliable. Our political police are not at the forefront of their profession, and the type of interrogation they conduct is worthless. Almost every page of the indictment has the phrases "according to information received by the security department," "information which reached the security department." What are those phrases? What is this information?[22]

I can imagine what would have happened to a Soviet judge or lawyer of the Stalin era if he had dared to criticize an NKVD investigation in these terms. (The phrases "according to information received by the NKVD" or "the NKVD Directorate possesses information" were at the head of virtually every indictment issued by NKVD investigators.) Indeed, I know for a fact what happened to lawyers who dared to try to defend detainees. To cite but one example, in the March 1939 "Youth Affair" in Northern Ossetia, a case that led to the execution of the local Komsomol leaders, a lawyer named Yasinsky tried to prove that his client had been subjected to unlawful methods of investigation. Yasinsky's act was one of civic courage as well as civic desperation—his defendant was about to be executed. The lawyer himself was arrested the day after the trial, and found guilty of slander. He died in labor camp.[23]

So, all external barriers to the NKVD's murderous rampage had been effectively removed. But where were the individual's own internal moral constraints? Shouldn't they have come into play? After all, Khvat wasn't raised by wolves. He had a mother; he had grandparents who were religious believers. He'd gone to church and learned the Bible in school. The peasant families in the Russia where Khvat grew up were godfearing people: surely some bit of that moral teaching must have sunk in, some must have remained despite his revolutionary "education"? Apparently, all too little.

Khvat was seven years old when World War I broke out, ten when the Russian revolution came, turning brother against brother, son against father; when revolutionary military tribunals decided cases as "their revolutionary Communist sense of law and revolutionary conscience dictated"; when all the laws of tsarist Russia were abolished. Khvat was eleven when the Civil War started, when the White Terror's gallows covered Russia, and the Red Terror was unleashed.

It took shape very quickly. On December 7, 1917, less than two months after the October Bolshevik coup, the All-Russian Extraordinary Commission (VChK, known as the Cheka) was created. At first, it was charged with fighting counterrevolution and sabotage, and with ideological and economic counterintelligence. But the Cheka soon took on broader tasks: fighting speculation, government corruption, and espionage; suppressing counterrevolutionary acts and banditry; maintaining security on public transportation and in the Red Army; and guarding the state border.

On February 21, 1918, the Council of People's Commissars ratified Lenin's manifesto entitled "The Socialist Fatherland Is in Danger!" The eighth point of this document stated: "Enemy agents, speculators, thugs, hooligans, counterrevolutionary agitators, and German spies will be executed on the spot."[24] And so they were, by the dozens and hundreds; and then, by the thousands and hundreds of thousands. People started saying that the initials VChK stood for *vsyakomu cheloveku kaput*, the Russian phrase for "every man *kaput*."

The great humanist Lenin, fierce campaigner against the abuses of the tsarist autocracy, wrote a historic memo: "Comrade Feyadorov: In Nizhny, a White Guard uprising is clearly being prepared. We must mount every effort, create a troika of dictators, immediately unleash mass terror, shoot and expose hundreds of the prostitutes who get soldiers drunk, and [shoot] former officers, etc. There isn't a moment to lose. We must take action everywhere. Mass searches. Shoot anyone who is carrying a weapon. Change the guards at warehouses and put in reliable people."[25] He sent telegrams: "Shoot all plotters and *those who are ambivalent* without asking anyone, and do not permit any idiotic red tape."[26] He dictated letters to the front: "It's damned important for us to put an end to [White Guard General] Yudenich (yes, put an end to him—finish him off). If the attack has begun, can't we mobilize another 20,000 Petersburg workers plus 10,000 bourgeoisie, *put some machine guns behind them, shoot a couple hundred** and place massive pressure on Yudenich?" Or another: "Put every effort into catching and shooting the Astrakhan speculators and bribetakers. These bastards have to be dealt with so that people will remember it for years."[27]

They did remember; for years, they remembered, and they have not forgotten to this day. That was how the foundations of the

---

* This is where the SMERSH barrage troops of the Great Patriotic War got their start—Author. (SMERSH was the Russian acronym for *smert shpiyonam*, "death to spies," an infamous unit of counterintelligence during the war. One of their techniques was to follow behind charging soldiers at the front and shoot any who turned back or deserted—Trans.)

totalitarian regime, and of totalitarian law and totalitarian justice, were laid—the foundations of Soviet morality.

On September 5, 1918, after the murder of M. Uritsky, chairman of the Petrograd Cheka, and an assassination attempt on Lenin, the Council of People's Commissars passed the official resolution imposing the Red Terror. That was a signal to lift all restraints. For the next four or so years, Russia drowned in its own blood.

"We will sweep all the filth out of Soviet Russia with an iron broom," vowed M. Latsis, chairman of the Ukrainian Cheka, in the journal *Red Terror*, on November 1, 1918. "Do not look in the file of incriminating evidence to see whether or not the accused rose up against the Soviets with arms or words," advised Latsis. "Ask him instead to which class he belongs, what is his background, his education, his profession. These are the questions that will determine the fate of the accused. That is the meaning and essence of the Red Terror."[28]

The All-Russian Extraordinary Commission had unlimited rights, and was answerable to no one. Its agents were allowed to conduct searches at will, make arrests, and perform executions. Hostage-taking became a primary offensive tactic: innocent people were seized—on the street, in their apartments, in train stations or theaters—and shot, solely in retribution for someone else's terrorist attack in some other locale.

For the sake of deterrence, the Cheka journal *The Weekly of the Extraordinary Commission on the Struggle with Counterrevolution and Speculation* began to publish lists of the executed.

In answer to the murder of Comrade Uritsky and the attempt on Comrade Lenin, the following were subjected to Red Terror: By the Sumsk District Cheka—3 pilots; by the Smolensk District Commission—38 merchants of the Western District; by the Novorzhev Cheka, Alexander, Natalya, Yevdokiya, Pavel, and Mikhail Roslyakov; by the Poshekhonskaya Cheka, 31 people (5 Shalayevs, 4 Vokovs).[29]

"By order of the Petrograd Extraordinary Commission," reported the *Weekly* (No. 5, October 29, 1918), five hundred hostages were shot.[30] "Class aliens"—princes, dukes, representatives of the ancien régime, members of opposition parties—were taken hostage and executed: "A total of 184 of the most prominent representatives of the bourgeoisie and social traitors [Socialist Revolutionary Party members] were taken," reports the Ivano-Voznesensk Cheka.[31]

Nor were members of "our own class" exempt:

In a single Kozhukov concentration camp near Moscow, 313 Tambov peasants were held as hostages in 1921–22, including children whose ages ranged from one month to sixteen years.[32]

In the Ural region, an uprising was crushed with medieval brutality. According to official data, 10,000 peasants were executed; unofficially, they numbered 25,000 or more. When you talk with the workers and peasants, it seems incredible that the Bolsheviks could have a foothold when about 99 percent of the population are against them. It can only mean that the people are desperately scared.[33]

"Looking at my card file for just 1918 alone, I tried to determine the social background of the persons executed," writes S. Melgunov, who was living in Moscow at the time. "According to the few statistics I could gather, I was able to obtain the following very arbitrary groupings:[34]

Intellectuals	1,286
Peasants	962
Ordinary Workers	468
Unknown	450
Criminal Elements	438
White-Collar Criminals	187
Servants	118

Soldiers and Sailors   28
Bourgeoisie   22
Priests   19

Wives were arrested for their husbands' offenses; husbands, for their wives'; children, for their parents'; parents, for their children's; neighbors, for their neighbors'; servants, for their masters'. A certain student P murdered Commissar N: for that, the student's father, mother, two brothers (the younger of whom was fifteen), his teacher (who was a German), and her eighteen-year-old niece all were murdered. After that, they found the student.[35]

A priest, an engineer, a medical orderly, a merchant, a factory owner, "the former editor of a newspaper," "a lumberjack," "a former prison guard," "a retired artillery man," "a leader of a local branch of the Popular Will Party," "a student pretending to be a sailor"—all of these appear on a list, published in various Cheka weeklies, of the professions of persons shot to death.

It was a bacchanal of violence.

"It would be inconvenient to conduct the operation of the Cheka within a legal framework," the Chekist Shklovsky explained simply in No. 6 of the Cheka's *Weekly*.

Throughout the country, without investigation or trial, the Chekists raged. They tortured old men and raped schoolgirls and killed parents before the eyes of their children. They impaled people, beat them with an iron glove, put wet leather "crowns" on their heads, buried them alive, locked them in cells where the floor was covered with corpses. Amazing, isn't it, that today's agents do not blanch to call themselves Chekists, and proudly claim Dzerzhinsky's legacy?

"Our terror was forced on us," cried the Bolshevik leaders. "Its source is the working class, not the Cheka."

No, that's not true; the terror clearly was the Cheka's own, as we can see from the Cheka's own instructions. Here is just one of the official Chekist directives from spring 1918, concerning the categories of people to be shot:

I. Application of Executions

1. All former gendarme officers on the special list approved by the VChK.

2. All gendarmes and police officers accused of suspicious activities based on results of a search.

3. Anyone in possession of unauthorized weapons, unless mitigating circumstances exist (for example, membership in a revolutionary Soviet party or workers' organization).

4. Anyone suspected of counterrevolutionary activity who is discovered to be in possession of false documents. Where some doubt exists, these cases should be transferred to the VChK for final review.

5. Anyone discovered consorting with Russian and foreign counterrevolutionaries and their organizations for criminal purposes, either within the territory of Soviet Russia or outside.

6. Active members of Socialist Revolutionary parties of the center and right. (Note: included among active members are members of executive bodies of all committees from the central down to the city and district level; members of armed groups and those who have Party-related dealings with them; anyone performing assignments for armed groups; anyone serving as a liaison between various organizations, etc.

7. Active members of counterrevolutionary parties (Cadets, Octobrists, etc.)

8. Cases in which the death penalty is to be imposed must be discussed in the presence of representatives of the Russian Communist Party.

9. Execution may only be implemented by unanimous decision of three members of the Commission.

10. Upon demand by a representative of the Russian Committee of Communists, or in the event of disagree-

ment among the members of the RChK [Russian Extraordinary Commission], the case must be transferred to the All-Russian ChK for final determination.

II. Arrest Followed by Imprisonment in Concentration Camp

11. Anyone advocating and organizing political strikes and other active measures to overthrow Soviet rule, if not already subject to execution.

12. Officers with no specific assignment who, after searches, are deemed suspicious.

13. Prominent leaders of bourgeois and landowners' counterrevolutionary groups.

14. Members of former nationalist and Black Hundreds organizations.

15. All members, without exception, of Socialist Revolutionary parties of the center, right-wing popular socialists, Cadets, and other counterrevolutionaries. Ordinary members of Socialist Revolutionary center and right-wing parties who are proletarians may be released after signing a statement declaring that they condemn the terrorist policy of their central [party] institutions and their [parties'] policy vis-à-vis the Anglo-French invasion and their general approval of Anglo-French imperialism.

16. Active members of the Menshevik party, according to the criteria enumerated in point 6.

Wide-scale searches and arrests must be conducted among the bourgeoisie, and arrested bourgeois must be declared hostages and imprisoned in camps, where forced labor will be organized for them. For intimidation's sake, the bourgeois must be deported immediately, given only the briefest period (24–36 hours) to prepare for departure . . .[36]

For the sake of some "bright future," the Bolsheviks turned the country into an enormous graveyard. As Melgunov wrote, "There wasn't a town or village where there wasn't a department of the almighty All-Russian Extraordinary Commission, which is now the *main nerve of state administration*, and has swallowed up the last vestiges of law. No other nation in the world has gone so far in sanctioning murder as an instrument of government."[37]

A top secret memo from Lenin, dated April 1921, instructed Molotov to have the VChK to draft a systematic plan for the rest of 1921 and early 1922, and report within a couple of weeks to the Politburo. The Cheka was to

1) complete liquidation of the Socialist Revolutionaries and tighten surveillance;
2) the Mensheviks—as above;
3) purge the Party: out with unstable Communists;
4) purge Saratov and Samar region;
5) purge special-assignment units;
6) purge academy students in the provinces;
7) purge village government apparats: lecture needed from the VChK, the NKVnudel [People's Commissariat of Internal Affairs], and Rabkrin [Workers and Peasants Inspectorate]. *Top secret. Eyes only. Retyping prohibited. Burn after use.*[38]

The actual document, drafted by Samsonov, the chief of the Cheka's Secret Department, is sprinkled with phrases like "massive operations," "liquidation," "group and individual isolation," and imperatives to "flush out" the Socialist Revolutionaries and Mensheviks "to the edge of the Republic." And it was all planned, months in advance, taking into account holidays and seasonal variations in working patterns. "During the summer period before the harvest, operations on a national scale (except for unusual instances, like the Kronstadt events, etc.) should not be carried out, but activists of all parties right up to the regional and territorial level should be individually beaten."[39]

At some point, Lenin, himself a lawyer by training, after all, seems to have comprehended the terrible force of destruction he had unleashed, and attempted to check its progress. At a Politburo session on December 1, 1921, he proposed a resolution that would narrow the jurisdiction of the VChK and strengthen the role of the judicial organs. But it was too late; his resolution was voted down.[40] (A year prior to this, in December 1920, the VTsIK [All-Russian Central Executive Committee] and Council of People's Commissars had suspended executions. That decision lasted only four months.) The avalanche could not be stopped.

No one knows how many people perished in the carnage; estimates run as high as an average of five thousand people a day, or 1.5 million people a year.[41]

The writer Maxim Gorky rationalized the brutality of the revolution by the brutality and ignorance of the Russian people. So, then, is the brutality of the French Revolution a result of the enlightenment of the French people? No, I think that, at root, revolution is beyond ethnicity. Russians, Jews, Ukrainians, Latvians, Georgians, and Armenians all took part in the slaughter in Russia, and each group had its own reason for doing so. (The reference book *Peoples of the USSR* could double as a list of the participating groups.) The very principle of revolution as a way to resolve social problems is flawed. By its very nature, revolution releases the most unbridled instincts of the basest elements of society. For them, revolution offers the chance to grab what life had denied them, whether because of their own insufficiencies or the injustices of the social system.

Revolution inevitably is violent. (As Lenin said: "A revolution is not made in white gloves"; "a revolution is only worth something when it knows how to defend itself.") And the violence inevitably corrupts those people who employ it. It's said that a person who has once tasted human flesh becomes a cannibal forever; the same is true for the person who has shed another's blood: he has already crossed some moral line, and once he has done so, he can do it a second time, and a third, and a tenth. "You only have to allow yourself to do it once," says Dostoyevsky's Raskolnikov, after murdering the old pawnbroker. Hundreds, thousands, tens of thousands of people all over the country *allowed themselves* to do it: is it any wonder, then, that this country and this people so easily accepted and justified Stalin's genocide?

"By the will of revolutionary power," wrote the first People's Commissar of Justice, the left Socialist Revolutionary Shteinberg, "a stratum of revolutionary murderers has been created who are fated soon to become the murderers of the revolution."[42]

But he was wrong. This was no "stratum" of murderers, but a whole country; and they were not "murderers of the revolution," but the most faithful incarnation of its principles. They always justified their bloody actions in the most uplifting terms, as necessary means to a noble end, the realization of the Communist idea.

But any idea, Communist or National Socialist, that separates people by class (exploiters and exploited), nationality (Aryans and non-Aryans), or on any other basis, is inherently corrupt. Any idea that declares some people better and others worse, and promises the "best" people heaven—at the expense, naturally, of the murder of the others, the worst—is fundamentally flawed. As the Chekist newspaper *Krasnyy mech* [The Red Sword] put it, "The victims we claim will bring redemption and pave the way to the Bright Kingdom of Labor, Freedom, and Truth."[43] Such an idea must entail the creation of a powerful security corps and punitive organs to ensure that the "worst" do not sneak into the ranks of the "best." (Lenin: "The power of the laborers cannot exist while exploiters *exist* on the earth.")[44] "We are a form of the same essence—the Party state," the SS officer Liss persuades the Bolshevik Mostovsky in Vasily Grossman's great novel, *Life and Fate*.[45] "It's not important which one of us wins in this war," he says. "If you win, we will go on living and continue on in you; if we win, you will go on living and continue on in us."

It was in the name of that "bright kingdom" that thousands of Soviet prisoners of war who lived through German labor camps were sent to the Soviet camps in Siberia, and in the name of that same kingdom that a mere three months after the Third Reich signed a treaty of unconditional surrender, the NKVD moved its own prisoners into Buchenwald—that symbol of the Fascist hell —which, along with ten other concentration camps, had come under Soviet control. According to West German estimates, about 65,000 political prisoners—men, women, and children—perished in the special camps of the Soviet zone of occupation.[46]

Although these camps were closed in 1950, a new wave of repression was unleashed in the Soviet Union, no less terrible than that of 1937. Owing to the shortage of executioners and the large number of "criminals" condemned to death, the Chekists used trucks camouflaged as bread vans for mobile death chambers. Yes, the very same machinery made notorious by the Nazis—yes, these trucks were originally a Soviet invention, in use years before the ovens of Auschwitz were built.[47]

In the name of "Labor, Freedom, and Truth," all moral order was reversed. "There is no morality in politics, there is only expediency," taught Lenin.[48] And people learned the lesson. But it was a hard lesson, and the earlier a child began to learn it, the better. Zalkind's *Revolution and Youth*, published in Moscow in 1924, spelled it out:

> "Thou shalt not kill" is a sanctimonious commandment. The proletariat should approach this rule in strictly utilitarian fashion, from the point of view of class utility. Murder of the most evil, incorrigible enemy of the revolution, murder committed in an organized manner by a class collective on the order of the class rulers in the name of salvation of the proletarian revolution, is *lawful, ethical murder*. The metaphysical values of human life do not exist for the proletariat, for whom there exist only the interests of the proletarian revolution.[49]

Murder became the norm. "A twelve-year-old girl is afraid of blood. Draw up a list of books whose reading will force the girl to reject her instinctive revulsion toward the Red Terror," recommends the *Anthology of Assignments for Extracurricular Library Work* of 1920.[50]

A boy named Sasha Khvat was thirteen years old at the time. He was twenty-two when the "great change"—collectivization—cut its cruel swathe through the villages, as the OGPU*, as the Cheka was called after 1923, carried out the deportation of millions of peasant families to Siberia—to starvation and death. And they were the flower of the peasantry, the prosperous (and therefore "undesirable") *kulaks*, and slightly less well-off (but still undesirable) *podkulachniki*.†

How could anyone's moral sense develop in all this madness? What could compassion mean to someone who learned not to think twice about shedding another's blood or taking a life? How else could the investigators of the VChK-OGPU-NKVD-KGB behave, when they, and their teachers and predecessors, all had been educated in this school of fratricidal terror?

But does that excuse Khvat (and his ilk), justify what he did? Does it lessen his guilt before the men he sentenced to death, or the wives who lost their husbands, or the orphaned children whose childhood was snatched away, who suffered neglect and abuse in the special homes for children of "enemies of the people"?

The children. There is no more painful topic. Consider the following letter to Joseph Stalin, found in the papers of NKVD investigator Lt. Gen. Alexander Lanfang. It is addressed to "Uncle," an affectionate term children often use even with unrelated adults in Russia, and the name and patronymic of that "Uncle" are those of Stalin:

---

* *Obyedinyonnoye gosudarstvennoye politicheskoye upravleniye*, Unified State Political Directorate—Trans.

† According to official statistics, about 1.5 million kulak families were deported. Each family had an average of six people—Author.

Dear Uncle Josif Vissarionovich,

My sister Roza and I go to School No. 151 of the Leningrad District in Moscow. I am in the fifth grade, and Roza is in the second. We decided to write you a letter so we could calm down and study better. Our father, Vasily Tarasovich Chemodanov, was taken September 15, 1937. Our mama was in the hospital at the time having a complicated operation, a Caesarean section, and they took out our sister, whom we called Svetlanochka. She is already three and a half months old. Two months after they arrested Papa, they came for mama. But they didn't take Mama, because Svetlanochka was three weeks old, and Mama was very sick. They asked her to sign a statement that she would not leave Moscow. Josif Vissarionovich, we ask you not to touch our mama, because she is good and we love her. We ask you to please answer our letter. And we promise you that we will study hard and always get good marks.

Leningradskoye shosse, d. 36, kv. 191. Written by Grisha Chemodanov, Roza Chemodanov, and Grisha Chemodanov for Svetlanochka.

This letter was written by the children of a Vasily Chemodanov, "Comrado Chemo," a man well known, even legendary, in the Russia of the 1930s, as the Komsomol representative in the Communist Youth International. Naturally, he was arrested and executed, as were so many people with international ties in those days.

Investigator Alexander Lanfang had been in charge of Chemodanov's case, which is why the letter from the junior Chemodanovs to "the children's best friend" (as the newspapers of that era called Stalin) had ended up in Lanfang's files.

I located the Chemodanov children in 1988. Grisha, the eldest, had been killed at the front in 1941. When I read his letter to his surviving sisters, Roza and Svetlanochka, the two women broke down in tears, and at first could not even speak. Then, they told me their story.

After their father's arrest, Grisha and Roza lived with their grandmother for a time, until their mother, Olga Abramovna, and baby sister, Svetlanochka, came home from the hospital. As a result of a botched blood transfusion, Olga had lost sensation in her legs and arms. The family had no money. The NKVD men had confiscated their possessions by the truckload, leaving only the bed on which the children slept. Roza, peeping from behind a door, saw how they divided up the family's things among themselves: "This gramophone is for you, that dress for me." They even squabbled over her mama's rose-colored powder compact.

Using Olga's passport, Roza and Grisha got a job in a workshop pasting together cardboard pudding packages. That was how they earned money to buy some bread for themselves, and some milk for Svetlanochka. (Their mother's own milk had dried up from all the worry.) Sometimes, there would be a knock at the door, and when they opened it, a bag of groceries would have been left behind: their neighbors were helping to feed them, but were afraid to visit the apartment of a man who had been arrested.

The children also scraped together five rubles a month to send to their father in prison—first to Butyrka, then to Lefortovo. The clerks at the window kept on accepting the money right up until the war in 1941, never bothering to inform the children that Vasily Chemodanov had been executed in November 1937.

One day, their mother's former manicurist called her and offered to teach her and fit her out with the tools of the trade. "Otherwise, you'll die of hunger." But, as the wife of "an enemy of the people," Olga Abramovna was unable to find a job anywhere. As soon as Roza turned thirteen, she had to leave school and go to work at a factory as a riveter.

When war broke out, Svetlanochka was turned over to a state children's home. Soon, an anonymous letter arrived saying the children at the orphanage were covered with lice, their stomachs were swollen from hunger, they were being buried by the busload.

If you want to see Svetlanochka alive, wrote the correspondent, get her out of here. Some old Moscow neighbors who had moved to a town near the orphanage took her in.

For a long time after, Svetlanochka would cry when she saw bread on the table—from fear that there wouldn't be any left for her.

In the mid-1950s, Vasily Chemodanov, like so many others, was rehabilitated. His widow and daughters received the proper piece of paper. But both "place of death" and "cause of death" had been crossed out on the form.

After my article about Khvat was published, I received dozens of letters: "By telling about Khvat's 'universities,' about the NKVD's codes of conduct, about the moral atmosphere in the country at the time, you are justifying Khvat," a reader wrote.

That wasn't it, I replied. I was just trying to understand how people like Khvat were formed; people who, as late as 1991, ranked Felix Dzerzhinsky, the founder of the Cheka, among their top five heroes.[51] For that's the point, really—the Khvats and the Lukhovitskys can't just be dismissed as aberrations or mutants. They are purebred Soviet types.

As for their guilt, is there any more difficult question? Determining the guilt of someone who was following orders is doubly difficult, in legal as well as moral terms.

It's true that the arrest of Vavilov, Khvat's "charge," was okayed at the top. No less a figure than Beria, People's Commissar of the NKVD, had secured permission from Molotov, the chairman of the Soviet of People's Commissars. And it's also true that Stalin himself would review the NKVD's arrest list and would "mark the names of the people who had to be arrested with crosses or arrows or all sorts of other signs, and often give orders as to what direction an investigation should take."[52] Leading government figures—Voroshilov, Kaganovich, and Malenkov—would take part in interrogations and sanction physical torture. Yes, the country was being run by a band of murderers (in gangsters' slang, *pakhany*, god-fathers). And except for Beria and his close comrades, none of them suffered any punishment.

But it is also true that many of the NKVD's victims were arrested because their fellow citizens—normal Soviet people—wrote informers' reports against them.

They wrote so that they could get rid of an undesirable boss. They wrote to get rid of a rival who stood in the way of their career. They wrote to improve their living conditions, to put a neighbor behind bars and as a reward get his room in a tiny communal apartment. Wives denounced their husbands to make way for a lover; husbands denounced their wives. Wives denounced their husbands' mistresses, then the mistresses informed on their lovers.

People informed out of fear, as a means of self-preservation. Many informed under pressure from the Chekists who had to fulfill an arrest quota and needed the informers' "evidence." Whatever the reasons, they wrote; they denounced; they informed. According to some estimates, one of every two citizens of the country cooperated with the NKVD. And that's not counting the millions who voted readily at meetings to expel "the wife of the enemy of the people" from the Party, or his son from Komsomol, knowing that the person would automatically be removed from a job or an institute or be barred from university, and would be branded for life as an outcast. Or the tens of millions who silently swallowed what was served up in the newspapers, not bothering to doubt what was written—thus assuring the Khvats of the world unopposed tyranny over the entire nation in the time when the adage about cannibals was put to the test daily.

I was not alive then, and so perhaps my position, that of someone born in a "vegetarian time," is too absolute. There were, of course, different degrees of guilt, but is that really an excuse simply to forgive oneself and forget?

I often think: What would we do if we didn't have our leaders—Stalin, Khrushchev, Brezhnev, Gorbachev, and now

Yeltsin—on whom to place exclusive blame for the actions of millions? And I ask myself: How much more time will pass before the public—the intelligentsia, the new democrats, and all the rest of us, too—will admit that we are all to blame for what went on during all these decades of Soviet rule? After all, it happened because of us—because we let them get away with it.

We allowed them to kill us in the 1930s and 1940s (we helped by informing and encouraging them with our support), and to humiliate us in the 1950s ("Thank God, at least they're not putting us in jail anymore"). We allowed them to have us fired, to forbid us to travel abroad, to send us to psychiatric prisons. And we let them jail and exile those who challenged their power in the 1970s and 1980s. We remained silent. The effect of our complicity is well known; a terrible statistic has made it into the Guinness Book of Records: 66.7 million people were killed by state persecution and terrorism from October 1917 through 1959—under Lenin, Stalin, and Khrushchev.[53] And how many lives were ruined after that, in the 1970s and 1980s, when we remained abjectly silent—who can count them?

Of course Khvat is guilty, regardless of the fact that the criminal case begun against him by the Chief Military Procuracy under Khrushchev in 1957 was closed in 1962.

Khvat is guilty because he has human blood on his hands, and because he was perfectly aware of what he was doing. Recall what he said about the charges brought against Vavilov, whom he prosecuted so vigorously: "Of course I didn't believe the espionage charge." He knew that he was sending innocent people to their deaths.

During his trial in 1955, NKVD investigator Leonid Shvartsman was asked, "Were you not aware of the fact that you were beating one of the great military leaders, a man who had served his country nobly?" (He was being asked about Army Gen. K. A. Meretskov, arrested in the summer of 1941.) Shvartsman replied: "I had orders from very high up, which were not subject to discussion."[54]

There were never any discussions; you simply did as you were told, and so earned medals and titles and salaries (along with bonuses adjusted for rank; officers' salaries were ten or twenty times higher than average people's). You were given an apartment, vacations in elite spas, and access to special, nonpublic distributors of scarce products. And you rose through the ranks.

In 1946, Khvat was promoted to head of Department T, the Department to Combat Terrorism of the NKVD's Central Office. Lambs of God did not advance in the NKVD, or get coveted apartments in the center of Moscow; Khvat must have earned it.

On the subject of apartments: given the Soviet Union's persistent housing shortage, especially in those years, if a potential "enemy of the people" had a decent apartment, that was always a serious incentive for arrest. For example, Investigator Boyarsky, who worked in Northern Ossetia, arrested a married couple, the Tsurovs, kicked their twelve-year-old daughter out onto the street, and moved into the apartment. He even took a liking to the furniture, and kept it. In 1950, the MGB and the Moscow city authorities actually signed a special agreement whereby apartments of detainees were transferred to the MGB in order to resolve the housing problems of their own employees.

But the greatest appeal of being an NKVD investigator was not the fancy titles and the high pay, but the power one held over other people. The neighbors of MGB officers feared them. Their wives were served first at the store. Bullies from the schoolyard suddenly became deferential, and former classmates sought their patronage. Academicians, and marshals, and even Politburo members—who only the day before could have pulverized them with a single word—now begged these investigators for mercy during interrogations. Oh, revenge was sweet for these petty little people; they actually seemed to enjoy it.

Lackeys! Perhaps this was the ultimate paradox of Communism: that, under its banner of absolute equality, the ignorant, the servile, and the unqualified felt entitled to grab the mantle of power. The idea that class should no longer limit a person became perverted and twisted, until its adherents felt that nothing should stand in the way of their ambitions. No longer barred from high positions, they began to feel that power, not just equality, was their right. And so, in the workers' and peasants' state, it became unprestigious to be a worker or peasant. Those more intelligent, more educated, and more successful were seen as impediments to be humiliated, crushed, and stamped out. Lackeys of Khvat's type could find no other way to claim their "birthright" than through brutality and murder. The same pattern has emerged in all of this century's communist regimes, in Europe and Latin America and Africa. It ensures that all the old classes, strata, and castes will rise again, with the aggressive mediocrities and nonentities now becoming the elite.

But let us return to the thirties and forties, to the Stalinist investigators. Didn't any of them resist the lawlessness, refuse to beat testimony out of people, to torture them with the "stand-up" or other methods? Yes, some did. I was told about Terenty Deribas, chief of the NKVD Directorate for the Far East Territory, who refused to conduct arrests on falsified testimony, and was executed.[55] Investigator Glebov wouldn't take the "testimony" of Commander Yakir. He, too, was shot. Kapustin and Volkov, heads of NKVD regional directorates, both committed suicide. S. Nuskulter, procurator of the city of Vitebsk, took it into his head to do something quite strange for those times: he investigated the legality of keeping people in the NKVD's pretrial holding cells. A firing squad put an end to his questions.[56]

I also heard of investigators who didn't take a public stance against the NKVD, or get shot, but who would shut the doors of the interrogation rooms and say to the detainee: "I will now scream and shout swear words and bang my fists on the table. You must cry out. That's for those who are listening behind the door." And no doubt there were others whose names I did not learn, whom I did not read or hear about, who simply disappeared. But the list of true people of conscience is heartbreakingly short, although 22,000 Chekists died during the years of the Stalinist Inquisition.[57]

God rest their souls! Still, few of them died fighting the criminal regime; they were simply victims of Stalin's purges of the NKVD organs, which destroyed layer after layer of Chekists, and put others in their place.

Common wisdom holds that the apogee of the punitive organs' power came in the Stalin years. But, for all that this was the bloodiest period in their history, the organs still remained subservient to the country's sole true power: Joseph Stalin. NKVD agents were relegated to the role of private henchmen, albeit henchmen with considerable initiative. In the depths of his heart, the dictator probably feared them. But they feared him even more.

Hanging over them was the Damoclean sword of the purges certain to come. They'd come under people's commissars Yagoda and Yezhov, under Beria, then under the NKVD-MGB chairmen Abakumov, Merkulov, and Ignatyev.

Stalin had both Yagoda and Yezhov executed; he would have done the same to Beria, if his own age and health hadn't caught up with him. But Khrushchev took care of it for him.

Right after Commissar Yagoda's death in 1936, all eighteen of the first- and second-ranking commissars of state security were executed. After Yezhov's death in 1938, 101 of the highest NKVD officials were executed—not only Yezhov's deputies, but almost all the department heads of the NKVD Central Office, the people's commissars of internal affairs of the Union and autonomous republics, and the chiefs of territorial, regional, and city directorates.[58]

Thousands of ordinary investigators were shot in the cellars of the Soviet Gestapo. (Khvat survived by a miracle; a warrant for his arrest had been signed in the early 1950s.)

"I cannot describe in words what happened to me during that time. I was more like a hounded animal than a tortured human being," wrote Investigator Z. Ushakov-Ushimirsky to the leaders of the NKVD from prison. Ushakov-Ushimirsky had been among those who in 1937 perpetrated bogus accusations of a "military-

Fascist conspiracy" in the Red Army, and had personally beaten a "confession" out of Marshal Tukhachevsky. "I myself had occasion to beat enemies of the Party and Soviet government in Lefortovo Prison (and elsewhere)," he wrote. "But I never had any idea of how terrible it felt to be beaten, the agonies people experienced. True, our beatings were never so brutal; and besides, we interrogated and beat them only when absolutely necessary, and when they really were enemies . . . What can I say? I gave up, I could no longer bear the beatings or even the mention of them."[59] He was executed in 1938, soon after his arrest.

Stalin was no fool. He realized that witnesses like Ushakov-Ushimirsky were liabilities, and he removed them in a timely fashion. He knew that mortal terror was the only way to keep these blood-crazed people under his control. Otherwise, they might attack the dictator himself, like a pack of wolves falling on their leader at the first sign of weakness. It was through fear—obsessive, haunting, animal fear—that Stalin kept the ever-growing state security system in line, and turned it into his instrument, the means by which his will became power.

In other words, a body such as the KGB can only be kept under control and prevented from seizing power through an absolute personal dictatorship. People raised in the language of violence do not understand any other. Every weakness, every concession only adds to the group's strength, and the instrument of power becomes a power in its own right.

At the end of the interview, Khvat cried. And I felt sorry for him. I pitied this old man who had lived a long and inglorious life, in which he had been both executioner and victim.

CHAPTER

3

Unnatural Selection

The dictator died. His chief henchman, Beria, suddenly "turned out to be" an English spy, and was deposed. The first, cannibal stage of the totalitarian state's development gave way to a more civilized stage: now, souls were destroyed, rather than bodies. And now, the KGB's infiltration of state and social structures began in earnest.

Years in the upper echelons of power had given Nikita Khrushchev a clear idea of what the Chekists were capable of when a strong controlling hand was absent. And he knew he was no Stalin.

Aware of the terrible danger the organs constituted to him, he wasted no time in instituting his own defensive purge of state security. This time, the purge was virtually bloodless—a shift from barbaric to bureaucratic measures that indicated a significant realignment of the balance of power between the head of the totalitarian state and the organs.

In retrospect, this can be seen as a clear portent of Khrushchev's eventual fall from power. Indeed, Brezhnev's coup against Khrushchev in 1964 was in large part engineered by the KGB, led by Vladimir Semichastny. Unlike Stalin, Khrushchev did not inspire terror in the organs. The lesson is clear: In a totalitarian state, nothing, neither punishment nor pardons, can be half-hearted.

Those whom Khrushchev punished became not frightened, but resentful; those whom he pardoned realized his vulnerability—and prepared for the kill.

This isn't to say that the organs didn't have a difficult time of it for a while. With the Stalinist past still vividly in mind, the Party hierarchy made panicky attempts to quash any initiative on the part of the security services. Beria was executed in 1953; shortly thereafter, his closest aides were as well. Kobulov was executed in 1954 (Bagirov in 1956), the same year in which State Security (MGB) Minister Abakumov and the MGB Chief of Investigation Leonov went on trial and MGB Gen. M. Ryumin, the instigator of the famous "Doctors' Plot" case, was sentenced to death.[1] Harsh experience told the organs that worse was likely to come.

In 1955, that fear seemed to be coming true. Khrushchev, driven by domestic economic crisis, especially in agriculture, by Cold War tensions, and by signs of unrest in Eastern Europe, moved to consolidate his political position at home. A series of amnesties freed thousands from the gulag at the same time that twenty-year terms given thousands more were coming to an end. A flood of returnees, all with distinct memories of their torturers, loomed. The Chief Military Procuracy assembled a special group under the direction of Maj. Gen. Boris Viktorov to review falsified cases and "rehabilitate" the victims.[2] Later, similar groups were set up country-wide. Many former NKVD-MGB employees were fired, replaced by "new brooms" from the ostensibly "cleansed" organs. "We were replaced by amateurs"—Khvat complained to me—"Central Committee types." (But it was the Party's Central Committee that had sanctioned the repressions in the first place . . . the KGB hadn't acted without an OK from above.) Some professionals remained, like Filipp Bobkov, who joined in 1945 and didn't retire until 1991 (if then). And, while the organs duly changed the sign on their door, replacing the word "ministry" with "committee"—the Ministry of State Security (MGB)* was now called the Committee for State Security (KGB)—they still carried on the business of fabricating new cases under the same old Art. 58–10 (counterrevolutionary agitation); although now it was jokes about Khrushchev instead of Stalin that could land a person in jail.[3] The new man at the head of state security was Gen. Ivan Serov, Beria's deputy in the late 1930s, the "hero" who had organized the massive deportation of the peoples of the Caucasus during the war, and the adviser whose words of wisdom Khvat had sought in the case of academician Nikolai Vavilov. (Gen. Serov even managed to reap some advantages of perestroika in the last years of his life, heading the Red Star Garden and Dacha Cooperative.) Nor was Serov's career atypical of the "revamping" of the secret police.

What happened to the thousands of NKVD-MGB investigators? Basically, nothing. Thirty-eight NKVD generals were stripped of their titles, for example Aviation Lt. Gen. Alexander Avseyevich, one of the officers who in 1937 had succeeded in beating Vitaly Primakov into "confessing" that he had participated in a "military-Fascist plot" in the Red Army. Unlike his colleague Ushakov-Ushimirsky, Avseyevich had managed to escape Beria's purge of the cadres, and had been transferred to another "cover" at the USSR Military Air Forces.

Over a period of time, hundreds of Chekists lost their Party cards. Khvat resigned (under pressure) from the organs, and then spent five years as Party secretary at one of the directorates of the Ministry of Medium Machine-Building (known as the "atom ministry" because it was responsible for design and production of nuclear weapons). But in 1962, when the criminal investigation against Khvat was called off "owing to the statute of limitations," Dmitry Terekhov, another deputy of the Chief Military Procurator General, managed to get the Central Committee's Party Control

---

* From March 1953 to March 1954, the MGB was merged with the Ministry of Internal Affairs (MVD) and known under that title.

Committee to expel Khvat from the Party—despite Khvat's exemplary record (the NKVD-MGB had been a fine school).

As for the rest of the old secret police, several dozen faithful servants near retirement age, including Khvat, lost their personal pensions. Out of a thousands-strong army of torture-masters, only a few isolated individuals were tried in court on charges brought by Gen. Viktorov of the Chief Military Procuracy, which was responsible for initiating the probe of the NKVD-MGB investigators. The first to go on trial were those who knew too much for the new government's comfort. For "security's" sake, the new regime tried to make short work of these affairs.

The press duly reported official assurances that these trials were open—just as the trials of dissidents in the 1960s and 1970s would be "open." In fact, the deck was heavily stacked, with "representatives" or "delegations" of the "public" given special passes: so many for activists from Factory A, so many for exemplary "shock-workers" from Factory B, so many for members of the Party's district committee, and so forth. Furthermore, the authorities tried to distribute these passes in such a way that no one could see the whole trial from start to finish.[4] The same reasons that lay behind this secrecy kept Khrushchev's speech at the 1956 Twentieth Party Congress, "On the Cult of Personality and its Consequences," from being published in the Soviet media until 1989: the totalitarian government preferred not to reveal the methods by which it ruled the people.[5] The organs, playing the victims while actually working behind the scenes as a part of that government, had reason to hide their techniques; not only did they not want Soviet citizens to learn too much about how the NKVD-MGB had operated, they wanted to keep citizens from finding out that nothing had changed.

"What changed? What changed?" taunted Vladimir Semichastny, flinging my question back at me. "They stopped putting people in jail—that's what changed."[6]

Sorry, General; but the fact is, they *didn't* stop putting people in jail. What changed? Not much; although I suppose we ought to be grateful to Khrushchev that mass persecution was no longer the order of the day.

Closed doors also helped to create an aura of secrecy, fostering the illusion that there were more trials going on than was the case in fact. Although Vladimir Kryuchkov stated in one of his perestroika-era interviews that about 1,500 NKVD-MGB investigators were tried and convicted *for violating legality*, I must beg to differ; I'm afraid the former KGB chairman's researchers were ill informed about the history of Soviet jurisprudence.[7]

To begin with, it is obvious that this figure includes those who were tried during the Yezhov and Beria purges of the organs— officers tried as "enemies of the people," but not for violating *legal* norms.[8] (And what law are we talking about, anyway?) Moreover, most of those who were tried were not punished, whether or not they were found guilty.

How did they evade punishment?

First, there was the amnesty of March 27, 1953.[9] Drafted by Beria's staff in memory of the recently deceased Great Leader and Teacher, Stalin, this amnesty passed over the issue of political prisoners in silence, but did extend beyond common criminals to those who had committed offenses of office ("abuse of power," "exceeding authority," "inaction," "negligence," etc., according to Art. 193–17, point B, of the Russian Criminal Code). Since the majority of NKVD-MGB investigators had been indicted under this article, they benefited directly from the amnesty. And even without the amnesty, the statute of limitations on this article was ten years. That's why, fourteen years after the fact, Khvat would not have been tried for his conduct in the Vavilov case anyway.

A few investigators did end up behind bars, those whose actions the Military Procuracy deemed to fall under the infamous Art. 58 (counterrevolutionary activities), the same article that had cost the lives of countless "counterrevolutionaries," "spies," "terrorists," "saboteurs," and "traitors against the Motherland"—that is, the victims of the NKVD. There was no statute of limitations on Art. 58.[10]

In December 1957, Alexander Lanfang (by the mid-1950s, a lieutenant general of the MGB), who had fabricated the cases against the Comintern leaders I. Pyatnitsky, V. Knorin, Ya. Anvelts, and V. Chemodanov, was tried under this article. Entered as evidence against him was an appeal to the Politburo from Pyatnitsky, head of the Party delegation to the Comintern, who had dared to speak openly against NKVD chief Yezhov in 1937.

> I have already been in prison for six and a half months. I had lived with the hope that the investigation would determine my absolute innocence. Now, evidently, all is lost. Overwhelmed with horror, I once again declare to the Party and Soviet government that I am guilty of nothing. I have been, and remain, a loyal adherent and defender of Soviet rule. I remain, as ever, prepared to lay down my life for the socialist Fatherland. But I cannot, will not, and should not be in a Soviet prison; should never have been charged with Trotskyite counterrevolution, a cause I have never propounded, indeed, have always fought.[11]

Lanfang was sentenced to fifteen years, as was Col. Nikolai Kruzhkov, who'd been so assiduous in imprisoning scientists during the Leningrad blockade. One of the most terrible NKVD investigators, Col. Leonid Shvartsman, creator of the so-called military-Fascist plot that had led to the "liquidation" of six top Soviet Army generals in October 1941, at a time when the Germans were at the very gates of Moscow, was convicted under this article and shot.

Gen. Pavel Sudoplatov, to take another example, was imprisoned for fifteen years for "treason against the Motherland." As head of the NKVD division engaged in terror and subversion, he was one of the secret police chiefs who arranged the murders of Trotsky and the Ukrainian leader Yevgeny Konovalets. Sudoplatov was also one of the founders and directors of the so-called Laboratories of Death, where experiments were performed on live human subjects, prisoners from the gulag, using poisons and other controlled substances manufactured by the chemists and phar-macologists of the KGB's own Laboratory No. 12.

Lanfang and Kruzhkov were tried as "saboteurs" (Art. 58–7); Shvartsman as a "terrorist" (Art. 58– 8); Abakumov, Leonov, Su-doplatov, and his deputy, Naum Eitingon, as "traitors against the Motherland" (58–1). Not one of these officials was charged with "violation of legality."

But a new means of evading punishment was on the horizon. In December 1958, a new Fundamentals of Soviet Law (the basic legal code) was passed. Under the revised version of Article 58, many cases against NKVD-MGB officers were dismissed auto-matically. Changes in the statute of limitations applicable to other articles were also manipulated by accused officers with inside knowledge of the proposed legislation; they simply dragged out the investigation with delaying tactics until the new legal code came into effect, and charges were dropped.

If none of these dodges worked, if neither the new law, nor the old amnesty decree, nor the statute of limitations could be used to derail the case, then entire volumes of investigative material the court might use to convict a defendant of committing offenses under the war crimes articles were simply made to disappear. This happened in the case of Lt. Col. Boyarsky, whom we will meet again later in this chapter.

If implemented properly, all of these strategies could look per-fectly legal. But, if required, other, less "proper" methods were available as well. The military procurators simply had their arms twisted. As Gen. Viktorov once exclaimed to me: "You have no idea the pressure we were under. They made it incredibly hard for us to conduct any investigation. For the most part, witnesses to torture and abuse simply weren't around to testify; they'd been shot, or beaten to death in prisons, or they'd died in labor camps. And, remember, there were thousands and thousands of people waiting in line outside the doors of our offices for certificates of rehabilitation for themselves, their husbands, fathers, mothers, so they could get on with their lives."

I was on the verge of blurting out to Viktorov that until the investigators were convicted, we wouldn't be able to get on with our lives. But I realized it was all too easy to accuse military procurators of hypocrisy, when 99 percent of us were equally lacking in principle. We were all a part of the system. And, until it changed, nothing would happen.

The only possibility of restoring justice and punishing the murderers would have been a Soviet Nuremberg that characterized the crimes of the Stalin era as genocide, the crimes against humanity that they in fact were. The acts of the NKVD-MGB investigators should have been held comparable to the crimes of those responsible for Auschwitz and Buchenwald, to the offenses of those whom Russian courts even today sentence to capital punishment.

But a Soviet Nuremberg was unthinkable, for, like the German Nuremberg, it would have revealed the criminality of the ideology, the system in whose name these actions had been committed.

By imprisoning or executing a few dozen NKVD-MGB officers, the regime provided scapegoats for Russia's ever-present thirst for revenge. Here, it told the victims, here are the torturers who are to blame for your shattered destinies and uprooted lives. None of our leaders was willing to admit that the system of state security (not to mention the system of government) itself was flawed. "One of the first acts of West Germany after the war was over," wrote Lev Razgon, "was the government's public act of apology to the victims of the Fascists and the most substantial material compensation for their relatives. The GDR, as soon as it got rid of its Communist leader, also joined in that apology."[12] The Soviet Union did not follow suit. "We have nothing to repent of," said Gen. Kryuchkov, chairman of the KGB.[13]

So where did all those NKVD-MGB investigators end up? None of them—none that I ever heard of, in any case—was deported from the USSR for discrediting his socialist Motherland. Faithful unto death to the organs because the KGB had protected them from trial and prison and possible execution, they became the KGB's most valuable resource—the permanent "active reserve," part of the shadow staff. I would like to describe one such person.

I'll start the story in the middle, on September 5, 1988, rather than at the end. I will start midway, not to be intriguing—I am not a novelist—but because on that day transpired an event unprecedented in Soviet history. On that day, a monster and a murderer, a Chekist with fifty years' experience behind him, was confronted with irrefutable evidence of his crimes and publicly told to his face (even if not yet in a court) that he was a monster and a murderer, by people who had spent their lives in mortal fear of his ilk (and some in fear of him, personally).

This man was a former NKVD investigator who had on his conscience at least 117 lives: fifty-seven people executed, four who died from torture during the process of investigation, and the rest sent to labor camp, where they perished.[14] He was Vladimir Ananyevich Boyarsky, a torturer accused of having used "methods particularly agonizing to a murder victim, exploiting her helpless condition"; who had also earned the highest KGB distinction, "Honored Chekist," for his work with the scientific and creative intelligentsia, and had remained a lt. colonel of state security in the reserves.[15]

But his friends and colleagues from the scientific world apparently knew nothing about his Chekist experience, his KGB affiliations, past and present. Boyarsky was a well-respected professor who held advanced degrees in history and technology. He headed a workshop on the history of mining at the Institute for Earth Core Exploration (IPKON), had taught at the Mining Institute, and was a member of the Journalists' Union. And he was quite the Romeo, a real heartbreaker, and a sought-after guest in the homes of celebrated Moscow artists and among the fashionable intelligentsia.

In May 1988, I devoted a couple of pages of a *Moscow News* article on the KGB to Boyarsky. It was enough to cause quite a stir.

My exposé of Boyarsky's double life distressed his colleagues. Some of the older ones were panic-stricken as they recalled the unwonted candor of their conversations with Boyarsky. Some spent sleepless nights worrying that they'd be tarred with guilt by association because of their intimacy with the colonel, the trust they'd placed in him.

Boyarsky himself treated my revelations with professional dispassion; he didn't panic. You had to hand it to him—the man had guts.

Of course, it could not have been pleasant for the professor to see, hanging under his portrait in the institute's gallery of those who had fought in the Great Patriotic War, a hand-lettered sign, "Executioner." It must have been unpleasant to reach out to shake hands and meet—air. The "chat" he had with the institute's new director, Kliment Trubetskoy, must also have put a damper on Boyarsky's mood. Trubetskoy made it clear that the unexpected "gift" of Boyarsky was the last thing he needed in his new job. (His irritation was understandable: wherever he went, people would ask him, "Is that *your* institute where that bastard works?") "If everything the newspaper says is slander, as you claim," Trubetskoy told Boyarsky, "only a court can restore your good name." Of course, Boyarsky did not take *Moscow News* to court; instead, he fought us on his own ground. To all questions, he gave the identical response: *It's a lie.* Yes, he had worked in the NKVD; but he had *never* been an investigator, and had *never* put anyone in prison. He waved papers with fine-sounding signatures, hinted at high connections, dropping the names of well-known Central Committee secretaries and Politburo members. And here, he wasn't bluffing; he did have connections, and of rather long standing—something I myself realized when I found his name mentioned in a letter Stalin had written to Klement Gottwald, head of the Czechoslovak Communist Party.[16]

And he was energetic. The professor began to collect *kompromat* against me, calling some geologists he suspected held a grudge against me for things I'd written about conflicts in their field. The people I'd "insulted" smelled a rat, and called me up to warn me, for which I am very grateful. Boyarsky's final move was to report to the institute's directors that *Moscow News* was just about to fire me—if it hadn't already done so—and that, under threat of being closed down by the authorities, the editors were preparing a retraction.

Boyarsky was no Khvat: this was a worthy opponent who kept you on your toes, dancing.

He got some help from the June 1988 Nineteenth Party Conference, at which Politburo member Yegor Ligachev, then the number two man in the Party and government, tore into *Moscow News*. "We'll have this cleared up in no time," Boyarsky concluded.

Shortly thereafter, Trubetskoy called me at home and asked nervously, "Are you still sure that the facts in your article are accurate? Is there any chance that Boyarsky is telling the truth?" None at all, I said. By that time, I probably knew more about Boyarsky than his family and friends. Trubetskoy's alarm was understandable, though; in his position as Academy member, institute director, Party man, there were plenty of openings through which to pressure him. I could just see him being summoned to the district Party office—or the discreetly anonymous (no sign on the door, just a little bell) district KGB office in the same building—to be lectured on the "sensitive" political aspects of the situation. In any case, said Trubetskoy, institute staff wanted to hear the evidence against Boyarsky so that they could decide for themselves whether or not my article was accurate.

And they heard. A general meeting was called for September 5, 1988, and on the appointed day, the hall was packed. I was one of the invited guests, as was Maj. Gen. Vladimir Provotorov from the Chief Military Procuracy.

Boyarsky heard everything as well—including things he had long been convinced were safely buried in his past, particulars from his

KGB personal dossier, No. OI-4630. (So as not to embarrass the KGB, let me say right away that it had nothing to do with the publication of these documents.) One of the most telling was an August 22, 1947, deposition signed by one Col. Gorodnichenko:

> I hereby testify that from 1932 to 1936, Comrade V. A. Boyarsky was engaged in secret work in the NKVD of the Northern Ossetian ASSR: from January to August 1932 as an informer, subsequently as a resident at the Northern Caucasus Zinc Factory in the city of Ordzhonikidze. From August 1932 to April 1936, he was a paid resident, himself recruiting and handling agents and processing materials.
>
> With the direct participation of Comrade Boyarsky, several intelligence cases were launched . . . against anti-Soviet Trotskyite groups among professors, teachers, and students in Ordzhonikidze schools, with complete success. As cover, Comrade Boyarsky was placed during that period as a student at the Institute of Nonferrous Metals. In 1932–1936, Comrade Boyarsky worked under my direction.[17]

Incidentally, although I read out this glorious biography at the meeting, I was not able to publish it until March 1990, when all the censors finally let go of it. In October 1988, right before my second article on Boyarsky was to come out, this document was excised from the text even as the newspaper was on its way to the printers. When the editors demanded an explanation, they were told that its publication would jeopardize the KGB's work.

Here is the continuation of Boyarsky's brave life from a character reference in his dossier at the MGB Special Inspectorate:

> From his period of work as an operative of the Fourth Department, Boyarsky directed and led an agents' group on "Academic Institutions, Professors, and the Intelligentsia." In a single year of overt work, he successfully conducted the investigation and liquidation of the following cases: the

Northern Caucasus Pedagogical Institute (a five-person counterrevolutionary Trotskyite group); the Fascists' Affair (an
eleven-person counterrevolutionary youth Fascist organization); the "Aggressive and the Agrarians" (a six-person
counterrevolutionary Fascist insurgent organization); the
"Combatant" (a nine-person counterrevolutionary Fascist
bourgeois nationalist organization). In addition, he conducted
intelligence analyses of various counterrevolutionary Fascist
cases: "Coryphaeus," "Acquaintances," "The Aryans," "Mid-
get," "Esperanto," "Nationalist," "Friends," "Fascists,"
"Jackal." Boyarsky has an active and scheming intelligence.[18]

The functions of the Special Inspectorate have since been assumed by separate directorates in charge of personnel and staff
oversight, but its brief—a crucial one during the Stalin years—
has given it continuing power as a kind of secret police within the
secret police. Vital information about state security employees
flowed through this office: promotions, character references, reports to superiors, directors' orders, and so forth. Here, all the
Chekist's dirty laundry was collected: each personal dossier contained a special section of *kompromat*, which typically contained
such items as reports on the Chekist by their colleagues, letters
from wives denouncing their husbands and their mistresses, neighbors' complaints, anonymous letters, allegations of infractions on
the job, and "information obtained" from various sources. It made
for fascinating reading.

According to this information, Boyarsky had made quite a stunning career for himself. He had started out in the early thirties as
an ordinary operative, and within a few years had become head
of the secret-political department of the Northern Ossetian NKVD
Directorate. In 1937, he became a newly minted sergeant of state
security in the just-introduced system of quasimilitary ranks.
Within two years, he was a lieutenant; a year later, lieutenant
colonel.[19] He finished the war as a colonel, head of counterintel-

ligence (SMERSH) at the Far Eastern Front. But let me backtrack
a moment and give the floor to Boyarsky, especially since he himself
viewed his career as a Chekist in quite a different light.

I was sure that Boyarsky wouldn't show up at the institute meeting.
I thought that no matter how cynical the man was, he would
experience—well, not shame, of course; that was too much to
expect—but at least some discomfort at the thought of having to
explain himself to the friends and colleagues with whom he had
worked for years. But he did show up, bringing along his grandson,
a young man of about twenty, who was going to tape the proceedings.

Boyarsky looked tired, even haggard, the very picture of a harried innocent. In any event, he had lost the air of ease and slightly
provincial sophistication with which he had greeted me five months
earlier, when we first spoke.

Boyarsky was first to take the floor. "I did not come here to
justify myself. I came to tell the truth."

His extended monologue was liberally sprinkled with fashionable buzzwords—"rule of law," "glasnost," "democracy." He had
always managed to adapt to circumstances: in the 1930s, his reports, in fine Soviet parlance, called for "Stakhanovite"—shock-
worker—methods; in the late 1950s, during the Thaw, his articles
and books had titles like "Entering a New World" and *Birthday
of the New World*.

On this day, he spoke skillfully, pausing for emphasis, modu-
lating his intonation and pitch, passing lightly over some facts,
lingering over others. He described his war service in great
detail—how he had trained partisans and sent them behind enemy
lines, how he had tracked down spies through the forests, how he
had been awarded five orders and ten medals, how he had entered
Manchuria in battle with the Fifth Army of the First Far Eastern
Front, where he had headed the SMERSH counterintelligence

department . . . All he had to say about his activity in the late 1940s, when a new wave of repression rolled through the country, was a brief "I worked in Moscow, then abroad."

"In Moscow" he'd been deputy head of the MGB office in charge of Moscow and Moscow Region, supervising the investigations department. According to the testimony of his subordinates, he'd been a tough manager, strict and severe. One told me: "Anyone who'd done only a few nighttime interrogations, who interrogated for less than ten hours a day, who didn't know how to 'crank up' the detainee and couldn't get a confession from him, was considered by the bosses to be no good, incompetent."[20]

Yefim Dolitsky, a journalist who was arrested three times and who had "become acquainted" with Boyarsky in 1948 in the torture chambers of Butyrka Prison, called Boyarsky "a bloodstained gendarme devoid of all humanity, a wholesale provocateur, a professional bootlicker, a careerist who stopped at nothing, whose interrogations served as models, who could force people to 'confess' to crimes they hadn't committed—or help real criminals sweep the evidence under the carpet."[21]

Boyarsky's reference to work "abroad" concealed equally noteworthy matters. In the *kompromat* section of his file, I read that "in the summer of 1945 . . . Col. Boyarsky, while stationed in Harbin, committed grand larceny against a resident of Harbin, citizen Arkus. After arresting her without cause, Boyarsky had all her valuables—gold, diamonds, silver, fur, porcelain, clothing, furniture—carefully packed and shipped to the town of Spassk-Dalny, where Boyarsky maintained his permanent residence. In June 1946, he loaded everything into a fifty-ton Pullman car and shipped it to Moscow. Arkus was unlawfully detained under guard for three months without a procurator's warrant. Boyarsky pressured Arkus into signing a statement that she had no claims against the organ that had arrested her . . . Boyarsky confiscated property from Arkus's apartment valued in the vicinity of one million rubles . . ."[22]

"My investigation team was involved with that case," I was told in 1989 by Zorma Semyonovich Volynsky, who in the postwar years had been a senior military investigator for the Fifth Army's Military Procuracy. After reading my article, Volynsky wrote to me from his home in Kharkhov, and later came to Moscow. "It was a crime, pure and simple; by any reckoning, Boyarsky should have been jailed for robbery, but the materials were taken to the NKVD in Moscow and disappeared."

Elza Aronovna Arkus, the owner of a perfume factory in Harbin, lost everything. The man who arrested her, Boyarsky, returned home to a promotion, and was transferred to the capital's directorate of state security. And then, in July 1950, he was appointed senior adviser to Czechoslovakia's national committee of state security (StB). He was to all intents and purposes the new socialist country's minister of state security, with a salary of 29,000 kroner, equal to that of a well-paid Czechoslovak minister.[23] In Czechoslovakia, too, he allowed himself, according to the *kompromat*, "great excesses in his life-style and abuse of his official position." But his real distinction was his role in the Slánský show trials, to which we will return.

It goes without saying that these were not the biographical highlights that Boyarsky emphasized at the Institute that day. Still, it is remarkable that he spoke without the slightest embarrassment, totally unfazed by the presence of at least two people in the hall, Maj. Gen. Provotorov and myself, who knew the real story of his career and could identify easily all the fabrications in his version.

Boyarsky gave a ringing description of his early years. The newspaper story was slanderous, he declared. The truth was, he'd been just a kid, busy running around to meetings and conferences, in charge of work highly esteemed in those days—here his voice gathered strength—*Komsomol* work. (It kept him busy, no doubt; but not too busy to inform on his fellow Komsomols in his spare time—he remained silent about that, however.) In 1936, upon recommendation of the Komsomol, he entered the NKVD straight from university. His duties there were exclusively secretarial: as was typical in a national republic, his bosses, not native speakers of Russian, were not comfortable writing in that language, so they asked him to keep the minutes of meetings. His voice trembling, he said: "Behind doors that were closed to me, crimes were being committed about which I, a mere Komsomol brat, had no suspicion."

Oh, yes, just a little Komsomol brat! "In 1938, at a troika session, Boyarsky reported on the case against the brothers Vladimir and Avgust Lats," Olga Slavina, secretary of the troika, told investigators in 1940. Slavina, who herself was sentenced to two and a half years for inserting the name of a person she didn't like on an execution order, gave the following details: "As far as I recall, there was more material on Vladimir Lats, more evidence, than on Avgust . . . When Boyarsky argued for the execution of Avgust, Mirkin [NKVD People's Commissar of Northern Ossetia] said that Lats was young, and ten years was more than enough." Boyarsky, however, insisted on execution, and by a decision of the troika, Avgust Lats was sentenced to be shot to death by firing squad. "When I had typed the record of the troika session and brought it to Mirkin for his signature, he said, 'We have to be more careful with Boyarsky, or he'll undercut us. I wanted to let Avgust Lats get by with the second category [not execution, but labor camp]—he was a young kid and there wasn't much evidence on him—but Boyarsky nixed it.' When I queried him as to why, as chairman of the troika, he had not insisted on his opinion, Mirkin reflected a little and then said, 'The hell with Lats, he was a German, anyway.' "[24]

The doors on such proceedings indeed were "closed," but not to Boyarsky. As Ivan Kuchiyev, one of Boyarsky's NKVD colleagues, testified: "I saw the poet Alibalov in Boyarsky's office with his hands tied: he had been beaten, and his face was bloody. Boyarsky demanded a confession from him. Alibalov ended up dying in Boyarsky's office, but Boyarsky reported on the case at the troika as if he were still alive. It was decided there to give him the death penalty, and an order for his execution was drafted, although he was long dead."[25]

In 1939, the "Komsomol brat" from the provincial town of Ordzhonikidze was transferred to Moscow—probably "for special services rendered"—to the NKVD's Central Office, in Second Chief (counterintelligence). He thus managed to escape the purge of Yezhov's cadres, although criminal charges had already been filed against him, and *kompromat* already collected. He was lucky: "Materials of the investigation in the case of V. A. Boyarsky are to be handed over for temporary filing," stated the decision of the NKVD Inspectorate.[26]

Clearly, someone was watching over Boyarsky. That "someone" was Viktor Ilyin, a commissar of state security and later a general in the KGB.

As Boyarsky's talk drew to an end, the audience seemed confused, dubious. But Boyarsky finished strong: "If we do not build a state based on law, then many of the terrible things that we are only now learning about are sure to happen again," he moralized in fine professorial fashion.

Provotorov, sitting next to me, was turning purple. He got up heavily from his seat and adjusted the gold epaulets on his general's uniform; for a moment, I thought he was going to challenge Boyarsky to a duel, or at least punch him in the nose. ("Are you kidding?" Provotorov said to me afterward. "Do you think I'd dirty my hands on that scum?") The general slowly opened up a file yellowed with age and began to read from the testimony of Sheshukov and Zarubin, students at the Kharkov Military Academy who had been assigned to the Northern Ossetian NKVD under Boyarsky's command:

Boyarsky investigated the case of an accused teacher named Fatimat from the Alagiro-Ardonsky district, whom Boyarsky called a Socialist Revolutionary. Boyarsky employed punitive measures during the interrogation of this detainee. He forced her to stand up in his office for prolonged periods . . . However, this detainee categorically denied her guilt, saying that her husband had been murdered for lying; she would die, but she would not take a lie upon herself. From the prolonged standing, the detainee's body was very swollen, and she weakened and, unable to stand, began to fall. Then Boyarsky proposed that Zarubin and I tie her to the wall. For that purpose he put handcuffs on the detainee's hands himself, with her hands crossed behind her back, and said we should tie a rope from the handcuffs to a hook stuck in the wall. In addition, Boyarsky said that we should string a rope across the detainee's chest, under her arms, and tie it to a nail in the wall. After that, Boyarsky himself grabbed her braids and tied them to a nail, so that she could not lower her head to her chest or let it rest on her shoulders. We took shifts guarding her in that position. We did not give food or drink to the detainee, we did not take her to the bathroom, and a strong odor began to come from her. Boyarsky came in from time to time and demanded testimony from her, but she did not give any, after which Boyarsky said, "You'll hang here till you rot, or till you give us testimony." Toward the end, the detainee began to hallucinate; she groaned, at first loudly, then more and more quietly. At around four or five in the morning, the detainee died. About thirty-five to forty minutes before her death, she raised her head and said: "Tell your boss that I'm dying, but I will not speak lies about myself."[27]

Fatimat Dodoyevna Agnayeva died on September 14, 1937. According to testimony from Olga Slavina, Boyarsky kept Agnayeva in a stand-up for more than seventeen days. "Right up to her last breath, Agnayeva kept shouting that her husband Mikhail was not an enemy, but an honest man."[28]

When the general finished reading this testimony, the audience, shaken, began to roar.

"It's slander, I'm being libeled," Boyarsky yelled, his voice cracking.

Provotorov took another yellowed volume, opened it to the page he needed, and showed it to the audience.

"These are the records of Agnayeva's interrogations," he said, turning over page after page. At the bottom of each page was Boyarsky's signature. "Boyarsky, do you recognize your signature?" Boyarsky remained silent. "Here is the record of the interrogation of Dr. Khait, who performed the autopsy and was pressured by Boyarsky into attesting that he had found no trace of violent death. Here is the testimony of other students, Smolev and Abramov, taken in 1958."

"Why wasn't Boyarsky ever tried?" a thin, pale young man asked from somewhere far back in the room. "I have a little girl, and I'm . . . I'm just afraid . . . Just how many of these bastards are around?" The young man spoke the word "bastard" with obvious effort; he had been brought up to respect his elders. He looked at Boyarsky. I looked at the Chekist's grandson; absolutely impassive, he was aiming a recorder microphone in the direction of the young man who had spoken.

Why weren't they tried? Because they were needed. They were needed as experts to work for the KGB under other "covers"— in Boyarsky's case, at the Academy of Sciences. They were needed as professional agents to keep people in their various institutes under surveillance (the amateur informers couldn't match them). They were needed to select and help promote people in all areas of science, culture, industry, and government, people unburdened by moral scruples who were prepared (for the right pay) to serve that unholy trinity, the Party, the state, and the organs.

Still, why hadn't Boyarsky been put on trial? There were plenty of moves in that direction. In 1956, the Party Control Committee had expelled Boyarsky from the Party "for gross violation of socialist legality in 1937–1939" (as if he'd been selling flowers in the 1940s!). That same year, the military procurator of the Northern

Caucasian Military District opened a criminal case against a number of investigators working in the Northern Ossetia NKVD, including Boyarsky, who was accused of sabotage under Article 58–7.

The investigation was somewhat half-hearted—obviously, pressure was put on the military procuracy—and the charge was finally reduced to abuse of office (Art. 193–17). Meanwhile the case was dropped "owing to the statute of limitations."

But there was an unexpected hitch; the first secretary of the Northern Ossetian Regional Party Committee refused to back down, and complained directly to Khrushchev, who, still interested in cleaning up the ranks, ordered the military procuracy to reopen the case.[29] In 1958, a group of military investigators led by Lt. Col. Dmitry Vasilyevich Kashirin took over the investigation of Boyarsky and his Northern Ossetian boss, Gorodnichenko.

I managed to interview Kashirin in 1988, not long before his death. He told me that his group had collected three hundred "episodes" concerning Boyarsky offering indisputable evidence that he had personally arrested and tortured people and sent them to execution. They also tracked down a number of Boyarsky's colleagues and several dozen surviving witnesses. "He was a real virtuoso, a master of the business of torture," Kashirin told me.[30]

But Boyarsky wasn't worried. He refused to admit to anything, even when confronted by his victims.[31] Later, in 1958, he was arrested and detained at Butyrka Prison. But the material on his activities in the '40s and '50s mysteriously disappeared from his file. As a result, those activities that did not fall under the amnesty of 1953 or the statute of limitations on Art. 193–17 could not be held against him. These activities included his work in Czechoslovakia and his 1951–1953 service in Lithuania as department head of the MVD Directorate of Saulai District, where he was in charge of suppressing the Forest Brothers, Lithuanian partisans opposed to the Lithuanian communist government and Soviet occupying forces. He left memories of himself behind among people like

Vitautas Volotko, who, "worked on" by Boyarsky, signed the usual record of testimony "in his own hand," but penned the Latin letters "Z P" in the corner, for the Russian phrase *zverski prinuzhdyon*, "violently coerced."

To make a long story short, Boyarsky was released from Butyrka after a month "because of illness,"[32] and in February 1959, Gen. Viktorov signed the decree closing the criminal case against him "owing to the expiration of the statute of limitations."[33]

"I took a sin upon my soul," Viktorov told me recently.

The Thaw was cooling off. And KGB Lt. Col. Vladimir Ananyevich Boyarsky, doctoral candidate in history, teacher at the Moscow Pedagogical Institute, senior science editor of the USSR Academy of Sciences publishing house, returned after a brief absence to his work as an agent in place.

I wonder: was the month spent in Butyrka counted as vacation, or sick leave?

I'd first heard about Boyarsky, the investigator turned professor, from retired general Boris Viktorov, whom I met in the Military Procuracy's archives during the course of my research on Khvat. Viktorov had kept up his connections with the procuracy, and, despite a series of heart attacks, he was poking around in the archives and working on a book. In the midst of one of our conversations, Viktorov happened to mention another investigator, Boyarsky: "He tortured people but we couldn't bring him to trial, they wouldn't let us." And he told me how, for years on end, Boyarsky had been bothering the procuracy with petitions to be "rehabilitated," a necessary step for reinstatement in the Party. His efforts had become even more dogged in recent years; apparently, he saw perestroika as his big chance.

By the way, I do not mean to idealize Viktorov. He was a man of his time, as they say. But I was impressed by his profound sincerity, so uncommon in a long-term veteran of Soviet military law enforcement. He'd gone from the Military Procuracy to the Ministry of Internal Affairs, and yet somehow—no one knows how—he'd managed to preserve his integrity.

In any case, Viktorov's comments on Boyarsky had piqued my interest, and I decided to find out more about him. I looked him up in the directory at the Academy of Sciences; they knew him well there. "Of course, of course, you mean our own Vladimir Ananyevich."

"Our own Vladimir Ananyevich" had a well-earned reputation as a courteous and pleasant conversationalist. Furthermore, unlike Khvat, he was smart, and, in his own way, talented. I wouldn't call him an intellectual, but he had a certain sophistication that kept him from being out of place among the intelligentsia.

He knew how to treat people well. Through his wife, who worked in the elite Health Resort Institute, he was able to supply his colleagues at the Academy with medicines that were in short supply in the Soviet Union. He was a great one for doing favors. In his capacity as director of the popular science editorial board of the Academy's Editorial and Publishing Council, he helped corresponding members and academicians get their monographs and books published without a lot of red tape, eliding the tiresome paper quotas and getting a time slot at the printers'. Naturally, he didn't help everyone, only those who were of some use to him or to whom he took a liking. If you'd told the people who knew him that he was a murderer and a criminal, they wouldn't have believed you. "But he's such a nice guy."

Especially the women. He unfailingly found the right chord to strike with them. Good-looking and self-confident, he had what it took to win the fair sex; and there's every evidence that he did. (My KGB contacts insist that women are particularly easy to recruit, especially if the recruiter is handsome, and often provide immeasurably more valuable information than do men.)

My own relations with Boyarsky started off on a rather strained note. After I had gathered some information on him, I decided to call up and make an appointment for us to talk. A secretary at the institute put me through and I introduced myself, saying that I was studying the history of the Northern Ossetian Komsomol, and had heard that he had worked there in the NKVD. "I was never an investigator," he said, cutting me off without taking a moment to collect his thoughts. "I never worked in Northern Ossetia. I studied at an institute there, got married, and then moved to Moscow."

Of course, he had no time to see me; he was completely tied up with an important government assignment, designing a comprehensive study of the USSR's natural resources. The work involved tremendous responsibility: he reported directly to the Council of Ministers and the Central Committee. In fact, the minute he hung up the phone, he was heading straight for the Central Committee building. A pass was already waiting for him at the second entrance, he told me.

For a foreigner, it would not have been a very noteworthy conversation. For a Soviet journalist, the subtext was glaringly clear: "Watch out. I have powerful connections, right at the top." (The Central Committee's second entrance was used by the General Secretary, the Politburo, and Central Committee secretaries—the power elite. It was as if Boyarsky were saying: They value and respect me there, so look out, little girl, better not bite off more than you can chew.)

"And, by the way, give me the telephone number of your editor-in-chief," the professor said to me quite sternly. "I'll find out who assigned you to call me, and why." He was dressing me down, like a fractious schoolgirl. I gave him the number (I had warned my editor that this might happen) and we said good-bye.

I could see that Boyarsky would be a tough nut to crack; I'd have to follow all kinds of circuitous routes to get the information I needed. And I did need it: without the hard evidence to back up my suspicions, there was no point in trying to confront him.

But I didn't have many cards to play. I'd already worn out my welcome, such as it was, at the Military Procuracy, trying to find out about Khvat and Vavilov. The State Procuracy claimed they had nothing in their archives; the KGB denied any knowledge of Boyarsky. Thus, I was forced to turn to Viktorov for help, and to one other person whose name I must withhold for the time being. They both consented at once. After searching the Procuracy archives, they brought me some documents, including the Procuracy's dossier from 1959 and records of testimony regarding the agonizing death of the schoolteacher Fatimat Agnayeva. It wasn't much, but it did the trick.

After reading these documents, I was glad that Boyarsky hadn't been willing to see me; I was afraid that I wouldn't have been able to control myself. A few days later, Boyarsky called me up at home. I didn't ask how he'd found out my home telephone number (I live in the suburbs of Moscow, and my number isn't listed with the city directory services). I knew he had his ways.

This time, Boyarsky was more than courteous; he acted like a friend of the family. He dropped a few references to my husband and my sisters, and mentioned that he had "conducted some inquiries" about me. He'd read the articles I'd published, and had great respect for my principles and my refusal to compromise. He mentioned some mutual acquaintances, people well known in journalists' and writers' circles, one of whom later called to tell me what a nice guy Boyarsky was, how helpful he'd been (in what ways exactly, I didn't ask), and how inappropriate it would be to go muckraking through the distant past, the days when Boyarsky had been just another "Komsomol brat."

Finally, I succeeded in making an appointment to meet Boyarsky on April 12, 1988. By that time, I had already spoken to Kashirin, the lieutenant colonel who had been in charge of the military procuracy case against Boyarsky. I'd also called Khasan Ikayev, who had been interrogated by Boyarsky in 1937 (at the time, Ikayev had been first secretary of the Iraf District Party Committee of the Northern Ossetian ASSR, but his Party credentials elicited no respect from his interrogator). "Boyarsky made me stand in his office for a couple of days. I wasn't allowed to sleep, or eat or drink anything but salty bouillon. When I begged for water, Boyarsky unbuttoned his fly and said, 'I'll give you some from my faucet.' "[34] (In a later interview, which was videotaped, Ikayev exclaimed to the camera, "Boyarsky, you were hoping we'd all drop dead; but some of us lived—including me, Khasan Ikayev!") After that interview, my telephone number was passed from hand to hand among Boyarsky's other victims and their children, and they found me.

I must confess that when I went to meet Boyarsky, I left his telephone number and address with my husband and told him: If I don't return within three hours, come after me, and bring some friends. (Why to that address, and not Lubyanka?) I'm not usually a coward, but I'm not a fool, either. I won't walk alone through a dark forest, and I always carry Mace when I go into unfamiliar Moscow buildings at night. But this was a special time in my life, not conducive to even such calculated risk-taking—I was five and a half months pregnant.

Boyarsky lived in an impressive Stalin-era building in a fashionable district near the center of Moscow, at the corner of Garden Ring Road and Kalinin Avenue. Not only was it a prestigious address, but the building was famous for being located next door to the U.S. embassy. Traditional wisdom had it that people weren't allowed to move in there unless they were willing to permit all sorts of surveillance equipment to be installed to keep watch over the embassy.

Boyarsky's apartment had the lovely, understated elegance associated with the intelligentsia: no ostentatious display of wealth, no crystal to blind one, but no sign of poverty, either. He didn't show me around the apartment, nor did I ask, although I did eye the furniture with interest: Were these the pieces he'd been accused of stealing from the Manchurian millionairess Elza Arkus in 1945? Or had he traded those in?

We spoke in his study, a typical professor's room, full of books. He showed me his own publications—a scientific monograph, some essays. There were fresh pastries on the coffee table, the kind that had to have come from the wonderful café at the Central

House of Writers, and coffee in a little Turkish pot, served in elegant demitasse cups. When I declined his offer to share the feast, he asked, laughing, "Are you was afraid I'll poison you?"

The conversation proceeded like a chess game. He told me in a sad voice that he had buried his wife a year ago. I lowered my head. He regretted that I had been left without a father at a tender age (the bastard knew everything!) and I lowered my head even further, hiding my irritation. Then he showed me his photographs from those beautiful Komsomol days. He'd been handsome, you had to admit, well-built, tall, and strong; his face was somewhat broad—he didn't have that "aristocratic" look—but he had gleaming brown eyes, strong eyebrows, a thick shock of black hair, swept back to emphasize the haughty line of his jaw. Even now, at seventy-five, he had the physique of an athlete. (His carefully clipped gray hair did seem a bit touched up to remove the yellowish tint that often comes with age.)

When I mentioned the name of Fatimat Agnayeva, his head jerked up. He seemed to be trying to figure out how I knew it. He let out a discreet sob ("Forgive me, I was thinking of my wife . . . we loved each other so much; why did she have to go first?"), then declared he'd been slandered brutally by people envious of his Komsomol successes. "I was a real leader," he boasted. "And I won't hide it—the girls liked me. But I repeat, I *never* was an NKVD investigator. It's true, I did work in counterintelligence; I was head of the department in charge of smashing the Americans' intelligence network—that much I can tell you. But an investigator? That's dirty work . . . heaven help me, the Military Procuracy's criminal case, that was all just Khrushchev trying to destroy me. Remember, I was proved innocent."

I questioned Boyarsky about his academic career. How had he managed to defend a doctoral dissertation in a field in which he had no previous background, a year after leaving the Ministry of Security, after seventeen years of strenuous work in the organs? The question hung in the air for a moment, unanswered. Suddenly, the papers on the table all slid to the floor. Grunting a bit, Boyarsky bent down to pick them up. He was practically crawling at my feet. "Oh, Zhenochka," he said to me, using the diminutive, as though he were a friend, "—old age is no picnic." By the time he'd picked up the papers, the question was forgotten. I asked another. "What was the dissertation topic?"

"The Eastern Slavs in the Hussite Movement," he replied. Jan Hus, the father of the fifteenth-century Reformation—whose work had he plagiarized? Catching my look of surprise, he hastened to add: "My father was a historian; I had access to his research."

It was all a lie. His father was a schoolteacher, not a historian, and Boyarsky's dissertation topic was "The Defeat of the Interventionists and White Guards at the Eastern Front (Summer 1918– Early 1919)."[35] I didn't find that out until later, when I searched the archives at the Academic Attestation Committee (VAK), where all advanced degrees were registered. But that afternoon I already had my suspicions.

Remembering that Boyarsky had served as senior adviser to the Czech State Security Committee, I figured that he had probably arrested some Czech academic, found a finished manuscript during a search, and—accustomed as he was to taking other people's things—put it in his pocket. He'd returned to Moscow, asked someone to translate the work into Russian (with his connections, it would have been a simple matter), and defended the dissertation. To prove that, of course, I'd have to get into the Czech archives somehow. But in the spring of 1988, the Velvet Revolution was still a year and a half away, and Prague's archives were guarded as fiercely as Moscow's.

In any case, my April 1988 visit ended on a pleasant note, with Boyarsky taking the time to dictate a weight-loss diet to me (just what I needed at the time), which I copied down diligently. The professor escorted me to the door, and kissed my hand in polite farewell. "I'm going to be out of town," he mentioned casually. "I'm heading a Journalists' Union delegation to Yugoslavia." "Oh, so we're colleagues?" I asked in surprise.

I looked Boyarsky up at the Union's Moscow branch, and discovered that the man who had tortured the journalist Yefim Dolitsky, and who had signed the indictment of the journalist Alexander Litvak, had been accepted into the Journalists' Union in September 1960—four years after being expelled from the Party. This was astonishing, given the Soviet understanding of the journalist's profession. Western-style independent investigation did not exist at that time in the Soviet Union; journalists were considered the Party's ideological front line, whose brief was to articulate to their fellow citizens a Party-approved version of reality. It was inconceivable that someone who had been kicked out of the Party could have been accepted into the Union: a nonmember, perhaps; a person who had compromised the name of the Party, never. But there was the name: *Boyarsky*. My colleague.

From the documents in the file, I learned that Boyarsky had been a working journalist as early as 1931. He had an abundant list of publications in newspapers, from the local to the national level. A curious note stated that one of Boyarsky's bosses at the Academy of Sciences publishing house "confirmed that V. A. Boyarsky had been expelled from the Party and not reinstated . . . reason unknown, since it involved Comrade Boyarsky's work in the organs."[36] Period. Signature. That was enough. The simple mention of the organs meant, Hands off. No further questions were asked; smart people do not ask questions of the organs. It's details like this that give a glimpse of how the KGB's shadow staff was formed during the post-Stalin Thaw.

All this information was too much for me to just sit on, so, while Boyarsky went off to Yugoslavia, I took off on an even more exciting adventure, trying to get my article into the paper. Need I mention that as soon as the censor (still on every editorial board at that time) read through the typeset galleys, they were forwarded posthaste to the Central Committee's Department of Agitation and

Propaganda? The Party bosses homed in on the pages about Boyarsky. "How do you know that? It can't be so; he's a respected man," they droned on. Still, I had the impression that the article's contents came as no surprise.

"Let us see the documents," came the demand from the Central Committee. Naturally, they didn't ask me—I was not even supposed to know about all these *vertushka* conversations. Besides, I was not a Party member, so I was not to be trusted in any case. They went instead to Yury Bandura, deputy chief editor of *MN*.

Two years before the Law on the Press officially abolished censorship, editors did not have the luxury of telling the censors to go to hell or to take their request to a judge. As for me, I still had all the documents, but to disclose them would be to jeopardize the safety of my sources.

It seemed as if everyone's hands were tied. But suddenly we had a brilliant idea: we called the Chief Military Procuracy, and asked them to confirm the facts cited in the article. Maj. Gen. Vladimir Provotorov, assistant to the Chief Military Procurator, read the article and was amazed: "Where did you get that?" I mumbled something vague, but then pressed him: "Is it true?"

The general called back later, apparently having checked the files in the archive. It was true. Still unable to get over it, he remarked, "Some of the wording in your piece seems as if it's been taken from the actual findings of the Chief Military Procuracy in 1959." I chose not to comment.

The article was published in May 1988.

Since the information was getting out anyway, the authorities chose to make it seem as though it had been their own idea, and I was allowed to see the Military Procuracy's eighteen-volume file on V. A. Boyarsky, Case No. 06–58.

Eventually I pieced the story together; and, in the process, learned the very interesting story of Boyarsky's event-filled fifteen months in Czechoslovakia.

He arrived in July 1950. By that summer the official investigation in the case of the robbery of Elza Arkus, the Harbin perfume factory owner, was drawing to a close. It had been going on the whole time Boyarsky served as deputy chief of the MGB for Moscow and Moscow Region, and its findings were a dead weight in the *kompromat* section of Boyarsky's personal file. But suddenly, to everyone's surprise, he received the plum assignment of senior adviser to the Czech State Security Committee. According to rumor, it was the sudden infusion of a million rubles that did the trick—the million that he had stolen from the unfortunate Arkus.[37] Everyone knew, after all, that Viktor Abakumov, then the head of the Ministry of Security, was "bribable" . . . though only by banknotes of large denomination.

But the disposable income wasn't Boyarsky's only instrument of influence with Abakumov. During the war, Boyarsky had cozied up to Gen. Belkin, head of the Counterintelligence Directorate of SMERSH at the Northern Caucasian Front, chief of the Soviet intelligence bureau for Central Europe, and coordinator of the show trials, the trumped-up proceedings against the leaders of Communist parties in the "people's democracies" (as the bloc countries were called at the time). Belkin gave Boyarsky a letter of recommendation to Abakumov.[38] Whether that letter would have been sufficient to secure Boyarsky's appointment, I cannot tell. A candidate for the job of senior adviser (naturally, introduced by the MGB) would have to be approved by the Central Committee, after all . . . as Boyarsky was, of course.[39]

Boyarsky lived high on the hog in Czechoslovakia. You have to hand it to him, he knew how to extract every last drop from life. Never one to shun luxury, Boyarsky took possession of a beautiful mansion in Prague, and kept four servants, a guard, and five dogs.[40] In the Soviet Union, especially in the Stalin era, such perquisites would have been available only to a member of the Politburo. Boyarsky's wife, Irina Akhmatova, overwhelmed by the sudden largesse, went a bit wild. At a loss for what to do with all the servants, she spent her time ordering up endless dresses, till the local stores ran out of fabric to sell her.[41] Boyarsky had about fifty Soviet advisers working for him in Czech intelligence, and they, of course, wasted no time squealing about all this to Moscow.[42]

Boyarsky had met Irina during the war, and had gotten her a job working at SMERSH, as he had done for his brother Georgy, who went on to study (or pretend to, as cover) at the national film institute.[43] Akhmatova was a faithful helpmate to the colonel (until they split up, that is; at which point she wrote a report denouncing him).[44] Back in Manchuria, she had worked the Elza Arkus case with him, befriending the old woman like a good neighbor, going over for little chats—and casing the joint. Arkus adored the Russian woman, gave her presents, and hid nothing from her; and so, when it came time to rob their neighbor, the Boyarskys knew just where all her hiding places were.[45] I imagine they anticipated an equally gratifying haul from Czechoslovakia.

Boyarsky's colleagues reported back that he was quite a gourmand: "In three months he spent 219,000 kroner on food for himself; the budget for the whole collective was 600,000."[46] They also complained that he pocketed money allocated for the agents' network. It's no wonder they were angry: Boyarsky, after all, was already getting paid an exorbitant salary of 29,000 kroner.

Even back in Moscow, Boyarsky's pay had been no pittance: 3,600 rubles base salary, 1,300 for his military rank, plus 15 percent (735 rubles) for his years of meritorious service. Altogether, his compensation package in 1949 was 5,633 rubles per month.[47] For comparison's sake, that same year Lev Razgon, a recently released political prisoner working as a senior academic researcher at the Stavropol House of Political Education, earned 600 rubles per month. My father, a radio engineer with postgraduate degrees, section head at a top secret defense research institute (and Stalin never skimped on defense), was earning 1,800–2,000 per month at the time (including bonuses), which was considered more than a decent salary.

But enough about the market value of Boyarsky's service; let's talk about what he was being paid for. "I made no major decisions without consulting the chief adviser," Ladislav Kopřiva, then Czech Minister of State Security, recounted. "The chief adviser had more weight than a minister among Communist bureau-crats."[48]

Boyarsky had been sent to Czechoslovakia to organize a new show trial. Such trials had already been held against László Rajk in Hungary (Minister of Internal Affairs, and one of the most popular leaders of the Communist Party) and Kostov in Bulgaria. Rudolf Slánský, General Secretary of the Czech Communist Party, was next in line.

The trials were Stalin's response to his postwar allies' talk of a "special path" to socialism, that is, for their taste for national independence. He would tolerate only one path—and he would be the one to forge it.

Boyarsky performed his assignment quite zealously. By February 1951, he'd arrested about fifty top Czechoslovak officials, including the heads of the National Committee for State Security, in a purge in the best tradition of the NKVD-MGB.[49] Otto Šling, first sec-retary of the regional committee of the Czechoslovak Communist Party in Brno, had been in the Czechoslovak version of Lubyanka since October 1950, apparently as a result of Boyarsky's unclear understanding of what Stalin wanted him to accomplish. Or per-haps it wasn't the orders from Moscow that were the problem; President Gottwald may not have been ready to betray Slánský, his general secretary. And it's not inconceivable that both Gottwald and Slánský himself, by giving the go-ahead for these arrests, were trying to "buy off" Stalin. Whatever the case, Boyarsky at first interrogated Šling with an eye to obtaining a "confession" that Šling had intended to do away with Slánský.[50]

Boyarsky himself later explained that despite the order from Moscow, he had tried to save Slánský, to "keep the sword from falling." Such mercy brought no thanks, though; his failure to complete the assignment got him demoted and recalled.

A sad tale, no doubt, but his account is more than a little difficult to swallow, if only because "Boyarsky" and "saving someone"—other than himself—are concepts that do not easily fit together; nor do they fit the facts. Historians of the Prague Trial all agree that it was Boyarsky who orchestrated the "Slánský Affair." Indeed, he'd been collecting *kompromat* against Slánský almost since arriving in Czechoslovakia. He kept the records in his desk drawer, waiting until the time was right, and then used them to convince the Czech leaders that Šling was only a pawn of those above him.

The show trials in Czechoslovakia were also intended as a stern warning to "world Jewry, Zionism, and international Jewish imperialism." The arrests took on an openly nationalistic, anti-Semitic tinge. Šling was only the beginning; Slánský, too, was a Jew, as were eleven of the fourteen people condemned at this trial. Meanwhile, in the Soviet Union, the war against the "cosmopolitans" was under way; Jews were being expelled from every institution and profession, and a plan was being drafted to deport them to Siberia and parts east. The cause begun by Hitler with the silent collusion of the world powers—England, France, and the U.S.— was being taken up by Stalin. The Nazi ideal, condemned in Nuremberg by the world's judges (including the Soviets), was alive and well.

As for Boyarsky, his problem was that he had slapped his case together too poorly—perhaps out of habit. In his experience, building a case meant putting people into the "stand-up" and the "conveyor," giving them salty bouillon or toilet water, waiting a few days—and then, presto! a "Trotskyite," a "Fascist," or a "terrorist" would emerge. Neither he nor the special conferences were required to provide specific evidence.

But he hadn't taken a number of factors into account. Czechoslovakia, after all, was not the Soviet Union; the year was 1951; and Slánský *was* General Secretary . . . and Stalin liked to have these types of trials look good, with at least some appearance of authenticity. Then, who knows, another Walter Duranty* might turn up, and declare to all the world that the charges were true.[51]

That's what Stalin wanted—but that's not what he got. When

---

* Duranty was the American journalist allowed into the infamous 1938 Moscow show trial of Bukharin and others who, according to Robert Conquest, believed almost everything that was said there and told the world about his support of the trial—Author.

he read Boyarsky's report from Prague, he hit the roof. "There's no evidence to back up the charges," he wrote to Gottwald on July 21, 1951. "It's clear that Boyarsky isn't serious about his work, and therefore, we have decided to recall him to Moscow."[52]

Gottwald protested that Boyarsky "has provided very valuable help to us at the Ministry of National Security," and urged that the colonel be allowed to stay.[53] But Stalin was intractable. "The results of Boyarsky's work in the ČSSR illustrate that he does not have sufficient qualification for fulfilling the responsible duties of an adviser."[54] Poor Boyarsky! Any dreams he might have had of becoming a general disappeared before his eyes. Gottwald agreed to replace Boyarsky with Aleksei Beschastnov, an MGB general. It was Beschastnov who had the honor of arresting Slánský, and who brought the case to its infamous conclusion—Slánský's execution—in November 1952: the laurels were Beschastnov's.[55]

Meanwhile, back at MGB headquarters, big changes were in the works. Abakumov, who had protected Boyarsky, had been arrested in the fall of 1951. Boyarsky's luck had run out, and a new storm was about to break over his head.

It began when his own deputy, Comrade Yesikov, informed the Moscow bosses that "the behavior of Comrade Boyarsky seems inappropriate and false." In particular, Boyarsky had "behaved improperly in connection with the presence of materials at the organs of state security of the Czechoslovak People's Republic regarding the hostile activity of Jewish bourgeois nationalists, a number of whom have wormed their way into the state and Party apparat." Yesikov further claimed that "Comrade Boyarsky has not facilitated the exploitation of these materials," and had notified the USSR MGB of them "only under pressure from the staff of adviser Yesikov and several other staff workers."

I can imagine Boyarsky's howls of indignation: after all, it was he who had been proclaiming publicly that "our chief enemy is international Zionism, which has planted its agents everywhere."[56] It was he who had labored to ensconce that ultimate anti-Semite, Andrej Keppert, in a position of power in Czechoslovak state security—Keppert, who'd said that "upon sight of a person with a crooked nose he would immediately either open a case against him or send him to prison."[57]

But Comrade Yesikov would not relent. Finally, the deputy minister of state security himself, Maj. Gen. Pitovranov, looked into the case. He sent the following memo upstairs to the Central Committee: "According to the allegations of a number of USSR MGB workers, Comrade Boyarsky has incorrectly reported his ethnic background as Ukrainian, although his manner and appearance show him to be a Jew."[58]

Boyarsky had suffered poor luck before, but this was the worst. Imagine—suspected of being a Jew! And not for the first time, either; a few years before, he'd been forced to "clear himself" of the same suspicion to Abakumov, and now it was starting all over again. "Verification of Boyarsky's biographical data," concluded Pitovranov, "did not confirm these allegations." Nevertheless, the mere suspicion of a Jewish background may have been one of the reasons for Boyarsky's recall from Czechoslovakia.

Actually, the question of whether or not Boyarsky is Jewish is of little interest to me (although recently discovered evidence indicates conclusively that he is not). As a Jew, I'm interested in another question entirely: Why were there so many Jews among the NKVD-MGB investigators—including many of the most terrible? It's a painful question for me, but I cannot evade it.

True, Jews' proportional representation in the NKVD was no greater than that of Russians or Latvians. As Vladimir Jabotinsky, one of the fathers of Zionism, said, "Every nation is entitled to its scoundrels." Why shouldn't Jews have them?

But the argument ignores our history: the turn-of-the-century pogroms in Kishinev and Odessa, the mass murder of Jews in Ukraine during the Civil War . . . With the particular agonies reserved for Jews in Russia, how could they forget that pain long enough to want to participate in its infliction?

No, the answer lies in the Jews' special relationship to the revolution.

During the Russian Empire, Jews were forced to live in *mes-techki*, "little places" or settlements. They were subjected to terrible pogroms, and to drastic abridgement of rights. The revolution meant a kind of liberation for them; and they embraced it because it granted them hope of survival, of raising their children in peace instead of sorrow, of finally gaining equal rights.

Yet, by its very nature, revolution brings everything to the surface, including everything that is vile. The revolution brought the nation's scoundrels out into the open; for those who found their way to it, the NKVD offered an opportunity to assert their power, further their ambitions, and suppress their fears. In that sense, Jews were no different from their colleagues of other nationalities who labored in the organs. They tended to be better educated, and therefore rose more rapidly up the career ladder; and, thanks to their "genetic fear," they were especially zealous, afraid they would be caught being "soft" on their own.

Boyarsky returned to Moscow. His final act, true to form, was to order the inventory records at the Soviet military mission destroyed. Of course, the report on him reached Moscow before he did.

To this day, I cannot understand why Boyarsky was kept on by the MGB. After that murderous criticism from Stalin (especially given that Abakumov was already in prison), why wasn't he simply retired, if not executed? By all the rules of the game, everyone around Abakumov should have been "removed," especially Boyarsky, who, among other things, had been accused of protecting Abakumov by "incorrectly handling information received from a source" about Abakumov's purported liaisons with women of ill repute. ("Boyarsky has a portrait of Abakumov hanging above the desk in his home in Moscow," was the word from his colleagues.)[59] But the much-maligned colonel clearly had friends in high places, and evidently even the Great Leader was getting tired and saving his strength for his chosen battles.

The MGB did not mention Stalin or his criticism of Boyarsky in its indictment. "For mistakes tolerated on the job and unworthy behavior, he should be reduced in military rank to a lieutenant colonel," stated USSR MGB order No. 5522, dated December 13, 1951.[60] Not only had Boyarsky's general's epaulets flown out the window; he hadn't even been able to hang on to his colonel's shoulder boards. He spent another two years in Saulai, Lithuania, but his career as a staff Chekist was essentially over.

Thus ended Boyarsky's first life; and thus began his second, as a professor-scientist. In 1979, in one of his own handcrafted biographies, Boyarsky wrote: "In 1950–51, I was in Czechoslovakia, working as an adviser and simultaneously collecting material for my dissertation, which served as one of the main reasons for my recall to Moscow in July 1951."[61] Astonishing, no?

I spent several weeks reading through the Boyarsky file at the Military Procuracy's archives—time that was inestimably valuable to my education as a journalist, a citizen of the Soviet Union, and a human being. I was shaken. Even in a country that has seen the publication of such monumental works as Solzhenitsyn's *Gulag Archipelago*, Yevgenia Ginzburg's *Journey into the Whirlwind*, or Lev Razgon's *Unimaginable*, I must say that the procuracy's documents—unpolished by a literary editor, not meant to be read—possessed an absolutely unique power. Reading them, I began to understand why they are so carefully preserved, and so obsessively concealed. I also felt, more strongly than ever, that all of the files concerning the inspection and rehabilitation of NKVD-KGB investigators, all of the dossiers kept in the archives of the Chief Military Procuracy, not to mention the investigation files buried at the KGB and prison files rotting in any of the old penitentiaries, should all be published in exactly the same form in which they were preserved. It is not only a question of people learning some information they didn't know before—although they will learn something, just as I did.

They will learn that a tailor could be arrested for sewing a suit that didn't fit, a musician could be arrested for playing badly at a concert and thus spoiling the sophisticated palate of an NKVD boss, and a teacher could be arrested for giving the wrong grade to a daughter of an investigator.[62]

They will learn that from pain and fear (of such tortures as enemas with boiling water), people turned into animals willing to do anything. They will learn how people went insane in cells 50 by 50 centimeters square, like the ones at the NKVD in Northern Ossetia, and how the investigators obtained testimony, even from those who had already been handed the death penalty.[63]

They will learn that people can be tortured without ever receiving a blow. The KGB officers could get by without beating them, just by not letting them go to the bathroom during the prolonged interrogations: "If you sign, I'll let you go." They could deny them food for several days in a row, and then have their own lunch in front of the starving prisoner. They could keep them awake for days. They could order them not to move their fingers or toes. They could offer toilet water to a prisoner suffering from intolerable thirst. They could send him for a cold bath in a shower with a cement floor. They could tie him to a hot radiator. Then, they could promise to do all the same things to his daughter.[64] All these possibilities come from the file of just one NKVD-MGB investigator.

From another: "Interrogated through the night—17 hours without sleep or food . . . demanded false testimonies . . ." The year was 1988, the third year of perestroika. The place was Moscow.[65]

I think that people should know what can be done—what has been done—to them in their own country, by their fellow citizens: *people like us.*

There, on the dusty archive shelves, are preserved the cries and groans of thousands of people: their fears, their letters before death, their pleas for mercy, the appeals from their children, wives, husbands, and mothers; the records of their interrogations, the testimonies of their abuse, and the tales they told to the military procurators. The tragedy of an entire people is preserved there, the true story of this country—a story whose moral escapes us, year after year.

While working on this book, turning over the pages of my notebooks (in which I had copied down pages from the criminal file; there could be no question of xeroxing them), I suddenly was overwhelmed by the sense that if I did not make all of this public, those terrible testimonies of other people's sufferings would simply disappear. They had been written by real people, very much alive. And I am hounded, literally persecuted by the feeling that I am burying them again.

The investigation was assigned to Tekayev. He summoned me to his office, then Gorodnichenko and Boyarsky came as well, and they asked one question, would I give a confession or not. They bound me hand and foot and began to beat me with a rubber hose, taking turns. Later, they didn't even ask me anymore, but just brought me into the office and began to beat me. I no longer had the strength to walk; the guards in fact were not escorting me to the interrogation, but carrying me. These torments continued from evening until morning each day, except for Sunday evening. They beat me until I lost consciousness, then poured cold water over me, revived me, and once again started hitting me. They punched me on the wounds on my back infected from previous beatings. The flesh on my thighs came away from the bones and pus came out in huge quantities, yet they didn't offer me any medical aid. I began to have nervous convulsions, and, fearing that I would go insane, I tried to commit suicide. For that purpose I pulled out a rusty nail from the shower, hid it in the crap bucket for several days, then stuck it into a vein in my left arm, keeping it there several days and nights, trying to cause blood poisoning. To my surprise, it didn't work. Then I tried to hang myself on a hook in the shower, but the hook broke off. The last time, they beat me from seven in the evening until sunrise on May 16, 1939, demanding that I sign a text that had been prepared in advance. At one point, they brought Anton Sharikyan to my cell, barely alive. He was the secretary of the Ordzhonikidze City Party Committee. He apparently had already begun to go insane, and kept asking if I knew whether there was still Soviet rule on the outside or not; he had been kept in a stand-up for twelve days, then beaten. Kokov and Maurer were brought to my trial. Despite the fact that I had known them very well before my arrest, I didn't recognize them; I only guessed it was them when I heard their voices. At the trial, I described the tortures to which Gorodnichenko, Tekayev, and Boyarsky had subjected me, and how they had forced me to sign false testimony. Before and after the trial I was kept in solitary confinement, did not see the procurator at all, and was not given paper for writing an appeal. Thus, I was forced to sew my statement on the back of my undershirt; and when that was discovered, I wrote it on the wall of my cell with a burnt match.[66]

I know that this testimony does not add much to what I have already written or what has been said by dozens of other people. But at least let this man's memory not die: Romazan Gaiteyevich Bitemirov. At least my conscience is clear now with him, a person completely unknown to me. But what about the others whose voices cry out just as terribly from my notebook?

Boyarsky's criminal dossier told me a lot about his first life as a Chekist. But how did he get away with it? Manage to play out his second life so perfectly? Manage to obtain status, recognition, authority?

I'm not talking about how Boyarsky wangled his history degree without any history education. To me, the answer is obvious: back in 1949, half of the Moscow intelligentsia was in solitary confinement in the MGB's investigation cells. Most likely, faculty members of the Moscow Regional Pedagogical Institute, which awarded Col. Boyarsky high marks in his exams, were among those incarcerated in those cells. Or, there is the possibility proposed by an anonymous "Chekist" whose letter turned up in Boyarsky's personal dossier at the MGB's Special Inspectorate: Boyarsky hadn't actually taken the exams at the Moscow Regional Pedagogical Institute, but had "exploit[ed] his official position . . . The exams were taken at the MGB Directorate building."[67]

More intriguing is the question of how Boyarsky succeeded in defending his dissertations. The range of his interests is truly breathtaking: from the "Defeat of the Interventionists and White Guards" in the Civil War to "Development of the Scientific Technical Bases for Open Ore Mining in the USSR: The Experience of Historical Research." Who wrote them? How did he get past all the red tape with only a fake diploma from the metallurgical institute in Ordzhonikidze? Why had this professional self-inventor scattered varying birth dates throughout his papers; removed personal data—education and birth—from his brother's dossier at the MGB? I still had to find out how the "legend" of a KGB secret agent was constructed, how the shadow staff was built.

Unfortunately, Boyarsky himself was not much help to me. At the Academic Attestation Commission (VAK) archive, I read an autobiographical note written in 1979: "In 1951–53, I worked in the Lithuanian SSR, where I completed my dissertation." Intriguing, given that the author had headed the Second Department of the MVD Department in Saulai. "In 1953, I was transferred back to Moscow, and in connection with my entrance into graduate school, was retired into the reserves." He might have cited some more pressing reasons for his retirement: Beria's arrest, the purges of the MGB, and the large collection of *kompromat* against him.[68]

But don't make the mistake of imagining that a move into the reserves meant a break with the organs. The colonel was simply transferred to the "active reserve," where he continued to remain involved in operational work. Not until 1963 did the USSR KGB clinic deliver the verdict: "No longer fit for operational service."

But even then, they added: "Fit for duty *outside the service* during peacetime. First-degree fitness with restrictions during wartime."[69]

"In 1954, I defended my dissertation," the colonel wrote of his peacetime career. "I transferred permanently to academic work, which I had always wanted to pursue."

I was unable to locate Boyarsky's history dissertation. It was not at the State Lenin Library, the depository for all dissertations except those with a "top secret" stamp, nor was it in the files of the Academic Attestation Commission. It wasn't a matter of old files having been dumped—people who had looked for it twenty years earlier had gotten no further than I had.[70]

Boyarsky's personal dossier was there, however, and contained plenty of interesting material. I was struck by comments made by Prof. Nikolai Volkov at an Academic Council meeting of the Moscow Regional Pedagogical Institute's history department: "The author [Boyarsky] makes generous use of collections of English documents, *Czechoslovak documents* [author's emphasis]." But "when the topic is our Soviet troops, the author does not have sufficient material."[71] Nevertheless, Prof. Volkov was "delighted" with the dissertation's "novelty."

So my theory of a Czech connection was not so groundless at all; Boyarsky did go fishing for materials in the fraternal country. And he probably reeled in quite a bit, enough so that he could pick one of two topics, either the Hussites or the Intervention, for his dissertation.

Why did he select the second topic? Perhaps an answer can be found in the evaluation of the dissertation made by the so-called black reviewer, that is, the reader whose name remains unknown to the doctoral candidate: "The dissertation consists of a compilation of previously known materials. Essentially, this is a not very complete retelling of brief extracts from Chapter 8 of the *Short Course of the History of the VKP(b)* [the Bolsheviks].[72] Who, in 1954, would have dared fail such a zealous student of the *Short Course*'s author—Stalin himself? (Interestingly, this review is dated 1956, that is, after the attack on the "cult of personality" made it possible for VAK to scorn the work of the fledgling "historian" Boyarsky.) The reviewer continued: "As a rule, the author does not indicate sources, that is, he does not name the original archival materials from which he is drawing various facts, numbers, and character references."[73]

Translated into plain language, this would read, "Dear Comrade! You forgot to cite your sources. Was your academic work stolen? Did you plagiarize it?"

A second signed critique offered a similar assessment of Boyarsky's work. According to I. Berkhin, an assistant professor and specialist in the history of the Civil War, "The archival citations are not properly made. There are no references to the library, the number of the file, or the page."

"Candidate Boyarsky's arguments are recognized as sufficient," the experts' commission of VAK nevertheless concluded.

Boyarsky continued, unperturbed, with his highly useful "research" at the USSR Institute of History. "He struck me as a very pleasant guy," his colleague, Viktor Farsobin, wrote to me. "The ladies were wild about him; he made a big fuss over them, kissed their hands . . . I have some vague recollection that we canceled some penalty the Party had given him. We were just too lazy to investigate." Lazy? What could they do? They were playing against a lieutenant colonel of the KGB.

Boyarsky's file contained another interesting document, dated 1954: "V. A. Boyarsky has been active in scholarly and practical pursuits for twenty-three years . . . During service in the NKVD-MGB-MVD of the USSR, he was also involved in pedagogical work."[74] Indeed, he taught his share of lessons.

"Boyarsky criticized the investigators for an insufficient number of night interrogations," reported Lt. G. Chernov, his former subordinate in the Moscow MGB. "He demanded that the investigation workers step up their work with the detainees for the purpose of obtaining confessions."[75] Was *that* the "pedagogical work" they were talking about?

Boyarsky's scientific career advanced almost as swiftly. In 1958, he was made senior editor of the Academy of Sciences Press; a year later, editor-in-chief; in 1960, he became a teacher at the Moscow Publishing Institute, a mentor of students. In 1967, he was given the title of senior academic researcher in his specialty, history of science and technology, and, as secretary of the editorial board of the journal *Popular Science Literature*, participated in the Academy's Editorial and Publishing Council. In 1968, he was named lecturer at the Moscow Mining Institute Department of Technology, Mechanization, and Organization of Open Mining. Author of fifty-three scientific articles, he also coauthored a textbook that would later form the basis for his doctoral dissertation, "Development of Ore and Loose Deposits." His coauthor, Mikhail Agoshkov, at the time already a corresponding member of the Academy, is now an academician who in 1991 was awarded the title Hero of Socialist Labor.

Agoshkov had begun his life in science back in the 1930s, at the Institute of Ferrous Metals in Ordzhonikidze, where NKVD resident Boyarsky was one of his "students."

I met Agoshkov at the Academy's annual general meeting in the auditorium of Moscow State University, where Soviet academicians, including Andrei Sakharov, were discussing the future of Soviet science.

Agoshkov was over eighty years old, and evidently hard of hearing. "Do you recall the name Boyarsky?" I asked him. "Boyarsky?" It was obvious that the academician was having trouble remembering him. "Boy-ar-sky," he said, drawing out the name. "Yes, yes . . . I think I had a student by that name. Yes, he was a talented young man, I recall."

"Did you ever run into him later on?"

"I don't think so . . . no. No, I don't recall that I did. Why are you interested?"

"He worked as an NKVD investigator."

"Really? But he was such a talented young man." And the academician hurried out to the foyer; just then, a break had been called.

The subject seemed to induce memory failure in so many people that I went back to check.

"You cannot make a rank-and-file soldier liable for conscientiously following the orders of his superiors," wrote Agoshkov in his petition to the Military Procuracy for Boyarsky's rehabilitation in 1965.[76] Agoshkov's wasn't the only vote of confidence. KGB Gen. Viktor Nikolayevich Ilyin, former commissar for state security, secretary for organizational matters at the Moscow branch of the Writers' Union, and Boyarsky's long-term protector, also went to bat for his protégé: "I had the opportunity to become convinced of Boyarsky's abilities," wrote Ilyin of his 1937 meeting with Boyarsky in Northern Ossetia. "Despite his youth, he was very knowledgeable about . . . the character and nature of various nationalist movements and their historical past, and also very skilled at dealing with the agent network."[77]

The late 1930s had been a difficult period for academic institutions throughout the country. In 1937–39, the Institute was accused of harboring myriad "counterrevolutionary," "Trotskyite," and "Fascist" organizations—groups whose "existence" owed a great deal to Boyarsky, who was posing as a student while heading the agent group responsible for "Academic Institutions, Professors, and Intelligentsia." Students, teachers, and professors were arrested by the dozens. Agoshkov was among the few who remained untouched—perhaps because, in 1936, he'd put his signature on a first-degree diploma (No. 8707) confirming Boyarsky's graduation from the mining department of the Institute of Nonferrous Metals and granting him the title of "mining engineer of ore industry."[78]

Interestingly, a special 1950 investigation by the MGB established the following: "There is no information about graduation from the institute and receipt of a diploma by V. A. Boyarsky. Boyarsky's diploma was issued illegally."[79] In 1990, a procuracy investigation confirmed: "Boyarsky was not among the people who graduated from the institute."[80]

On the fake diploma, Agoshkov's signature is notated, "for the dean of the mining department"—that is, the dean himself was either absent or (more likely) was supposed to be unaware of the falsification. And this was not the only official document in Boyarsky's file that bore the annotation "for ———."[81]

In 1978, when Boyarsky defended his second dissertation, an anonymous denunciation was sent to the Academic Council: "I don't know the scientific merits of the dissertation, although Boyarsky has never been a mining engineer, but his moral character is well known to me. Boyarsky is guilty of the slander and ruination of Party workers in both our country and Czechoslovakia . . . He concealed his expulsion from the Party from the Academic Council."[82] For the second time, Agoshkov turned out to support his former student. "As a person who has known V. A. Boyarsky very well for almost fifty years, I can assure you . . ." reads the transcript of the meeting of Special Council K-003,11.03, at the Academy's Institute of Natural Sciences and Technology.[83]

Agoshkov hadn't recalled ever coming across Boyarsky after his graduation . . . Well, people do forget; it happens.

The author of the anonymous denunciation of Boyarsky has given me permission to use her name here. Marya Grigoryevna Malkova is the widow of Yefim Semyonovich Likhtenshtein, the secretary (or director) of the Academy's Editorial and Publishing Council. Her husband's acquaintance with Boyarsky dated back to the period when Likhtenshtein was head of the Academy Press, and Boyarsky was a senior editor. According to Marya Grigoryevna, Boyarsky had been recommended to her husband as an energetic man who'd gone through a lot of pain. They were curious about what had happened. "He seemed so downtrodden," she told me.[84]

When Likhtenshtein became head of the Editorial and Publishing Council, he brought along Boyarsky, who quickly found his footing.

"You see, the Council set the schedule for the press, and the academicians would go there as petitioners, prepared to do anything to get their work published quickly. Who wants to wait for years for their book or monograph to come out? You could make a lot of connections there, major ones," Marya Grigoryevna told me.

And these connections, it did not escape Boyarsky's notice, could mean power and favors owed to him. As his network of influence began to grow, he began to interfere in Council business, creating great difficulties for Likhtenshtein, who was now in the way. Likhtenshtein, deeply wounded by Boyarsky's treachery, fell ill. His wife chose her own way of fighting for her husband.

How did she learn about Boyarsky's past? Her husband had told her from his sickbed. But how had Likhtenshtein found out? Boyarsky had signed a statement promising not to divulge facts connected with his work at the NKVD-MGB. Maria didn't tell me, but it wasn't all that hard to figure out.

The head of an official Soviet publishing house had to be approved by the Party Central Committee; after all, the publishing houses, like all mass media, were on the front lines of the ideological war. The résumé of an editor-in-chief would be very carefully vetted by the KGB. If all was in order, the applicant would be summoned for an interview with officers of the KGB's Fifth Directorate. There, he would be advised that on his staff, as on the staffs of all large media editorial organizations, there were KGB representatives—and that their work was not to be interfered with. Yefim Likhtenshtein must have had just such a conversation with the KGB about Boyarsky.

Marya Grigoryevna ended her anonymous letter: "I am a decent Communist, but I am not signing my name, because he [Boyarsky] has been the ruin of more than one decent person." This provoked a bit of a fuss, but it was more than compensated for by the avalanche of panegyrics that promptly emerged from the academic and scientific world. "In all areas of science and productive activity he has shown himself to be loyal to the Party, exceptionally hard-working, morally upright, a modest and responsible comrade," wrote one of Boyarsky's scholarly defenders.[85]

Others pointed out that anonymous letters were an unfit basis for investigation, something that should not be used against a person. Some were more temperate, preferring to demand verification: Was it true that Boyarsky had concealed his expulsion from the Party?—certainly, that would be a serious offense—and had he "never been a mining engineer"?[86]

At Boyarsky's insistence, the Moscow City Procuracy started an investigation in search of the anonymous letter writer. The Central Committee also chose to keep a vigilant eye on the proceedings.[87] Not because they were shocked by the charges: to them, it was all old news. But the person accused was so respected *over there*, at Lubyanka.

The anonymous tipster was quickly found. Her age saved her from formal charges, but she was given a strict lecture, warned, and then let go.

Boyarsky, for his part, received his colleagues' congratulations graciously: "Well, thank God, everything's been cleared up."

The Academic Council reconvened. This time, though, everyone knew whom they were dealing with, and the kind of allies he could count on. Even in the transcript of the meeting—an affectless official document—it is clear how deferentially, even timidly, those eminent professors questioned Boyarsky.

One of the academicians, a Hero of Socialist Labor, one of the inventors of our space-based missile defense system, said awkwardly: "Ah . . . now, about Czechoslovakia, in the sense stated in the anonymous letter, were there any claims against you?"

"No," Boyarsky answered flatly. "There were none in Czechoslovakia. And there were none during the whole period of my membership in the Party. And there are none today."[88]

That satisfied them. The Council concluded: "In his scientific and productive activity as in his everyday life, Comrade Boyarsky follows the norms of Communist morality."[89] Well, that much was true; and thus, Boyarsky won another round.

"How does he get away with all this?" readers would ask me in letters. How? Part of the reason was that he had a perfect, professional understanding of the psychology of the world of scientists and artistic intellectuals in which he moved. He knew what these people—often talented and very decent—were and were not capable of, to what limit he could push them, and where they would not budge. For some reason, I think Boyarsky had contempt for these members of the intelligentsia. And perhaps, from his narrow perspective, his scorn was justified.

A few years later, Vladimir Boyarsky, doctor of technical sciences, would receive the academic title of professor. By the time we met, his official biographies credited him with "more than two hundred scientific works, including twelve monographs, textbooks, and handbooks," and described him as "a leading scientist in the field of the history of mining science and technology." A brilliant bastard, you had to hand it to him—brilliant. Because no matter how much his home office helped, no matter what doors were opened for him because of people's fear of the KGB, no matter what connections he had, Boyarsky's talents were very real.

I never did learn how Boyarsky wrote his first dissertation. I believe the name of the author of the original historical work is forever buried in the lists of people executed by the MGB. The author of the second is more transparent: most of the articles and monographs on which it was based had been coauthored with Academician Agoshkov and his students. Well, consenting to plagiarism wasn't a high price to pay for one's life.

As for the question of Boyarsky's date of birth—sometimes, 1913, at other times, 1915—it was finally solved by Col. Viktor Shein, a special cases investigator with the Chief Military Procuracy. Shein checked the record of births at the Vladikavkaz Ecclesiastical Consistory for 1913 and 1915, and discovered that Boyarsky's father, Anany Vladimirovich Boyarsky, had been a cleric who taught at the Theological Academy and held a rank in the tsarist civil service equivalent to that of an army major, and that Boyarsky's godmother had been the daughter of a colonel in the Tsar's army. He was born in 1915, before the revolution, and his birth certificate noted his baptism and also gave the name of his godmother. His tinkering with his birth date and his brother's dossier were meant to make information on the family background difficult to find.

Boyarsky had good reason to worry: the birth certificate would show that he was the son of a clergyman—a "social alien," a class enemy. The revolution's bright future and the doors to higher education would be locked to such an alien; and, of course, there could be no chance of a career in the NKVD or MGB. By 1937, in fact, such information was sufficient to get one arrested and declared an "enemy of the people." Boyarsky preferred to arrest other people.

And now, the requisite happy ending.

After my series of articles on Boyarsky appeared, VAK stripped him of his degrees of candidate of history and doctor of technology. After petitioning from the Moscow Mining Institute (there was a stormy meeting there as well) and the Institute for Earth Core Exploration, the USSR State Education Committee also withdrew his titles of professor and assistant professor. The Academy's Presidium removed his title of senior scientific researcher. The Moscow branch of the Journalists' Union expelled Boyarsky from its membership. No matter how flattering this reaction from official institutions was to me as a journalist, I must say that all of these expulsions and stripping of degrees were completely unlawful. No one examined Boyarsky's dissertations, no one compared the texts, no research was done—and, certainly, no confession was offered. The lieutenant colonel lost his titles solely on the basis of the infamous par. 104 of the Statute on the Conferment of Degrees, for "actions incompatible with the title of a Soviet scientist." Ironically, it was a paragraph that had been used just as successfully against dissidents—a feature it shared with the other penalties assessed against him.[90]

It felt like the Thaw all over again. The public thirsted for blood, and they got it. The KGB offered up one of its own as a scapegoat: Here you go, we'll be big about this; take him and be grateful.

But the Committee for State Security lost nothing. Boyarsky had been a lieutenant colonel, a meritorious worker in the organs, and an honored Chekist; and so he remained. That's not to say that the KGB displayed no reaction at all; on the contrary, the Chief Military Procuracy experienced some unpleasant moments. Nonetheless, it managed to open an investigation (for the third time on this case), though the KGB made sure one of its agents was on the investigative team. Boyarsky went along with it: with all the talk of demotions and expulsions buzzing around him, he figured he could buy himself some time with the plea "innocent until proven guilty by trial." Fair enough. He also assumed that the new investigation would be nothing more than a gesture on the part of the Military Procuracy. Who wants to hunt down witnesses from fifty years ago, after all?

After several months of probing, the procurator, Victor Shein, served Boyarsky with a warrant that accused him of a number of crimes, including murder committed by "methods particularly agonizing to the victim, exploiting her helpless state." Boyarsky appealed to the procurator, demanded a court hearing, and hired a lawyer. (Thinking one attorney insufficient, a group of veterans of the Fifth Army, where Boyarsky had headed the SMERSH unit, hired him an additional counsel.) The public defense was led by a retired KGB colonel, Petrenko, who had once worked under Boyarsky, and was one of the authors of a report on Boyarsky's criminal behavior in Harbin.

Well, Boyarsky was wrong about the long-lost witnesses. Shein found them, and interviewed them, and got it all on videotape, including Khasan Ikayev's defiant "I survived." Viktor Shein explained to these people, many of whom were very elderly, others of whom were the children of people executed or killed in the labor camps, that, as victims, they could, at the very least, bring a civil suit against Boyarsky for material compensation. But not a single one of the eighty witnesses did this. They didn't want to relive those harsh memories with a trial that would have added a whole new layer of pain—for, under Soviet law, the burden of proof was on the plaintiff. But perhaps most important of all was their revulsion at the thought of dealing with *them*—the KGB—again, on any terms.

Boyarsky's willingness to put his head in the noose must also have been a function of his firm conviction that there would be no hanging—that his beloved Committee, which he had served faithfully and sincerely throughout his life, would not betray him, would not permit an open court hearing.

He was wrong there, too. The KGB didn't need him anymore: he was old and he'd blown his cover. Even so, there was no trial—nor is there one to come. For the case to go before the court, Boyarsky would have had to sign in accordance with Art. 201, that is, he would have had to go in person to the procuracy and sign the indictment and thereby register his understanding of the charges. Boyarsky simply chose to ignore it—and, once again, the threat of labor camp faded away, as time passed and the statute of limitations came to his rescue.

Meanwhile, Boyarsky continued to write complaints about me to officials. First it was to the Central Committee; then to the Russian parliamentary Human Rights Committee chaired by Sergei Kovalyov, the prominent human rights campaigner and former political prisoner. Boyarsky complained, among other things, that it was on the basis of my articles that his degrees and titles had been unlawfully removed from him, and that I had been allowed to view his dossier at the Chief Military Procuracy, while he had not. What can I say? He was right; laws mean nothing here. But I will not come to Boyarsky's aid, even though I realize that the authorities who treat him like this today could treat me the same way tomorrow. I cannot help it; I find him repugnant. I cannot forgive him for the schoolteacher Agnayeva, who was hung by her braids to a hook on the wall because she refused to give testimony against her husband. I cannot forgive him for the twelve-year-old Tsurova girl, whom he kicked out on the street after he put her parents in prison, or for hundreds of others whom he tortured and killed, all of whom are now part of my life.

And yet, despite everything I learned about the investigators of the NKVD-MGB-KGB—and they do not instill any positive emotions in me—I am categorically opposed to changing the law to make it harsher and more punitive. In our country, people have become so hardened, so thirsty for revenge, that such an escalation, I fear, could one day become a trap for us all.

Anyway, it's too late for that. What's done is done. The Committee, which once might have been brought under public control, had long since become its own empire.

Boyarsky's story was not exceptional. Thousands of NKVD-MGB investigators went into the reserves or the *active* reserves, and settled into new professional identities. They got jobs in the "first departments" that oversaw employees' contacts in ministries doing secret work; in scientific research institutes dealing with classified subject matter; and in various so-called post office boxes, research institutes and secret plants identified only by their box numbers. They landed positions as heads of personnel departments, jobs as deputies overseeing classified work and contact with foreigners in universities and academic institutes or supervising the "ideological correctness" of people in the arts or the army. Gen. Ilyin, for example, ended up in the Writers' Union. Abakumov's deputy, Gen. Yepishev, became head of the Main Political Administration (MPA) of the Soviet Army and Navy. Other former NKVD officers took jobs as directors of operations at local city or regional government offices, or were placed in newspapers, publishing houses, police administrations, and procurators' offices. This continued throughout the 1970s and 1980s, and into the 1990s, even though Yeltsin initiated a number of reforms.

"Officers of the KGB who have at any time served in the organs and have transferred to work in other organizations remain in the active reserve of the agency," a KGB official explained to me.

Not only have the Chekists successfully moved into their new positions and made themselves at home, not only have they brought with them the ideology nurtured by their institution, but they have also continued to keep old informers in line through threats of exposure, while recruiting new ones as well. They have become a network of their own, with sponsors (Boyarsky was not the only agent to have his Agoshkov) and apprentices and successors.

Thus, the enormous shadow staff expanded to a size unimaginable even in the glory days of Stalin's Cheka. It is through this staff that the KGB managed to infiltrate government offices and public organizations, and gradually to become an integral part of them. This relentless encroachment is what makes any comparison of the KGB with the CIA or the FBI seem naïve to me. The CIA and the FBI may have their secrets and informers, but these are finite institutions, and so they do not bear being equated with the Russian secret police.

Perhaps the most terrible legacy of this infinitely proliferating NKVD-MGB-KGB is what I call "unnatural selection"—the decades-long process (aided and abetted by the political organs) of selecting and breeding a special type of *homo sapiens: homo Sovieticus*.

At first, many of the most decent people from the aristocracy, intelligentsia, working class, and peasantry were simply killed. Then, out of those who remained, the organs carefully selected the most eager and obedient, and gave them the top posts. Boyarsky is a brilliant example of such selection, but he is not alone. Khrushchev and Brezhnev (for all that we are so quick to disown him) and Gorbachev, and even Yeltsin, are all of the same strain.

I remember being rocked back on my heels by a letter from a former prisoner, D. Alkatsev, whose case Boyarsky had been in charge of investigating:

First of all, please accept from me lots of good wishes from faraway Taymyrskaya tundra, now the flourishing industrial city of Norilsk, the "pearl of the polar regions," as the journalists picturesquely call it. Yes, there was only bare tundra here when, in August 1939, we were brought on the *Budyonny* from the Solovki Central Prison to the port of Dudnik, and then along a rapid rail line [in cattle cars, where thousands perished without water or air] to this town. Almost barefoot, tortured and exhausted, I began my labor. And although I aged prematurely and now suffer a serious heart condition, I am proud that my life has not passed in vain, and not without use to our Great State.[91]

"Our Great State." And there were millions of people like Alkatsev, whose passivity and allegiance in spite of everything made Boyarsky possible.

We can congratulate ourselves for that. With such support, such might—hundreds of thousands of full-time Chekists, and millions of freelancers—the KGB could make use of the relative softening of the post-Stalin regime (truly, it was no longer something to fear) and move to assume an even greater share of the nation's power. A new oligarchy was born: the Communist Party, the military-industrial complex, the KGB. And with each generation of negative selection, the KGB extended its influence further.

CHAPTER

4

Who Was Behind Perestroika?

In the fall of 1990, a new book by Christopher Andrew and Oleg Gordievsky, *KGB: The Inside Story*, created quite a stir in the American press with its claim that the KGB had stage-managed perestroika.[1] The buzz had not yet subsided when some Western political commentators made another sensational claim: the KGB had engineered Gorbachev's rise to power. (A. Avtorkhanov, a prominent émigré Sovietologist living in Munich, had made a similar claim some years before in his book *From Andropov to Gorbachev*; this time, however, the media picked it up.)

Western readers stricken by Gorbymania and with only limited knowledge of the nuances of the Soviet power structure found such "exposés" shocking and treated them as right-wing attacks on the "fledgling Soviet democracy" and its leader, Gorbachev.

Then, the Berlin Wall fell. Now every single taxi driver, whether in New York, Washington, Chicago, or San Francisco, felt it his duty to tell me how much he admired Gorbachev. It's not that I minded these conversations; I had my own personal reasons for gratitude to Gorbachev. For one, under Brezhnev, Andropov, and Chernenko, I'd have been strictly prohibited from traveling abroad. It wasn't till the fourth year of perestroika that I managed to get a passport to travel outside the Soviet Union. So I said yes and amen to the cab drivers' paeans to Gorby, although I must admit I thought it a bit much when one of them tried to tell me—a

Soviet citizen—that Yeltsin was a bad guy for criticizing the leader who could grant instant bliss to the entire Russian populace if only he'd follow the cabby's advice (thank God, it was a short ride). Clearly, the First Chief Directorate and Service A (disinformation) had done their jobs well. According to retired KGB Col. Oleg Nechiporenko, a special group was formed within intelligence with the sole aim of discrediting Yeltsin abroad. There is no doubt that Gorbachev okayed this, although there's no proof that he ordered it. It was amusing to see this disinformation—for example, the Italian newspaper *Repubblica*'s sensational tale of Yeltsin on a drinking binge during a U.S. visit, replayed in the Soviet mass media, citing Western sources.[2]

"You Russians take such a dark view of everything that happens in your country. You think the KGB is behind everything, even the good things," my Western opponents would retort. "After all, is it really so important who started perestroika—the KGB, Gorbachev, or the two of them together?"

Indeed it is. Knowing who initiated perestroika helps us to understand its original purposes, as well as its sadly inevitable outcome.

The notion that the KGB was the initiator of perestroika seems absurd, even heretical, especially to "gloomy" Russians, who are incapable of thinking about the KGB as anything but immutably conservative, unlikely to take such a bold initiative, and certainly lacking any noble impulses. Yet, it is not so paradoxical after all, when you consider the KGB's true purpose. But to discover that, we must first discount the stereotype of the KGB as just a secret service (it's never been) or even a secret police. Rather, we must understand that the KGB was—and in a way still is—one of the most powerful and important components of the oligarchy that ran the USSR, and still runs Russia. And second, we must resist the impulse to reduce the KGB's complicated history to the stuff of cheap spy thrillers, tempting though it may be.

In fact, you could almost picture the opening scene: The year is 1985, and several KGB directors—let us say, Chairman Viktor

Chebrikov, Filipp Bobkov, his first deputy for intelligence, and Vladimir Kryuchkov, head of the FCD and future KGB chief—are gathered to sip tea and ponder the future. At last they hit upon an idea: Let's make the next strike at the West through a global campaign of disinformation; tell everyone the Soviet Union's going to abandon its status as "Evil Empire" and become an open, democratic society. The Westerners will lap it up: they'll be so relieved they'll send us aid by the planeload, and presto! our economic woes will be history, too.

Let's get Gorbachev in here, they told each other; we've got enough dirt on him to make sure he'll stay in line. "Go for it, young man," they told him. Plausible, no?

Unfortunately, the credit for that scenario belongs to others, for example Anatoly Golitsyn, a former Soviet intelligence agent who defected to the West in 1961. In *New Lies for Old* he claims that as early as 1959, the KGB was working up a perestroika-type plot to manipulate foreign public opinion on a global scale.[3] The plan was in a way inspired by the teachings of the sixth-century B.C. Chinese theoretician and military commander Sun Tsu, who said, "I will force the enemy to take our strength for weakness, and our weakness for strength, and thus will turn his strength into weakness."[4]

Of course, the KGB is no stranger to *deza*, its nickname for *dezinformatsiya*; in fact, that's Service A's job. But perestroika was a far different undertaking than planting a bogus story or discrediting a minor official. And it would be an error to overestimate the intellectual and imaginative capabilities of the KGB to that extent. No, in real life, perestroika was much more complex than a mere *deza* plot.

The reader will recall that the KGB's penetration of Party and state structures began to take new forms after Khrushchev's speech at the Twentieth Party Congress denouncing the Stalin "personality cult." The organs had always had their own agents and investigators in the regional committees and ministries, but the infiltration that followed Khrushchev's purge of the organs was of a different order altogether, as ex-Chekists took off their uniforms and went off to civilian jobs in the bureaucracy. Their pride had taken a beating, but their greed for power was still intact, and it soon became clear that Khrushchev's "perestroika" of the organs was merely a game of musical chairs. The Committee continued to function as a secret police, conducting political investigations and crushing dissent. These former officers were, if anything, even more valuable to the KGB in their new bureaucratic positions.

But while the Chekists were stashing their uniforms in their closets, yesterday's Party and Komsomol bureaucrats were donning brand-new outfits and picking up military epaulets and special military provisions at KGB warehouses for the privileged. A number of Party ideologists entered in the wake of Alexander Shelepin, who became KGB head in 1959 after putting in several years fighting for the "radiant Communist future" as first secretary of the Komsomol.

In his three years (1959–1961) as KGB chairman, Shelepin apparently made great efforts to recruit well-educated individuals who had worked in scientific research institutes and universities. By building up its scientific and technological base, the KGB laid the groundwork for its future power. If before, under Stalin, the organs needed people with good, strong shoulders, now they needed people with good, strong heads on those shoulders.

In 1961, Shelepin transferred to the position of Central Committee secretary. Three years later, in 1964, he was a key player in Khrushchev's ouster. The leading role in this palace coup was played by Vladimir Semichastny, another Chekist who had also served as first secretary of the Komsomol, and Shelepin's pick for KGB chairman.[5] Under Semichastny, the ranks of the KGB once again swelled with hundreds of ideological watchdogs from the Party and Komsomol. And just as the old Chekists had not lost their connections with Lubyanka, so had the old Party people not lost their contacts with the matrix that had nurtured them. And so the two organizations were brought even closer together.

These infusions of new blood into the KGB were prompted by the most honorable of intentions. Rid of their most grotesque elements, the organs would become more civilized, more professional. But what naïveté that was, to think that the juggernaut of state repression would fail to pulverize any attempt at reform! On the contrary, infusion of Party blood had the effect of revving up the KGB's crackdowns on dissent—ideological policing being the newcomers' chief claim to professional expertise.

The end of the Khrushchev Thaw was heralded to the world by the shooting of workers in the city of Novocherkassk in the summer of 1962, demonstrators who had gathered to protest the raising of prices on bread and milk, and to demand an increase in their wages. The demonstration itself—economic, not political—was an outcome of Khrushchev's liberalization; nothing of the kind could have been imagined in the Stalin era. However, as the following secret document, recently released from the archives, reveals, the regime's violent response was utterly congruent with its principles, which the Thaw hadn't altered in the least. Dozens of workers were killed, hundreds were wounded, and the "instigators" of the demonstration were sentenced to execution by firing squad.

The August 23, 1962, secret memo No. 2170-I to the Central Committee is signed by USSR Procurator General Rudenko and KGB Deputy Chairman Ivashutin:

We report that on August 20 of this year, in the city of Novocherkassk, Rostov Province, the open trial in the case of the organizers of and most active participants in the mass disorders that took place June 1–3, 1962, was completed . . .

All but one of the accused pleaded guilty and recanted the crimes committed.

About seventy witnesses were examined in the trial. They fully corroborated their testimonies given during preliminary investigation and exposed the criminal activity of the defendants.

Seven criminals—Zaitsev, Mokrousov, Kuznetsov, Cherepanov, Korkach, Sotnikov, and Shuvayev—were sentenced to execution, and the rest to lengthy terms of imprisonment, from ten to fifteen years.

The court's sentence was received by prolonged applause in the overflowing courtroom . . . a welder in the iron shop at the electric locomotive factory stated: "A dog's death for dogs!" . . . a railroad engineer stated upon hearing the sentence: "Those low-down crooks! They went against their own brothers and fathers. It's right that they're being executed."

At the request of the workers, a discussion of the progress of the trial was held in the assembly shop at the electric locomotive factory. Vilyayeva, a painter, stated: "They did the right thing, organizing a show trial; people should know who the ringleaders were . . . People like that shouldn't get any sympathy. They're rejects from the human race."[6]

This document is a near-twin of documents from the era of Stalin's show trials. The same elements were present: witnesses who obviously had been beaten bloody in Chekist dungeons so that they could now denounce the "criminal activity of the accused"; the public's applause after the handing down of the death sentence; the worker's words, "A dog's death for dogs."

Still, the influx of new cadres that changed the KGB's image forced it to find more "civilized" methods of fighting its fellow citizens—and also stimulating it to combat dissent with renewed vigor.

The secret memorandum prepared by the KGB on the trial of writers Sinyavsky and Daniel and sent to the Central Committee over the signature of KGB Chairman Semichastny and Procurator general Rudenko on December 23, 1965 (No. 2343-s) was an example of the ideologists' new, creative approach to state security—what you might call a Chekist literary critique.

The investigation has established that, during the period of 1956–1963, Sinyavsky and Daniel, under the pseudonyms

Abram Tertz and Nikolai Arzhak, wrote a number of works whose slanderous anti-Soviet content defamed the Soviet state and social order, and sent them abroad through illegal channels.

Arzhak's short story "Moscow Calling," for example, represents a malicious lampoon of our reality. In this work, the Soviet Union is depicted as an enormous concentration camp where the people are oppressed, intimidated, and angry. In the author's fantasy, the people are so "brainwashed" that they blindly submit to any unrestrained abuse from the authorities, and even help them implement the most preposterous measures to hurl the country practically back to the Stone Age . . .[7]

This is followed by almost five pages of exhaustive analysis of the writers' works, something that would be the envy of Mandelstam, or Babel, or dozens of other writers and poets executed or sent to labor camps by Stalin's Chekists—who had never seen, much less read through, their works.

Semichastny and Rudenko finish with a proposal that a "public accuser" be recruited to provide testimony damaging to the defendants, and suggest that the Writers' Union provide this member of the trial's cast.

Central Committee officials supported their Chekist colleagues' call for a trial, and drafted a program for media coverage:

APN, in conjunction with the KGB, is assigned to prepare appropriate articles about the trial to be published abroad . . . Foreign correspondents are not to be allowed to attend the trial . . . A special press group [of Central Committee and KGB officials] is to be formed to prepare special reports and to review [Soviet] reporters' coverage of the progress of the trial . . .[8]

The members of the press group included our old friend Filipp Bobkov, who would go on to become chief of ideological counterintelligence and a leading specialist on the artistic intelligentsia; and Alexander Yakovlev, now known to the world as the architect of perestroika, but at that time deputy head of the Central Committee's Department of Agitation and Propaganda.

For Soviet writers, being tried and jailed wasn't anything new. But the trial of Sinyavsky and Daniel was a landmark date for the "new" KGB, the occasion on which the KGB and the Central Committee relinquished their previous mutual fear and hatred. The trial of poet Joseph Brodsky furthered and strengthened this rapprochement.

It is no coincidence that under Shelepin and Semichastny the FCD's Disinformation Service was greatly expanded and accorded special status. This Service had every reason to view regional, city, and district Party and Komsomol committees as being under its aegis, since they had always played fast and loose with the facts and had been ready to rewrite the past. "If the Soviets were as enterprising in the areas of industry and agriculture as they are in disinformation," wrote Admiral Stansfield Turner, CIA director under President Carter, "they would have overtaken us by all parameters."

As the grafting together of the Party and state apparats began to take hold, a new type of rule came into being—the Party-Chekist-military oligarchy. The KGB and the military-industrial complex (MIC) occupied a peripheral role for the time being, ceding authority to the Party. But not for long.

I don't want to oversimplify here; the mechanisms of repression didn't merge with the power structures overnight. As we saw, the organs went through a rough period under Khrushchev. But the totalitarian state was on the rise, and the machinery of coercion would not remain a subordinate instrument forever.

The process came to its logical culmination in 1967, when Yury

Andropov assumed the leadership of the KGB under Brezhnev (he remained in that post until 1982, when he replaced Brezhnev as General Secretary), the first time since Stalin's death that a man who had held such a high position in the Party hierarchy (Andropov was a Central Committee secretary) was coming to run the KGB. And the first time since Beria's day that a KGB chairman was made a member of the country's governing body, the Politburo. "That appointment signified a degree of rapprochement between the Party and the KGB, and they began to operate almost like two divisions of one and the same organization," writes Geoffrey Hosking in *A History of the Soviet Union*.[9]

Under Andropov, KGB directorate heads, both national and local, were installed at corresponding levels within the executive bureaus of the regional and city Party committees. With the oligarchy locked firmly into place, there now began one of the most dismal periods in the post-Stalinist USSR.

"It was precisely with the coming of Andropov," claims Shelepin, "that the KGB once again became the state within a state it had been in the pre-Khrushchev era. Andropov restored everything I had tried so hard to liquidate at the KGB."[10]

I remember August 1968 very well. I was nine years old, and my parents and I were vacationing on the Black Sea near Odessa. One day, the sky above the beach was suddenly filled with aircraft. The roar of the planes blended with the rumble of tanks rolling somewhere nearby. My father, who had fought at the front during World War II, was certain that war had broken out. But the war wasn't on USSR territory; these were Soviet tanks headed out to crush the Prague Spring.

Years later, in December 1979, I was with some fellow students, studying for an exam, when we were stunned to see on television that our troops had "responded to the request of the Afghan leadership" and entered Afghanistan. Bitterly, we calculated that the regime's bloody interventions occurred in a twelve-year cycle: Hungary in 1956; Czechoslovakia in 1968; Afghanistan in the winter of 1979–80. And we realized that each of these dates was linked to the name of Yury Andropov: in 1956, Andropov had been ambassador to Hungary, while in 1968 and 1979 he had sanctioned the bloodletting in his capacities as KGB chairman and Politburo member. This was the man Gorbachev hailed in the early years of perestroika as godfather of the nation's democratic reforms.

According to Oleg Kalugin, it was the KGB, arguing that the Prague Spring was an American plot to undermine the East Bloc, that insisted on using "extreme measures" in Czechoslovakia—arguing that otherwise Czechoslovakia would escape from the Soviet sphere of influence, fall prey to NATO, and that would be that. Kalugin, at that time one of Soviet intelligence's top officials in the U.S., transmitted documentary evidence that the CIA had nothing to do with the Prague Spring. But, according to Kalugin, the document was simply filed away.

The shedding of foreign blood was not Andropov's only achievement during his long career (although that career's crowning glory may well have been the downing of South Korean Airlines flight 007 by Soviet fighters in 1983, during his tenure as General Secretary). It was Andropov, that father of democracy, who in 1968 created the KGB's Fifth Directorate—ideological counter-intelligence—and put it to work churning out a fine harvest of political prisoners. And it was Andropov who, on April 29, 1969, submitted to the Central Committee a thoroughly worked-out plan for the establishment of a network of psychiatric hospitals—the infamous *psikushkas*—to protect the "Soviet government and social order" from dissidents.[11]

Thus did the Chekists reap their revenge for the Thaw. Stalin was returned to the pantheon as national hero and savior of the Fatherland, and any mention of the "Terror" again became taboo.

Yaroslav Golovanov, biographer of the Soviet aircraft designer Sergei Korolyov, tried to obtain Korolyov's case file from the KGB.

Korolyov had done time in both Kolyma and a *sharashka*, a special prison where top scientists and engineers were forced to continue work in their fields.

"What do you need it for?" asked Filipp Bobkov, then in charge of cases involving the intelligentsia.

"Because it's the truth," replied Golovanov.

"Soviet people don't need that kind of truth," retorted Bobkov.

From Moscow's Lefortovo and Lubyanka prisons, to Vladimir Central and Chistopol jails and the Perm and Mordovian labor camps, special trains ferried away political prisoners—those who had tried to speak out loud the truth that, in the opinion of Filipp Bobkov, the public didn't need.

A January 21, 1977, top secret memo No. 123-A to the Central Committee signed by Andropov and Rudenko delineates "measures to terminate the criminal activity of Orlov, Ginzburg, [Mykola] Rudenko, and Venclova":

> The enemy's special services and ideological centers are applying serious efforts to invigorate and extend the hostile activity of anti-Soviet elements on the territory of the Soviet Union. Especially notable is the effort of Western special services to organize an association of persons opposing the existing state and social order in our country. The Committee for State Security possesses reliable information that officials in the U.S. embassy in Moscow are especially involved in this matter . . .
>
> According to available information, correspondents accredited in Moscow from the U.S., West Germany, England, France, and Italy have made persistent attempts to convince the ringleaders among the anti-Soviets to further their subversion by means of "appeals" to the governments of various countries containing malicious slander against Soviet reality, "press conferences," and open protests against the Soviet government's measures . . .
>
> The organs of state security and the USSR Procurator's

Office have employed prophylactic measures . . . However, the most hostile-minded ringleaders among the so-called dissidents have not ceased their activity. Moreover, in ignoring official warnings, they have become more active and more persistent in attempts to legalize their criminal activity . . . their behavior is explained by their confidence in their impunity and in the protective measures that the West may take in their support . . .

The need has thus emerged to implement measures to terminate the actions of Orlov, Ginzburg, and others definitively, on the basis of existing law . . .

With respect to other individuals, the KGB will undertake to issue warnings and terminate their hostile activities using standard procedures . . . we can see no alternatives, given that Orlov, Ginzburg . . . and others (not to mention Sakharov) are growing bolder, providing an extremely negative and dangerous example to others.[12]

Informers seemed to be lurking everywhere: and, in fact, they *were* everywhere. A nice young fellow once brought some typewritten copies of poetry by Nikolai Gumilyev, then still banned, and poems by Osip Mandelstam and Anna Akhmatova, who were still partially censored, to the Moscow State University (MGU) journalism department, where I was a student. I purchased the three handbound, onionskin booklets for twenty-five rubles, half of my monthly stipend. A few days later, I was called in by the senior comrades in the journalism department's Party bureau. They reminded me that possession and distribution of prohibited literature could easily land me seven years in labor camp.

Leonid Shebarshin, former chief of foreign intelligence, has confirmed what students in my day suspected. Each year, the KGB's foreign intelligence section (and others, I imagine) drafted a list of young people whom it recommended for acceptance into special places in MGU's journalism department. Thus, the Committee ensured the training of its cadres for the Soviet media, while preparing a cover for those whom it was going to send abroad. You can be sure most of these people were willing to show their gratitude by informing on their colleagues from time to time.

No aspect of Soviet life escaped the KGB's scrutiny, no matter how banal or how personal. They practically hid under the beds! One document on marriages to foreigners, written by KGB Chairman Fyodorchuk on November 11, 1982, was typical:

> Recently, as the overall number of mixed marriages with foreigners has grown . . . an increase has been noted in registration of marriages by Soviet cultural figures with foreigners from capitalist countries . . .
>
> Marriages with citizens of Western countries have been registered by the poet Y. Yevtushenko, filmmaker A. Shlepyanov, Vakhtangov Theater actress L. Maksakova, film director A. Mikhalkov-Konchalovsky, film actresses M. Bulgakova and E. Koreneva, pianist A. Gavrilov, ex–world chess champion B. Spassky, composer A. Zatsepin, Bolshoi Ballet soloist B. Derevyanko, and others. Some of them virtually live abroad full-time.
>
> After having left the Motherland as a consequence of marriage, some representatives of the intelligentsia have embarked on the path of committing hostile actions against the USSR . . . The bourgeois mass media . . . claims that the marriage of Soviet citizens with foreigners and departure abroad serves the goals of "the flourishing of creative potential under conditions of free self-expression" . . . In some individual cases, refusal to grant permission to travel abroad to Soviet citizens who have married foreigners on such grounds as protection of state secrets has on occasion provoked predictably hysterical protests against "the forcible separation of families," while those who have been denied permission to travel have made efforts to incite various antisocial actions . . . The artistic intelligentsia exhibits a widespread belief that family ties with foreigners can be parlayed

into a means of obtaining all sorts of "goods" abroad, cutting all sorts of deals—the net effect of which is to glorify the Western life-style while threatening leakage of damaging information abroad.[13]

Sometimes the KGB's determination to find a conspiracy was almost comical. In secret memo No. 1479-f to the Central Committee, Fyodorchuk wrote:

According to information that has reached the KGB, elements of negative behavior have been observed recently among certain categories of Soviet viewers present at various international cultural and artistic events.

On July 9 of this year, the closing ceremony of the Seventh International Tchaikovsky Competition took place in the Grand Hall of the Moscow State Conservatory, during which the results were officially announced, and a final concert was given by the winners. During the award process, the majority of viewers demonstrated a clear tendency to overestimate some of the foreign performers, primarily representatives of the U.S. and Great Britain, who were greeted with prolonged applause that at times clearly was meant to be provocative . . . At the same time, the presentation of awards to the Soviet performers who had taken even higher places generated no more than a courteous acknowledgment. This contrast was even more marked during the winners' concert. Thus, P. Donohoe, a pianist from Great Britain, was brought back for repeated encores and showered with flowers. In the opinion of a number of those present, the reaction to his performance was not entirely objective, but had been artificially incited. There was evidence for this in the fact that after the ovation given the Englishman, many viewers left the concert, and the performances of Soviet winners V. Ovchinnikov and L. Zabilyasty took place before a half-empty hall.

Of course, not everything was so funny. On March 29, 1983, the Central Committee voted to "accept the proposal from the Central Committee Propaganda Department and the USSR KGB to create the Anti-Zionist Committee of the Soviet Public" and to "assign the Soviet Peace Fund to undertake financing and the Joint Administration of Public Committees to provide material and technical support for its work." (Comments excerpted from the minutes, marked "top secret," of the 101st session of the Secretariat of the CPSU Central Committee, no. st-101/62gs.) An initiative group's appeal to the Soviet public was to be published in the newspapers *Pravda, Izvestia, Sovetskaya Rossiya, Literaturnaya gazeta*, the magazines *Novoye vremya, Sovetish Heimland*, and the newspapers of the Union republics and the Jewish Autonomous Province. The Central Committee's Department of Propaganda and the KGB were to review jointly the work plans of the Anti-Zionist Committee, and to provide "necessary assistance."[14]

The formation of the Anti-Zionist Committee, which worked under the direct supervision of the KGB's chief ideologist, Filipp Bobkov, was nothing more than an attempt to provide a civilized front to a long-standing policy of state-sponsored anti-Semitism, which had grown during the Brezhnev years to epic proportions.

Anti-Semitism is a kind of recurring theme in my life. I remember how neighborhood girls a little older than my sister and I tore off our Pioneer kerchiefs during the Six-Day War, at a time when Soviet newspapers were trumpeting about the "filthy intrigue of the Israeli Zionists." I remember how in 1975, when we were applying to university, my sister and I were told before we'd even taken entrance exams that our Jewish last name meant we had no chance at all of being accepted. Back then, the most prestigious universities had stopped letting in even "halfers"—people with only one Jewish parent.

In the U.S., the word "Jew" primarily defines a religious affiliation. In Russia, the word "Jew" connotes a nationality, what Americans would call an ethnic group. Most Jews in Russia, if they know anything at all about Judaism, know it only as a cultural and historical phenomenon. Russian passports to this day contain a line that states our "nationality"—not our citizenship, but our ethnic affiliation. In the 1970s and 1980s, passport identification as a Jew was a virtual bar against making any sort of career. Universities, offices, ministries, newspapers, journals, and scientific research institutions had a "five-percent quota": no more than five percent of their employees could be Jewish. When I graduated from university in the spring of 1980, three different departments of a large and popular newspaper for which I had been freelancing offered me a staff job. Finally, I was put on the agenda of the editorial board as a candidate. "Couldn't you find a young journalist with a different last name?" asked the editor-in-chief. Everyone got the hint: any other last name would do, so long as it wasn't Jewish. The only work I could find (despite finishing first in my class at Moscow State University) was stuffing envelopes in the letters to the editor department of a fairly good weekly. Its editor explained to me, "Surely you understand, I can't take you as a correspondent—the Central Committee won't let through a last name like that." He himself was no anti-Semite; he published my articles at a time when many others wouldn't even consider it unless I used a pseudonym.

But let's get back to those "two divisions of one and the same organization" who were now working together, sometimes amicably, sometimes quarreling over who was more important and who had more government clout. Under Andropov (and later, under Brezhnev and Gorbachev), transfers from the KGB to the Party-state structures and back became increasingly common; in fact, an entirely everyday affair.

At the top, for example, Givi Gumbaridze shifted from the post of Georgia's KGB chairman to become the republic's Party chief in the heyday of perestroika. An even more notable figure, Geidar Aliyev, who'd headed the Azerbaijan KGB under Andropov, later became his republic's general secretary, that is, its Party boss.

Under Gorbachev, Aliyev also became first deputy chairman of the USSR Council of Ministers. After a military coup in the late spring of 1993, Aliyev, speaker of the now-independent Azerbaijan's parliament, removed E. Alchibeyev, the country's president, from office. Moscow sources claim that the Chekists played a major role in putting their chief and colleague back at the helm.

At the middle level—or, more precisely, at the next-to-the-top level, whose inhabitants may have lacked *de jure* authority, but nevertheless exercised enormous power *de facto*—there was Arkady Volsky, former aide to KGB Chairman Yury Andropov, who became director of the Central Committee's Department of Industry; in other words, the chief commander of Soviet industry. From there, he became president of the Science and Industry Union, a rather curious organization that, according to rumor, functioned as a key channel for commercial investment of Party and KGB money to the tune of billions of rubles. Other middle-level figures included Gen. Abramov, former head of the Fifth Directorate, who became deputy procurator general (in one of perestroika's more ironic moments, he was assigned to oversee the rehabilitation of Stalin's victims); Gen. Yevgeny Ivanov, who replaced Abramov in ideological counterintelligence after doing yeoman work as sector head in the Central Committee's administration; and Gen. Vorotnikov, who came from the Party to take over Ivanov's old job. To cite yet another example of the middle level, in the spring of 1991, A. Sterligov, operations director of the Russian Council of Ministers, returned to his original home at the KGB with a promotion to major general. Previously, then colonel Sterligov had headed the Economic Directorate of the Council of Ministers (the most powerful directorate, which controlled the distribution of goods for the nomenklatura), and then, under Prime Minister Nikolai Ryzhkov, the Sixth Sector of this directorate. This sector was charged with tracking the status of Soviet industry and verifying the accuracy of information reported to the government (i.e., checking whether the ministers were lying). It was also supposed to oversee the activity of employees at the

Council of Ministers. Sterligov had six KGB officers working under him, officially seconded to the Council from the KGB, and representing a whole range of Chekist directorates: economic counterintelligence (Sixth Directorate); counterintelligence in transportation (Fourth Directorate); counterintelligence (Second Chief Directorate), and so on. Sixth Sector reported to both the KGB and the Council of Ministers, and its employees had two sets of official work identification papers.

On August 21, 1991, Gen. Sterligov was part of the group that arrested his former boss, KGB chief Vladimir Kryuchkov. Sterligov went on to become chief of staff for Alexander Rutskoi, the new vice president of Russia, but that relationship foundered as Sterligov veered far to the right, becoming the leader of an extreme quasi–National-Socialist group, the Russian National Assembly (later renamed the National Salvation Front). Sterligov is firm in asserting that most KGB officers share his views. In the summer of 1993, he quarreled with his Front colleagues over the question of purging Russia of democrats, Jews, and members of other religious faiths. He figured prominently in the October 1993 parliamentary rebellion, and, no doubt, will surface again.

Another middle-level figure, KGB Col. Yevgeny Kalgin, an officer of the KGB Secretariat under Chairman Yury Andropov, went on to become Andropov's personal secretary when Andropov became Party chief. He continued as secretary to Chernenko, and then to Gorbachev. At the Central Committee's Administrative Organs Department, I am told, many people, including the executives, reported to both the Central Committee and the KGB. In this context, it is intriguing to note that Anatoly Lukyanov, chairman of the USSR Supreme Soviet (the standing parliament) at the time of the August 1991 coup, had been simultaneously a Central Committee secretary and director of the Central Committee's Administrative Organs Department.[15] To take one more instance of cross-fertilization, in December 1990, after persistent entreaties by President Gorbachev and a repeat vote at the Fourth USSR Congress of People's Deputies, Gennady Yanayev was elected Vice President. For eighteen years, Yanayev had been a top official of the Committee of Youth Organizations and the Union of Soviet Friendship Societies, organizations traditionally used as cover for KGB agents.[16]

It's no wonder that during the years of the much-ballyhooed perestroika, people who were closely connected with the KGB advanced to the highest offices of the country. Obviously, as the regime became softer at the top, the center of gravity began to shift toward the oligarchy's repressive component, the KGB.

Who's doing what to whom? was the question that fascinated the press, foreign as well as Soviet; what's the KGB to the Party, and vice versa? According to the KGB, the Party was top dog, always meddling in Committee affairs. Thus, for all the latitude granted the KGB in keeping tabs on organizations and individuals, top Party officials were off-limits. You could bug anyone else's telephones, collect *kompromat*, amass a dossier, even if they had parliamentary immunity—unless they were Party brass. At that point, Oleg Kalugin explained, an "internal directive went into effect prohibiting any operations against these people, that is, against bugging their telephones, putting them under surveillance, or filming them with a videocamera," while negative material already collected or newly acquired had to be destroyed.[17]

Kalugin noted one important exception: the regional Party nomenklatura could be bugged, if necessary, but in that case, Party authorities had to decide whose telephones were to be bugged.[18]

Kalugin added this qualification for a reason. According to my sources in the KGB (who continue to work at Lubyanka), it was all a matter of the Party member in question and the rank of the KGB officer who had compromising evidence. For rank-and-file officers, such matters were off-limits. But no regional chief was without a roster of individuals to whom such tasks could be entrusted, especially if the orders came from higher up. All this may give the misleading impression that such cases were rare. Precisely the opposite was true, as the wave of criminal trials and investigations that followed the death of Leonid Brezhnev and the accession of Yury Andropov to General Secretary made clear. As a major housecleaning operation began, it became obvious that for years, Andropov had been gathering information and maintaining a dossier of abuses in the Party-state apparat.[19] (Even Brezhnev's own son-in-law, Churbanov, got caught in the cleanup, and eventually ended up in a labor camp.)

In short, the KGB kept a constant watch on everyone, including the country's highest officials.

Did the Party exercise similar surveillance over the KGB? Of course. Each KGB directorate harbored individuals on whom the Party bosses could rely, people who would inform on their co-workers for material rewards—a new apartment, say—and career advancement. But unfortunately for the Party comrades, their technical capabilities were nothing compared to the KGB's, with its specialized services and equipment for electronic and human surveillance, interception of correspondence, and so forth.

So, naturally, there was always a certain tension between the KGB and the Party. The *komitetchiki* were always irritated by nonprofessionals interfering in their affairs—especially Party functionaries, with their proclivity toward larceny and their lust for awards and medals. And those from the Party also found it a tad disconcerting never to be sure when they picked up the telephone or went to visit a girlfriend whether the KGB was there, too.

Although the KGB's official charter nominally placed it beneath the Politburo and the Council of Ministers, it makes little sense to speak of any real subordination of the KGB to the Party and state apparats. Like the members of a true oligarchy, the Party and the KGB had become full and equal partners, officers of "different divisions of the same organization."

Alexander Yakovlev, former Politburo member and close adviser to Gorbachev, who worked for many years in the Central Committee, explained: "There was always a mutual and silent mistrust between us, but with an observance of all the rules of propriety. That is, the officers of the KGB always demonstrated their respect for us and their readiness to fulfill our assignments;

there was a discipline. But you always felt, all of us felt, that they had the most information, that they always knew more, including information about you. Over the years, an invisible fear came to encircle us as we saw comrades dismissed abruptly from the Central Committee for unspecified reasons: all we knew for certain was that the compromising evidence had come from the KGB.[20]

Until the last years of perestroika, the KGB's relations with the third pillar of the oligarchy, the military-industrial complex (MIC), which provided the material foundation of the totalitarian regime, were significantly different from those with the Party.

The definitive book about the Soviet military-industrial complex—"The Monstrosity," as *Moscow News* called it in a March 1991 "morality tale"—has yet to be written. What we do know is that as of December 1991, the Soviet MIC numbered 14.4 million people, including soldiers, officers, engineers, technicians, and designers who were kept occupied with an uninterrupted stream of work (not all of it productive) at hundreds of factories, closed towns, proving grounds, and testing ranges. This included an army nearly 4 million strong. In comparison, the U.S. armed forces numbered 2,133,000—about half as large.[21] (The new Russian army is currently said to number about 1.5–2 million.) When the war against Fascism broke out in June 1941, in the year when the USSR was under the greatest threat, the Red Army had only 1,333,000 more people under arms than its successor did during the perestroika years, in peacetime—a peacetime in which Russians had a hard time getting enough to eat.[22]

Each year, the MIC produced 1,700 tanks, 5,700 armored personnel carriers, and 1,850 units of field artillery—respectively, 2.3, 8.7, and 11.5 times as many as the U.S.* In 1989, the USSR produced 3 times as many nuclear submarines as the U.S., 1.5 times as many destroyers, 15 times as many intercontinental missiles, and

---

* Figures for 1989. In 1988, more tanks were produced: 3,500, or 4.5 times as many as in the U.S.—Author.

more than 6 times as many short-range intercontinental ballistic missiles.[23]

Needless to say, this cost quite a bit of money. The MIC's official budget, according to Gorbachev, was 96.5 billion rubles—more than a third of the Soviet Union's entire budget.[24] But the International Institute for Strategic Studies in London, disinclined to believe even Gorbachev's statistics (Gorbachev's predecessors cited the ridiculous figure of 20 billion rubles), suggests that the military expenditures of the Soviet Union reached 200–220 billion rubles, or almost half of its budget, in 1989.[25] Soviet specialists estimate that in real costs, our expenditures on troops and armaments prior to 1972 were between 236 and 300 billion rubles a year.[26] Thus, the budget of the USSR Ministry of Defense, according to official figures, was approximately equal to the sum total of expenditures for the subsidy of the national economy, science, social and cultural programs, maintenance of law enforcement agencies, cleanup of the Chernobyl disaster, and the program to save the endangered Aral Lake region.[27]

No wonder the citizens of one of the richest countries in the world felt so poor.

The military monster ate up 25 percent of the GNP, 80 percent of the country's scientific potential, 80 percent of its industrial production, 42 million hectares of land (housing for troops, bases, airports, etc.), plus another 22 million hectares for testing of space launches, etc.[28] The MIC used the lion's share of all steel production (60 percent) and the entire yield of ferrous metals production.[29] According to some estimates, more than 87 percent of all of the Soviet Union's factories worked for the MIC.[30] In February 1991, Gorbachev admitted that the Soviet Union had "the most militarized economy in the world and the largest defense expenditures."[31]

The normal reader, especially the normal Western reader, may well wonder: how on earth can you say the KGB and the Party had all the power, when the MIC had such control over the economy? The normal reader, raised under socialism, will wave his hand wearily and say, Oh, come on, what does the economy have to do with it? And he will be right.

Throughout the history of the USSR, except perhaps for the last few years of perestroika, ideology prevailed over and dictated everything, including the economy. Of course, the economy was important; ideology could not be maintained very well without all the tanks and machine guns rolling off the assembly line, ready to be aimed at the Soviet people—not to mention at the world outside the USSR. But the well-being of the economy was hardly the main concern. Ideology, the domain of the KGB and the Party, ruled the 14.4 million servants of the MIC. The Party/KGB regime could not survive without the MIC; when it began to show signs of disease, they woke up and declared perestroika.

But there was another factor in the ideologists' reluctance to let the military get too close: politicians' traditional (and justifiable) fear that the machine guns might be turned on them. Before the war, Stalin ordered the execution of three of the five marshals of the Soviet Union, the nation's highest military officials; the execution of *all* military district commanders; and the internment or execution of the commanders of corps, divisions, and brigades, and up to fifty percent of troop leaders. By the start of the war, one in five officers of the Red Army had become a victim of the Terror.

During the Khrushchev era, the officers were no longer killed, and were jailed less frequently, but their access to power was strictly limited. The classic example is Marshal Georgy Zhukov, who helped Khrushchev get rid of Beria, then supported Khrushchev in the power struggle against Molotov and Kaganovich, who had been close to Stalin. Khrushchev displayed his gratitude by exiling the marshal, who was popular with both the troops and the public: Zhukov was forced to leave the capital, and his followers were never again welcomed in the corridors of power. The army was even excluded from the palace coup of 1964; the KGB preferred to rely on the KGB to oust Khrushchev.

I know of only two cases of insubordination by people in uniform under Brezhnev. Each incident had a political coloration, though how deep is open to question. In 1969, Second Lieutenant Viktor Ilyin staked out the Kremlin's Borovitsky Gates and took a potshot at the car in which Brezhnev was supposed to be riding. Pronounced insane, Ilyin spent the next eighteen years in solitary confinement in Kazan Psychiatric Hospital. As for the validity of the diagnosis, who can say?[32]

Four years later, Third Captain Valery Sablin steered a large antisubmarine vessel, the *Storozhevoi*, off course into international waters, and broadcast the following appeal: "We have not betrayed the Motherland, and we are not opportunists looking for fame at any price. The time has come to air a number of urgent questions about our country's political, social, and economic development, and its people's future. Genuine, public, nationwide discussion is needed without pressure from state and Party organs." It's difficult to figure out what Sablin thought he'd achieve. His ship's radio operator, who transmitted the appeal, signed off by saying "Bye-bye, guys!" Ten hours after "Sablin's mutiny" broke out, his ship was attacked by a Soviet YaK-28 bomber. A squad landed on deck and arrested Sablin and several seamen who'd supported him. The Military Collegium of the USSR Supreme Court pronounced Sablin guilty of treason and sentenced him to "execution without confiscation of property owing to the lack of same." Sablin was shot by firing squad.[33]

Officers of the Chief Military Procuracy told me of several such incidents that alarmed the comrades from the Central Committee and KGB, but they admitted that these had more to do with the refusal of subordinates to obey their superiors' orders than politics per se.

Still, no one was taking any chances. The armed forces were not to be trusted, and so they were kept under a number of watchful eyes. First, the KGB's Third Chief Directorate (military counter-intelligence) functioned as the political watchdog within the MIC. Although its main brief was combatting foreign espionage in the armed forces, it was equally alert to internal subversion.[34]

In the KGB's opinion, if the army were given authority over military counterintelligence, the state would lose its last vestige of control over its armed forces. (To date, the military has not been granted that authority.) While it's hard to believe our country will ever suffer from a shortage of informers, it is true that such a move might well endanger long-established information channels—the "special departments" made up of KGB agents that traditionally have been part of every regiment and military unit.

A certain colonel—I'll call him Col. Salmatov—came to visit me at *Moscow News*, bearing a two-hundred-page typewritten man-uscript. To put it mildly, the colonel was better armed with the sword than the pen (although the manuscript revealed that it was the pen that had enabled him to achieve his elevated rank; Salmatov had penned reports informing on his fellow officers).

His story was a mundane one. Soon after graduating from mil-itary academy and finding his bearings in the army, Salmatov had been summoned to the special department. The KGB explained to him what a great help he could be to the Party and the entire Soviet people, if only he would . . . in short, inform. Salmatov tried to refuse—or so he claims in his manuscript—at which point the special department officer pulled out a document, and, cov-ering up the signature at the bottom of the page, invited Salmatov to read an excerpt from his own dossier. It was just the usual petty charge: once, while out drinking with a group of people, he had permitted himself some liberties, making a few rude remarks about the military leadership, telling a joke about the General Secretary. The officer gave Salmatov a detailed description of how his life could be ruined—or his career made: all he had to do was co-operate. Salmatov agreed. In his manuscript, he goes on for seventy pages about how the officers pestered him with requests for in-formation, and how remorseful he felt toward those against whom he was made to inform (not an unusual claim in such narratives). What intrigued me most was his claim that the special departments worked particularly hard to recruit the wives of officers as informants: these women were ideal candidates because they were great gossips, and very concerned about their husbands' careers. Many worked in officers' mess halls, clubs, barber shops, and other places where people were likely to loosen their tongues. By some estimates, from 30 to 40 percent of the people serving in the armed forces were KGB sources or "reliables."[35]

The ideologists were also able to monitor the armed forces via another channel, the "political" offices. These were abolished in early 1991 and replaced by "military-political" offices—that is, they changed their name. According to information from the Directorate to Protect the Soviet Constitutional Order, the political offices always worked in close tandem with their Party offices and ideological counterparts; they were birds of a feather, after all.

There had been occasional mention in the Soviet press of the somewhat complicated relations between army officers and their *zampolit*, the Russian abbreviation for *zamestitel po politicheskoy chasti*, deputy for political affairs. One day, I happened to speak with a commander of an army unit in a certain region. (Here as elsewhere I will withhold the names of my sources whose jobs might be endangered by disclosure.) He made no attempt to conceal his hatred of the *zampolit* in his unit—nor his fear.

"Why are you so afraid of him?" I asked. "You're a lieutenant colonel; he's a major." The commander laughed sarcastically. "Why? Because he writes reports to the political directorate, and if he writes me up in one of his reports, the game is over. It's a hundred kilometers to the city from here, so there's at least some semblance of civilization. But if they want, they can send me out to the sticks, where there aren't any decent schools, or stores, or hospitals, let alone a theater. I've got a family and kids. My wife has a job here; she's a university graduate. But up north, in some godforsaken place . . . she'd leave me."

"You can't refuse to go there?" I asked, naïvely. "Refuse?" He looked at me as if I were an idiot. "I'm a military man. Well, sure, I could resign from the army. But then, what would I do? Where would I get an apartment? I want to go to the Academy, but to get in, I need a character reference from the political organs. So I'm sitting here and worrying about what kind of stories those bastards are going to come up with. If I don't get in, I'll be stuck here for the rest of my life." He was silent for a while. "You civilians have no idea how enslaved we military people are."

"The KGB has enormous clout in the army," another officer from a different troop unit and type told me. "At headquarters, where I served, there were three hundred people. The most important person was the KGB man: he could call in any officer and do whatever he liked with him."[36]

"Whatever he liked" might entail arrest, a military tribunal, or a psychiatric ward. A special department officer, Maj. Boris Bugrov, wrote ruefully to *Komsomolskaya pravda*: "Yes, I am a former senior operative of the KGB's special department in the same military unit where you, Ivan Ryabov, served as a private. You decided that only the UN could bring order to our country." [Ryabov had written to the UN about abuses in the Soviet army.] "I had you put in a psychiatric hospital, not because you were really ill, but because I really believed we needed official certification of your mental instability."[37]

They didn't necessarily "like" ordering such complicated persecutions. In a country where your chance of having sausage, meat, or milk in your refrigerator, or of having any degree of civilization around you—sidewalks instead of knee-deep mud, for example; or a toilet instead of an outhouse, an apartment instead of a miserable little corner in a crowded barracks where even cattle would have a hard time—depends in large part on where you live, you really can get a person to do anything you want without having to resort to extreme measures. The very conditions of our existence ("survival" might be a better word for it), our miserable everyday life, engenders informers and augments the KGB's power.

Far more than in the army, the security organs (particularly the

Sixth Directorate) made their presence felt in a critical part of the MIC: the scientific research institutes, factories, laboratories, and proving grounds where weapons are designed and tested. In fact, the Soviet MIC, especially its nuclear weapons plants, was created under the aegis of state security. The famous *Sredmash* (the Ministry of Medium Machine-Building), the "atomic ministry" where nuclear armaments were designed, was created by Beria himself, who remained in charge of the nuclear program right up until his denunciation as a "British spy" and execution in 1953. The "Beria boys" and their successors kept careful watch over the chief designers, as well as the designers' wives, lovers, and friends. After Khrushchev "sorted out" the organs, the MIC also became the perfect home for displaced security people. Take, for example, Lt. Gen. Ogoltsov, who had been a deputy to Abakumov, the Minister of State Security who'd been shot on Khrushchev's orders. Ogoltsov was expelled from the Party and fired from the organs, but he then spent the rest of his working years as deputy director of security at the top secret Scientific Research Institute No. 1. Regardless of perestroika, the security chiefs at such institutes are all still colonels (give or take a rank) of the KGB.

According to people who have worked for decades in the MIC, all institute employees' work telephones, and often their home phones as well, were routinely tapped by the KGB. The KGB also had authority over any work-related trips the scientists might take. And under the aegis of the first ("personnel") department found in every defense plant, the KGB also handled all classified candidate-level and doctoral dissertations. These departments, incidentally, were also a channel for recruiting new Chekists among factory or institute employees.

On the subject of relations between the directors of defense research institutes and laboratories and the KGB, all my sources had the same view: life was complicated enough without walking into that mine field. "Usually the director cannot sign even the most meaningless paper if the signature of the deputy for security is not already on it," I was told.

The Western reader may be just as quick as our citizens to understand the significance of these signatures; bureaucracy knows no national boundaries. "Without a little piece of paper you don't exist" has long been the axiom ruling our lives. In a closed scientific institute, that "little piece of paper" may be the key to a joint experiment with colleagues from another institute, for which you need permission to a) conduct research in a classified area, and b) enter a closed institution. But they don't give it to you—oh, they don't come out and say no; they just drag out the process, check your background all the way to the Stone Age, find out whether you have relatives abroad or, of course, if you are a CIA agent—and, as a result, your experiment is disrupted, work grinds to a halt, your dissertation stalls . . . everything falls behind schedule, and your nerves are shot. A scientist who has invented a unique weapon is reduced to pacing back and forth outside the door of the deputy for security, trying to catch his glance, waiting to grovel for a signature. And then, there are the favors to be done, markers to be called in, the heart-to-heart "chats" . . . Who needs them?

But you have no choice. Say, your nerves snap, and you take out your frustrations on the deputy for security: if you then go complain to the director, do you think he'll want to get involved? "You're on your own," he'll tell you; and now, anything can happen. For violation of security regulations, they can rescind your access to secret documents, forcing you to leave the closed institute for a civilian one with far inferior equipment and funding—and there goes your life's work.

Military secrets, especially those connected with new technologies, must be protected. The problem is, however, that without a law defining just what constitutes a state secret, the KGB was at liberty to use "security" as an excuse for all manner of harassment and persecution.[38]

Of course, when we speak about the MIC's subordination to the oligarchy's ideological structures—the KGB and Party—we should not forget that the MIC itself was the largest supplier of cadres of the nomenklatura, the bureaucratic elite. Only the youth detachment of the Party, the Komsomol, could compete. (According to statistics gathered by sociologist Olga Kryshtanovskaya, 28.3 percent of the Chekist elite began their careers at defense plants; 20.8 came from the Party apparat; 13.2 from institutions of public education, mainly universities; and 47 percent from the Komsomol.)[39] And as soon as the ideological reins were loosened slightly in the years of perestroika, the MIC began to turn into an extremely conservative political force in its own right.

By 1985, the KGB had successfully grafted itself on to the Party-state apparat, and the old political elite had grown decrepit, corrupt, and generally degraded. So, when that unholy trinity—the KGB, the CPSU, and the MIC—cooked up the plan for perestroika, the KGB was in a prime position to run the show and man the engine for reform.

Of course, it's a safe bet that the lucky historians who someday will be allowed to see the secret papers of the KGB and Party from the first half of the 1980s will not ever find a "smoking gun" document to prove definitively that the KGB was perestroika's prime mover. All the evidence will be circumstantial—but undeniable.

What will they find? Memoranda from the KGB's Sixth Directorate (economic affairs), written to the KGB's directors, warning that the Soviet economy was on the verge of collapse; studies from the FCD's Department T (scientific and technological intelligence) chronicling the West's successes in electronics, computers, and invention of new technologies; analytical reports from MIC scientists giving evidence that the Soviet MIC was beginning to fall hopelessly behind that of the enemy—for, despite the production of thousands of tanks and missiles and the infusion of many billions of rubles, any notion of the USSR's defense capabilities, especially in strategic weapons, was rapidly becoming a myth.

They may also find the reports of a secret group of economists created during the 1980s on Yury Andropov's orders. This group, which was attached to the government's Interagency Council to Study the Experience of Socialist Countries, prepared analyses of economic reforms in China, Yugoslavia, and Hungary, and on this basis proffered recommendations for the liberalization of the Soviet economy.[40] (The group was disbanded in 1984, when Andropov died and was replaced by the doddering Konstantin Chernenko, for whom walking was enough of a trial, let alone economic initiatives.)

Historians may find the Soviet press of the perestroika era a richer lode. For example, a 1990 interview with then–first deputy KGB chairman and Central Committee member Filipp Bobkov: "The KGB in 1985 understood very well that the Soviet Union could not develop without perestroika."[41] And even more intriguing, an early 1991 comment from then KGB Chairman Vladimir Kryuchkov: "The state security organs were the first, even before 1985, to say the words that are now resounding on every corner: 'We can't go on like this!' "[42]

I imagine this was one of the rare occasions when the chairman was not lying. Of course, the KGB didn't mean the same thing as the democrats did when they said "we can't go on like this." Genuine reform, which was the great promise of perestroika, would have destroyed a secretive and outlaw organization like the KGB; but somehow that never happened, did it?

The KGB's own motives are easy to understand. The regional Party offices and the KGB had long been sheltering the doddering Politburo members from all but the most sanitized reports of the nation's condition, in order to both placate the senile rulers and preserve the perks that accrued to the bearers of good news.

Georgy Arbatov, head of the Institute of the U.S.A. and Canada, said very aptly about that glorious period of our existence: "Physiology became the most important factor in politics." In the early 1980s, the life of a nuclear superpower had come to depend on how well an incapacitated General Secretary was feeling and what side of the bed the people around him, who were just as incapacitated and ill, got out of in the morning.[43]

Inserting lies in reports and statistics was not just the way the authorities communicated with the public; it was a widespread practice within the ruling structures. But while the KGB spared the nerves of the hierarchs—who, in any event, were heading off to the next world, one after another—it did not deceive itself. The KGB alone knew, or cared to know, the true state of the Soviet economy. It knew that the price of oil was plummeting and that the government's foreign currency revenues were falling (and, with them, the possibility of purchasing equipment for the MIC's plants). They knew that labor productivity had dropped drastically, and that the sporadic investment in machine-building (80 percent of which went to the MIC) was failing to yield returns. Economic analysis warned that in 1984, for each ruble invested in plant, the country was gaining 25 percent less product than fifteen years earlier.[44] In short, the material foundation of the totalitarian regime, the only thing that enabled the USSR to be a great power feared by the rest of the world, was starting to crumble.

By the mid-eighties, it became obvious that the country's economy had reached its limit. Its inability to meet the MIC's demands was jeopardizing the country's very system of government. The MIC's cries for help finally convinced the oligarchy that reforms were needed—but what kind? And how were they to be maintained without destroying the very soul of the regime?

With the "body" of the great leviathan sick unto death, its nerve center went to work.*

The next step was to find a front man to claim responsibility for the ensuing changes, and thereby divert attention from the backroom maneuvering that was really shaking things up. The

---

* There is evidence that the KGB also had a hand in the perestroika of Eastern Europe. Jan Ruml, a prominent Czech dissident and member of Charter 77 who became the deputy minister of internal affairs, testified, "Even as early as 1988, Moscow had drafted a plan to replace the ruling groups in Czechoslovakia, Bulgaria, and Romania with reform Communists." The KGB may have been involved in the toppling of Ceauşescu's regime in Romania. And I am certain that the KGB was behind the overthrow of Honecker in East Germany (he was actively opposed to Soviet perestroika, and had banned the distribution of *Moscow News* and the APN digest *Sputnik*). After all, the durability of the military-economic Warsaw Pact required a more or less stable political situation—Author.

KGB found their man in Mikhail Gorbachev. Young, sophisticated, and in the loop, he appealed to members of the oligarchy
sensitive to the need for a new image to go along with the Soviet
Union's vaunted "new" policies.

Gorbachev had been in line for the job once before. According
to Arkady Volsky, Andropov's close aide, Andropov had written
a deathbed testament that included the following lines: "Comrade
members of the Central Committee, for reasons known to you, I
cannot in this period take an active participation in the direction
of the Politburo and the Secretariat of the Central Committee. In
connection with this, I would ask the Central Committee Plenum
to review the matter and assign the running of the Politburo and
Secretariat"—that is, the position of General Secretary—"to Comrade Mikhail Sergeyevich Gorbachev." But what happened next
seems like something out of a detective novel. By the time the
typewritten copy of this document was read at the Central Committee Plenum, the paragraph about Gorbachev was missing, and
Andropov had been succeeded by Konstantin Chernenko, already
himself mortally ill. Gorbachev was forced to wait another year,
until April 1985, to assume the throne.[45] (Chernenko's aide, Vadim
Pechenev, denies Volsky's version of these events; though, who
knows, Pechenev may well have been one of those who "edited"
Andropov's testament.)

Gorbachev performed his task well. He understood the required
policies, and what they were meant to accomplish. The man who
in December 1984 gave a speech sharply criticizing "market socialism" because the "main historical advantage of the countries
of socialism is the planned nature of the economy," who, according to Pechenev, had quietly but systematically suppressed
any attempts to introduce any radical notions of restructuring
into the speeches of chief officials, a year and a half later was
hailing perestroika.[46] "Our main task," he said in an April 1985
speech, "is to move rapidly to the production of new genera-
tions of machines and equipment that will ensure the introduction of new technology . . . Primary attention must be given to

improving machine-tool building, accelerating the development of computer technology, instrument-building, electric technology, and electronics as catalysts for scientific and technological progress."[47] It is no coincidence that Gorbachev was essentially listing the branches of industry in the MIC.

Pick any one of Gorbachev's speeches from the first years of perestroika at random, and you will find the key buzzwords: "acceleration," "scientific-technological progress," "development of machine-building." For a more detailed reflection of the government's agenda, look at a speech from Gorbachev's comrade-in-arms, Nikolai Ryzhkov. At the 1986 Twenty-Seventh Party Congress, Ryzhkov, who had recently come from the MIC to become chairman of the Council of Ministers, stated: "Machine-building must grow 1.5 times faster than industry . . . Capital investment in machine-building must increase by a factor of 1.8."[48]

All economic reform was directed toward bolstering the MIC, but the shelves in the stores steadily grew emptier. With scarcity the only visible result of the much-touted need for change, social tension grew, and very nearly erupted. So our prudent leaders came up with a cost-free outlet: they declared the advent of glasnost, the symbol of perestroika. (True freedom of speech, for which it is commonly mistaken, was still far away.)

This cunning trick, diffusing social tension by manipulating the media, had actually been conceived by Joseph Stalin. In 1947, at a meeting in the Kremlin, he suddenly started talking about the need to change the image of the writers' newspaper *Literaturnaya gazeta*:

All newspapers are official newspapers in one way or another, but *Literaturnaya gazeta*, the newspaper of the Writers' Union, should raise issues unofficially, including those that we cannot or will not raise officially. *Literaturnaya gazeta* as an unofficial newspaper can be more outspoken than we are on some issues; it can be more to the left, it can differ from the officially expressed viewpoint in how candidly it raises an issue. It is quite possible that we will even criticize *Lit-eraturnaya gazeta* for this. But it should not be afraid, despite the criticism; it should go on doing its job.[49]

But Comrade Stalin's diligent pupils clearly overestimated their abilities. They mistook the Soviet Union of 1985 for the labor camp of 1947. After seventy years of repression, citizens would not be satisfied by this limited allowance. The new freedoms would be seized upon and stretched further and further, with the "reform-ers" the first casualties of the expansion. It would not be possible to push back the reforms without bloodshed and tanks.

The story is fascinating, but let me not oversimplify it for mere dramatic effect. I am not trying to say that Gorbachev was simply and utterly a creature of the KGB—that's just the kind of crude thinking that inevitably leads to formulations like "Gorbachev is a KGB agent."

The story is more complex than that: it's about subtle timing and overlapping interests. Gorbachev suited the group within the oligarchy who were capable of seeing how close the Soviet Union was to economic collapse. That meant he suited the KGB as well. So, it was natural for the Committee to guide him through the bureaucratic maze. Of course, it was understood that Gorbachev would have to pay for this favor someday. Yes, he had debts . . .

Consider this interesting episode: in 1984, when Gorbachev was still only second in command, he traveled to England. At that time, the head of FCD was Gen. Vladimir Kryuchkov, who had risen through the ranks at Andropov's right hand (first in Hungary, when Andropov was the Soviet ambassador; then as his aide at the Central Committee; and finally, as the KGB chairman's chief of staff). The FCD took a particular interest in Gorbachev's visit, and went to great pains to ensure that it was a success and that Gorbachev played well both abroad and at home.[50] Significantly, in 1988, four years after the London visit, Kryuchkov was appointed head of the KGB, becoming the first head of foreign intelligence to assume that post. It was commonly said that he was one of the people closest to Gorbachev.[51]

But the question of who chose Gorbachev for the role of reformer is finally less relevant than the fact that the reforms themselves were undertaken for the sake of salvaging the MIC, which meant the regime itself. The result was the greater impoverishment, and ultimate destruction, of the rest of the country. But these reforms did not appear to threaten the security of either the MIC or the KGB—and that's what was most important.

As for the third branch of the oligarchy, I'm afraid that the KGB ascendant had little interest in defending a corrupt and enfeebled Party against the democrats' lethal blow. The KGB no longer wanted to remain the force behind the scenes. And that would prove to be one of its greatest mistakes.

This, to be sure, is only my version of the story. But one thing is certain: perestroika opened the way for the KGB to advance toward the very heart of power.

CHAPTER

5

Realities of the Glasnost Era

A man hanged himself.

Once upon a time, he'd worked as a tram driver in Rostov-on-the-Don. He'd been an active member of Defense, a civic club born in response to Gorbachev's call for popular involvement in perestroika—a club whose very existence evinced citizens' faith that they could now defend themselves against government abuse.

His name was Anatoly Otreznov. He was thirty-five years old, an ordinary, hard-working man, just another face in the crowd. His social life was minimal; he had no friends or family. If anything distinguished him, it was his big mouth: even in company, he'd damn the Party, the government, and the Constitution. In 1988, especially in the provinces, this was risky behavior.

And then he hanged himself. His suicide note—his "Confession," as he entitled it—ended with the words: "People are no-good trash." And only then, after his death, did people learn that Otreznov had been a KGB agent: oh, not on the payroll; just a petty informer planted in Defense to keep an eye on things and, if possible, discredit it. As payment for his services, Otreznov had been promised his lifelong dream, an apartment of his own. (He'd grown up in an orphanage, served in the army, and then had alternated between dormitories and corners in other people's places.) But, despite his superiors' promises, all they could come up with was a room in a communal apartment. All he'd wanted was a room of his own—not a trip to Hawaii, not girls on the beach in Fiji—and still, it fell through; they lied. Perhaps he hadn't done his job for them well enough? In despair, he took his own life.

By December 1989, glasnost had reached the point where Nikolai Popkov was able to publish Otreznov's tale in *Literaturnaya gazeta*.[1] "The Noose" was the first account of a KGB plant in perestroika-era, democratic citizens' organizations to appear in the Soviet press. But despite its exposé of the hypocrisy underlying officially declared perestroika, glasnost, and "new thought," it had little impact. People had become too accustomed to the KGB even to raise an eyebrow. "Stop following people altogether? . . . then what role would the Committee for State Security have?" Vladimir Semichastny, Khrushchev-era KGB chairman asked in surprise in a perestroika-era interview. "If [the Committee] fails to keep up with things—people's moods, opinions and just where we're all headed—and something goes wrong, everyone will jump on us: Where were you, guys? Is that how you earn your pay?"[2]

Gen. Oleg Kalugin gave a graphic example of the way the Committee earned its pay vis-à-vis the new organizations. "When Leningrad's stages began to fill up with rock-oriented musicians, a rock club was formed at the KGB's initiative to keep the rock movement manageable and under control." By now, both sides take this sort of thing for granted. It's not very nice, but what can you do? There's no point in yelling at the weather; it's easier just to take your umbrella. And it's not as though the methods are any different from thirty or fifty years ago. "Only the objects of attention have changed; now it's workers' strike committees and new political parties."[3]

In December 1989, around the same time that the article on Otreznov appeared, KGB Chairman Kryuchkov held a reception at Lubyanka for women journalists from the International Press Club. He was a model of warmth and tact; and, of course, no one broached the subject of the Otreznov article. In fact, no mention was made of agents, informers, plants—the sorts of things that interest a wide range of readers. Instead, Kryuchkov went on about safeguarding the liberties of Soviet citizens ("our actions must protect human rights") and the training of Chekists who "work within the law." Kryuchkov seemed to be proud of the KGB's achievements in the area of glasnost.[4] He cited a recent scholarly conference on "Democracy, Perestroika, and the Organs of the KGB," and a newly passed resolution on "The Committee for State Security and Glasnost." The KGB had started publishing an *Information Bulletin*. (Of course, it was impossible to get hold of a copy, but Kryuchkov remained understandably silent about that.) And let's not forget the Public Liaison Center that had been established, with KGB Gen. Alexander Karbainov at its helm. Karbainov's years at the head of Fifth Directorate's First Department apparently had given him a lively interest in the work and private lives of writers, artists, and musicians, an obvious plus in this very visible public relations post.

Ever faithful to his concern for the KGB's image, Kryuchkov took great pains to explain his institution's attitude toward dissent and dissidents: "The security organs did not combat 'dissent,' only specific unlawful activities; therefore, the terms 'dissidents' and 'political prisoners' were never acceptable to us." So that's how it was! It was the terminology that made them uncomfortable; putting people in jail didn't bother them. According to a 1987 memorandum to Gorbachev prepared by the KGB and the USSR Procurator, there were at that time 288 political prisoners in labor camp. "Of these, 114 had been sent to correctional labor facilities for anti-Soviet agitation and propaganda, 119 for knowingly disseminating fraudulent and defamatory tales about government and society, while 55 people had been exiled for criminal offenses."[5]

In November 1989, a month before Kryuchkov smooth-talked the ladies at Lubyanka, Sergei Kuznetsov, an active member of Sverdlovsk's fledgling Democratic Union, had been sentenced to three years' imprisonment for civil rights activism. By that time, the articles previously used to jail dissidents had been repealed (the infamous Art. 70, "anti-Soviet agitation and propaganda," and

Art. 190–1, "dissemination of deliberately false fabrications defam-
ing the Soviet state and social order"), and a "Law on Rallies and
Demonstrations" had been passed, granting citizens freedom of
assembly (while preserving the government's right to deny that
permission should those assembling "misbehave").[6] According to
the authorities, Democratic Union had a track record of such
misbehavior, and so the police were sent out to disperse their rally,
billy clubs swinging. Kuznetsov was brought up on ordinary criminal charges (just as Kryuchkov said: the KGB's only interest was
"criminal" activity). Thus, the activist whose crimes consisted of
distributing leaflets critical of the Soviet state and organizing rallies
banned by the authorities found himself charged with Art. 130
(libel) and Art. 191–1 (resisting a police officer). Within a few
months, however, Kuznetsov was released: the international community had raised quite a fuss about the arrest, which cast a pall
over the era of "new thought." By the end of 1989, the Committee's
nerves had settled, and it no longer jumped at every perestroika
skirmish. (As the Russian saying goes, the dog barks, but the
caravan goes forward. And go forward it did.)

Kryuchkov did face one slightly unsettling question from a
woman journalist who inquired about the privileges enjoyed by
the KGB's top brass. Kryuchkov's reply was typically straightforward and sincere, in the best tradition of Soviet demagoguery.
"The only privilege of rank in the KGB is a greater degree of
responsibility." True, he did add later that a certain category of
Chekists were entitled to a state dacha—"as payment for services
rendered," he emphasized—as well as access to government car
service, vacation homes, and clinics, and their own vegetable garden plots. No doubt the KGB rank-and-file found it fascinating
to hear how modest were their superiors' demands . . .

The *komitetchiki* themselves had nicknamed the fourth floor
of the KGB's grim new charcoal granite building on Lubyanka
Square the "Zone"—a bit of Chekist black humor, since here the
"Zone" didn't keep labor camp prisoners in; instead, it kept ordinary Chekists out. Yes, here in this Zone (classified top secret)

was the special dining room for the chairman, his deputies, and members of the KGB collegium. Here, diners feasted on organic produce such as neither ordinary Chekists nor ordinary Soviet citizens would ever know in their lifetime. So much for the classless society—perestroika or no, some things never change.

Another carefully guarded secret was that the Committee's elite would order housewares unavailable in ordinary Soviet stores from Western catalogues. Officially, these men earned a salary in rubles, which have no value outside the USSR, but between the various Soviet foreign trade organizations, there was always a way to work out the arrangements.[7]

The journalists further asked Kryuchkov how the radicals and conservatives in the KGB were getting along with each other, and who was dominant. That gave Kryuchkov an opportunity to expand on the "monolithic unity in the ranks of the KGB" . . . an interesting question, indeed, since the "monolithic unity in the ranks," in Kryuchkov's meaning of the phrase, had long since disappeared.

Although not so visible, the flame of confrontation had been flickering for years between those who called themselves "professionals" and those they referred to as "Party apparatchiks." The Party hacks had begun their careers in Komsomol and Party committees, had moved up through the ranks of the military reserves, and had taken these ranks with them when they transferred to the KGB. The professionals, those who'd started out in the organs as rank-and-file operatives, deeply resented their colleagues' career jumps. The professionals believed that their Party competitors were incapable of handling real Chekist's work; they hadn't earned the power, the pay, the trips abroad. And they probably were right, although the KGB's chief function (as Semichastny reminded us) was to keep tabs on the populace; and on that, the Party comrades were the real experts.

The perks of high office played a very significant role in the competition between the two camps, and none more so than the coveted prize of foreign travel. This was especially true for intelligence officers. A trip abroad—or better yet, a long-term posting under the cover of an embassy or a foreign news bureau—unquestionably would set a Soviet citizen up for life. Abroad, one could use one's salary to buy goods that at home for years had been available only on the black market at exorbitant prices. And money itself could be multiplied by "buying for trade-in": the commission on a VCR or TV sold through a consignment store or a private individual more than made up the purchase price at cheap foreign rates. (It wasn't just the *komitetchiki* who took advantage of this; other Soviet workers abroad also bought cheap to sell dear.) Besides, given the plethora of KGB "covers," who knew which of the Soviets abroad were KGB?[8]

According to KGB Lt. Col. Valentin Korolyov, material incentive attracted many young people, particularly children of the Party and state nomenklatura, into the organs (especially the FCD), which also contributed to the merging of Party and KGB structures.

"Only ten to twenty percent of those in the First Chief are 'mongrels,' " that is, without connections or parents in the nomenklatura, claimed Korolev. "Those with slightly more of a 'pedigree' graduate from the KGB Academy into Second Chief . . . the institution's central counterintelligence organ. I was personally acquainted with only two 'mongrels': one Academy student placed in First Chief, and one in Second Chief. They were decent people. But the other 'mongrels' assigned to Second Chief informed on their fellow classmates to school officials."[9] Again, we get a view of the Committee's prevailing moral ethos.

In our impoverished country, the possibility of financial gain is also a powerful means of drawing people into cooperating with the organs. In the past, the KGB could refuse permission to travel (as they refused me for eight years) without citing any reason. The personnel department people at my newspaper told me point-blank, "Don't even submit your documents—it's hopeless." I recently learned that in 1989, Gely Ageyev, deputy KGB chairman, had personally signed permission for me to travel. "That means they must have had something serious on you," my source said. But what? Will I ever learn?

Today, the Committee operates more delicately; they simply take their time processing your documents, until it's too late for you to get to the conference you want to attend. You're reduced to begging for a visa, or trying to chalk up a favor or two: after all, who needs trouble with the organs? In 1991, when I was scheduled to deliver a paper on "The KGB and Perestroika" at a conference of investigative journalists in the U.S., I had to threaten to involve the Western press before my visa finally came through, on the very day of my departure.

But to get back to the Committee itself: as its vaunted internal cohesiveness began to dissolve in the last years of perestroika, a series of so-called KGB dissidents emerged. The wave of "renegades" was launched by Col. Yaroslav Karpovich, a retired ideological counterintelligence officer, who was followed by Maj. Gen. Oleg Kalugin. Kryuchkov was satisfied to strip Karpovich of his title of Honored Chekist; in Kalugin's case, the KGB demanded that President Gorbachev strip him of all his ranks and medals. Prime Minister Ryzhkov ordered Kalugin's pension revoked, and a criminal case was opened under Art. 74 of the Russian Penal Code ("divulging state secrets").* His former colleagues made every effort to compromise him. From March 1987 on, the Twelfth Department of the Second Chief Directorate maintained surveillance over "Petrov" (Kalugin's code name), claiming "signs of possible operations of an agent of American special services on USSR territory." They subjected him to "episodic ES" (external surveillance) and "periodic OTM 'A' " (operational technical measure for audio surveillance, i.e., bugging a telephone).

From June through September 1990, "Petrov" was prohibited from leaving the USSR or entering the bureaus of foreign organizations accredited in Moscow. Later on, by direct order of

---

* After the coup, Gorbachev issued a decree that, without explanation or apology, restored to Kalugin his rank, medals, and pension—Author.

V. A. Kryuchkov (a personally signed assignment), "OTM 'A' was performed on 'Petrov' in order to reveal his connections with foreigners and further monitor them from the perspective of a possible relationship to the enemy's special services."[10]

Others followed the lead of these two by publishing articles that were quite damaging to the KGB: retired colonel Mikhail Lyubimov (another former intelligence agent who had been the Soviet resident in Denmark); Korolev, whom I have already mentioned; Col. Vladimir Rubanov, an analyst from the KGB's research institute; Lt. Col. Alexander Kichikhin, of ideological counterintelligence; Maj. Alexander Mavrin of the Volgograd KGB Directorate; and a few others. In the summer of 1990, the Western press carried an open letter from four KGB officers who claimed that the KGB was torpedoing all legitimate efforts at reform in the Soviet Union. Thereupon, three hundred Central Office employees signed a letter to the USSR Supreme Soviet protesting this "mudslinging against the KGB." In November 1990, *Rossiyskaya gazeta* published a statement from sixty-four officers of the Sverdlovsk Region KGB Directorate regarding the "potential danger posed by the KGB organs to the democratic changes being made in the country" and warning that the Committee still was not under parliamentary oversight.[11]

For all the attention it attracted, however, the rebellion within the KGB collapsed without the need for any harsh measures; a few promises were all that was needed to quiet things down. After all, Sverdlovsk was Yeltsin's home base, and the last thing the authorities wanted was the sort of confrontation that would add to the Russian leader's growing popularity.

I take issue with those of my colleagues who view Soviet intelligence agents who have defected to the West as genuine political opponents of the KGB. I am thinking, for example, of *Rabochnaya tribuna* [Worker's Tribune] correspondent and FCD Third Department agent Mikhail Butkov, whose 1991 defection raised some questions among Western colleagues aware of his intelligence connections. The KGB published a written denial that Butkov was an agent working under journalistic cover, but Butkov's own statement belies this:

Taking advantage of a convenient opportunity which became available with the arrival in London of my father, I would like to inform you of the motives of my action, that is, petitioning for political asylum in Great Britain.

My appeal to the British authorities for political asylum in May 1991 was dictated by political motivations. This was a completely deliberate and independent step and I was not subjected to any pressure. I considered it my duty to oppose the attempts of reactionary forces in the USSR, above all the CPSU and its instrument, the KGB, to strangle the process of democratic reform. I believed that the assignments received by the KGB's foreign staffs were simply criminal and aimed at preserving the power of the elite to the detriment of the people and the state. The firm conviction that the real enemy must be sought within the country and not outside and that the interests of the West coincide with the authentic interests of the people (but not the ruling elite, of course) has led me to the decision to help the political leaders of the West evaluate accurately the processes under way in the USSR, despite the disinformation actively disseminated by the KGB about the democratic movement and its leaders. I believe I have fulfilled my duty.

I would also like to note that the operative damage caused by me is limited to my personal contacts with agents who in my opinion were already known.

As a Russian and a patriot, I cannot reject my Motherland, and will return to Russia as soon as I can be completely sure that the legislation of this country will protect me completely from any abuse and guarantee me the essential freedoms accepted in the free world.

Although I have no doubt that ideological differences with their native country played a large role in such agents' defections, it's hard to square their form of political protest with any notion of moral heroism. In defecting, they often exposed their agent networks—live human beings who had no voice in their colleague's decision—to terrible punishment, including the death penalty. Then again, what sense does it make to talk about morality in *that* line of work?

By any accounting, the Committee was hardly overflowing with dissidents and rebels. I may have left out a few names, but with about 89,000 people employed at the KGB in Moscow alone, we're still only talking about a drop in the ocean.

Moreover, something prevents me from calling these renegade agents "dissidents." Their courage unquestionably commands respect; clashing with the KGB while still wearing Chekist epaulets is no job for the faint-hearted. Perhaps it's just that these so-called dissidents managed, despite their misgivings, to work so many years in that institution. They chose to join the KGB; no one forced them. They knew what the KGB was up to, and they served, anyway. Or maybe what bothers me is that in all their articles, I've never perceived a sense of personal, individual guilt, or any hint of personal repentance. In any case, I find it more comfortable to call these officers "critics of the KGB."

As far as I'm concerned, there's been only one genuine dissident in the KGB in the entire post-Stalin era—Viktor Orekhov.

Orekhov was a willing recruit who entered the KGB's Dzerzhinsky Academy from military service in the border troops. He studied in the prestigious Second Department (intelligence and counterintelligence). But for all his dreams of foreign intrigue, he got no further than the Moscow River District KGB Directorate, where he started out as a junior operative with the rank of lieutenant, keeping a watch over the foreign students at the Institute of Textile Industry. His "flaw" was simple enough: he lacked a nomenklatura pedigree. Talent wasn't enough; without connections, you started at the bottom.

Orekhov didn't uncover any spies, but he succeeded in "attracting for cooperation" (recruiting) his assigned quota of students. This led to his transfer to the Moscow Region Directorate Fifth Directorate (ideological counter-intelligence). He sincerely believed in the battle against dissidents' "slanderous fabrications" impugning the country's honor, and he worked assiduously to convince them of the error of their ways, calling them in for "prophylactic" talks, tapping their phones, making every attempt to recruit them.

Wiretapping doesn't come cheap, Orekhov explained to me.

First, you have to see who lives in the adjacent apartments and on the floors above and below and sometimes in the whole building. Then you have to find a way of getting the residents out of their homes. You go to their workplace and set things up with the personnel people . . . you find the tickets for a decent spa . . . or you simply tell the person that for reasons of state security, they'll have to get out of town . . . Then, a special team from Twelfth Department comes in and installs the device: a microcamera is wired through the ceiling of the apartment above, or put in a place where it's less noticeable, like behind a shelf in one of the rooms. Once it's installed, a special artist on the team paints over the damaged wallpaper so you'd never guess anything's gone on. All this, of course, assumes that the subject under observation is away . . . if the person in whom we are interested never travels . . . a team of *komitetchiki* is sent to keep him at work; another team detains his spouse, while a third one enters the apartment and fulfills the assignment.

Orekhov was sent on his share of clandestine searches, checking over dissidents' apartments, keeping a special eye out for banned literature. Once they knew where everything was, it was easy enough to come back later with an official warrant in hand.

In short, Orekhov did his job well. It wasn't a bad life. As he explained to me, "You have to understand, I was the elite. My salary was 330 rubles, pretty good money in those days. I could enter any store through the back door; I never had to stand in line. I could get my foot in any minister's door—everyone was afraid. I could call up any director and say, 'This is Orekhov from the KGB,' and he'd ask, 'When would it be convenient for you to come in?' "

There were bonuses as well: a tour to Japan with the Bolshoi Theater during which Orekhov ostensibly was keeping tabs on the ballet stars, making sure none of them was defecting or making contact with foreigners; in fact, he was out on a spree amidst "capitalist decadence." Back home, he returned to his job following dissidents and reading banned writing (some of it confiscated from the dissidents themselves). To make a long story short, at some point it dawned on Orekhov that they were telling it the way it really was. Oh, they might be laying it on a bit thick, but basically, it was the truth. "The chaos and filth; the fact that we put people in jail who only want good for this country—it was all true," he told me.

Once Orekhov "invited in for a chat" (that is, detained) Mark Morozov, an outspoken opponent of abuses of workers' rights. Orekhov knew from listening to the bug in Morozov's phone that he was carrying a copy of Solzhenitsyn's *Gulag Archipelago* in his briefcase. They talked; and Morozov began feeding the captain with literature on human rights. But self-education wasn't enough for Orekhov. Once, he told Morozov to warn a certain person— Anatoly Shcharansky—that his coat had been bugged with a tiny miniature radio. Another time, Orekhov called from a public phone (more difficult to trace) to warn that Yury Orlov, the well-known physicist, human rights campaigner, and founder of the Moscow Helsinki Group, was about to be picked up. Orlov was able to elude arrest for a few days, even though his apartment was under surveillance—and when you are facing years of prison and labor camp, even a week means a lot.

Alexander Podrabinek, a prominent human rights advocate and

editor-in-chief of the newspaper *Ekspress-khronika*, published underground for many years, told me about his contact with Orekhov:

Fate brought me together with Orekhov in a very strange way. On October 10, 1977, he came to search my Moscow apartment with a team of KGB agents led by Investigator Katalikov. Two months later, he informed me (using a pseudonym) of a criminal case being prepared against me. On May 19, 1978, agents from his department came looking for me, but I had learned of the arrest date from Orekhov three days earlier. When the KGB was trying to force me to leave the USSR in December 1977, using the threat of a criminal case against me and my brother [Kirill], Orekhov gave me information that helped me determine the seriousness of the KGB's intentions. Orekhov warned us in advance of at least a dozen searches.[12]

Orekhov could not prevent searches or arrests, but not being caught unprepared made a big difference to the dissidents. It gave them time to hide what had to be hidden, alert friends and acquaintances, and warn those liable to be arrested next. And Western reporters could be informed, which meant a public outcry, something the KGB hated. Orekhov's criminal file contained the following charges:

In January 1977, Orekhov warned of the impending arrest of Orlov. In February 1977, Orekhov warned of the special operational and technical measures being used against [Anatoly] Shcharansky and of forthcoming searches of [Alexander] Lavut. Since Orekhov knew that Morozov had some relationship to the production and distribution of some anti-Soviet leaflets, he let him know about the operational and technical measures being taken against him and also [Irina] Grivnina and [Vladimir] Skvirsky. Morozov passed on the information he received from Orekhov to his fellow dissidents.[13]

Eventually, the KGB learned of Orekhov's unorthodox approach to his job, and in August 1978, he was arrested and jailed. From prison, Orekhov mounted a letter-writing campaign. He wrote to Andropov, then head of the KGB; to Suslov, the Politburo's hard-line chief ideologist; and to General Secretary Brezhnev, naïvely trying to convince them that he'd only acted in the interests of state security. The dissidents truly cared about their homeland; attacking them wasted money and compromised the state. Of course, he got no replies.

At the trial, Mark Morozov described Orekhov's relations with the dissidents in detail. (Morozov's own fate was a sad one; he eventually hanged himself in Chistopol Prison.)

Orekhov received a sentence of eight years under Art. 260, par. *a*, to be served in a special zone for former law-enforcement employees in the Mariisky labor camp. "When you heard the sentence, weren't you afraid?" I asked Orekhov. "Oh no, on the contrary, I felt like singing; I was sure that now the truth would finally emerge. Listen, this wasn't an ordinary case—I was a captain of the KGB. Now, they would investigate properly and realize that the people I was helping were patriots, not thieves."

Orekhov continued to fight for justice from labor camp, even going on a hunger strike in defense of prisoners' rights. Local Chekists were stupefied: "How could you? A KGB captain . . . you had a job in Moscow, you traveled abroad, you were being recommended for a leadership post . . ."

"How could I? So that people like you never again have the opportunity to ask such questions," replied Orekhov.

Orekhov served his sentence in full and was released from prison in 1986. The sentence meted out by the tribunal was not reduced by a single day or hour: here was a man who truly paid on all accounts! His illusions about the regime were gone, and so was his health: when we met for our first interview, the ex-captain was wearing slippers; he couldn't pull boots over his ravaged feet.

After his return to Moscow, Orekhov started his own cooperative. To this day, he and his new colleagues continue to turn out fall and winter jackets—good ones.

I have not profiled Captain Viktor Orekhov in reproach of anyone; or, if it is in reproach, then it is against all of us who lived in those years. Rather, I have told the story to say there was such a man in the KGB—one, out of hundreds of thousands. And, in that sense, Kryuchkov was not lying about the "monolith of the Chekist ranks."

Although a fierce opponent of Kryuchkov, Kalugin does agree with him about the uniformity of the ranks, but from a different premise. Kalugin says that despite the presence in the Committee of the sort of radically minded people who appeared in the years of perestroika, the core of the Committee remains extremely conservative. Regardless of the KGB's own glasnost and the pressure placed on it by democrats, these hard-liners have been unfazed.[14] Why?

To begin with, the Committee's paramilitary nature forbade resistance to orders. I asked one agent whether they could refuse to carry out unsavory tasks. "What do you mean, refuse?" he replied. "We're military men; an order is an order. I could lose my job for disobeying an order, and someone else would just destroy the documents I was ordered to destroy."[15] M. Lyubimov, a KGB reserve colonel, explained:

> If an officer dared to express indignation at something, they would not only fire him, but blacklist him so that no decent organization would ever give him a job. And where would he go to complain? To court? To the Commission on Defense and State Security? Who would be in a position to defend him? . . . the KGB could always say that the comrade's

dismissal was connected with some top secret matters . . .
That's why even honest officers hold their tongues or excoriate those who dare to speak the truth. Fear has always reigned
at the KGB, disgusting fear, I would say . . .[16]

There is a somewhat more complicated reason for the absence
of dissent: in a country suffering from shortages of everything but
misery, it is unlikely that a KGB employee would choose to jeopardize his privileges. As Orekhov said: "I was the elite, I could go
into any store through the back door, I could get my foot in any
minister's office." Even if he is exaggerating here, he is in essence
right. Chekists may not be very popular, but their ID cards still
work magic.

The main reason for the Committee's uniform conservatism,
however, lies in something intangible—what is euphemistically
called *KGB mentality*. To quote Gen. Kalugin:

> Gorbachev proclaimed the priority of universal human values, rejecting old stereotypes and ideas. But masses of Committee officers had worked to maintain these very stereotypes
> . . . When the Party said "international imperialism," the
> KGB decoded this to mean foreign intelligence agencies, hostile émigré organizations, centers of ideological subversion,
> international Zionism, the Vatican, Radio Liberty. Whole
> structures of the Committee were involved in the campaigns
> against these institutions. It was clear who the enemy was. So,
> now they were talking about universal human values? What
> happened to the Vatican and Radio Liberty? What were people to do, as all they'd believed in collapsed before their very
> eyes? This kind of situation either breeds demoralization or
> sparks resistance, and resistance inevitably develops into a
> certain political philosophy, namely, conservatism.[17]

A prominent colleague of mine who was invited to the KGB
Academy to meet with the new perestroika-era generation of stu-

dents returned utterly shaken. "You can't even imagine the depth of the audience's hatred for the independent press, the new entrepreneurs, and the democrats," he told me.

"The country that reads *The Gulag Archipelago* will already be a changed one," according to Solzhenitsyn himself. The Chekists were granted that privilege before the rest of us. But by 1989, the people standing in endless lines for sausage and cheese were more concerned with damning Gorbachev for "wanting to sell the [Soviet] Union off to foreigners"; the Balts for demanding independence; the democrats for betraying everything, including socialism. The word *vreditel* ("wrecker" or "saboteur"), which was repeated in Solzhenitsyn's book hundreds if not thousands of times—the accusation that under the Stalin era the government had sent millions of people to labor camp or execution—could now be heard more and more frequently on these lines.

I asked Alexander Kichikhin, a KGB lieutenant colonel (now in the reserves), a former ideological counterintelligence officer and a serious critic of the KGB, when his department would finally be abolished. He answered: "It should not be abolished under any circumstances." Was he serious? Did he really think the Chekists should continue keeping tabs on their fellow citizens?

"Of course," he replied. Like Semichastny, Kichikhin explained that agents had to keep a close watch on any shifts in the public's moods and opinions, or else society would have their blood.

A survey conducted by the KGB's sociological service in May and June of 1991, the sixth year of perestroika and glasnost, revealed that half of the USSR KGB Academy's students—tomorrow's Chekists—believed in a double standard of morality, that is, different codes of ethics for Chekists and for other citizens. A bit more than a third (35.5 percent) felt that "the end justifies the means"; more than three-quarters of the students (77.6 percent) were convinced that the "saboteurs" were to blame for the country's impoverishment; while 75 percent accused the CIA and other Western intelligence agencies of aggravating ethnic conflict within the Soviet Union and financing democratic groups' attempts to destroy the country.

Meanwhile, 62.6 percent of permanent staff Chekists justified the use of force to disperse peaceful demonstrations, even if it led to bloodshed. The Chekists believed that anti-Soviet, anti-state actions should be violently suppressed.[18]

"A type of thinking specific to the profession," the sociologists explain. Um-hum . . .

So, don't hold your breath waiting for the KGB to transform itself. And democracy in our country is not possible so long as the KGB, despite all the new slogans, continues to do its job—with the same methods, the same hands, the same brains, and the same mentality. A nation serious about ridding itself of a totalitarian regime starts by getting rid of its state security apparatus. (When Jan Ruml, one of the current directors of the new Czech Ministry of Internal Affairs, was asked how he expected to cope without the trained professionals of the old security service, he replied: "We don't need the kind of professionals who worked under the previous regime."[19]) It's a harsh truth, but I'm afraid there's no other way.

Our perestroika has proved that point.

So, if not genuine reform, what was really going on behind the KGB's façade of glasnost and perestroika so reassuringly served up by Kryuchkov to the assembled women journalists and the rest of the country?

Well, for one thing, the foreign intelligence office was keeping up its everyday work, maintaining close contacts (again, sometimes financial) with friends in the West, mainly representatives of Communist parties and various national movements. It routinely supplied couriers who acted as conduits for funds that were passed by hand from Vneshekonombank [the Soviet Foreign Trade Bank] ("Deposit No. 1")—via a special bank teller and a chain of KGB agents—to a designated recipient in the West. A signed receipt from the recipient would then be returned to the Central Committee.[20] At this very moment, I have before me documents that are in themselves evidence that this long-established system did not cease to operate during the perestroika years.

Reading the signatures on these documents from the Politburo's top secret files, one is treated to a virtual history of KGB operations abroad.

For example, one 1953 letter signed by then–KGB chief S. Ignatov notes the receipt of $300,000 sent via the "KGB resident in Paris" to Marcel Servon, head of the personnel department of the Central Committee of the French Communist Party. "The transfer was made in observance of all the safety precautions, and successfully completed."[21]

In 1967, Andropov reported that

on assignment from the Central Committee of the CPSU, the KGB residency in New York maintains secret contacts with the head of the U.S. Communist Party to exchange information with friends and send them money . . . Taking into account the abovementioned, I ask that the question of establishing an additional post of First Secretary of the USSR Representation at the UN in New York, to be assigned to V. A. Chichurin, be investigated.[22]

In 1976, Andropov signed a document allocating $1 million to the Italian Communist Party, assigning the KGB to transfer the funds.

These documents were typical; in fact, in the mid-1970s, special forms were printed with blank spaces for the recipient's name, the sum, and the date. A document identical to the one affirming the Italian Party's good fortune records even greater fortune for the French Communist Party—$6 million.[23] Between 1981 and 1991, the French Party received about $24 million; the U.S. Communist Party, more than $21 million. (By the way, in 1987, as an impoverished Soviet Union requested loans from America,

U.S. Communist chief Gus Hall was notified of an allocation of $500,000; in 1989, the U.S. Communist Party was awarded $2 million.)[24] These are not poor countries; this certainly wasn't charitable aid.

A letter signed by Viktor Chebrikov, who replaced Andropov as head of the KGB in 1982, noted: "The USSR KGB maintains contact with the son of Premier Minister Rajiv Gandhi [of India] . . . R. Gandhi expresses deep gratitude for benefits accruing to the Prime Minister's family from the commercial dealings of an Indian firm he controls in cooperation with Soviet foreign trade organizations. R. Gandhi reports confidentially that a substantial portion of the funds obtained through this channel are used to support the party of R. Gandhi."[25]

The practice of supporting foreign Communist parties continued into the perestroika era. In 1991, *Moscow News* published a document recording the transfer of 1,189,213 Finnish marks to the leadership of the Communist Party of Finland [Unity].[26] The publication of this document had unexpected ramifications. Its signer, Vladimir Silvestrov, a colonel of FCD's Third Department (the UK, Australia, New Zealand, and the Scandinavian countries), was still working as the KGB's deputy resident in Finland under diplomatic cover. The Finns, who for so long had put up with the Soviet Union's unneighborly behavior (in the summer of 1991, forty out of fifty officers in the Soviet embassy in Helsinki were KGB or GRU), suddenly lost their patience and ordered the "diplomat" out. Silvestrov was recalled within a week.[27]

In the last ten years of the USSR's existence, more than $250 million in cash found its way abroad in the briefcases of intelligence agents. (And this still leaves billions of dollars of interest-free loans to "friends" and supplies of "special equipment" (arms) in exchange for, say, raisins.) This, from a country where two-thirds of the population was living below the poverty line. My grandmother, who worked for the state for her entire life, received a pension of 43 rubles a month, the equivalent of 480 dollars a year. But at the same time, the General Secretary of the Central Committee of the

Israeli Communist Party wrote his rich "uncles" in the CPSU: "To pay Party functionaries in Israel a salary of less than three thousand dollars a month is simply inhumane."[28] On February 19, 1991, in a memorandum addressed to the CPSU leaders, Valentin Falin, a Central Committee secretary, insisted that debts to "firms of friendly parties" be paid. "In Vneshekonombank's calculation, *the country is on the threshold of bankruptcy*, with all the ensuing economic and political consequences." Falin concluded that money should be returned to the "friends" from state (not Party) funds as quickly as possible, or "the CPSU will be faced with the need to hunt for resources to support friendly parties at the expense of the Party budget."[29]

Cash was vitally important for intelligence work, helping to establish contacts with Communist friends who were influential in their parliaments and governments (such "friends" included ministers, members of parliament, and major businessmen who sometimes appeared in state security documents as "competent sources of the KGB"). I have no faith in the altruism of intelligence or the Soviet government: the money undoubtedly had to be returned in the form of, for example, scientific and technological information, long an expensive commodity.

Intelligence clung to another old line of work in the Gorbachev years—training in . . . I almost wrote "terrorism," but let's just call it "special training on matters of ensuring the security of the Party," as does the Special File of the Central Committee. A typical document from the perestroika years marked "SPECIAL FILE: Top Secret" assigns the International Department of the Central Committee to review and fulfill the requests of the Communist Party of Argentina for "assistance in preparing Argentinean passports, identity papers, and containers for their transport and storage." It is signed by Yakovlev, Ligachev, Razumovsky, and other top leaders of the time.[30]

After the failure of the August 1991 coup, the new government discovered a room in the International Department (intelligence's branch) in the Central Committee building in which blank passports from many countries were stored, forged with different years. There were inks used by various countries, makeup, wigs, and other articles of espionage tradecraft. The media expressed shock; International Department officials declared themselves equally amazed, claiming that the items had been stored there since the days of the Comintern. Documents from the Special File reveal an unbroken chain from the days of the Comintern, through the Khrushchev and Brezhnev eras, and into Gorbachev's time. Even during perestroika, this department did more than forge passports; it also instructed officers in tradecraft, provided special military training, offered a course in "equipment and organization of radio broadcast interception," supplied high-caliber Walther pistols and foreign-brand weapons (more difficult to trace), taught message encryptment and personal disguise, and trained agents to set up field radio transmitters—the stuff of spy novels. By the way, speaking of foreign weapons, among the documents in the Politburo's top secret Special File, I came across a curious letter from KGB chief Andropov to the Politburo dated December 31, 1975, with a notation that it had been coordinated with the Defense Ministry, and the heading "On Obtaining Captured American Weapons from the DRV [Vietnam]."

Upon assignment from the Central Committee of the CPSU the Committee for State Security provides assistance to individual foreign Communist parties and representatives of national liberation movements, supplying them with modern weapons manufactured in the capitalist countries.

At the present time, the KGB of the USSR Council of Ministers is experiencing a shortage of such weaponry. The Committee has appealed to the heads of the DRV Interior Ministry to review the possibility of allocating ten thousand captured American machine guns and ten million bullets.

In December of this year, DRV Interior Minister Comrade Chan Kuok Hoan informed our representative confidentially that in principle, the Vietnamese Politburo is prepared to take a favorable view of this matter. In addition, Chan Kuok Hoan, noting that the DRV Defense Ministry has control over the captured military technology, recommends appealing to DRV Defense Minister Comrade Vo Nguyen Giap for the abovementioned quantity of weapons to be supplied gratis.

We consider it expedient to make this request to Comrade Giap after informing him that the weapons will be used to combat imperialism and assist the national liberation movement.

In the event that Comrade Giap agrees to transfer the weaponry free of charge, we consider it expedient, after thanking him, to offer him in exchange an equal quantity of weapons of Soviet make.[31]

This letter bears the signatures of ten Politburo members, but it's not the autographs that interest me, rather the question of where, and when, the weapons left behind by the Americans in Vietnam have been used.

Intelligence, of course, kept a sharp eye on the Third World, meddling in the affairs of sovereign states by providing financial aid to selected election campaigns. A memo from Kryuchkov to Gorbachev, dated March 2, 1989, reads:

As a result of parliamentary elections in Sri Lanka on February 15, the country's leading opposition party, the Party of Freedom for Sri Lanka (PFSL), headed by S. Banna, which received financial aid during the election campaign (Resolution of the Central Committee of the CPSU No. 216 K/OV of 3.02.89), increased its representation in the highest legislative body from eight to sixty-seven deputies. In addition, with our material encouragement, a number of reliable connections between the USSR KGB and both the PFSL and the United National Party (UNP) were advanced.

This . . . makes this party the most numerous and influential opposition force in parliament, where the ruling UNP holds 125 seats.

S. Bandaranaike asked to convey to Moscow her sincere gratitude for the support which, she says, was largely responsible for the PFSL's success . . . The chairman of the PFSL has announced that the party's increasing influence in parliament will be used to block the pro-Western and anti-democratic domestic course of the UNP . . . The Committee for State Security continues to maintain confidential contacts with S. Bandaranaike, and will use both her personal political authority and the growing influence of the party she heads in the country and the parliament in the interests of the Soviet Union. Our reliable connections in parliament will also be employed to these ends.[32]

What I liked most about this document is that the KGB "materially encouraged" the advancement of both opposition parties in the Sri Lanka parliament.

I'm sure that the CIA and British intelligence and the Israeli Mossad all do the same sorts of things. No doubt, even the governments of democratic countries finance political parties favorable to them, just as the CPSU financed the Communists—and the money for this, too, is taken from the taxpayers' pockets. But I'm less interested in the company the KGB kept than in the misery it brought. The money that flowed out of the USSR was used to bolster regimes distinguished by labor camps, torture, executions, thousands of deaths. Moreover, the Soviet Union often supplied money and arms to purely criminal organizations for whom abstract "ends" justified anything, from the theft of national treasures to terrorist street bombings.

A top secret memo from Andropov to Brezhnev, dated April 23, 1974, reflects the Soviet government mentality, which remained unchanged even in the years of perestroika and "new thought."

Since 1968, the Committee for State Security has maintained clandestine contact with Vadia Haddad, Politburo member of the Palestine Liberation Popular Front (PLPF), and chief of the PLPF's foreign operations.

In a confidential conversation at a meeting with the KGB resident in Libya in April of this year, Vadia Haddad outlined the PLPF's prospective program of subversive and terrorist activity, summarized as follows:

The chief purpose of the PLPF's special actions is to increase the effectiveness of the struggle of the Palestinian resistance against Israel, Zionism, and American imperialism . . . at the present time, the PLPF is preparing a number of special operations, including a strike against the major oil reserves in various regions (Saudi Arabia, the Persian Gulf, Hong Kong, and others), the destruction of tankers and supertankers, operations against American and Israeli representatives in Iran, Greece, Ethiopia, and Kenya, a raid on the diamond center building in Tel Aviv, and others.

V. Haddad appealed to us to help his organization obtain several types of special technical devices necessary to conduct subversive operations.

In appealing for assistance, V. Haddad clearly recognizes our aversion in principle to terrorism, and so is refraining from raising with us any matters related to this direction of the PLPF's activities.

The nature of relations with V. Haddad enables us to oversee to a certain extent the operation of the PLPF's department of foreign operations, to influence it in ways favorable to the Soviet Union, and to carry out active measures in our interests with the forces of his organization, while observing the necessary secrecy.

Taking the abovementioned into account, it would seem expedient at the next meeting to treat favorably Vadia Haddad's request to help the PLPF with special devices. As for the specifics of providing aid, it is intended that these matters be decided on an individual case basis, keeping in mind the interests of the Soviet Union and avoiding any possibility of damage to our national security.

We request your consent.[33]

The consent was forthcoming; the first page of this document carries the signatures of most of the Politburo members of that time.

On May 14, 1975, the next page of the Special File reveals, the KGB transferred to V. Haddad a shipment of foreign-made weapons and cartridges (53 machine guns, including 10 with silencers, plus 34,000 bullets). "The illegal transfer of weapons was made in neutral waters in the Bay of Aden at night without making contact and with strict observance of security, using a reconnaissance ship of the USSR navy. Haddad is the only foreigner to know that the weaponry in question was transferred by us."[34]

Despite Soviet leaders' hypocritical claims of aversion to terrorism, they remained willing to accommodate Palestinian requests for weapons clearly destined for such use. The summary of Minutes No. 185 of the November 27, 1984, Politburo session includes the following notes:

a) Assign the USSR KGB to inform the leadership of the Palestinian Liberation Democratic Front (PLDF) of Soviet agreement in principle to ship special goods [that is, armaments] to the PLDF valued at 15 million rubles, in exchange for a collection of art treasures of the ancient world;
b) Accept from the PLDF requests for delivery of special goods within the stated sum;
c) In cooperation with the USSR Ministry of Culture, carry out measures concerning the legal aspects of the acquired collections . . .
4. Assign the USSR Ministry of Culture to:
a) Receive from the USSR KGB by special list a collection of art treasures of the ancient world;

b) Determine in coordination with the USSR KGB the place and conditions for special storage of the collection ("the gold fund"), covert scientific evaluation, and future exhibition. Together with the USSR Finance Ministry, submit according to standard procedure a proposal regarding the necessary allocations;

c) With the USSR KGB, decide on the exhibition of individual objects and groups of articles for the collection.[35]

According to experts, this collection of art treasures stolen by PLDF from one of Lebanon's banks and placed in storage in Moscow is valued at $9 billion, while the value of the weapons transferred to PLDF was approximately $20 million. The FCD's officers still recall this operation proudly as one of their finest, from the viewpoints of both intelligence and financial gain.

In 1990, a year after Soviet troops had been removed from Afghanistan, where civil war was raging, Politburo members exhibited no reluctance to agree to the shipment of "special goods including 150 R-17E missile sets, 2 Luna-M missile launchers, 380 tanks, 1,925 infantry combat vehicles and armored personnel carriers, 2,382 guns and mortars, 700 antiaircraft cannon and mounts, 12,800 jet flamethrowers," and so forth.[36]

In this context a letter to the Central Committee from some Latin American petitioners for funds no longer surprises:

Dear Comrades,

We are of course trying to obtain financial means through our own efforts, including a ransom from representatives of the local oligarchy, if we succeed in kidnapping them. However, the progress of the armed struggle has caused almost all of them to flee the country, and they now live abroad. . . .

What childlike candor—no one to kidnap![37]

What else was on the KGB's agenda during the perestroika years? Domestic affairs, of course. And they were undergoing significant changes. Gorbachev's "new thought," which was supposed to give a breather to the Soviet military-industrial complex, gasping from the crazy marathon of "catching up to and overtaking America," gave the KGB an unexpected break: now, it could really get to work inside the country, concentrating on its cherished raison d'être—political surveillance.

Not that the KGB had ever lacked work in that department, of course. But never before, except perhaps under Stalin, had the KGB had such a scope for maneuvering. For the first time in the seventy-odd years of the regime's existence, people were stepping forward to be counted. There was so much work to be done:

> Comrade, you must believe, the star
> Of our glasnost will set
> And the Committee for State Security
> Will take down our names . . .

This parody of a famous verse by Alexander Pushkin made the rounds in 1989 after the First Congress of People's Deputies.* Politics was in the air. Could the Committee be far behind?

Now that its talents in supporting international terrorism and establishing autocratic regimes in Africa were slightly less in demand, the FCD redirected its efforts to the area of disinformation. Of course, for the foreign KGB residents this work was nothing new; Service A (disinformation and intelligence) had been created for this very reason. But the department's intellectual might was

---

* Pushkin's "To Chaadayev": Comrade, you must believe,/The star of our amazing fortune will rise,/Russia will awake from sleep,/And on the shards of despotism/They will write our names!—Trans.

now shifted away from foreign climes, especially the Third World, to the home front.

Two imperatives took precedence: Gorbachev had to be put in his place with daunting reminders of the West's "dirty tricks"; at the same time, public opinion abroad had to be manipulated to suit the FCD's purposes—with foreigners' perceptions of the Soviet President's opponents a primary target.

Boris Yeltsin was especially hard hit by this propaganda, particularly at home. Starting in 1989, at closed meetings of KGB directors, direct orders were issued to discredit Yeltsin and other members of the Interregional Group, the parliamentary opposition that had been organized during the Congress of People's Deputies.[38] In the spring of 1991, when Yeltsin was running for President of Russia, KGB directors sent their officers a coded telegram directing them to vote against Yeltsin.[39] The right-wing press (*Pravda, Sovetskaya Rossiya*, and others) fell right in step with this anti-Yeltsin propaganda, which took the form, not of political attack —there's plenty to attack there—but of personal vendetta, including a ludicrous article in *Sovetskaya Rossiya* claiming that Yeltsin had ties to the Italian mafia.

Deza—disinformation, or as it is officially called, "placement of information to our advantage"—was also placed in the West, disseminated by every means imaginable. Considerable use was made of church officials (as we saw in chapter 2, the KGB had devoted significant resources to compromising the integrity of clerics). Often, Service A and ideological counterintelligence worked together "to influence clerical circles in the West."[40]

Foreign correspondents working in Moscow were another favorite target of disinformation, whether by stoking competition for sensational exposés of Soviet life, or by cutting off access to information. All of this helped to give the journalists a rather superficial picture of Soviet realities and the political games going on behind the scenes.

How did the KGB involve the foreign journalists in its games? Well, for example, only through the Foreign Ministry's press department (strictly speaking, also KGB) could permission be obtained to travel to some hot spot closed to everyone else. Further, "materials selected to support a certain version of a story would be planted with an unsuspecting Western correspondent," as a well-informed source explained the Chekist technique to me. Did that explain the story in the American weekly *The Guardian* in September 1990 under the byline of Sarah Demont? Reliable sources such as Gen. Oleg Kalugin claim that *The Guardian* has long had a relationship (including financial) with Soviet intelligence. One such reporter filed a September 1990 story claiming that the Interregional Group was being backed by people closely associated with the CIA—clear interference in the internal affairs of the Soviet Union. Within a month, this sensational news had found its way back into our country, reprinted in the conservative paper *Sovetskaya Rossiya*.[41] In February 1991, President Gorbachev seemed to be citing the same *deza* when he claimed (without revealing the source) that the democrats were being run by "foreign think tanks and alien mentalities." And then, in June of that year, KGB Chairman Kryuchkov raised the specter of the CIA's "agents of influence." Great minds think alike . . .

Let me make clear that I'm not interested in casting aspersions on my Western colleagues. It was a pleasure to read David Remnick's reporting for the *Washington Post*, Bill Keller for *The New York Times*, Jeff Trimble for *U.S. News & World Report*, Hedrick Smith's *The Russians* (to my mind, one of the best books on Russia), and many other Moscow correspondents from Western publications. They had spent years living here, and were properly wary of believing "facts" gleaned from "reliable" sources. They were aware that the real import of a piece of information—often directly contrary to the ostensible "fact"—had to be read between the lines, from a context difficult for an outsider to grasp, especially one raised to expect freedom of information. Hence the naïveté of so much that has been written about the Soviet Union in the Western press and the KGB's success in manipulating foreign correspondents. Have my colleagues from the other world ever wondered why the KGB and some other institutions were so eager to hold "exclusive" press conferences for foreign correspondents? Because the Chekists' fellow citizens could easily catch them in the act of lying, and might even say so, publicly.

Need I add that these same Western journalists were under the vigilant eye of the KGB during the years of our glasnost? Here is a report, dated December 6, 1988, from A. Kapto, Director of the Department of Ideology of the Central Committee:

> The USSR Council of Ministers Chief Directorate for Protection of State Secrets in the Press reports that by Resolution of the CPSU Central Committee No. 177/77gs of March 7, 1961, clandestine surveillance has been established at USSR Glavlit [the chief censorship agency] of information transmitted by foreign correspondents abroad, to facilitate reception of necessary reports and timely organization of counterpropaganda.
>
> As an increasing number of Western news agencies switch to transmission of materials using rapid computer technology and other modern means of communication (for example, the "telefax"), the work of the special service of USSR Glavlit, which is outfitted with outmoded equipment (teletypes), has become significantly more difficult. Without appropriate renovation of its technical equipment, this special service soon will be unable to fulfill all its assigned functions.
>
> Therefore, it is proposed that the USSR Ministry of Communications, together with the USSR Committee for State Security and USSR Glavlit, be assigned to review the matter of technical support for the special service of USSR Glavlit. The matter has been coordinated with the USSR KGB (Comrade F. D. Bobkov) and the USSR Ministry of Communications (Comrade V. A. Shamshin).[42]

First Chief even maintained a special office, the Department of Political Publications, to print its own books and articles used in counterpropaganda. Its employees were officially on the payroll of the official news service, News Press Agency (APN), but the fact that their real bosses were at FCD's Yasenevo headquarters was an open secret (I myself always enjoyed the irony that this department was located right next door to the editorial offices of *Moscow News*).

The FCD's traditional sphere of intelligence-gathering widened as the country advanced toward glasnost and democracy. Lt. Col. V. Aksyonov of the FCD's Seventh Department testified:

> The First Chief Directorate has begun to interfere actively in internal domestic political processes. Intelligence officers and illegal agents are being recalled from abroad to the territory of the Union, primarily to the areas of maximum tension (the Baltic, Azerbaijan, Moldavia), for the purpose of gathering information and conducting active measures.[43]

My, my, how the bluebloods of the KGB had fallen! What had happened to their vaunted "clean hands" and distance from "dirty Lubyanka business"? These were the elite of the FCD. They spoke foreign languages like natives, and fantastic sums had been spent to train and plant them abroad—and now this. Now, coded telegrams were going out from the Center to the residencies abroad with orders to turn the Beau Brummels of intelligence into banal *toptuny*, spying on people's deputies, leaders of democratic movements, and other prominent figures—their own fellow citizens.

A letter from Gen. Vyacheslav Zhizhin, deputy chief of FCD, to the directors of ideological counterintelligence, describes in detail the surveillance of Soviet and Russian people's deputies abroad. Revisionists today claim that Kryuchkov forced the FCD to become involved in such unsavory affairs against resistance on the parts of intelligence officers; it's not true.

A selected cadre of FCD officers especially close to Kryuchkov (who, as we will recall, headed intelligence for fourteen years) had the very delicate task of surveillance of the country's top leaders, including former Politburo members Alexander Yakovlev and Eduard Shevardnadze, not to mention President Gorbachev himself.

Following the August 1991 coup, official investigators checking the safe of Valery Boldin, Gorbachev's chief of staff, found "a substantial quantity of KGB surveillance material with information from 1989–91 (annotations of agents' reports, transcripts of electronic surveillance, external surveillance, analyses of the Western press, various analytical documents) . . . concerning Yakovlev, A. N.; Shevardnadze, E. A.; Khasbulatov, R. I.; Boris Yeltsin, Galina Starovoitova, and other people's deputies during their trips abroad." The official report also notes that aides to the President were kept under surveillance; Gorbachev himself is not mentioned as the subject of surveillance.[44]

At the Russian Procuracy I was able to get a look at an internal memo, dated June 20, 1991, from Gen. Leonid Shebarshin, at that time chief of intelligence, to Vladimir Kryuchkov, then KGB chairman. Much of the memo concerns events of little interest now, but one part is relevant to our story:

> According to information from *those close to* M. S. Gorbachev, over the next few days, he will be making decisions that have a vital impact on the USSR's future . . . According to the *source*, it would be expedient to create a situation whereby Gorbachev would virtually concede Pavlov's line [Pavlov, then prime minister, joined the coup plotters later that year] while at the same time offering him a chance to correct publicly some elements of his program and political line. According to the *source*, Gorbachev's intimates believe that the most influential figure capable of coordinating such tactics with the President would be Kryuchkov.

Who was that "source," the KGB's secret agent in Gorbachev's entourage? Who gave Shebarshin and Kryuchkov information they could have received no other way? Former Politburo member Alexander Yakovlev told me point-blank that it was Yevgeny

Kalgin—the same KGB Col. Kalgin who had worked as secretary to General Secretaries Andropov, Chernenko, and Gorbachev. "He was Kryuchkov's personal agent," Yakovlev told me. In 1989, however, with Gorbachev's approval, Kolgin had been appointed chief of the KGB's Electronic Surveillance Department. While this was evidence of the trust with which he was regarded, it removed him from the everyday affairs of the President's staff, making it unlikely that he was the source.

KGB Gen. Viktor Ivanenko, chief of Russian state security in fall 1991, and a member of the KGB's own commission that investigated the Chekists' role in the August events, claimed that the informer was Gorbachev's press secretary at the time, Vitaly Ignatenko. Well known—or perhaps "infamous" is a more appropriate term—in journalistic circles as a devout careerist, Ignatenko had been shifted to an executive position at the chief state information agency immediately after the coup—according to Ivanenko, as a result of information Gorbachev had received about Ignatenko's ties to Kryuchkov. (Ironically, Ignatenko managed to hang onto this job even as Gorbachev was removed from the scene.)

I was unable to find confirmation of Gen. Ivanenko's claim that Ignatenko informed on Gorbachev to the KGB. Gorbachev himself remains silent on this point. A number of my other informed sources doubt that Ignatenko could have been the source. But then who was it? Most likely, someone from FCD—who else would Kryuchkov have trusted with such a task?

One way or another, intelligence labored valiantly in service of the Motherland, from one end of the country to the other, and beyond its borders. And no matter what the official line, the record is clear: all KGB directorates, even such elite national security outfits as intelligence, are inherently political police, first and foremost.

Second Chief (counterintelligence) also continued to toil assiduously, never deviating from its purpose. There were CIA agents to tail—according to the Soviet press, their numbers were growing astronomically—and the usual tabs to be kept on workers' attitudes. For this, tried and tested channels remained open, the so-called active reserves of Committee officers assigned to various Soviet institutions.

There was such a "reserve" at the newspaper where I worked, consisting of a nice, mild-mannered fellow named Volodya, a KGB major. His job was to watch the foreigners who worked as copy editors and translators in the foreign language departments of *Moscow News*. His duties also included keeping his bosses up to date on articles to be published, especially those critical of the KGB. I always felt sorry for Volodya, who obviously found his role onerous. I recall the spring of 1990, when my article "Lubyanka: Will There Ever Be an End?" appeared: it had been inserted at the last moment, the typesetting done in secret. Volodya was under fire for not alerting his bosses in time (he couldn't; or wouldn't). He managed to hang on, and the next time my coauthor and I were about to do something on the KGB, we warned Volodya to take a sick day.

Glasnost journalism really put the KGB to the test, especially during the final years of perestroika, after the passage of the new Law on the Press and the removal of censorship. No longer was it just a question of taking out objectionable material and replacing it with something else; now the KGB had to be fast on its feet.

For example, "secret helpers" published articles such as "Through Agent 'Motherland'" (*Nash Sovremennik* [Our Contemporary], No. 5, 1989) on the émigré writer Lev Kopelev, "exposing" his connections with anti-Soviet centers in the West. The KGB also produced newspapers and journals disguised as independent publications: "The first issue of an unofficial journal, *Slovo* [Word], has been issued [June 1988] and distributed to the religious community with the sanction of the KGB, in order to prevent religious extremism in the church community."[45] (Just an aside, while we're speaking of the Church. Many people were enthusiastic when the Soviet parliament in June 1990 passed the Law on Freedom of Conscience, ostensibly signaling the end of the government struggle against the Church. Interestingly, a draft of this law was first vetted at the KGB, of all places; the arena of the decades-long battle *against* freedom of conscience. KGB Col. V. Timoshevsky even submitted a review of the draft legislation.)[46]

There were other ways of "working with" the press. We have to take the Committee's line on, say, Lithuania, an ideological counterintelligence officer told me. "But it shouldn't be written too bluntly, with our fingerprints all over it; it should be done professionally, so the reader will believe it." "A well-known journalist—let's call him 'K'—from *Moskovskaya Pravda* is invited to visit us at the directorate. An operative prepares a rough draft for him, choosing the style and material carefully: good material, obtained through agents' channels. An article comes out—trenchant, not without some jabs at the authorities. It creates quite a stir.

"Or, another example: Ksenya Myalo's article in the November 1989 *Nash Sovremennik* on the problem of the ethnic Germans in Russia, which was influential in postponing the resolution of the issue of restoring the Volga German territory. That was ordered, edited, and largely written by the KGB's Directorate to Protect the Soviet Constitutional Order. We all did assignments of that sort. Your boss would call you in and ask, 'Do you have a man at such-and-such a newspaper?' 'Sure.' 'Then go for it.' A panoply of articles appears across the spectrum from right to left, but always with a certain tilt in favor of the KGB. And of course none is signed 'KGB': no, the reader sees the byline of special correspondent 'A,' or columnist 'B.' "

"What if the editor-in-chief doesn't want to publish the article?" I asked.

"Well, of course things fall through sometimes. But don't forget, this work didn't start yesterday with glasnost and perestroika; we've been doing it for years. Often, we'd take note of a young, promising journalist and plant some sensational material with him; and mind you, we didn't ask for anything in return. We'd just help him out, find him housing, give a boost to his career . . . Eventually he'd reach an important post and we'd exercise our influence through him . . ."

"What influence? Why would independent publications listen to you?"

"We might ask for a little favor—just to give a certain article a bit of a push before it gets dated. And then . . . don't forget, we still control the processing of documents for trips abroad."*

Valentin Stepankov, the Procurator General of Russia, confirmed that the Chekists had planted their agents throughout the media. He was reluctant to name anyone, but he did identify one person, Sergei Drozdov, formerly deputy resident of Soviet intelligence in Tokyo, who worked there under cover of *Komsomolskaya pravda*. Toward the end of perestroika, Drozdov became founder and chief editor of the newspaper *Rossiya*. Drozdov's KGB past was actually no secret to other journalists. And it's always been known that 70 percent of the Soviet news bureaus abroad were infiltrated with *komitetchiki*, mainly intelligence officers.

Of course, journalists were not the chief focus of the Committee's attention. Not at the bottom of the list, perhaps; but not a top priority, either. The gray mass of "silent cattle" (as my fellow citizens are customarily called) had awakened suddenly from decades of complaisance. They were setting up political parties and civic organizations, promoting one of their own kind as leader. A plan was needed to deal with this phenomenon. The KGB set to work behind closed doors. Rank-and-file Chekists (mainly from ideological counterintelligence) who had been assigned to recruit "silent helpers" in opposition circles were taken aside and told in simple terms that they had a new subject for scrutiny. These new political organizations had to be watched, they were told, lest they unwittingly threaten the state order and Constitutional rights of citizens.[47]

Not a single rally or demonstration passed without Chekists in

---

* The Russian Ministry of Security still controls foreign passports—Author.

attendance, not even an informal gathering of democratic intelligentsia. A 1989 ideological counterintelligence report notes that "a tape recording of the speeches of the leaders of the so-called Moscow Tribune, which has an antisocial orientation, has been received from Agent 'Andrei.' "[48] It wasn't clear why information had to be obtained from Agent "Andrei"; Moscow Tribune was an intelligentsia forum whose meetings were open to the public. But the KGB maintained its vigilance, filmed the outspoken speakers with hidden videocameras "to protect public order," while officers of the Defense Ministry's GRU were enlisted to keep an eye on street corner demonstrators.

In the summer of 1989, as the first powerful wave of miners' strikes swept through the country, the workers' movement, too, became the subject of KGB vigilance. The proletariat, tormented by daily cares and plagued with vodka, suddenly awoke and began to organize into a rather serious political force. The KGB had somehow learned to keep the intelligentsia under control, but labor protest was something new, at least for the younger generation of Chekists. Their elders remembered the June 1962 Novocherkassk rebellion of workers who had marched to the town square to protest price hikes. But the authorities could no longer get away with shooting people; now, they had to operate more subtly. Maj. Gen. E. F. Ivanov, chief of the Directorate to Protect the Soviet Constitutional Order, and Maj. Gen. N. A. Savenko, chief of the Sixth Directorate, reported on June 3, 1990:

From April 30 to May 2, 1990, the First All-Union Congress of Independent Workers' Movements opened in the city of Novokuznetsk, Kemerov Region, with representatives from strike committees in Vorkuta, Kuzbass, Donbass, Karaganda, and other regions . . . Heightened interest in this conference was shown by foreign correspondents accredited in the USSR who are involved in the enemy's special services, representatives of Poland's Solidarity, overt members of the NTS, as well as other organizations of an anti-Constitutional orientation such as Sajudis, Rukh, and others.

In order to provide practical assistance in the organization of measures by the Novokuznetsk KGB, officers of the USSR KGB Sixth Directorate and the Directorate to Protect the Soviet Constitutional Order, along with covert sources [secret agents], were sent on assignment.

As a result of the measures taken, the subversive intentions of the enemy to gather negative information on the situation in the workers' community were neutralized. Joint operations in managing *sources who came to the congress as delegates, consultants, and guests* prevented the passing of extremist resolutions on extremist actions on the part of individual workers' delegations and their leaders, disrupted the coalescing of a central leadership of the strike movement, and prevented submission to radically minded political opportunists and organizations of an anti-Constitutional orientation.

For personal initiative and persistence displayed, high professionalism and political maturity in carrying out of operative measures involving foreigners and certain Soviet citizens representing informal politicized organizations during the so-called First Congress of Independent Workers' Movements, and for the positive results achieved, we propose that the following officers be awarded . . .[49]

This remarkable document probably needs no commentary. But there is one small addendum. Such KGB operations often elicited the desired response from factory managers. Typical was the Volgograd Tractor Parts Factory, where a strike committee had been formed. The administration banned it. Then, protest leaflets appeared on the plant's walls. A memo followed to the Volgograd City KGB Directorate over the signature of Deputy Director B.

Atopov, requesting "assistance in the normalization of the situation at the factory."[50]

Finally, there was another important area where the KGB intervened with a heavy hand—the Popular Fronts that were leading national liberation movements in the colonies of the last empire on earth, the Soviet Empire. Let me start by saying there was no shortage of xenophobia and chauvinism in these fronts and movements. But while the KGB may not have initiated these tendencies, it showed no reluctance to fan the flames of ethnic rivalry. Future investigators will have to determine specific responsibility for bloody ethnic clashes in Sumgait, Osh, Uzgen, Baku, and Nagorno-Karabakh, but in no case will the KGB be able to claim complete innocence.

Just before violence broke out in Alma Ata (the capital of Kazakhstan, now known as Almaty) in 1986, according to reliable sources, KGB officers passed out arms to workers (as elsewhere in the Soviet Union, the proletariat was predominantly ethnic Russian), and set them against "nationalist-minded" Kazakh students.

On the day before the terrible night of April 9, 1989, in Tbilisi, the capital of Georgia, KGB regiments were deployed on orders from Moscow. KGB glasnost took a bitter turn as agents videotaped the *spetsnaz* assault on unarmed demonstrators.[51]

In 1990, when pogroms were unleashed against Armenians in Baku, capital of Azerbaijan, a republic dominated by Muslims, First Deputy Filipp Bobkov exhibited glasnost, KGB-style. When a journalist asked whether it really had been necessary to send troops into Baku on the night of January 19–20, he admitted: "We had to do it. It's not a question of Armenians here. If we didn't bring in troops, there would have been a completely different government in Azerbaijan."[52] That "different government" was the Azerbaijan Popular Front, which to all intents and purposes had been running the republic since earlier that month. But, with the aid of the KGB *spetsnaz*, the Popular Front was smashed and its leaders jailed.

(More than a year later, a police investigation of the Armenian massacre revealed that the pogroms had been provoked by the KGB in order to justify—especially to the world outside the Soviet Union—armed intervention in Baku.)[53]

In the summer of 1990, there were mass killings of Meskhetian Turks in Uzbekistan's Fergana Valley. In 1991, Kyrghyz and Uzbeks clashed in the city of Osh. According to Lt. Col. Kichikhin, "The Committee knew that a massacre was being planned there. They knew, but for some reason, they buried the information in their files."[54]

During the same period, Kichikhin was involved in the KGB's aggravation of Russian resentment against so-called Volga Germans seeking restoration of their autonomy in the Saratov Region. The ethnic Germans were under constant KGB surveillance, he noted: "About 3,500 agents operated within the Russian German movement . . . In 1989, the Russian German Renaissance Society held its constituent assembly. A governing body was elected, with a presidium of thirty-three people, of whom twenty-one were KGB agents."[55]

And, of course, the KGB was particularly active in fanning ethnic rivalries in the Baltics. Back in 1988, as a counterweight to the Popular Fronts, the KGB had established organizations (Intermovement, Unity, and others) to defend the Russian-speaking population. The Russians indeed were beleaguered—but the KGB's intervention only exacerbated the situation. The logical culmination of the KGB's efforts came on January 12–13, 1991, in Vilnius, when Group A-7, the Alpha Group *spetsnaz* from the Seventh Directorate, attacked Lithuanians defending their central television station, and chalked up several more murders to its tally. According to my information, this operation, had it succeeded in Vilnius, would have been repeated in Latvia and Estonia. But the operation was conducted clumsily; the authorities had not wanted bloodshed and corpses. Consequently, Filipp Bobkov was removed from office and replaced by Gen. Viktor Grushko, head of counterintelligence, a man quite close to Kryuchkov.

After the January 1991 Vilnius tragedy, a series of mysterious bombs exploded in Russian neighborhoods in Latvia and Estonia. As might be expected, the terrorists were never caught. Among those who were injured in the blasts was Maj. Sapunov of Directorate Z. His colleagues expressed their sympathies for his misfortune, but described his contusion in the official report as the result of a fracas at a dance, even though, as Kichikhin pointed out, "It's hard to believe that an agent on assignment would go to a dance, let alone get involved in a brawl with the locals."[56] And anyway, people in Riga were hardly in a dancing mood; they were too busy building barricades. With reason: in January the OMON (riot police) went on a rampage, killing four people.

One might ask why the Committee, with its deathlock on power, felt it necessary to incite or aggravate nationalist conflicts or support the extremist wing of the anti-Semitic Pamyat group in the Center.[57] There are at least three reasons. Ethnic tension garnered support for totalitarian power from the Russian population of the republics, who had every reason to fear discrimination from the native residents.

Nationalist conflicts also compromised the democrats in the eyes of Russians in Russia: Look what you've let loose; now they're beating up our group out there, was a popular sentiment. "They did the right thing by bringing troops into Vilnius, otherwise the Lithuanians would have butchered the Russians there," said a colleague of mine, a nice, intelligent woman. When *Moscow News* ran a post-Vilnius editorial entitled "The Crime of a Regime that Does Not Want to Leave the Stage"—a historic act on the part of our editor-in-chief, Yegor Yakovlev—the editorial offices were inundated with calls and letters echoing my colleague's views. In this regard, the incident in Vilnius was a way of preparing the public for a justification of possible bloodshed in Russia.

Third, and perhaps most important, ethnic clashes roiled things up and helped the KGB convince the public that a "strong arm" was needed to maintain order and save the nation from ruin and civil war. Naturally, this strong arm was closely identified with the KGB.

As perestroika wound down, the Sixth Directorate (economic affairs) was promoted to the front line of attack. Although, as we've seen, the paths of all the directorates crisscrossed; they operated in concert against a common enemy—dissent. Thus, the "economists" (Sixth) and the "ideologues" (Fifth) shared coverage of the workers' movement. Vladimir Lutsenko, chief of the Department to Combat Organized Crime, worked side by side in Riga with Maj. Sapunov from ideological counterintelligence.[58] Military counterintelligence (Third) was supposed to be tracking down spies within the military; instead, it picked up members and sympathizers of Shield, a civil rights organization of military personnel. "What do you mean, spies?" said Maj. Sergei Petruchik, the senior operative of the KGB special department in the motorized division in Vladikavkaz (Northern Ossetia), surprised at my naïveté. "I have worked here for three years, and I've never seen a spy and or even heard of them, and there haven't been any for decades, since before my time. What's going on here is total surveillance, following the situation in the armed services among soldiers and officers. For the whole area of Vladikavkaz, you would need two agents at most from military counterintelligence, but we have two departments with ten people . . . What else do we do? How do we earn our pay? Obviously, by reporting who said what and who thinks what."[59]

But, returning to the Sixth, it's easy to see that perestroika's pioneering private property owners, cooperative workers, landlords, and entrepreneurs, all of whom claimed some degree of personal freedom, were a source of avid interest to the KGB "economists." The Committee made no bones about the fact that joint ventures with foreigners would be under Chekist surveillance. As Kryuchkov explained, "The KGB knows that Western special services are paying close heed to how joint ventures are being set up and run."[60] Could the Committee do any less? In fact, a good many of these joint ventures were founded by the KGB itself: they provided perfect cover for contacts with foreigners and a respectable starting point from which to infiltrate the burgeoning class of Soviet entrepreneurs. They also provided a nice front for the agents' personal financial transactions. And, in fall 1990, Kryuchkov issued an order permitting the KGB to engage in its own commercial business.

No wonder work with joint ventures acquired special prestige at the KGB. Three major services—economic, intelligence, and ideological counterintelligence—were all involved. Nor did the "economists" of the Sixth limit themselves to oversight: according to my sources, funds from the oligarchy (KGB, CPSU—it's impossible to distinguish) were used to found nearly 80 percent of the new banks, stock markets, and companies. Why not? After all, the entire country was their personal treasury.

The KGB had a jump on commercial projects, anyway, since its agents had acquired the practical experience needed to start firms and companies in developing "covers" for illegals scattered around the world in countries with every variety of market economy imaginable. As a 1990 report from one KGB Col. Veselovsky explains, he was transferred from the FCD to the Central Committee's Administrative Department. "The reason for my transfer," he writes, "was the urgent need of the directors of the Administrative Department to create a division capable of coordinating the economic activity of the Party's management structures in the changing climate . . . The choice fell to me, since by education I am an international economist, *I have experience working abroad* [author's emphasis], and am well known to the majority of Central Committee executives for my work in the Komsomol and All-Union Central Trade Union Council. Furthermore, [Party officials] thought that such a serious matter as organizing economic activity could be assigned only to employees of the Department . . ."[61]

Veselovsky agreed to inform Bobkov regularly about his "activities" in the Administrative Department.

Col. Veselovsky made good use of his background, developing a joint stock concern with a Swiss-Canadian firm, Seabeco Group.[62] After the August coup, Seabeco's Moscow office was closed for a spell, but then it reopened. Veselovsky took off for Canada, dropped out of sight for a while, then surfaced in the great banking city of Zurich at the Indosuez Bank, through which the KGB is alleged to have transferred funds in July 1991 to Seabeco, using Soviet front organizations.

One of the KGB's first successful ventures was the company known as ANT, a covert operation founded in 1986 with the help of the FCD and the Sixth Directorate. Its director of ANT was KGB Captain V. Ryashentsev, a former officer of the Ninth Directorate who had entered the reserves. According to a parliamentary inquiry by the USSR General Procurator, thirty out of ANT's thirty-seven executives had previously worked for the KGB or the Ministry of Internal Affairs, or had been employed at factories of the military-industrial complex.[63] ANT was a strictly covert organization.

According to some sources, ANT engaged in secret export of Soviet weapons to various flashpoints around the globe. The Sixth Sector of the USSR Council of Ministers, a branch of economic counterintelligence in the country's chief governing body, was involved. "Do you believe the information from the Sixth Sector?" a correspondent from *Izvestia* asked Nikolai Ryzhkov, prime minister at the time. "Yes, I do. The information is reliable."[64]

An immense scandal broke out over ANT in 1990; the firm eventually was dissolved and the Committee slapped its own wrists for allegedly breaching laws forbidding the sale of military technology (in this case, tanks) abroad. But matters were much more complex than they seemed on the surface; the ANT scandal was in fact a case of the KGB being forced to choose political over commercial and intelligence interests. The scandal compromised the Yeltsin government in the eyes of the man in the street, since Yeltsin's Vice Premier, Gennady Filshin, had signed one of the ANT contracts. It also allowed the KGB to publicly disparage the embryonic market even further ("Those cooperative owners are selling the country out from under us"). And the ANT affair let the Committee shore up the sorely battered façade of the Party, a "favor" it turned to its own advantage as it plunged on with financial deals that included investing the Party's considerable assets.

The oligarchy is known to have invested about 3 billion gold rubles (at an exchange rate of approximately 65 cents per ruble) in some six hundred commercial enterprises and banks. These include Avtobank, Tokobank, Unikumbank, International Commercial Bank, the firms Galactic, Jobrus, Holding Ltd., Moscow Municipal Association, the Azerbaijan Association (which reportedly has a volume of several million dollars), the Russian Exchange House, the Russian Trade House, and the Scientific and Industrial Union.[65] We probably will never know how many firms have been opened using the oligarchy's funds in our country and abroad. And what difference would it make if we did find out? The money is already invested and bringing in interest, and so far as some people are concerned, there's no taint on success.

KGB interests had a way of turning up in all sorts of fascinating places. Consider the case of Sergei Danilovich Kauzov, whose marriage to Christina Onassis was headline news around the world. In an April 20, 1985, top secret letter to Mikhail Gorbachev, who had just assumed the office of General Secretary, KGB Chairman Viktor Chebrikov states: "Using the financial aid and influence of C. Onassis, S. D. Kauzov founded several of his own companies abroad, acquiring total or partial ownership of ten ships, and concentrating about 25 million dollars of capital in his own hands, of which 3 million were deposited in Swiss and London bank accounts . . . Starting in July 1982, S. D. Kauzov, in accordance with an agreement reached with him, transferred large sums of foreign currency as his Party contribution for the trust vested in him by allowing him to remain in the ranks of the CPSU. To date he has transferred $450,000. The last contribution, in the sum of $100,000, was made in April of this year."[66]

I'd have been prepared to believe that S. D. Kauzov's Party contribution was based exclusively on ideological considerations were it not for a single additional phrase, the statement that the FCD had "since 1979 performed its work" with the abovementioned citizen. The phrase is vague, but the zealousness with which intelligence hastened to demonstrate that Kauzov had no relationship with them after I published this remarkable document in *Izvestia* in June 1992 gives me pause. Not that it really matters . . .

Foreign businessmen have never been particularly bothered by the prospect of doing business with the KGB; perestroika hardly changed that. An extremely top secret KGB memo to Soviet leaders stated:

> In 1978, American Senator Edward Kennedy appealed to the KGB to assist in establishing cooperation between Soviet organizations and the California firm Agritech, headed by former senator J. Tunney. This firm in turn was connected to a French-American company, Finatech S.A., which was run by a competent KGB source, the prominent Western financier D. Karr, through whom opinions had been confidentially exchanged for several years between the General Secretary of the Communist Party and Sen. Kennedy. D. Karr provided the KGB with technical information on conditions in the U.S. and other capitalist countries which were regularly reported to the Central Committee.[67]

The "prominent financier" D. Karr has passed away. He was in fact a Soviet agent who provided the Soviet Union with a great deal of useful information, especially involving science and technology. As for Edward Kennedy, I don't mean to imply that he was an informer or a traitor or anything of the kind. According to the official transcript, during a March 1990 meeting with KGB Chairman Kryuchkov, the senator even took the opportunity to express his devotion to democratic ideals and his concern for the plight of the Baltic republics. But I think it's worthy of note that this esteemed statesman and longtime hero of American liberalism—with greater access to information about totalitarian abuses in the Soviet Union than any Soviet citizen—felt no reluctance to approach the KGB as if it were a legitimate government institution. He was willing to ask it for favors and look for its help in making profitable contracts for his old school friend John Tunney.

After I published this KGB memo, an AP correspondent tried three times (so far as I know) to reach Edward Kennedy's lawyer, but to no avail. Kennedy's press secretary refutes any claim of his boss's contacts with the KGB.

The KGB's involvement in a company apparently instills confidence in foreign investors. With so vast an institution backing it, a new venture seems less likely to vanish into thin air. Clearly, moral considerations aside, the foreign businessmen are right— these partners *do* know their business.

What was it that Martin Bormann said? The Nazi Party's funds will come in handy for those who continue the cause of national socialism in the future. Will the same be true of the KGB's joint ventures, domestically and abroad?

The Sixth Directorate's finest hour came on November 23, 1990, when the USSR Supreme Soviet directed the KGB to "combat economic sabotage." The Committee's right to exercise control over the management of both state and private enterprises had been legitimized. (By then, KGB officers were already acting as bank guards.)

Economic counterintelligence set up a "headquarters to combat economic sabotage." The propaganda started to flow, and *Pravda* (the organ of the Central Committee) and *Sovetskaya Rossiya* (organ of the Russian Communist Party) didn't even bother to hide their Chekist sources or sympathies as they printed meticulously documented reports of the KGB's discoveries of freight cars stashed with onions, matches hidden in warehouses, machinations of cooperatives, and "Russian treasures" going under the auctioneer's hammer.[68] This "nationwide inventory of canned beef," as the leftist press ironically called the obsession with sabotage, was not a stupid tactic. Of course, it didn't put any more food on the shelves—provisions grew scarcer with each passing month, and life on the whole worsened—but accusations of "wrecking" gave angry shoppers' complaints a neo-Stalinist ring. Increasingly, letters coming into my office had an admonitory tone: "Hands off the KGB, our homeland's last line of defense." The Committee knew well how to tap the resentment of those for whom perestroika had meant only new burdens and deprivations.

To a sociological survey that asked, What do the people around you feel? 42 percent of those polled replied, "exhaustion and indifference," "anger and aggressiveness"; 22 percent said simply, "fear."[69] Glasnost won't feed your family. And though a plot of private land, a home of one's own, might have given people a sense of greater independence, perestroika provided neither.

The "man in the street" was clamoring for law and order. According to the National Center for the Study of Public Opinion, in January 1991, 69 percent of the population agreed that what the country needed was "stringent order."[70] Its surveys also showed that the number of those who put their faith in the army as the best hope for restoring order was growing. In September 1990, 8 percent of those polled had held these views; by January 1991, 20 percent supported military intervention to restore order.[71]

The Party, split into factions, was exiting the scene. Polls showed that 62 percent of the Russian population held extremely negative views of the Party.[72]

The democrats, splintered into countless parties and factions, squabbled endlessly in the press. They were united on only one thing: "Down with the CPSU!" In 1989, there was literally not a single rally or demonstration at which the CPSU was not denounced. That was the year the Party really gave up the ghost, despite the fact that the infamous Article 6 of the Soviet Constitution, which stipulated the CPSU as "the leading and ruling force of society," had not yet been repealed. The KGB, with its finger on the nation's pulse, was perfectly aware of the Party's humiliating predicament. The democrats weren't alone in storming the CPSU Bastille.

The oligarchs understood that it was time to cut their losses. The Party would have to go. As the "leading and ruling force of society," the Party was always in the limelight. The very essence of the regime, and all its crimes, were inextricably linked to the Party in the public mind. Widespread awareness of the Party elite's corruption and greed, their dachas, special apartments, clinics, and spas, added fuel to the fire so far as the public was concerned. The fact that the oligarchy's other components, the military-industrial complex and the KGB, enjoyed identical privileges, somehow escaped attention.

The newspapers were full of exposés of Party apparatchiks: they were inciting the army to shoot at their fellow citizens, compelling the obedient KGB to eavesdrop and spy on neighbors and colleagues. There was plenty of truth to this; not the whole truth, though. The bosses of the Party, MIC, and KGB for years had operated in concert, in complete harmony. The Party, assigned the role of scapegoat, was supposed to distract public dissatisfaction from the oligarchy as a whole. The Party accepted this role, and performed it well. The Bastille was trembling—but it was a changed Bastille. Strangely, at all the rallies in 1990 or 1991, I never once heard the slogan "Down with the KGB!"

The democrats succeeded in overthrowing the Communists, but it was a shortsighted victory; they failed to see that an independent political force had formed in the country, a force that no longer had much need for the Party.

In 1989, twelve KGB officers, mainly from the republic committees, were elected as people's deputies of the USSR. For the first time, KGB officers had been awarded the powers and responsibilities of popularly elected representatives.[73] A year later, according to sociologist Olga Kryshtanovskaya, 2,756 KGB people were elected to republic-level and local parliaments. Moreover, 86 percent won their seats in the first round of elections, which is to say that people supported them unreservedly, hoping that "law and order" candidates would whip our poor country back into shape.

The Committee had been taking great pains to improve its image. In July 1989, a commission had been formed to work on "non-cliché methods of propaganda" for "Party political support of the operative and administrative activity of the KGB."[74] There were occasional setbacks, but such was to be expected. For example, there was the time when Kryuchkov said that in the camps of Lenin and Stalin, only about 3 million people "had departed by reason of death." To tell such a blatant lie in a country where absolutely every family mourns relatives killed in those torture chambers was, of course, an error. There were cries of outrage, mainly from the intelligentsia. But Kryuchkov was forgiven, and people's sights were redirected to their primary enemy, the Party.

Meanwhile, the Party, or, to be more precise, its ruling elite, continued to defend the KGB when it came under attack. In late July 1989, Kryuchkov sent an angry memo to the Central Committee entitled "On the Intention of Antisocial Elements to Conduct an International Seminar on 'The KGB and Perestroika' in Moscow." This seminar was obviously being proposed by "agitators from abroad, antisocial elements from among the so-called human rights activists, and Jewish nationalists," the KGB chairman wrote. "Masking themselves behind the process of glasnost and democratization," these elements were intent on "discrediting the USSR Committee for State Security" by drawing public attention to controversial aspects of its operations. And how did the country's chief Chekist propose to quash this damaging propaganda? A list was attached of people to put under surveillance, names and addresses included. A piquant addendum was a memo stapled to the letter: "This event simply must be cut off at the root," signed "M. Gorbachev."[75]

In March 1990, the Third USSR Congress of People's Deputies voted to remove Art. 6, which codified the special leading role of the Party, from the Soviet Constitution. The democrats celebrated victory—as did the Chekists. Having sacrificed "quantity," the oligarchy now placed its stakes on "quality."

The tragic paradox of perestroika is that the democrats removed the Communist Party from the political arena before they were ready to step in and take over. Unwittingly, they'd disrupted the balance of power in favor of the KGB. Harmonious cooperation notwithstanding, the Party bureaucrats had never stopped looking warily over their shoulders at their Committee comrades; they'd always been careful to strew a few obstacles in their course. But now the obstacles were gone, and the KGB and MIC were advancing across an open field.

Sociological surveys in early 1991 confirmed unprecedented disaffection with all government institutions. One third of the Soviet public did not trust President Gorbachev or the USSR Supreme Soviet. Nearly half (48 percent) rated the government's record as "poor." Public disapproval of local authorities and informal political or civic organizations ran at about 50 percent. (In such politicized cities as Moscow or Gorky, the figures were 51 percent and 45 percent, respectively.) While the KGB didn't escape the general critical mood, it fared better—40 percent of respondents expressed a negative opinion about it.[76]

"When destruction and chaos reach the level of panic, the pendulum of social support may swing to the right, toward the power of the person with the gun," sociologists warned.[77]

By spring 1991, the pendulum had long since swung to the right side of the political spectrum. The KGB had long since won the battle in the upper echelons of the government. In a sense, its victory had always been assured. Its control of society had long been locked into place. Political surveillance and "all-out war against economic saboteurs" were simply means of maintaining an end already attained: control of every sphere of public and personal life. Through its monopoly on information, it controlled government decision-making as well. The KGB didn't so much seize power, as disclose power already seized.

Nothing was more vital to the Chekists' consolidation of power than their monopoly on information. Like any monopoly, it thrived on the lack of viable alternatives. In the U.S., for example, the government receives information from the CIA, the FBI, military intelligence, the State Department Bureau of Intelligence, the NSA, the Congressional Research Service, various public organizations, and so forth. The information comes through channels independent from each other, making it possible to check it out, and the various intelligence agencies compete to provide the most current and accurate information. This competition is one of democracy's prime guarantors. Secret services everywhere have a habit of regarding themselves as being above the law, and congressional and parliamentary oversight committees are not nearly so effective a control as a competitor vying for the same slice of the government's budget.

In my country, however, all information was filtered through the KGB, including much of the intelligence gathered by the Defense Ministry's Chief Intelligence Directorate (GRU). Information gathered by intelligence abroad was screened at the FCD; domestic intelligence went to the Directorate of Analysis, to which local Chekists sent all serious documents and data. Next, the information went to the heads of the chief directorates of intelligence and counterintelligence. From there it was placed on the desk of the chairman of the KGB, who, as my sources explained to me, "could send it further up, to the President, for example; or not."

Information "sent up" would come to the country's leaders in the form of memos, usually signed by the USSR KGB chairman, or telegrams (which by definition were under the jurisdiction of directorate chiefs). Interestingly, there were several classes of the so-called first distribution that was sent to Gorbachev and his closest aides; the second went to lower-ranking executives who had no "need to know."

The government's top officials were avid consumers of all sorts of intelligence information. "N.N. spent several days in the Hawaiian Islands with the Soviet citizen M.M., with whom he was intimate," read a typical report, a February 1990 top secret letter from the KGB addressed to Comrade M. S. Gorbachev. At the bottom of the letter was a handwritten note: "Reported to Comrade Gorbachev. Comrade Lukyanov informed." In 1990 alone, Gorbachev received sixty-seven different memoranda from KGB intelligence reporting on what his opponents were doing and saying and whom they were sleeping with.[78]

As a high-ranking *komitetchik* told me, "It's like getting hooked on the needle. All a politician has to do is read the information from, say, a wiretapped telephone conversation, just once, and he won't be able to refuse such 'memos' in the future."

Information could also be "commissioned." As KGB Col. Vladimir Rubanov put it in an interview with me, "The KGB calls the tune."

This is how it worked. KGB directorate offices at the district and municipal level would be sent a directive—for example, "On the Submission of Information on the Current Situation among Workers"—with the leadership's specific requirements. For example, the abovementioned document requests material on the development of the independent labor movement and its ties to international organizations and trade unions and an analysis of the media's "negative influence on workers." There's a stock vocabulary for just about everything, Maj. Alexander Mavrin, an officer of the Volgograd Region KGB Directorate, reported. "Acts . . . have to be 'extremist'; activity is always 'destructive'; demonstrations are always 'negative.'" The major weighed his words carefully. "Information prepared in this fashion may mislead the leadership of the KGB and the political bodies that ordered the reports. There is a danger that they will take inappropriate actions . . ."[79]

Maj. Mikhail Shevtsov, an officer of the Rostov Region KGB Directorate, agreed with this analysis, and added a point: the KGB also had a stock vocabulary of public reactions ranging from out-rage to heartfelt approval, which it would seed as necessary.

Consider the following February 21, 1990, report from Vladimir Kryuchkov, addressed to Gorbachev and marked "top secret":

> Through operative channels documents prepared by the Interregional Group of Deputies (IGD) have been obtained by us (see attached). Among them is an "Appeal to Citizens, Democratic Organizations and Movements," calling for ral-lies and demonstrations of opposition forces throughout the country, and a "Declaration of the Civic Action Movement" about which we have reported previously (No. 56-K/OV of January 12, 1990) . . .
>
> These documents, which legitimize plans for a political provocation being prepared for the next few days by the IGD, were discussed today at a meeting with [Party ideology chief—Trans.] Comrade V. A. Medvedev. It seems vital to support the proposals made at that meeting regarding the preparation of measures to expose the incendiary nature of these "papers." In our opinion, such attacks should not re-main without a worthy reply. Otherwise, they may become a source of serious future political complications.[80]

It's clear from this memo how much influence the KGB wielded. So it should not surprise us to hear the KGB's unmistakable voice in Gorbachev's speeches during the last years of perestroika, bristling with such phrases as "extremist elements," "antisocial forces," and "destructive actions," warnings like "we know where you got that" and "don't think we don't know who your sources are" (the "democrats" were the unnamed enemy), threats like "the people will not tolerate this," or "we still have to find out who is behind the miners' demands." After all, there are quite a few empty labor camps up north, awaiting new prisoners.

Theoretically, of course, there were channels through which information could bypass the KGB on the way to the top leadership, including Gorbachev. There were TASS reports, Party and government newspapers. But the leaders had no faith in these sources; they were known for sending only sanitized and favorable information to the top. In fact, the Sixth Sector of the Council of Ministers' branch of the KGB's Sixth Directorate had been set up primarily to verify information received from various ministries and agencies. It was KGB information they trusted, first and foremost.

As for other potential information channels—the Ministry of Foreign Affairs, Gorbachev's personal correspondence, other newspapers and journals, the President's own eyes and ears—we must remember that all the decoding services of the country, including the Foreign Ministry's, the government's, and even the President's, were (and are) controlled by the KGB, even if technically the cipher clerks were on the payroll of other organizations or agencies.

Boris Pankin, former Soviet ambassador to Czechoslovakia, briefly foreign minister after the coup, and subsequently ambassador to Great Britain, claimed that about half the people at embassies were KGB. His figure was not precise. In fact, two-thirds of the officials at Soviet embassies abroad were Chekists. The exact figures were as follows: out of 3,900 employees of the Soviet Union's Foreign Ministry, 2,200 were officers of the KGB or the GRU.[81] "They kept the employees under surveillance, including sometimes even the ambassadors themselves . . . Even our authentic diplomats, in order to raise their status, would put out rumors that they were on assignment [from the KGB]." Pankin further recounted: "I once invited a deputy minister [of foreign affairs] into my office and asked him, 'Is it really true that the embassies exist as cover for intelligence?' He looked at me in amazement, not comprehending, as if to say, 'What else would they be for, Boris Dmitrievich?!' "[82]

And the press? Gorbachev's reaction to the glasnost he himself had proclaimed was one of antagonism. He didn't like what his clipping services handed him to read (he didn't read the newspapers themselves). In his book *Against the Grain*, Boris Yeltsin criticizes the top leaders for their practice of allowing the Security Service—the Ninth Directorate of the KGB—to prepare "press releases" for them.[83] Nowadays, however, Yeltsin is pleased to accept the same kind of service.

But surely the President of the country had other sources of information, people whom he trusted? Starting in 1991, unfortunately, Gorbachev's inner circle began to disintegrate. First, Eduard Shevardnaze resigned; then Alexander Yakovlev stepped down, followed by economic advisers Nikolai Petrakov and Stanislav Shatalin. (Several months later, an old acquaintance, a KGB colonel, called Yakovlev and warned him to be careful: a car "accident" was being planned for him.) These were the people who had integrity, and kept it. They were replaced by Gennady Yanayev, longtime head of the Committee of Youth Organizations of the USSR and the Union of Soviet Friendship Societies, organizations traditionally used as cover by the KGB; Boris Pugo, the new interior minister, previously chairman of the Central Committee's Party Control Committee (the Party's internal watchdog) and chairman of the Latvian KGB; and Anatoly Lukyanov, close to both Gorbachev and the KGB. If the list sounds familiar, it's because these names recurred in August 1991: all of these men were among the "putschists."

But Gorbachev, in appointing these individuals to their high positions, had made his choice. His greatest trust, according to Alexander Yakovlev, was reserved for KGB chief Kryuchkov: "Gorbachev had a particular predilection for the information he received from the KGB and GRU."

"Whoever has the information calls the tune," as Col. Vladimir Rubanov told me. The KGB was indeed calling the tune.

———

To Kremlin-watchers, the fall of 1990 became known as "Gorbachev's right turn." The pivotal issue was the "500 Days" program developed by reform economists Stanislav Shatalin and Grigory Yavlinsky, which proposed to transfer the authority of Moscow Center to the constituent Soviet republics. This threatened the very right of the oligarchy to claim the entire nation, with all its republics, as their property. They reacted with a display of force.

On September 6, *Pravda* published the manifesto of the military-industrial complex, "Status for the Defense Industry"—a public warning that the MIC would not give up one iota of its power or property.

On September 11, Boris Yeltsin informed the Russian Supreme Soviet that troops were moving on Moscow. The information came from a member of Shield, the military's civic rights association. A Ryazan Paratroopers Regiment was moving on the capital, along with units from the Tula Division and the Pskov Military Commandos Division. They had been issued ammunition and equipment.[84] Confronted with these reports, the defense minister nervously countered that the troops were being transferred to Moscow for the potato harvest to rehearse for the November 7 parade on Red Square. But Shield objected. Did the soldiers need full battle kit to pick potatoes?

That same day at a session of parliament, Mikhail Gorbachev told members he was inclined to support the Shatalin-Yavlinsky economic program.[85] Only a week later, he changed his mind and more or less rejected it wholesale.

In early October, the Council of Ministers, at that time still chaired by Nikolai Ryzhkov, convened to discuss emergency measures to combat the crime wave that was sweeping the country and leading it to the brink of chaos. KGB Chairman Kryuchkov reported that virtually all of the divisions under his command had been mobilized for the war on crime and on those grounds requested an increase in the KGB's budget.[86] Producing evidence to the contrary, Interior Minister Vadim Bakatin reported that crime rates in fact had fallen 250 percent in the preceding year.[87] But, by the end of the month, the requested resolution from the Council of Ministers had been approved, and the media received copies of the "Proposals for Emergency Measures to Combat Law-breaking," in which the KGB was assigned a prominent role.[88] Soon afterward, Vadim Bakatin was suddenly replaced as interior minister by former Chekist Boris Pugo.

In November, a hitherto obscure "Centrist Bloc of Political Parties" appeared on the political scene. Its leaders were received warmly by Prime Minister Ryzhkov and USSR Supreme Soviet Chairman Anatoly Lukyanov. The bloc's members included Vladimir Zhirinovsky, chairman of the so-called Liberal Democratic Party, who a month earlier had been expelled from his own party "for cooperation with the KGB."[89] The leftist press assailed the Centrist Bloc as a cynical attempt to exploit the slogans of perestroika and glasnost as a means of squeezing the democrats out of the political arena.

That same month, Leonid Kravchenko was named head of USSR Gostelradio, the regime's powerful propaganda machine. Kravchenko previously had headed TASS, widely recognized as the KGB's cover abroad.

On November 18, Gorbachev demanded, and was granted, "extraordinary powers." The "500 Days" program, long languishing, was declared officially dead.

On December 11, KGB Chairman Kryuchkov appeared on Central Television and in no uncertain terms made it clear who was holding the reins of power in the country.[90]

His hard-line speech aroused panic at home and abroad, to the point that Western news agencies sent out wires from Moscow claiming "a bloodless coup has taken place in the Soviet Union." Most anxiety-provoking was Kryuchkov's claim that "destructive elements" with "extreme radical political tendencies" who were "very well funded and morally supported from abroad" had vowed to "shatter our society and government and destroy Soviet rule." The Soviet audience, trained for decades to read between the lines, understood that by "radical political tendencies" and "destructive elements" Kryuchkov meant primarily the national liberation movements in the Soviet republics and the democratic forces at the center of the empire.

In addition, the KGB chairman made repeated mention of "economic sabotage" orchestrated by those same "destructive elements." The intent of his words was clear: to explain to Soviet citizens the reason for bare store shelves and to give them villains to blame for the dire economic situation. And it was true that in December 1990, the food crisis in the country had reached critical proportions. In Moscow, there were lines even for bread; such staples as matches and salt had disappeared altogether. The public had not seen such shortages since the immediate postwar period. No wonder average citizens' angry opposition to any government, democratic or not, had reached the boiling point.

Obviously, if an enemy was responsible for all this, it was the KGB's duty to fight it. So Kryuchkov called on "all honest citizens" to report to the KGB any attempts to undermine "the socialist state and social order"—that is, to inform.

Among those citizens who still preserved a scrap of faith in perestroika, the peremptory tone of Kryuchkov's speech crushed all remaining hope. In fact, we all assumed that the first arrests were imminent: but they did not occur.

What, then, was the import of Kryuchkov's speech? It was a show of force. On December 11, 1990, the Soviet KGB for the first time publicly declared, through its chairman, that the real power in the country was vested in the political police. The economic and political chaos unleashed by perestroika and the concomitant weakening of all other government bodies, including the Party's Central Committee, had allowed the KGB to become the uncontested leader of the country's oligarchic government.

Later in December, at the Fourth USSR Congress of People's Deputies, Kryuchkov announced: "Concerns are being heard that if decisive measures are not taken today to impose order, then we must knowingly concede that blood will be shed . . . But is not blood already being shed? . . . I do not want to frighten anyone, but the Committee for State Security is convinced that if developments in our country proceed further in the same vein, we will not be able to avert more serious social and political upheavals with damaging consequences."[91] Eduard Shevardnadze's resignation in protest was accepted by Gorbachev, seemingly with little attempt to dissuade Shevardnadze. As the Soyuz group exulted in its triumph, Shevardnadze warned: "Dictatorship is coming."

In January 1991, blood was shed in Vilnius. By the end of January there were corpses in Riga as well. Journalists learned that in areas around the country a clandestine power structure was being set up, the so-called SZ (from the Russian *suzhonnye zasedaniya*, or "closed sessions"). In the event that a "state of emergency" was declared, the SZ would coordinate the work of local military boards, KGB directorates, and legal affairs departments—all in strict secret, of course.[92]

On January 26, President Gorbachev issued a number of directives to be implemented by the KGB, including the Decree on Combating Economic Sabotage. Another decree instituted joint patrols by the police and army on the streets of Soviet cities. The groundwork was being laid for KGB administrative control over businesses and factories under a state of emergency. Law enforcement agencies were on the alert.

In February, speaking in Minsk, Mikhail Gorbachev echoed Kryuchkov's December address, calling the democrats "forces of destruction" and accusing them of being guided by "outsiders." The democrats' slogans, Gorbachev fulminated, are "useful to someone, but not to you and me."[93]

A KGB analytical report entitled "The Political Situation in the Country" was placed on Gorbachev's desk. In it, Kryuchkov declares that "interests of protecting the Soviet Constitutional order urgently dictate support of the necessary governmental control over the mass media to prevent erosion of their personnel and even more their becoming a mouthpiece for antisocialist forces," and questions the "appropriateness" of democratization and glasnost under current conditions. He warns that antisocialist circles have turned these concepts into an implicit acceptance of the notion that perestroika constitutes not a renewal of socialism, but an inevitable return to the "course of world civilization"—capitalism.

Kryuchkov went on to say that in light of the depth of the crisis and the likelihood of further complication of the situation, the possibility could not be excluded of, at the appropriate moment, forming temporary structures (within the framework of implementing emergency measures granted to the President by the USSR Supreme Soviet). Such a step would require powerful propaganda support and direct communication with the people, calling on them to unite to preserve the Union of the SSR, and protect public order.[94]

President Gorbachev's speech signaled a public break with the democrats. Shortly thereafter, Prime Minister Valentin Pavlov (who replaced the discredited Ryzhkov) publicly accused Western financial capital of waging war against the Soviet Union.[95]

In March, the head of the KGB's Directorate of Analysis, Lt. Gen. Nikolai Leonov, addressed the First Congress of Soyuz (now a national association). He spoke frankly: "The overwhelming majority of my colleagues and I are with you—under your banners."[96]

As for the public, disillusionment was rife. The National Center for the Study of Public Opinion conducted a survey throughout the fifteen republics of the USSR. To the question "What is perestroika?" 18 percent replied: "an attempt by the ruling elite to preserve power at the price of some democratization"; 17 percent said it was a "cover for a struggle for power at the top"; 14 percent felt that it was "a slogan that had outlived its usefulness." Only 7 percent continued to believe perestroika was a "revolutionary transformation of society."[97]

In April, a KGB Special Forces Command Directorate was formed by decree of the KGB chairman.[98]

Alexander Yakovlev wrote Gorbachev a memo: "As far as I am informed, and analysis as well dictates such a forecast, a coup d'état is being prepared from the right. Something like a neofascist regime is advancing. The ideas of 1985 will be trampled. You and even your comrades-at-arms will be anathematized." There was no reply from Gorbachev.

Yakovlev tried to persuade Gorbachev to drop the "shackles" of the General Secretary past—the whole weight of the dying Party—and remain just President. Gorbachev rejoined, "I can't. I don't want the Party to turn into the OMON [riot police]."[99]

In May, the USSR Supreme Soviet passed the Law on the KGB (with only one vote against), legitimizing the KGB's status in the country and making mail surveillance and telephone wiretapping legal. Art. 14, par. 9, states that Chekists may "enter unimpeded at any time of the day or night residential and other buildings belonging to citizens" if the KGB suspects a crime is being committed. A court warrant or procurator's sanction is not required for such entry. Not since the Stalin era had the chief institution of repression in the country been granted such broad and arbitrary power. The law had been drafted by the KGB and the parliamentary Committee on Defense and State Security, whose brief was oversight of the KGB. Of its 38 members, 26 were representatives of the army and the military-industrial complex, 2 were Chekists, and 5 were Party regional committee secretaries.[100]

On June 21, at a Supreme Soviet session, Prime Minister Valentin Pavlov demanded that he be granted "extraordinary powers." Defense Minister Dmitry Yazov, Interior Minister Boris Pugo, and KGB Chairman Kryuchkov spoke at a closed session of parliament. To the frightened deputies, they held up the specter of chaos and collapse in the country. "CIA agents of influence" were successfully operating in the country, placing pressure on top leaders, claimed Kryuchkov.[101] Gorbachev, concerned that his advisers were now trying to call the shots, publicly rebuked the four men for what the press dubbed "a parliamentary putsch." Rumors abounded that the KGB chairman would lose his job, but he stayed in place. The two sides were reconciled.

In July, a Union Treaty was drafted at Novo-Ogaryovo, the President's country residence, a kind of watered-down political version of the "500 Days" in which the bulk of power was vested in the republics, with Moscow reduced to a coordinating role. Nine republic leaders, plus the President, were willing to sign it.

On August 17, former Politburo member and Presidential Council member Alexander Yakovlev responded to his expulsion from the Communist Party with an open letter: "An influential Stalinist group has formed in the Party's leading core . . . The Party leadership, despite its own declarations, is ridding itself of the democratic wing of the Party, conducting preparations for a social revanche, and for a Party and state coup . . ."[102]

On August 19, 1991, at 4:00 a.m., I finished the first draft of this chapter. I had no intuition or premonition; it was just a coincidence that at 4:00 a.m. on August 19, a state of emergency was declared, and tanks entered Moscow. But I knew nothing about it. I was just tired, and I went to bed.

CHAPTER

6

The Coup

From my journal:

August 19. So it's happened, after all . . . My husband woke me this morning with the words, "Get up, Cassandra, there's a coup." A State Committee for the State of Emergency (which we're calling by its Russian initials, GKChP) announced that Gorbachev has been taken ill and therefore could not perform his presidential duties. They really are idiots—they couldn't even come up with something more original than the 1964 formula when they kicked Khrushchev out: "The President has been taken ill and is therefore incapacitated."[1] The duties of the chief of state have been assigned to Yanayev. In addition to Yanayev, the GKChP includes the Holy Trinity—Kryuchkov, Pugo, and Yazov—as well as Prime Minister Pavlov; Tizyakov, president of the Association of State Enterprises; Baklanov, first deputy chairman of the USSR Defense Council; and Starodubtsev, chairman of the Peasants' Union. Here it is, the "pleiad of talent" Kryuchkov promised us last June!

It's easy enough to see what the Trinity—representing the KGB, the Interior Ministry, and the Army—are doing on the State Committee. Yanayev is there to give everything an appearance of legality: The President is unexpectedly and inexplicably incapacitated; naturally, the Vice President takes over. It's happened on the eve of the very day the Union Treaty was supposed to be signed—what could be more natural? Pavlov's presence is no mystery, either; hadn't he requested emergency powers back in June? Baklanov and Tizyakov represent the defense people, the MIC. As for Starodubtsev, well, the old Soviet-style mentality demands that there be a "representative of the people" on the committee, and how fine to have a country boy and firm defender of the collective farm system. But where's Lukyanov? Is he sticking with Gorbachev? Or is he doing his usual, running things behind the scenes?

The putschists explain that the country's chaotic conditions demanded a restitution of order. A state of emergency is to be in effect for six months; activities of political parties and movements have been suspended, and censorship of the press is imminent. "Taking advantage of the freedoms granted, trampling upon the fresh shoots of democracy, extremist forces have arisen which intend to liquidate the Soviet Union"—that's their explanation. Oh, how afraid they are of losing their property . . .

Fine if they can do it; right now, I'm more worried about my family, especially my little girl, if . . . I don't want to think about that. And then, what do I do with my manuscript? I can't believe it, that after all these years of writing about the KGB, knowing just what to expect from them, I didn't arrange a hiding place! My office is full of materials, documents, drafts, *tamizdat*. I'll throw a file into my bag and take the bag with me; I'll try to give it to a typist to be transcribed and send it to the West somehow. If it doesn't work out . . . well, I did my best.

This is the second time this year I've started a journal. Seven months ago, when the Chekists and the military began killing people, it was in Vilnius, far away. Now, the trouble's right next door, under my windows. A column of tanks just rumbled past the newspaper office; people ran into the street and started shouting at the soldiers, shaking their fists. One tank deliberately aimed for a man, who just managed to avoid being run over.

There's quite a crowd here at the newspaper: members of the staff, writers, some strangers, too. Our editor-in-chief is in the thick of things: Yegor [Yakovlev] is over at the parliament building, the "White House." It's clear the paper won't be coming out today; men with machine guns are stationed at the printing presses. CNN shows columns of tanks moving along Kutuzovsky Prospect and the Garden Ring Road. Across from *Moscow News*, on the other side of the square near the *Izvestia* building, there are more tanks (or armored personnel carriers—I can't tell the difference) from the elite Taman Motorized Rifle Division. The word from the soldiers is that they were roused at 5:00 a.m. and told they were being sent to pacify draft evaders in Moscow. In addition to the Taman Division, the Kantemir Tank Division and the Tula Paratroopers Division have been sent to Moscow.

News from the White House: Yeltsin has issued a decree declaring the GKChP an unconstitutional body, and calling on people not to obey it. He managed to get through to Gorbachev's summer residence at Foros, but was told that Gorbachev was resting and couldn't come to the phone. He tried getting Yanayev, and was told that he couldn't come to the phone, either: "He's resting after a difficult night and asked not to be disturbed." All of Yeltsin's government telephone lines have been cut off. Chekists have been pulling deputies off the streets and arresting them; the head of Shield was picked up near the White House, right in front of a gaping crowd. No one can figure out why Yeltsin hasn't been arrested. Is the GKChP afraid? Certainly, they'd have no problem taking him in. The White House has been under armed guard for hours; when Rutskoi got there he immediately ordered that machine guns be issued to policemen and the building be secured.

14:00. Yakovlev's back. Yeltsin's holding steadfast. The situation is grave. Since we can't publish, we'll put out xeroxed leaflets. Each one of us will have to decide whether or not to remain at the editorial offices. There is no guarantee we won't see armed guards here as well, no guarantee of . . . anything. Grim smiles; but nobody leaves.

16:30. Well, it's about time. The *gekachepisty* are finally getting on the ball; a TASS wire reports that independent democratic newspapers, including *MN*, have been shut down. The right-wing papers—*Pravda, Sovetskaya Rossiya, Rossiya, Krasnaya zvezda* [Red

Star]—will appear as usual. The rest must "reregister" at GKChP's new media control office. Our colleagues at *Kommersant* have already found out that neither they, nor we, have any more chance of registering than of seeing our own ears.

An anonymous voice just attacked Yegor over the *vertushka*, saying, "You tried to do me in; now listen to the radio, you son-of-a-bitch." On the radio, the GKChP's decrees were being repeated for the hundredth time. Yegor is perfectly calm; he thrives on tension.

Some *Izvestia* reporters have come over (to their great embarrassment, their paper wasn't shut down). There was a scuffle at their printing presses; the printers refused to set the newspaper unless they could run Yeltsin's decree. *Izvestia* editor-in-chief Yefimov, back from vacation, burst into the print shop floor, yelling—and that's where the story ends, for now. The outcome's still in doubt. We add what we've got to our leaflet, which begins with an apology to our readers: You won't be seeing the next issue of our paper; unfortunately, there's a coup going on here.

I call up the KGB's Center for Public Liaison to find out what they're thinking over there, but all their perestroika politeness has vanished, and they cut me off brusquely. You want an interview? Write down your questions, drop them in the box in the KGB's reception area, and we'll take a look. I could hear the smirk in their voices.

More news comes in: Moscow KGB has shut down the independent radio station Echo Moscow and taken Radio Russia off the air. There are Chekists at every elevator and studio at Central Television; tanks surround the building, journalists are being searched at the entrance. The guys from *Vesti*, the Russian Television news program, thought fast—they lowered their equipment out the window on ropes and then slid down after it. But then how come our telephones are still working? People are calling in from all over the country; in fact, the international lines are still open. Sherry Jones, a documentary filmmaker and director of the Washington Media Association, actually managed to get through to us from Washington, D.C. To be more precise, the Washington-Moscow line wasn't working, but she got through via Helsinki. Like us, they were sitting and watching CNN, and I think they were more worried about us than we were ourselves.

19:00. Great news: an acquaintance from the KGB called one of our colleagues to say that seven thousand people are going to be arrested in Moscow, including eleven *Moscow News* journalists—I'm on the list, as is Natalya Gevorkyan, with whom I've often worked. Thanks for the honor, guys; it's nice to know our work hasn't gone unnoticed.

Night. I'm going to stay at a friend's. There's no way for me to get home—Kutuzovsky Prospect and Minsk Chaussee are wall-to-wall with tanks and armored personnel carriers. Everything at home is fine.

August 20. We're churning out leaflets on an assembly line; we can't keep up with the demand. There's a line outside *MN*, as though it were a store with some rare commodity. Our schoolboy couriers can't get past the waiting crowd to distribute the leaflets—people snatch them right out of their hands, then grumble when they're told it's one to a customer. There's a scarcity of news sources in the city: Central Television is showing *Swan Lake*, and CNN isn't generally available. Our Xerox machines are already smoking, even though the Soros Foundation brought over two more.* Now, we're running out of paper.

Our sources have called to tell us that practically the entire staff of the Moscow KGB has been sent out on the street to monitor the situation and prevent demonstrations. There are a lot of KGB agents in the crowd gathering around the White House to defend the Russian government. It's a real tinderbox over there.

Editors from eleven of the shut-down newspapers met with Yegor—we're going to pool our efforts in an underground newspaper. Arrangements have already been made with a printing press in Tallinn. We've been sending news out by fax to Paris, New

---

* The Soviet American Cultural Initiative, founded and co-chaired by the American businessman George Soros—Author.

York, Berlin, Rome: it's coming out in *Libération, The New York Times*, and *Repubblica*, with a *Moscow News* byline. But why are the faxes working? Why are the airports letting flights land? Why are the trains running on their regular schedules throughout the country? Why are they letting us put out our leaflets, even letting our boys plaster them to the sides of tanks? ("Tanks are the best place to advertise *MN*" is the latest marketing wisdom at the office.) What kind of a coup is this, anyway?

Yeltsin has issued a decree declaring himself Commander-in-Chief of the Army. He hesitated for a long time before making this move, fearing—and rightly so—that it would split the army.

15:00. I took a ride through the city. Apart from heavy congestion here and there, traffic seemed normal. There were two armored personnel carriers in front of the Main Post Office; crack troops surrounded Central Television; on the Garden Ring Road, eight tanks and two APCs thundered past me. Most of the military vehicles were on Kutuzovsky, not far from the White House.

16:00. The square around the White House is packed with people. Announcements are made over megaphones: "Seventh chain is forming; fifth chain, meet by Entrance No. 8." It's anticipated that the building will be stormed within the next hour. A chain of people with arms linked blocks our passage, saying, "No women allowed here." Andrei Makarov, a well-known attorney, is just behind us; he shouts: "They're not women, they're journalists." There's no time or energy to retaliate in kind. People grab our leaflets—and any others they can find.

21:00. The dancing swans are replaced by the *Vremya* news program, on which a 10 p.m. curfew is announced for Moscow. Yegor orders everyone to leave the editorial office. Sasha Shalganov, our managing editor, has gone with the typists and printers to set an underground issue of *MN*. The joint underground newspaper planned earlier is being put to bed at *Kommersant*. Our parliamentary correspondent, Volodya Orlov, is still at the White House. Natalya Gevorkyan, Tatyana Menshikova, who heads our political reform department, and I have decided to spend the night at the newspaper; we have to hustle information over the faxes and into the underground issue.

August 21. 00:30. We've gotten hold of the White House. There are about forty thousand people outside. It's raining. Japanese umbrellas are being handed out. Shots have rung out nearby, but it's hard to tell whether they are blanks. Something terrible is happening in the tunnel directly across from the American embassy, where people are trying to stop tanks from coming through with a barricade constructed out of trolley buses. The embassy's press office is no help; they tell me, "Call the State Department in Washington, we're not giving out any information." "According to our information, people are being killed right now under your windows," I snap back. "Call Washington," they respond.

1:40. Another call from a colleague at the White House. There seems to be a lull in the gunfire. Military people tell us these operations have their own rhythm: the next attack should be expected about 4:00 a.m.

2:10. Tatyana has gotten through to Burbulis on the *vertushka*.* "Sound the alarms, girls," he says, "spread the news: the putschists are getting mean. We're surrounded by tanks and APCs. There are about two hundred deputies in the building, plus a ton of reporters. Everyone's been issued a machine gun." "Where is Yeltsin?" we ask. "Yeltsin is here."

It's a disaster. It's all over. We open up a bottle of cognac and toast all the wonderful things that—*were*; including *MN*. I feel a twinge of regret for our editorial faxes and computers; whatever the OMON doesn't smash, it'll carry away. I try to fax some friends in the States: "If something should happen to me, please take care of my little girl." The fax doesn't go through. Domestic fax lines are still working. Igor Korolyov, the *MN* telecommunications engineer, transmits our information to *Kommersant*.

2:47. We call Burbulis again. "I spoke to Yazov and Yanayev,"

---

* Gennady Burbulis, at that time State Secretary of the RSFSR [Russian Soviet Federated Socialist Republic], was later forced to step down—Author.

he tells us. "They say they weren't responsible; it's the Russians at the White House who are causing all the trouble."

Three of us are trying to reach the coup leaders—Yazov, Pugo, Kryuchkov. No luck.

3:45. Called Burbulis again. "We just heard that the Vitebsk KGB Paratroopers Division is moving toward Moscow. I called Kryuchkov. At first he denied it, then he said, 'I'll look into it.' "

Where is Yeltsin? "Yeltsin's still here."

4:30. According to Burbulis, the KGB division is still advancing on Moscow. Some troops are being withdrawn from the White House. Burbulis: "Vehicles are leaving and new ones are coming to take their place."

5:25. Burbulis: "The troops stopped advancing. Things seem to be turning around. They'll pay for this . . ."

At dawn, our "underground" crew is back. We're ready to go with a leaflet entitled "Chronicle of a Bloody Night"—and it was bloody; three people died in the clash near the American embassy. Sasha Makhov, *MN*'s international columnist, who was an eyewitness, recounts: "Three APCs were moving along. A barricade made of six trolley buses and a crowd of 2,500 people, blocked their way. People unfurled a banner reading *Brataniye* [Fraternization]. Two of the APCs came to a halt. The third—No. 536 —refused to stop, but the crowd surrounded it. Instead of halting, it began to pick up speed and tried to ram the barricade. Several people climbed up on it; it churned along, and two people fell under the treads in a mess of blood and guts. I was standing about ten yards away. The crowd went crazy; they started asking the residents of nearby buildings for empty bottles, which they filled with gasoline from the vehicles. They set the APC on fire. The crew jumped out and began firing; one guy had half of his skull blown away . . ."

9:00. Our typist, Anya Oreshechkina, and our technical editor, Natasha Senina, were arrested while pasting up leaflets near Lubyanka. At 9:00 a.m., the GKChP issued an order prohibiting the distribution of "provocative leaflets." The decree calls for up to thirty days detention, or a fine of a thousand rubles, but Anya and Natasha were released anyway; they asked for a copy of the leaflet as a "memento."

Evening. Well, it's over. The putschists are under arrest. Gorbachev has been brought from Foros. He looks terrible, with black circles under his eyes. Everyone at the office is kissing and congratulating each other in euphoria.

I went home during the day for a few hours to sleep. My three-year-old daughter Lyolka met me, asking, "Mama, did you beat the junta already?" I almost cried. What kind of country is it where three-year-old children can so easily add the word "junta" to their vocabulary?

22:00. Gorbachev's first press conference since his house arrest in Foros. He's obviously not thinking about what he's saying: "I'll never tell you the whole truth, anyway." Well, that's true enough. I feel a bit sorry for him, but it's just human compassion: I wouldn't want my worst enemy to go through what he did. Still, he brought the whole three-day nightmare on himself, and all of us. And yes, the three boys who were killed are on his conscience.

Coincidentally, August 21 is the twenty-third anniversary of the invasion of Prague by Soviet troops. The regime marked it in its finest tradition—with blood and corpses.

Gorbachev was right; we will never learn the whole truth about the events of August 1991. But information has a way of leaking. Those who have ears to hear, hear. Those who have eyes to see, see.[2]

My informed guesses turned out to be all too plausible: behind the August coup, as I always knew they'd be, were the KGB and its chairman, Gen. Vladimir Kryuchkov.

It all began three days before Kryuchkov made his dramatic December 11, 1990, "call for order" over Central Television. That day, Kryuchkov summoned to his office KGB Maj. Gen. Vyacheslav Zhizhin, formerly the chairman's chief of staff and now deputy chief of FCD, and KGB Col. Alexei Yegorov, of counterintelligence. Kryuchkov, citing a request from Gorbachev,[3] assigned the two men to prepare a memorandum recommending top priority measures to "stabilize" the situation in the country in the event that a state of emergency were to be declared.[4]

The memo was submitted. Attached to it were drafts of a decree for President Gorbachev to sign and a resolution on declaration of a state of emergency for the USSR Supreme Soviet to approve. According to Yegorov, colleagues were simultaneously working up plans (again, per request) on the implementation of direct presidential rule in Lithuania. A month later, in Vilnius, their first "trial run" was disastrous.

By March, the leaders clearly anticipated trouble closer to home. When several hundred thousand people took their calls for democratic representation to the streets prior to the opening of the Russian Congress of People's Deputies, troops were brought into Moscow. By secret order of Kryuchkov (No. 0036 of March 19, 1991) the KGB Directorate for Moscow and Moscow Region, previously under the jurisdiction of democratic municipal authorities, was placed directly under the KGB's Central Office. In addition, three special tactical groups were created in the Directorate for the Protection of the Soviet Constitutional Order (ideological counterintelligence).[5]

For the next four months, Kryuchkov worked intensively to get Gorbachev on his side. Kryuchkov forced the issue by placing the draft state of emergency declaration on the table at a Politburo session.[6] Gorbachev, as usual, looked for a compromise. While he agreed that the country had to be whipped into shape, he was reluctant to tarnish his image in the West (or jeopardize the financial assistance the West had promised to provide).

But the KGB didn't exactly sit around waiting to see what would happen.

Throughout the hard winter and spring of 1990–91, KGB surveillance was ratcheted up. The Chekists literally had the country in a fishbowl. Constant tabs were kept. The telephones of most of the Interregional Group, more than two hundred people, were tapped. Telephone conversations between deputies of all levels, from the Union to the local, were recorded with varying degrees of regularity all over the country. Telephones were bugged in offices, apartments, dachas. A special KGB system that reacted to certain words or phrases and automatically recorded the number of the telephone on which they were spoken was retooled for the moment. The old trigger phrases, like "Down with the CPSU," were changed—during the August coup, for example, they included "coup," "tanks," and "KGB."[7]

Prominent democratic political figures like Yury Afanasyev and Galina Starovoitova were also tailed (or "taken for thorough vetting," as Committee slang would have it). Reports on political figures were done up in duplicate, one copy for the KGB's active files, the other deposited in special archives of the Central Committee's secretariats (who'd often been the ones to commission such reports in the first place). These "Documents of the USSR KGB" were secured at the end of August, as the authorities sealed the Party offices.[8]

But the KGB's watchers extended their brief beyond political opponents, eavesdropping on Raisa Gorbacheva's hairdresser and Boris Yeltsin's tennis coach. Yeltsin in fact had been in the "fishbowl" for years; his daughters' telephone calls were tapped, and the sauna where he frequently took steam baths was "see-through."

This is how it was done, according to an explanatory memo written after the coup and dated September 11, 1991, from Col. M. I. Vedenin, deputy chief of the KGB's Twelfth Department:

In September 1989, Comrade E. I. Kalgin, the chief of Twelfth Department, summoned me and told me that it was necessary to determine the conditions for implanting technical devices in the sauna at the Friendship Sports Complex. The subject was not named. Throughout September and October, I studied the possibility of implanting the technical devices in the second sauna. Since the saunas were located in the basement and the walls and ceilings were of thick construction, it did not seem possible to use wire-type devices. I decided to use a radio. I contacted the KGB Moscow City Directorate, which served the sports complex operationally, and asked approval of the option of entering the sauna in the guise of regular users. We purchased tickets, and then conducted a technical reconnaissance. Between December 10 and 20, we outfitted the saunas with two remote-control radio transmitters. During the next period of surveillance, I saw B. N. Yeltsin approach the building with associates; they proceeded to enter one of the saunas. I turned on the tape recorder. The control center was in a car; reception was imperfect owing to the clandestine nature of the installation. When it was later determined that the subjects only used one of the saunas, the equipment in the other was dismantled.

We learned that after playing tennis and visiting the sauna, the subjects habitually visited the office of S. A. Muranovoi [Yeltsin's tennis coach]. Relations were established with a reliable person, I. V. Martsissov (a radio operator), and his office was then used to equip Muranovoi's office with the same type of remote-control radio transmitter. Surveillance was continued throughout January, February, March, and April 1990. In April, the equipment was dismantled.

In all, there were approximately 16–18 sessions of surveillance. The taped cassettes were turned over personally to E. I. Kalgin. Subsequently, the cassettes were returned after having been erased. I do not know how the information was used. Comrade Kalgin warned me of the covert nature of the operation, and told me not to involve other officers of the division.[9]

This document contains a rather interesting postscript that describes surveillance of the Italian correspondent Andrea Bananni, whose only crime was to play at the same tennis club as Yeltsin.

The KGB bugged the phones of other top state officials, too. For this purpose there was (and still is) a special room at the Directorate for Government Communications that enables operators from the Twelfth Department (electronic surveillance) to tap into government lines. No written authorizations were required for this; Kryuchkov's verbal instructions were sufficient.

Other prominent political figures subjected to surveillance during this period include: Prime Minister Ivan Silayev; State Secretary Gennady Burbulis; Moscow Government Chairman Yury Luzhkov; Moscow Mayor Gavriil Popov; Russian Press Minister Mikhail Poltoranin; Interior Minister and member of the Presidential Council Vadim Bakatin; Ivan Laptev, chairman of one of the houses of the USSR Supreme Soviet; Foreign Minister Eduard Shevardnadze; and Alexander Yakovlev, the "father of perestroika." Yakovlev was also subjected to "thorough vetting." When Yakovlev had to speak with Oleg Kalugin on August 8, 1991, they chose a noisy Moscow street near Miusskaya Square in Moscow; even so, their conversation was taped by seventy-two officers of the Seventh Directorate (external surveillance—the *toptuny*) with invisible microphones, who posed as passersby.

The list of those who were bugged is far from complete. I have only included those documented as coming from the source "Sergei" (which in KGB slang means a tapped telephone) and the source "Tatyana" (which means a bugged apartment or tailing).

Understandably, the eavesdroppers were particularly attentive before and during the coup. A memo from Col. Zuykova details the surveillance maintained on key players during the period August 15–22:

A. V. Korzhakov—home telephone
N. V. Ivanov—home telephone
M. N. Poltoranin—home and office telephones
I. S. Silayev—home telephone
Yu. M. Luzhkov—office reception and home telephones
G. I. Yanayev—home telephone

E. A. Shevardnadze—home and office telephones

A. N. Yakovlev—office telephone and other work telephone and home telephone under surveillance beginning August 9:

Yu. N. Afanasyev—home telephone

"Petrov" [KGB Gen. Oleg Kalugin appears under this code name in KGB surveillance reports]—home telephone

The information was mostly reported verbally. Only a small portion of it was presented in reports that were subsequently burned.

Their "eyes" and "ears" had no scruples; one of my very reliable sources told me, with a grimace of revulsion, that the safe of Valery Boldin, Gorbachev's chief of staff, contained tapes of what should have been the most private, intimate moments between people. Yeltsin was one of these people.

Kryuchkov trusted no one, not even his fellow believers. During the coup, short-lived as it was, the KGB had taps installed on "their" Vice President, Gennady Yanayev, Supreme Soviet Chairman Anatoly Lukyanov, later indicted as one of the plotters, and Central Committee Secretary Dzasokhov.

In the matter of surveillance, the relations between Kryuchkov and Gorbachev remain unclear. The post-coup investigation revealed a document from Kryuchkov attesting to the necessity, "given the ongoing hostile activity of the former KGB Gen. Oleg Kalugin, deleterious to both state security and the USSR's relations with other countries," of placing the renegade general (code-named "Petrov") under high-powered KGB surveillance. An addendum from Col. V. V. Nechayev, chief of the SCD's Twelfth Department, notes: "In April 1991, on orders from V. A. Kryuchkov, a letter was prepared and sent to the President of the USSR with a request to sanction the thorough examination of 'Petrov.' In June, the President's sanction was received."[10] I am curious to know whether

Gorbachev also sanctioned the surveillance of Yakovlev and Shevardnadze.

Late in November 1991, journalist Yury Shchekhochikhin put the question to Gorbachev: had he known that the telephones of Yakovlev, Shevardnadze, and Lukyanov were being monitored by the KGB? Gorbachev seemed shocked, especially by the latter—"They bugged him, too?" And yet, only two weeks earlier, the President had received a complete report from the State Commission to Investigate the Activity of the KGB during the Coup, in which all of these names were mentioned. That is, until Gorbachev ordered them excised.

Later, long after Gorbachev had relinquished the presidency, with former KGB chairman Kryuchkov remanded to Sailors' Rest Prison awaiting trial, Yakovlev asked Gorbachev whether he'd approved the surveillance the Chekists had kept on Yakovlev. I didn't even know they were watching you, Gorbachev replied, although he did add that in the winter of 1991, Kryuchkov had reportedly warned Gorbachev about an "intelligentsia cabal" headed by Alexander Yakovlev.

I asked Yakovlev whether he believed Gorbachev. He shook his head, No. "That's why I quit the Gorbachev Foundation," he told me, referring to the think tank Gorbachev set up after resigning from the presidency, on the board of which Yakovlev had served.[11]

Whatever responsibility Gorbachev accepted or denied for surveillance oversight, however, it's clear that in the end he wasn't calling all the shots: his own phone lines were tapped right along with the others'. Not that Kryuchkov lacked information on the President, or opportunities to exert influence on him. He had successfully drummed into Gorbachev's mind that only a "firm hand . . . could save the Soviet Union from collapse"—and in that, his only reliable supports would be the army and, of course, the KGB. But Kryuchkov liked to be sure; and there was nothing like "hands on" surveillance for that. So the KGB kept "Subject 110" (Gorbachev) and "Subject 111" (Raisa) under its eagle eye, recording such vital matters of state as: "18:30. III is in the bathtub. 19:04.III has stepped out of the bathtub." (When I read portions of the surveillance logbook at the Russian Procuracy, all I could think was, poor Raisa!)

And of course the KGB also had the Security Service to keep tabs on Gorbachev. According to my informed sources, the Security Service's First Department alone (the former KGB Ninth Directorate) included some 1,500 officers charged with maintaining surveillance over the President and other chief officials, their families, and everyone in presidential circles. Yeltsin inherited this cocoon of security. The First Department's staff includes maids, cleaning ladies, cooks, drivers, gardeners, etc. For example, the staff at the dacha in Foros where Gorbachev was placed under house arrest in August 1991 numbered about five hundred people, almost all of whom, from the security guards to maids, were employees of the KGB.

These operatives were there primarily to observe rather than persuade (presidents are rarely receptive to the political perspectives of their maids). Influencing Gorbachev's views was left to selected members of his executive staff—most notably, his chief of staff Valery Boldin, who kept tight reins on the flow of information in and out of his chief's office.

But somehow, their efforts were not enough. The decree on the state of emergency lay on Gorbachev's desk, unsigned. Gorbachev left Moscow for a much-needed vacation. And on August 5, Kryuchkov and friends held their first meeting at an FCD safe house code-named "Object ABC." The GKChP was born.[12]

The State Committee for the State of Emergency continued to meet over the next couple of weeks. Military strategy was placed in the hands of Maj. Gen. Pavel Grachev, paratroop commander, Afghanistan War hero—and, when push came to shove, the unexpected hero of the August crisis (in recognition of which he became Yeltsin's defense minister). Grachev, Yegorov, and Zhizhin repaired to a FCD dacha in Mashkino, where they prepared a further briefing on the projected state of emergency. Introducing a state of emergency, they warned, might backfire; among other reasons, "a substantial portion of the Soviet population has not yet experienced difficulties in obtaining food and necessities to the extent that they will support strict rationing and forced restoration of economic ties."[13] Apparently, however, Kryuchkov and the GKChP weren't particularly concerned about adverse public opinion.

On August 15, E. I. Kalgin, chief of Twelfth Department, and A. G. Beda, chief of the Directorate for Government Communications, received a verbal order from Kryuchkov to institute round-the-clock monitoring of all conversations on government lines. Kryuchkov's first deputy, Gen. G. Y. Ageyev, held a special briefing on audio surveillance. Yegorov and Zhizhin sat down to compile a "comprehensive program for the most urgent measures of an emergency nature."[14] (This program later formed the basis for Resolution No. 1 of the USSR State Committee for the State of Emergency broadcast over all Soviet radio stations at 6:00 a.m. on August 19.)

On Saturday, August 17, the KGB chairman convened a meeting of his deputies and chiefs of directorates and informed them about the impending state of emergency in the country.[15] There were no objections. He'd assessed his colleagues accurately; they backed the plan wholeheartedly.

That same day the *spetsnaz* of the KGB's Seventh Directorate (the A-7, or Alpha Group, which had dynamited the Baku TV station in January 1990 and stormed the Vilnius station in January 1991), the *spetsnaz* of the FCD, "Cascade," and a separate training regiment (sometimes called Group B) were placed on combat alert. They were moved from bases outside of Moscow into the city and billeted at the Dzerzhinsky Club. Group A-7 was supposed to arrest Yeltsin.

That evening, the coup-plotters gathered again at "Object ABC." The group included Prime Minister Valentin Pavlov, Defense Council Deputy Chairman Oleg Baklanov, Politburo member Oleg Shenin, Presidential Chief of Staff Valery Boldin, Defense

Minister Dmitry Yazov, his deputies Varennikov and Akalov, and of course Kryuchkov with his retinue, Grushko and Yegorov.[16]

Materials from the Procuracy's investigation give us a vivid portrait of the scene. The staff and guards had been given the night off; the table was set with a few bottles and some snacks. Yazov, Pavlov, and Shenin drank vodka; Kryuchkov and the rest drank whiskey. They talked. Pavlov talked about how poorly the harvest was going: hunger would be a real threat in the coming winter. Were the Union Treaty to be signed as announced on August 20, the country would simply disintegrate. It was high time they declared a state of emergency. Yazov said, Yes, it's time we imposed some law and order. Kryuchkov suggested that they go see Gorbachev and try to persuade him to transfer power for a month to the Committee for the State of Emergency; when matters were back in hand, Gorbachev could take back the presidential reins.[17] (Whether or not under the control of the GKChP, Kryuchkov did not specify.) Kryuchkov's colleagues balked at this: Gorbachev should just be told, Either declare a state of emergency or transfer power to Vice President Yanayev. At this point, the vodka ran out. Col. Yegorov was sent to get another bottle.

The next day, a delegation from the GKChP left for Foros. The group had chosen Baklanov, Gen. Valentin Varennikov, commander-in-chief of the land forces, Lt. Gen. Yury Plekhanov, chief of the KGB Security Service (and therefore empowered to admit outsiders onto the grounds of the dacha), Shenin, and Boldin. Boldin was invited at the suggestion of Yazov, who argued that the sight of his trusted long-time aide on the other side of the fence would let Gorbachev know in no uncertain terms that the jig was up. A connoisseur of both the human heart and of literature, Yazov recited "Et tu, Brute" in support of his argument.[18]

At 5:50 p.m. on August 18, Lt. Gen. Alexander Beda, chief of the Directorate for Government Communications, gave the order to cut all Gorbachev's direct phone lines and route all his calls through an operator: "Channels of communications with Moscow, Kiev, Sevastopol, Simferopol to Yalta and Foros are to be transferred to manual service."[19] (The next day, Yeltsin and Prime Minister Silayev would receive the same treatment.) A regiment of the Sevastopol KGB Directorate blockaded Gorbachev's dacha on land, and a group of Border Guard ships, under direct command of Plekhanov and his deputy, Generalov, blockaded the dacha from the sea.[20] Inside, the President's own guards kept a close watch on him—whether for protection or containment, it wasn't clear. Gorbachev's personal bodyguard, Gen. Vladimir Medvedev—"Uncle Volodya" to his comrades—left his President, and flew to Moscow.

The same day, the KGB's Fifteenth Directorate (the "bunker" division that acted as liaison between Lubyanka and the Party headquarters on Old Square) was put on combat alert. Its underground offices, dormitories, TASS branches, etc., were stocked with water, food, and oxygen.[21]

At the Directorate for Protection of the Soviet Constitutional Order, operational groups were assembled to take charge of the arrest and internment of those who, as the coded instructions phrased it, "might rouse the people."[22] That duty also fell to the Moscow KGB Directorate, for which purpose 300,000 blank arrest warrants were printed; only the names of the arrestees would have to be filled in.[23] These bore the signature of Lt. Gen. Nikolai Kalinin, commander of the Moscow Military District, who, with the imposition of the state of emergency, became the commander of Moscow.[24] Chekists in the capital were instructed to place the state Bank, Mint, and Treasury buildings, Central Television, and the central telephone and telegraph stations under armed guard.[25]

In Telegram No. 14555, Moscow KGB chief Gen. Prilukov ordered an operations headquarters to be opened "to intensify the work of counteracting subversive enemy activities against industrial buildings, public transportation and communications, enterprises producing staples and necessities for the population, and to prevent confrontations, sabotage, wrecking, and antisocial manifestations." By his order, plainclothes combat-ready operational and investigatory groups were placed on code *Volna* [wave] alert, "awaiting special instruction from the center." Thousands of Chekists sat by their telephones awaiting the signal for code *Plamya* [flame], emergency mobilization.[26]

The capital's *komitetchiki* were then sent out to work the streets and squares, and to mingle with defenders of the White House. GRU officers provided substantial assistance here, along with officers of the General Staff's Diplomatic Academy, who donned civilian clothes and went in search of information about "rabble-rousers" and "instigators" at rallies and at the barricades.[27] The GRU was also ordered to jam independent radio stations.

The Third Chief Directorate (military counterintelligence) also put up special squads and made sure that army units were deployed to Moscow. Some KGB officers were issued weapons and orders without the command location listed. Some of these officers later ended up in Vilnius and Riga.[28] Meanwhile, the military itself was keeping on top of events and coordinating its actions with those of the KGB.

On the night of August 18–19, when push came to shove and the members of the GKChP signed the announcement of Gorbachev's sudden illness and the institution of a state of emergency, there was an all-night drinking party; only Kryuchkov remained sober.

The rest of the story is public knowledge. Alpha was supposed to arrest Yeltsin, but they did not. They were supposed to storm the White House, but they did not. Their colleagues were supposed to exile seven thousand people from Moscow to the back of beyond. No one was exiled.

The coup had failed; and the world applauded the victory of democracy. But after a brief euphoria, the country sank back into depression. Soon, only journalists were bothering to ask such questions as, Who orchestrated the August events? The rest of the country was too numbed by the realization that for all the commotion, all the supposed triumph of righteousness, nothing had changed. How did we all play our parts so earnestly, everyone wondered; how did we fail to see that this was just another staged spectacle? Even more frightening, had we just seen a dress rehearsal for something more sinister?

So just what did happen? Why did the coup, which had been so carefully prepared by the KGB all throughout 1991, fizzle out so rapidly? In a mere twenty-four hours, the coup-plotters had already lost, turning into a huddle of broken, frightened men. It seemed almost inconceivable. The KGB had wiretapped half the country. They had kept all the top government leaders under surveillance, shadowed the democrats' every step. They'd been backed by the military-industrial complex, the army, and thousands of their own Chekists. In the country's provincial backwaters, people were too busy scrounging for salt and matches to take much notice of the turmoil. "Something's going on in Moscow but it doesn't concern us." When "it's none of our business" is the reigning ethos, seizing power shouldn't be much of a problem. And so—why *did* the coup fail? We simply can't avoid that question, especially now that another coup has been attempted.

Several theories have been circulated, none of them quite adequate. Some people say that the KGB underestimated Yeltsin's popularity. It's possible; but he'd been doing such a good job of flaunting that popularity over the past few years that it seems unlikely to have escaped anyone's notice. How could they have overlooked the evidence of a survey conducted on the very morning of August 20 which found that 52 percent of the Russian population supported Yeltsin, only 28 percent the GKChP, with 20 percent expressing no preference? Especially since those who favored Yeltsin made it clear that it was the man himself they applauded, not some abstract notion of "the people's choice" or "democracy in action."

Another theory has it that the coup-plotters had entirely misread the mood of the country, that the people were not ready to jettison Gorbachev. Unlikely; his endless compromises and maneuvers had embittered all of society, especially the intelligentsia. Six years of steadily decreasing prosperity had lost Gorbachev his last shreds of popular support. Furthermore, the GKChP's first resolution, in which they promised to fight "mismanagement and squandering of the national wealth," to freeze prices, raise wages, and give all interested urban dwellers small plots of land for vegetable gardens, was evidence of their feel for what mattered most to the average citizen. (People still think longingly of those gardens.)

Were the plotters, as popular lore would have it, shocked into paralysis by Muscovites' bravery? The resistance may have taken them by surprise, but it's hard to believe they considered it a serious obstacle.

On that terrible night of August 20–21, most of the nine million people of Moscow were sleeping. About 40,000–70,000 by some estimates had decided to camp out and defend the White House. They were mostly young people, and it would have been no trouble for the Alpha Group to sweep them off the square. As Maj. Gen. Viktor Karpukhin, chief of A-7, later pointed out, his agents had thoroughly infiltrated the White House defenders' ranks. "At night, we inspected all the barricades . . . they were like toys, it would have taken no effort at all to crush them . . . fifteen minutes at the most."[29] But why bother? The White House was already full of Chekists, some of them among Yeltsin's own security people. They could have shot Yeltsin at any point.

Those who explain the coup as the result of "social disintegration"—a country in chaos, an ineffectual government, and a floundering KGB—are mistaking the symptoms for the disease itself. The KGB was having its problems, along with the rest of the country, but it hadn't yet given up the ghost.

As for the bruited "resistance from within," the State Commission to Investigate the Activity of the KGB during the Coup (of which I was a member) has confirmed my suspicion that tales of mass mutiny from within the ranks have been wildly overblown. The investigator found that on August 19, the first day of the coup, only a few isolated Chekists opposed the GKChP. The majority either took part in the coup or sat it out. The KGB's ranks undoubtedly had been impressed by developments in Eastern Europe—but, if anything, those events had convinced the Chekists that it was time to dig their heels in. The examples of Czechoslovakia and East Germany made it painfully clear that a truly democratic government would have no use for their services. Helping to install such a government would be tantamount to signing their own death warrants.

No, none of these reasons was sufficient to doom the putsch to failure. Something else happened: what the plotters failed to understand was where they themselves stood in the scheme of things. Vanity forbade them to turn their eagle eyes on themselves; and so they underestimated the mistrust they evoked in the public, and especially within their own institutions. They just didn't realize how unpopular they were.

Prime Minister Pavlov had compromised himself in everyone's eyes by raising prices on necessities and suddenly decreeing that all fifty-ruble notes be turned in and withdrawn from circulation —a move that caused brutal suffering among the poor without accomplishing anything positive. Vice President Yanayev had long been dismissed as a clown, Gorbachev's lackey. At the August 19 press conference his hands, shaking from a hangover, made him the butt of jokes countrywide: "Poor putschist, he's hung over . . ." Starodubtsev had lost the peasantry's backing with his resistance to any reform of the collective farm system and refusal to acknowledge widespread desire for private land ownership. Yazov was despised by the new crop of generals for his ineptitude in management, and by the public for sending so many young men to certain death in the Caucasus. Tizyakov lacked the crucial support of the Scientific and Industrial Union and its director, Arkady Volsky. And Baklanov, during his tenure at the Council of Ministers and as the Central Committee secretary in charge of defense, had alienated influential members of the MIC. Pugo, who had replaced Vadim Bakatin as interior minister, was taking the heat for rampant police corruption. Besides, he was Latvian, and therefore viewed as an unwelcome foreigner. Finally, as a former Party apparatchik, Kryuchkov was the object of intense resentment from KGB professionals, although many gave him credit for his intelligence, commitment, and organizational ability. Indeed, Kryuchkov's colleagues had long sought to remove him from the office of chairman of the KGB. It was only the support (or dependency?) of Gorbachev that enabled Kryuchkov to hang on until summer 1991.

But if these men were unable to perceive their own decline, then immediate underlings were acutely aware of it. They could see that the sun was setting on their bosses, that history was passing them by. So the members of this second echelon of power seized the opportunity the coup provided, a moment of chaotic destabilization, and did the one thing that can bring any military leader to his knees: they broke the chain of command.

The second echelon of power stood aside. The "command center" of the totalitarian state—the shadow cabinets of the KGB, MIC, army, Party, and provincial authorities—did not support the coup. Communications faltered, and the plotters' intricately devised strategies came to naught. By the end of the coup's first day, the second echelon was convinced that it would fail. And with that, they moved from a "hands-off" stance to a game of their own in which the members of the GKChP were simply an impediment.

On the first day of the coup, FCD head Leonid Shebarshin sent a coded telegram to 130 KGB residencies abroad, ordering them to distribute the GKChP's official statements.[30] Earlier, the special training center under the FCD was put on combat alert and transferred to Moscow. But on August 20, he instructed the *spetsnaz* troops to wait for his personal authorization before following any of the GKChP's orders.[31] And that authorization never came.

On August 19, the operations group of Directorate Z (ideological counterintelligence) sat with their weapons at the ready, while the directorate's deputy chief led a group that supervised the closing down of printing shops and radio stations.[32] But by the evening of August 20, the weapons were stashed and the officers were awaiting further instructions. The instructions never came.

By the account of experts from the Russian Humanitarian Association (made up of former officers of the information directorate of the FCD), "During the first stage of the coup, Gen. Grachev —the very same one who drafted the military strategy for a putsch, and by whose command paratroopers entered Moscow—acted in accordance with Yazov's orders. But he did not lose contact with the Russian government. By the afternoon of August 20, he and Defense Minister Shaposhnikov were trying to stave off any storming of the White House, with the tragedy that would ensue."

On August 19, Lt. Gen. Prilukov, chief of the Moscow KGB, gathered together his deputies, division chiefs, and the directors of district KGB offices to explain the task facing the directorate —to arrest the key activists and maintain surveillance over their comrades on the streets of Moscow. No one at the meeting objected. By the afternoon of the next day, however, Prilukov's deputy, Maj. Gen. Alexander Korsak, was claiming that the leadership of the Moscow KGB "had decided not to take part in this escapade."[33]

On August 19 at 5:30 p.m., the A-7 *spetsnaz* allegedly received an order to clear the square in front of the White House and arrest the leadership of the Russian Republic. By the next day, according to numerous, virtually identical interviews, the A-7 leaders had arrived at a decision "not to permit any bloodshed." Perhaps . . . but when asked whether he had been prepared to obey whatever order was handed down, the response of Major General Karpukhin was simple: "Absolutely."[34] Col. Sergei Stepashin, head of the State Commission to Investigate the Activity of the KGB during the Coup, told me, "If you could have seen Karpukhin's eyes then, you would have understood that people like that do not refuse an order to kill." But no such order came.

Shortly before midnight on August 20, while tens of thousands of citizens gathered on the square, ready to defend the Russian leadership with their own lives, Kryuchkov summoned together tactical units trained to infiltrate the White House via secret tunnels that ran under, and into, the building. The summons was the last order he, or any of the KGB leadership, would issue; although he still held the title of chairman, it had become clear that he no longer held the reins. At 4:30 a.m., his officers returned to their homes.

The next evening, Maj. Gen. Alexander Sterligov of the KGB, along with officers of the Russian Procuracy, arrested Army Gen. Vladimir Kryuchkov. At one of his early interrogations, Kryuchkov said: "I do not regret anything that was done. And if I had to do it over again, I would have done it more energetically, so as to decapitate the leadership of Russia."[35]

Other members of the junta were also arrested that day. Boris Pugo was found dead at his home, his wife mortally wounded, in what authorities concluded was a murder-suicide.

Maj. Gen. Sterligov immediately became the chief of staff of Vice President Rutskoi. Lt. Gen. Pavel Grachev became defense minister. And the heads of most directorates were replaced by their deputies.

Thus, the second echelon of power, which had remained un-involved in the coup, was able to remove from the political scene those who had played the leading roles. I am afraid that now, in the chaos of our current power vacuum, this second echelon of power will simply take over the running of the country.

That is, if they haven't already.

But back on the evening of August 21, 1991, we all celebrated victory. At midnight, watched by unseen eyes behind the darkened windows of the KGB building, a jubilant crowd—with me in it—cheered as a heavy crane upended and hauled away the statue of the founder of the All-Russian Extraordinary Commission, the father of the Chekists, "Iron Felix" Dzerzhinsky.

And yet, as God is my witness, on that night, we left worse Chekists in place.

CHAPTER

7

Lubyanka–Now and Forever

Marx himself observed that history repeats itself, first as tragedy and then as farce. It would be interesting to know which was which, where the August coup is concerned.

The situation of the KGB since those tragic August days is strikingly reminiscent of the false promises of the mid-1950s, when the death of Stalin was followed by thunderous exposés, vows that such things "will never happen again," and a shake-up of the Committee's ranks. False promises were followed all too soon by a dismaying renaissance, as the KGB regained its power. Soviet tanks rolled into Prague . . . and then into Afghanistan . . . and the stage was set for the end of perestroika, when tanks rolled into . . . Moscow. Will we never learn?

The months following the August coup were hard for KGB officers. Having seen the statue of "Iron Felix" toppled from its pedestal, they had every reason to believe that they, too, were ripe for a fall. This came in the form of massive layoffs, the dismantling of the secret police as an institution, and the creation of a security agency bound by more civilized standards.

On August 27, 1991, the post-coup government's press organ, *Rossiyskaya gazeta*, ran the headline "The KGB Must Be Liquidated."[1] Lubyanka was in a state of shock.

"For the first time in the many years I've worked at the Committee, I saw KGB officers gulping down vodka in their offices," a lieutenant colonel told me.

"The Committee isn't really doing any work," Lt. Gen. Vadim Bakatin, whom Gorbachev had appointed KGB chairman immediately after the coup, told me in September. "Everyone's sitting and waiting to see what their fate will be."[2]

They may have been waiting, but they weren't sitting around idly. A contingent was busy burning documents—first and foremost, of course, anything to do with the coup.

The paper shredders were already working at full tilt on August 21, when an angry crowd threatened to storm the building on Lubyanka, just as their East German comrades had taken the Stasi building in Berlin in January 1990.

Fortunately, however, the Muscovites were dissuaded from their attempt. Whatever finds they might have made scarcely would have been worth the bloodshed: and blood certainly would have been shed; not only would the Chekists have fought back, but the Moscow authorities would have come to their aid. As it was, the KGB archives were hastily protected by makeshift barriers, as officers threw dossiers and agents' card files into plastic bags and hauled them from the archives' cellars into secret underground tunnels and bunkers.[3]

At 4:00 p.m. on August 22, KGB officers were ordered to gather all documents and prepare them to be destroyed. It remains unclear whether this order came from former intelligence chief Leonid Shebarshin, acting chairman of the KGB in the first days after the coup, or from someone lower down. Whatever the case, the order was canceled within an hour. The next day, the officers of the Directorate of Analysis received the same instruction; within a few hours, this order, too, was rescinded.[4] Later, all the most important documents, including lists of KGB agents and their personal dossiers, were removed from Moscow to KGB-commanded military bases in remote areas of Russia.[5]

Yes, back then I thought, Thank God that the crowd was dis-

tracted by the bone they were tossed, that they were satisfied by
toppling Dzerzhinsky's statue. Now, looking at a resurgent KGB,
I have second thoughts: perhaps the Germans who vandalized the
Stasi building had it right, after all. Did we miss our one chance
to put an end to Lubyanka forever? (On the other hand, the fact
that the West German Bundeswehr stood ready to back the crowd
helped cow the Stasi agents into acquiescence. But who would
have helped us?)

One of Vadim Bakatin's first orders was to seal the archives.
But it's one thing to give an order, quite another to enforce it; and
this still left the materials strewn on desks and stowed in officers'
locked drawers—places a wax seal couldn't secure.

Former ideological counterintelligence officer Alexander Kichikhin was quick to predict that "whoever enters our offices after
we're gone will find only empty drawers." He added, "The Fourth
Department has already destroyed everything that concerns the
Church hierarchs."[6]

When the temporary head of the Directorate of Analysis, Col.
Vladimir Rubanov, entered his new office, he found nothing but
bare walls and empty shelves and safes. His ultra-correct prede-
cessor, Lt. Gen. Leonov, had left behind only a small, gray note-
pad (on which, ironically, Rubanov noticed his own name).[7]

On August 22, the Seventh Directorate (external surveillance)
torched or shredded its documents. According to a later internal
KGB investigation, "Following eight orders, 164 documents were
destroyed. These included handbooks of the Seventh Directorate,
information bulletins, some operational documents produced during the coup d'état, and special notebooks."[8] But how many materials—and of what sort—were removed or destroyed without
any official orders? For example, what happened to the documents
hurriedly stuffed into bags and brought by Alpha Group couriers
to the KGB Security Service firing range near the village of
Kupavna?

Archives in the Russian autonomous and former Soviet republics also "disappeared" during this period. KGB archives were taken out of Tatarstan, Bashkiria, and Chechnya. The shelves in the state security buildings in the former Baltic republics were also emptied; Kryuchkov himself had seen to that.[9]

Twice, after the coup, I requested my own file from KGB directors, first from Viktor Ivanenko, chief of Russian state security at the time, and then from Vadim Bakatin. Both times, I was told it could not be located. "It's probably already been destroyed," Ivanenko said. A highly placed source from law enforcement circles raised an eyebrow at that tale. "They didn't destroy the file; they just don't want to give it to you," he said.

How many KGB documents were lost to the shredders? In the end, I think not all that many—probably only what concerned the Chekists' personal participation in the events of August 19–21.

More to the point: how many compromising papers did officers carry away stashed in their pockets and briefcases? Will they ever surface? And at what price: hard currency; high positions?

In the short term, there were real changes in the KGB. Media optimism in Russia and the West was genuine, and, for the moment, not unwarranted.

At the end of August 1991, all of Kryuchkov's generals—the so-called KGB collegium—turned in their resignations. A number of these "retirees" soon found themselves undergoing a "rest cure" —joining the first rank of putschists in Sailors' Rest Prison. But, before long, they were transferred again, this time to quarters of their own. They took up new careers—some, like former intelligence chief Leonid Shebarshin, started up private security services for banks; others, like former counterintelligence director Vladimir Grushko, took up teaching posts at the KGB's academies and schools. So far as I know, no one was left unemployed. And there was money to be earned on the side, as well; ex-generals wasted no time organizing an Association of Intelligence Veterans to market interviews and documents (many of them phony). It was all quite straightforward; an interview with Shebarshin, for example, cost $500.

Local Chekists received a rude shock in mid-September, when Yevgeny Savostyanov, a mining geophysicist and senior lieutenant in the reserves—and, more to the point, a recent aide to the mayor of Moscow and one of the founders of the Democratic Russia movement—was appointed chief of the Moscow KGB. They'd learned to live with directors from the Party apparat, but a scientist whose first step was to renounce his rank of lieutenant general was just too much. "I come to the KGB as a politician," Savostyanov told his staff; apparently, he thought this would allay any fears that he might interfere in their business. But if this placated the professionals, it left outside observers doubly anxious; traditionally, the KGB's "politicals" were those who concentrated on their political opponents. Still, the appointment of Savostyanov seemed to some to offer a glimmer of hope.

At the end of September 1991, Vadim Bakatin announced the exhilarating news that he was eliminating the Directorate to Protect the Soviet Constitutional Order, the ideological counterintelligence unit that throughout the years of Soviet power had targeted dissent.[10]

But it wasn't just units of the KGB that were disappearing; the Soviet Union itself was ceasing to exist, as republic after republic declared its independence. Thereupon, each would announce the nationalization of KGB property within its borders and the creation of its own state security forces. Except for the Baltics, none of the republics made even a token attempt to rid itself of political police—the very idea was unthinkable.

On October 24, 1991, two months before the Soviet Union ceased to exist, Mikhail Gorbachev signed into law the formal end of the KGB. But instead of "abolition," the official term for the action was *dezintegratsiya*, dismantling. The KGB was to be split into a number of independent agencies: it had been altered, but not abolished. (At least they were honest about that.)

To onlookers, the empire appeared to be crumbling. The "state within a state" was disintegrating before our very eyes. By the end of November, *The New York Times Magazine* and the London *Observer* were running stories headlined "Closing Down the KGB" and "The KGB Is Liquidated"—sensational news . . . if only it had been true.[11]

On December 17, 1991, Gorbachev announced that the Soviet Union would cease to exist as of January 1, 1992. He himself vacated his Kremlin office on December 26, 1991, and took a much-needed vacation.

For those of us who had carved our professional identity out of the struggle to catch even a glimpse of the Cheka's inner workings, the period just after the coup was indeed stunning. The doors of Lubyanka were swung open. As a member of a government commission authorized by both Gorbachev and Yeltsin, and headed by Sergei Stepashin, chairman of the Russian parliamentary Committee for Defense and Security, I was even allowed to walk the corridors of the holy of holies, the new state security building that housed the KGB's top brass. It was a far cry from the KGB's Public Liaison Center, the only part of Lubyanka that previously had been open to journalists.

I walked along the long, highly polished corridors, with nothing on the walls to distract the eye or help you to remember your way. I climbed up the side staircases, which were covered with netting to prevent arrestees from jumping over the rail to avoid interrogation; gazed at the dark wood of the massive office doors, which bore no signs, merely numbers to distinguish them; wandered up to the fourth floor, where, only a month before, Gen. Kryuchkov had gone from being the most powerful man in the country to an accused criminal to be removed summarily to Sailors' Rest Prison. I went into the cafeteria, where the Chekist generals had dined at an enormous oval table seated in high-backed chairs. KGB officers pointed out spots of particular interest ("That's where Kryuchkov used to sit").

Finally, completely emboldened, I took to entering Lubyanka through the KGB chairman's entrance, an unobtrusive doorway at the right side of the building. I would be met there by a tall, broad-shouldered fellow in his mid-thirties, whose plainclothes jacket seemed about to burst at the seams, unable to contain his muscular frame. "Are you from the *spetsnaz*?" I asked him. "Yes," he grinned. "Zenith? Cascade?" I queried, showing off my knowledge of the names of intelligence's *spetsnaz*. "Cascade," he nodded.

My brashness was in part pure reporter—getting in!—but it was also the boldness of authority. In the eyes of the Chekists terrified by their uncertain future, I represented the new order: not the Kremlin—it was clear even to them that Gorbachev's time was gone—but the new, "democratic" (or so they styled themselves) government of Boris Yeltsin and the Russian parliament.

By that time, the Chekists knew me quite well. They were aware that I'd published numerous articles calling for the liquidation of the KGB, convinced that state security would inevitably launch a coup and plunge the country back into the gulag from which it had so recently begun to emerge. They'd seen their attempt fail, and my comrades of the barricades ascend to power. They'd watched me saunter through the halls of Lubyanka, accoutred as a legitimate representative of state commissions investigating the KGB's role in staging the flubbed coup.

Somehow, the Chekists decided that I had a say over their fates. They rushed to provide me with documents and to rat on each other, looking me sincerely in the eye all the while. And I began to understand truly that the power of the political police rested squarely on the absence of our resistance, on our passivity and fear. Theirs is a coward's ideology, nervously dependent on shadowing and spying and trusting no one. Ultimately, the years of looking over their shoulders cripple them; they fall apart the moment their "monolithic unity" is breached. Individually, alone, they are not wolves, but jackals. With Kryuchkov locked up, his loyal KGB officers vented their disdain. "He's hung us all out to dry," could be heard in every corner of Lubyanka.

If either Gorbachev or Yeltsin had been bold enough to dismantle the KGB during the autumn of 1991, he'd have met little resistance from the Chekists. But Gorbachev and Yeltsin were too busy jockeying for personal power.

My own authority didn't last long; a few months after my appointment, I was expelled from the commission for what amounted to insubordination: I'd argued that a resolution we were drafting should include a call for the KGB's end and a statement of the irreconcilability of true democracy with a political police. My proposal raised some influential hackles, and I was bounced. Not a good sport, they'd clearly concluded of me; and likely, therefore, to be an inconvenient witness.

It was the inevitable ending to what had started out as a unanimous assumption that we'd be recommending that the KGB be dismantled. Our draft paper to this effect had prompted *Rossiyskaya gazeta*'s article "The KGB Must be Liquidated." But the tirade this provoked from Yeltsin intimidated commission chairman Stepashin, and other topics began to replace the KGB: the tortuous political situation; the Ukraine and its announcement that it was nationalizing all KGB property within its borders ("stealing Russian property," as my colleagues chose to put it); the need to keep a close watch on Gorbachev and other former Communists.

It was then that I realized that the KGB was a necessary part of this political game, a dangerous weapon used by Yeltsin against Gorbachev, by Gorbachev against Yeltsin, by the Russian president against the speaker of parliament. Later that fall, I learned that government telephone lines in both the Russian White House and the Kremlin (property of the as-yet-extant Soviet Union) were still being tapped; reports on opponents' confidential conversations were still being delivered to the desks of various officials.

It's no surprise, given this climate, that within a week of my comment the commission, by a majority vote, politely asked for my resignation. One of its members offered a rationalization: "We're concerned for your life. It's dangerous being a member of a commission like this; you could get yourself killed." But, if anything, membership in such a high-profile commission might have offered me a bit of protection. Furthermore, the commission was just beginning to receive fascinating materials from the Chekist archives, and KGB brass, past and present, were testifying. Still, I wasn't terribly upset; I had always kept as my maxim the lines from Griboyedov's brilliant satirical comedy, *Woe from Wit*: "Deliver us most of all from sorrows, both the master's wrath and the master's love." Their action just doubled my investigative zeal: if they were hiding something, then there was something to look for.

The KGB itself didn't appear to be aware of conflicts with the commission; not that it would have made much difference, with near anarchy prevailing at Lubyanka. The formal power structure was still in place, but the bosses were too busy squabbling and spying on one another, picking fights and digging up *kompromat*, to get anything done. For once, ordinary Soviet citizens really could sleep soundly—the Cheka was otherwise engaged.

The Stepashin commission held court in the office of former counterintelligence chief, Gen. Grushko. On another floor, the KGB's own internal commission was creating a bizarre Chekist purgatory, with dirt flying everywhere, and not a pair of clean hands in sight. I was not permitted access there, but in the course of my strolls through Lubyanka, I managed to sneak a look at this commission's materials, not without some profit. (As the great Russian satirist Saltykov-Shchedrin said, "All of Russian literature has emerged because the bosses were looking the other way.") On the fourth floor, Vadim Bakatin presided over an empire whose power was shrinking like wool in the dryer. Already, the tastier morsels of the Soviet Union's state security—the department of wiretapping, the directorate of external surveillance—had been swallowed up by Russian state security. Yeltsin was stealing from Gorbachev's plate.

Bakatin found himself between a rock and a hard place. As former chief of the Interior Ministry, he was ill at ease among the

Chekists. He persistently told interviewers that he found the "ide-ology of Chekism" repugnant.

On the other hand, the Russian authorities did not favor him, considering—and rightly so—that he was Gorbachev's man. And even Bakatin himself felt quite uncomfortable in his new position. He realized that the Chekists were wrapping him around their little fingers every step of the way, withholding information from him or falsifying what information they did give. "How much control do you have over the KGB?" I once asked Bakatin. "Very little," he replied. "I am absolutely convinced that whatever the *komi-tetchiki* don't want me to know, I won't know."[12] I had the op-portunity to verify Bakatin's statement; his analyses were even too optimistic.

He hated rooting around in that "Chekist slime," as he himself said. "Once, they brought me two volumes of wiretap transcripts from the telephones of democratic leaders—they'd been in Bol-din's safe. It was disgusting, realizing how they'd spied on people in their kitchens or taped conversations between a wife and a husband, a son and a mother. I told my staff to take them away and not bring anything like it again."[13] Clearly, this was not stan-dard behavior for the chief of state security, and no way to earn respect from his underlings.

Meeting repeatedly with Bakatin that autumn, I was always amazed to find in him a basic sincerity and decency that I thought had been destroyed forever in Soviet Party leaders. Bakatin had a pretty good reputation; although he was not an advocate of in-dependence for the Baltic republics, as interior minister he had opposed the use of force in the Baltics, advocating dialogue rather than violence (his stand had cost him his post, as Gorbachev yielded to hard-liners and replaced Bakatin with future putschist Boris Pugo).

Bakatin was a product of the rural Russian intelligentsia; his mother was a village physician. Perhaps it was this background that made him stand out like an alien organism in the Chekist halls of Lubyanka. Perhaps some favorite uncle had been one of Stalin's victims—who knows? Whatever the reason, even while traversing the Soviet power structure, he had managed to keep his soul.

I was the one to tell him that his office—the office of the chairman of the USSR KGB—had been bugged by his own Chekists. I'd come to get a statement from him following Gorbachev's decree ordering the intelligence division to be separated off from the KGB. I tried to catch him off-guard with an unexpected question: "Why do you favor the appointment of Academician Primakov as chief of intelligence?"

"How do you know that?" Bakatin didn't bother to conceal his surprise.

"It's true, isn't it?"

"Only three people know: myself, of course, my aide, Vyacheslav Nikonov, and the stenographer." Bakatin pushed the intercom button and barked, "Tell Nikonov to get in here at once."

Nikonov had barely managed to shut the massive double door and taken a few steps toward the KGB chairman's desk before Bakatin thundered, "I'll fire you! Who did you mention Primakov to?" Nikonov, a soft-spoken, tactful historian who had previously worked at the Central Committee, threw up his hands.

"Don't take it out on him," I told Bakatin. "It's not Nikonov, and not your stenographer. And Primakov's appointment isn't a secret any more than *anything* you say in this office or over those phones is a secret." I nodded at the battery of government telephones on a little table at Bakatin's left. They included direct lines to Gorbachev and Yeltsin.

"How do you know?"

I shook my head.

"Well, anyway . . . the hell with them, the . . . bastards . . ." Bakatin, restraining himself with difficulty, clearly had something stronger in mind.

Across the street, in the old yellow building where thousands had perished in the dread cellars of Lubyanka, where each brick was a grave marker, a new order had taken over. The fifth-floor office that had belonged to Kryuchkov's first deputy now housed the head of what was then called the Russian KGB (now called the Federal Security Agency), Lt. Gen. Viktor Ivanenko.

The Federal Security Agency had been created in the spring of 1991 at Yeltsin's behest. Until the coup, however, it had been more mirage than reality: a chief, two deputies, and twenty officers. But, by December 1991, Lt. Gen. Ivanenko had under his command twenty thousand regional directorate officers in the Russian provinces, plus another twenty-two thousand Chekists in Moscow.[14]

Chekists were comfortable with Ivanenko; he was one of theirs, having started out as an ordinary operative in Tyumen and worked his way up to the Inspectorate at Moscow Center. He was not known as a liberal, nor had he proposed anything so radical as the dismantling of state security, but he was willing to talk about reform, and he spoke of the new KGB as a bastion of Russia's new government system. His colleagues assumed that sooner or later his close relationship with Russia's leaders, including Yeltsin (he'd spent the entire three days of the coup together with Yeltsin's people in the besieged White House), would assure Ivanenko of the top security post. Bakatin would have to go.

When, on December 19, 1991, Yeltsin dismissed both Bakatin and Ivanenko with one decree, Ivanenko was devastated. "They betrayed me" was his only comment. The rumor sped through the corridors of power that Ivanenko had attempted to grab more authority for himself, but it wasn't true. The reason for his dismissal was far more mundane: having come into possession of materials exposing corruption among newly appointed Russian government officials, including then Interior Minister Barannikov (a close friend of Yeltsin's) and Deputy Interior Minister Dunayev, Ivanenko naïvely went to the top with his discoveries—only to be made the scapegoat.

The position shared for a time by Ivanenko and Bakatin was

freed for Yeltsin's choice, Gen. Viktor Barannikov. For chairman of state security, Yeltsin had wanted not just his own man, but someone personally close to him. He would live to regret it.

By now, the reader is well aware that there had never been any real question of disbanding the Committee for State Security. Oh, a bit of patching had to be done, not so much for the benefit of the Russian public, which was much too busy looking for bread (that hungry autumn, there wasn't a loaf left by noon), as to dazzle the West. And it worked.

So what did this "repair job" consist of? The KGB had been one big (and moderately happy) family, living together in reasonable harmony, its essential unity unthreatened by occasional squabbles. Now, after the coup, the leader was removed, names were changed all around, and new signs were to be hung over the door to each room.

The FCD changed its name, first to Central Intelligence Service (CIS), and then, after the collapse of the Soviet Union, to the Russian Intelligence Service. At the head of Intelligence was Academician Primakov, sixty-two, who'd previously been adviser to Gorbachev after stints as director of the Institute of Oriental Studies and the Institute of the World Economy and International Relations (IMEMO) of the USSR Academy of Sciences.

Although his academic reputation rested on his articles and books on the "third way," the theory that Third World countries are developing according to a model that lies somewhere between "capitalism" and "socialism," Primakov was better known internationally as a "friend of Baghdad," in close touch with the Iraqi dictator Saddam Hussein.[15]

The intelligence staff gave Primakov a rather chilly welcome, assuming he'd be only a temporary figure. But they were mistaken: Primakov has become one of the most influential people in the country in a variety of fields, including intelligence. The latter was not a new game to him; according to his colleagues, "Maxim" (his code name) was recruited by the Chekists back in the late 1950s, and began to cooperate actively with intelligence in 1965 as a Middle East correspondent for *Pravda*.[16] At his first press conference as chief of foreign intelligence, Primakov publicly denied any affiliation with the KGB, although he hinted that he was "not completely a novice."[17] (Reproving me for breaking the story that he'd done courier service for the KGB, he scoffed: "You really are naïve, Zhenya. No one who wanted to work abroad got away without some contact with the organs.")

Primakov promised that intelligence would no longer use Soviet news bureaus abroad as covers. The news services were delighted to think that they'd finally be able to fill their offices with real correspondents instead of hoping that they'd be left two or three slots for full-time journalists. No more giving away half, even all of their salary money to FCD agents . . . But who were the "civilians" who immediately began showing up at newspaper offices, claiming that intelligence was being "downsized" and offering their aid as press consultants? I tried without success to convince the new editor-in-chief of *Moscow News* that employing such sources made the paper an easy target for disinformation or use as espionage cover. The three lieutenant colonels who'd constituted themselves *MN*'s new "department of political investigation" were notably unforthcoming about their pasts and connections, preferring to sign their articles, "political commentator." Primakov, forced by budget cuts to reduce his staff, assiduously searched out such berths for them, to the point that in May 1992 I felt obligated to leave the paper. I valued my reputation; I could not work alongside Chekists. I later learned that Primakov had offered to subsidize three of one influential paper's overseas bureaus if they would reserve one correspondent's position as intelligence "cover." Such deals were not new: in 1990, the Central Committee approved the replacement of correspondents for *Rabochnaya tribuna* [Workers' Tribune] in Austria and Poland with KGB officers; in 1991, a similar deal was worked out for *Komsomolskaya pravda*'s Canada bureau.

As the security renaming game proceeded, what was briefly called the MSB (*Mezhrespublikanskaya sluzhba bezopasnosti*, the Interrepublic Security Service) became the Ministry of Security of Russia (MBR). The MBR contained the counterintelligence chief directorates and their subordinate divisions as well as the directorate to combat organized crime; an enormous Operations and Technology Directorate of top-notch scientific and engineering personnel, the "bunker" directorate, the department that coordinated special services of allies, and so on.

The new security configuration also included the Committee to Protect State Borders (the Border Guards) and the Federal Agency of Government Communications and Information, which united the directorate for government communications, the encryption departments of the Eighth Directorate (which not only guarded channels of information, but also controlled them), and the Sixteenth Directorate (electronic stations for surveillance and communications interception; so-called Sigint).

The great "transformation" of the KGB was turning out to be mostly cosmetic. For example, joint operations of counterintelligence and specialists from the Eighth Chief Directorate previously had required only mutual agreement among the directors. Now "we write papers and carry them to the next floor or the next building entrance" for written approval, Chekists explained; a mere telephone OK no longer sufficed.

Some bosses were replaced by their former deputies; a number of others survived the purge without incident. "I was conservative in the matter of replacing the directors," Vadim Bakatin admitted to me.[18]

Bakatin's successors generally hewed to this line, although some changes did take place. Under Barannikov, Gen. Kishin, who'd not long before succeeded his former boss as head of counterintelligence, lost his job when his underlings were discovered to be making their own transition to the free market—renting out agency safe houses for hard currency. (Needless to say, the money went straight into their pockets.)[19]

Those of pension age were sent into retirement. Anyone whose loyalty to the KGB was in question was fired or forced to resign. Col. Rubanov, who had fought against excessive secrecy regulations, was forced to leave. Lt. Col. Kichikhin, who opposed his colleagues during the first day of the coup, was dismissed, as was similarly minded Col. Rogozin of the Karelia KGB. Mayboroda and Ilkevich, officers of military counterintelligence, were dismissed for having resigned from the Party in protest on August 19. "We don't need any dissidents in the KGB," they were told.[20] The era of democracy was over. The middle ranks, the colonels and lieutenant colonels who set the whole tone of the KGB, remained in place; in fact, they cooperated in setting up a Public Committee to Protect State Security, a kind of unofficial "trade union" to insulate the Chekists from the whims of the new authorities.[21] In a not unsuccessful attempt to influence their colleagues, they also organized an underground center for both domestic and internal KGB situational analyses.[22]

There were some exceptions to this retrenchment. Over the past few years, various private detective bureaus, agencies to protect commercial secrets and information, personal security services, and research departments for major private companies created by former Chekists have begun to spring up like mushrooms after the rain. I suppose we can hope that they won't rush to cede their new businesses to future seekers after power, but they are a small drop in a huge ocean. For the most part, the security people go on doing what they were doing before, albeit with decreasing enthusiasm as the atmosphere becomes more chaotic. Their time will come, they know.

But rather than speculate, I will cite the explanation offered by Andrei Oligov, the former head of the Center for Public Liaison of the former Federal Security Agency, as to why the signs over the doors of the KGB's directorates had to be changed: "In order to quell public unease and prevent threats of reprisal against KGB officers, destruction of buildings, and theft of file documents, a decision has been made to announce that the Committee will be rapidly dismantled and separated into several independent agencies."[23]

In an interview with me, Bakatin explained: "Everyone says Bakatin destroyed the KGB system. For God's sake, that's not true—go to Kazakhstan and you'll see; not a single hair of a single officer's head has fallen. Or go to Kyrgyzstan—everything's stayed just the way it was. Same in the Moscow Directorate, and the Kemerovo Directorate . . . All the structures remained the same."[*24]

A dispassionate look at the post–August 1991 situation will show why such a "dismantling" was doomed to failure. The "state within a state" and the state without were like Siamese twins with a single set of vital organs. And yet, properly conducted, this process might have been a first step toward destroying the monster. If strict parliamentary oversight had been established, along with judicial review of operational and investigative activity, and if the newly formed Chekist agencies had been subordinated to other government agencies, real change might have been possible. But nothing of the sort happened.

"How fast could the dismantled KGB reunite into a single force?" I asked a GRU officer who was trying to persuade me that the old Chekist clan was coming apart.

"Instantly," he replied.

In December 1991, Boris Yeltsin surprised everyone by signing the Decree on the Formation of the Ministries of Security and Internal Affairs, which united the KGB and the police in one agency. People of the older generation noted immediately that Yeltsin was not

---

* Bakatin's comment came two weeks after David Wise's article "Closing Down the KGB" was published in The New York Times Magazine—Author.

being particularly original; secret police chief Lavrenty Beria had united these institutions in 1953, within twenty-four hours of Stalin's death. Nikita Khrushchev had separated these bodies of armed specialists in conspiracy. "History proves that when the agencies of security and the police are united, repressions always begin," wrote democratic newspapers at the time.[25]

But before long it became clear that this was just a tactical move on the part of Yeltsin, who was impatient with Bakatin (the Chekists hated Bakatin, and Yeltsin did not want to protect him) and Ivanenko, who had been too hasty in exposing corruption. Yeltsin's real purpose, as we have seen, was to free up the position of security chairman for his personal favorite, General Viktor Barannikov.

Poor Bakatin; he was the only decent person ever to have headed that criminal organization. And with Ivanenko's Federal Security Agency disbanded, the hope that one Chekist agency would monitor the other vanished; and, with it, our best chance for a respite from secret service attention.

The Constitutional Court declared Yeltsin's decree unlawful, which discouraged the President not at all; he had his man in place, which was all he'd ever really cared about.

Barannikov was greeted coolly—"Now we'll all get police whistles . . ." Relations between the KGB and the police had long been tense. The *komitetchiki* regarded police as lower-class thugs (not without reason: the police were known to be corrupt and closely linked to the criminal underworld). Under Kryuchkov, bribe-taking at the KGB had been kept to a minimum, although nobody was about to call the Chekists upstanding citizens. The police feared state security because they knew that their every move was watched by Directorate V of the KGB's military counterintelligence. In fact, about the only good KGB officers could see in Barannikov's appointment was that they'd get rid of Bakatin.

The last straw for the KGB officers had come when Bakatin handed over to the U.S. ambassador in Moscow blueprints for bugs the KGB had planted in the new American embassy building in the mid-1970s.[26] American intelligence agencies no doubt treated the blueprints with due skepticism. But the KGB regarded Bakatin's action as treason.

The criticisms leveled against Bakatin offer some useful insight into how special services (American secret agents, too, I imagine) go about bugging and spying:

There were not only surveillance devices in the American embassy, that is, microphones, but also special technology enabling us to monitor the electronic machines in the embassy, to tape information from computers, faxes, and so on. These same devices helped our agents working in the embassy. Special sensors were built into the steel framework of the construction panels. Without an exact blueprint, it would be difficult, if not impossible, to find such devices. Complex methods are used for this—high-frequency lasers and ultrasound tomography among others—to enable an investigator to obtain an electronic image on a computer. But, without the blueprints, it is hard to understand whether the images are intelligence equipment or seams and flaws in the building's framework. No wonder it costs $100 per cubic meter on the international market to clean intelligence equipment out of a building. For stripping government buildings like the embassy, the budget would be much greater. That is why the Americans figured that it was cheaper to raze the new embassy building than to try to clean it out. But now that they have the blueprints and know roughly where the bugs are located, the Americans can correlate the image on the computer screen with an actual technical device. And that means they can develop a methodology to detect Soviet espionage equipment (which, as we may surmise, may be planted elsewhere besides the American embassy).

"Would the Americans be able to use the new embassy building after a proper cleaning?" I asked my sources, who included specialists from the GRU's science and technology division.

"Yes, they might . . . but it's unlikely. After all, we know that in addition to the electronic bugs, they put in so-called passive devices—metallic corners hidden within the construction of the building that can be induced to 'talk' by means of distant X rays or by using the natural radioactive background."

These sources also noted that some of the panels containing bugs were imported from Finland. Presumably, the Americans would be able to find out which factory "stuffed" these panels, and determine who was helping the Soviets; thus, Bakatin had exposed these firms to reprisals from Western intelligence agencies. Equally competent sources insisted that the bugs had been installed after the panels reached Soviet territory: the trains and tractor-trailers hauling the panels had been held up at some remote junction, while specialists from counterintelligence worked with the sensitive load.[27]

I've already mentioned my aversion to spy novels, so I will stop here. I'll just add that Bakatin didn't decide alone to give the blueprint to Ambassador Robert Straus; both Gorbachev and Yeltsin certainly approved.[28] But in fine Soviet tradition, they kept their mouths shut and let him take the blame.

As soon as Viktor Barannikov took over the reins of security, all talk of "dismantling" the KGB came to a halt. At one of his first organizational meetings, the new minister asserted that security forces and the army were the "only real forces that can protect reforms in Russia. You cannot name a single structure in the Russian state mechanism that has such potential. The people are tired from all of this perestroika [reconstruction] and *nedostroika* [uncompleted construction]. Our trouble is that too much has been left to run its own course," he told his employees, who had despaired of ever again hearing such speeches.[29]

The doors of the KGB slammed shut once again. Parliamentary

oversight commissions, including the one I'd been a member of, ceased to exist.

In the spring of 1992, I went to see what would happen if I tried to reenter those so recently wide-open doors of Lubyanka. I came bearing an imposing document from the Supreme Soviet Presidium that declared me a consultant to a parliamentary commission to investigate KGB activity and requested that I be allowed to view state security files. The lieutenant guarding the entrance I'd chosen turned the paper over and over in his hands, then called his bosses, who called their bosses; and so on up the line. Several minutes later, they reported back: "There is no order to let you in."

"To whom does the Ministry of Security report?" I asked the lieutenant.

"To the Supreme Soviet of the Russian Federation," he replied with military brusqueness.

"Do you see here the seal of the Supreme Soviet and the signature of the chairman's deputy? Aren't you obligated to admit me?"

"That's true," he said, embarrassed. "But there are no orders."

Just for the hell of it, I went around to five other entrances to the KGB building. The same dialogue was repeated. At the last doorway, they were not so polite as they had been at the first; rather stern, in fact.

Shortly thereafter, my letter lost any power it might have had. Ruslan Khasbulatov, then chairman of the Russian Supreme Soviet, took it upon himself to close down the KGB investigation commission. In truth, he had long been unhappy with the commission's activities; and then the head of the Russian Orthodox Church, Patriarch Aleksy, came to visit him. It seems that through the commission's efforts, the patriarch had been exposed as an agent (code-named "Drozdov") of the KGB, who'd even been nominated for a KGB medal. What Speaker Khasbulatov and Patriarch Aleksy said to each other behind closed doors remained a secret, but afterward, Khasbulatov ordered the commission to disband and turn in its documents, and that was the end of that.

In April 1992, we learned that the Committee on Border Troops—the two hundred thousand-strong Border Guard whose charter also allows for them to be used to suppress unrest inside the country—had been reintegrated into the KGB.

Next, the special assignment (*spetsnaz*) groups that had been made directly subordinate to the President were returned to their original home at state security, as were the special KGB divisions that had been transferred to the Ministry of Defense after the coup.

In July 1992, Sergei Shakhrai (out of favor then as now, but deputy prime minister in the interim) told reporters that the Federal Agency of Government Communications and Information would soon be returned to the KGB. The press kicked up a huge fuss, but the *komitetchiki* shrugged: "What difference does it make if there's a resolution or not, we'll just go on working as we did under Kryuchkov, anyway."[30]

They were happy; I can understand that. But I'm furious. I'm furious at my hopes and illusions. The new authorities—I can't bring myself to call them "democrats"—lost a historic opportunity to abolish the political police without bloodshed or resistance. Why didn't they seize the moment?

More than any other perestroika-era politician, Boris Yeltsin had suffered at the hands of the Chekists. They had tried to discredit and ruin him—at home and, especially, in the West. They lay in wait for him at every turn, bugging his sauna, his home, his office, the bedrooms of his girlfriends, even recruiting women with whom he had been intimate. What stopped him from deciding to liquidate the political police? He'd spent his life in the upper echelons of Soviet power; he knew that the KGB was a force to conjure with. Was he afraid? Possibly. Did the euphoria of the August victory make him careless? That, too, is plausible. But I think the main reason lies in the mentality of a Party bureaucrat: he simply could not imagine a government structure in which the KGB was absent. Many of my contacts told me that he was a victim of that old delusion of new regimes: under the old regime—the bad guys, Gorbachev, Brezhnev, Andropov, and all the rest—the KGB was bad; but under the new (good) guy, Yeltsin, the KGB would be good. He'd be able to keep them in line; he'd take care of it personally.[31] What a tragic mistake of judgment that was . . .

In April 1993, Kirsan Ilyumzhinov, the newly reelected thirty-one-year-old president of the tiny Russian autonomous republic of Kalmykia, announced that he was abolishing his republic's secret police. "We have no spies," he said. The Russian authorities, incensed, leaned on the novice politician until he was forced to compromise and form a department of state security within the Interior Ministry.[32] Need I say more?

What about the political police? Now that the Central Committee has been shut down and the KGB's ideological counterintelligence has been eliminated, is it merely a thing of the past? Hardly.

"There will always be political police," one of the Russian KGB press center spokesman proclaimed back in that blessed autumn of 1991.[33] He wasn't kidding.

I went to visit Yevgeny Savostyanov, the new director of the Moscow Chekists and the new deputy minister of state security, as if he were an old and good friend. Back when I was working on the Boyarsky story, Savostyanov, who was then on the staff of the same Institute for Earth Core Exploration at the USSR Academy of Sciences where Boyarsky was professor, did a lot to help me organize the meeting where Boyarsky got his due.

After that, we somehow lost touch with one another. I heard that Savostyanov had become co-chairman of the liberal "Scientists for Democracy" movement that successfully fought the conservative Academy of Sciences to nominate Andrei Sakharov for parliament. Savostyanov went on to become one of the organizers of Democratic Russia, left science, and became involved in politics. Eventually, he became an aide to the first democratic mayor of

Moscow, Gavriil Popov, who immediately after the coup recommended him to the KGB.

We started off by speaking about Boyarsky. Savostyanov told me that soon after he'd started his new job, he was invited to a meeting of veteran Chekists. "I see Boyarsky about thirty feet away, coming toward me with his hand outstretched. I say to him, Vladimir Ananyevich, I'm sorry, but I won't shake your hand. Boyarsky's not at all embarrassed."

We spoke about how his democrat friends had reacted to his appointment to the KGB. (I should explain that in Russian intelligentsia circles—both in old tsarist Russia and to a lesser extent in Soviet Russia—service in the secret police, the Tsar's *okhrana* or the KGB, was considered dishonorable. If people did go to work for them, it was under coercion; in prerevolutionary times, the doors of decent homes were usually closed to such people.) Savostyanov replied that he himself had been taken aback at the idea, but hadn't hesitated for long. "Somebody has to clean out the stables."[34]

Soon after he had settled into his new office, he told me, he'd asked his staff to bring him some ideological counterintelligence files: like any normal Soviet person, he was curious to see if his own name was in there. He didn't find it; everything regarding the Democratic Russia movement had been whited out. Savostyanov asked the Chekists why they'd been spying on the democrats. To prevent the consolidation of extremist forces, came the stock response.

Savostyanov and I got a good laugh out of that one. You could accuse the democrats of just about anything but consolidation; they spent most of their time fighting each other.

Asked about informers, Savostyanov made a wry face and said that he preferred to call them "secret helpers." I raised my eyebrows at his little emendation; after all, we shared the same views. But then I thought, Well, it's his office, he's probably saying that for the benefit of the hidden microphones. But Savostyanov went on to say that he'd sent a memo to the Mayor's office recommending that prospective mayoral office employees or candidates for public office be required to submit to a background check that would screen out former KGB collaborators. The Mayor's office hadn't responded, probably because such a regulation would have forced too many people to step down. Savostyanov had chosen to let the matter drop.

"Well, what about the Fifth Service?" I asked Savostyanov. In Moscow, as elsewhere, ideological counterintelligence had the largest staff of any of the KGB's divisions.

"It's working," he replied.

"What do you mean, working? Ideological counterintelligence was supposed to be abolished," I said in surprise.

Savostyanov clammed up.

"So, you mean it's still there?" I queried.

"It depends on the assignments the authorities give to the directorate," he replied.

What the authorities had asked it to do was to keep an eye on Communists. And so, the same people who only yesterday had been battling anti-Communists and dissidents now began performing "thorough analysis" on their former Party comrades.

Some of them balked, however. One, called in by Savostyanov to be offered a promotion, asked what the new job was. "Organizing surveillance over members of the CPSU." "I'm a Communist by conviction," the Chekist answered. "I've never been involved in that sort of dirty job, and I don't intend to begin now." He quit state security, probably not the only one to do so. (A third individual, who'd overheard the exchange, told me about it, but Savostyanov confirmed the account.)[35]

No, I'm not so naïve as to believe that the millions of former Party members have simply disappeared, or that the bureaucratic structure within which they operated has dwindled away. Now that an autumn 1992 Constitutional Court ruling has overturned Yeltsin's November 6, 1991, decree banning the Party, the CPSU undoubtedly will make every attempt to regain power (albeit under a new name, the Union of Communist Parties—according to former Politburo member Yegor Ligachev, some six hundred thousand-strong by the summer of 1993).[36]

I have never been a member of the CPSU, or any other party, on principle; but what guarantee do I have that a KGB that shadows Communist bureaucrats suspected of breaking state constitutional order will not go after me on the same grounds? What's to stop them from intercepting my mail, bugging my telephones, shadowing me on the street? What right does state security have to spy on communists? Have they reason to suspect a terrorist act or a coup attempt?

"Now they all say they were against the coup, against Marxism-Leninism, that they are all pro-market, for pluralism and democracy," said Bakatin of his new colleagues in the KGB. "But in reality?" I asked. "It is vital that we de-ideologize state security," Bakatin replied. "Otherwise, we'll have the Socialists, if they come to power, persecuting, say, the Christian Democrats. . . . But no one can force people to forgo ideology, I can't . . . they have to make that decision for themselves." I heard no optimism in his voice.[37]

I ended my article on Savostyanov with the observation: "Only time will tell whether Savostyanov will instill a democratic mentality in the KGB, or the KGB will infuse him with their own mentality."

When we met again six months later, in the spring of 1992, he was a changed man. On vacation at a KGB spa outside Moscow, he clearly reveled in his newfound power, in the bodyguards and plainclothes Chekists at his beck and call. Nothing remained of Savostyanov's former candor. "We don't follow people any more. Ideological counterintelligence is gone," he said.

"Where are the Fifth's officers working now?" I asked.

"All over, but mainly in the Directorate to Combat Terrorism."[38] That was true enough: Barannikov, newly appointed minister of state security, had ordered that ideological counterintelligence be given the name of one of its subdepartments, the Directorate to Combat Terrorism. Once again, a name had been eliminated, but functions had been retained.

"Considering all the crime and chaos in our country, I hope to God we don't end up on the Chekists' list of potential terrorists who require stringent surveillance," I said. "You know—journalists who criticize the new authorities, that sort of thing. Doesn't it worry you?"

"Don't be so dramatic. I *told* you, we can't force anyone to do shadowing today," Savostyanov answered.

And I realized he'd been co-opted.

The day before, I had interviewed the liberal legislator and onetime Yeltsin adviser, Galina Starovoitova, who described how, during the Gorbachev era, the *komitetchiki* had beaten her husband, bugged her telephone, and tailed her constantly. "Once, I went to Yeltsin and complained about this completely unpardonable surveillance. I came out of the office and ran smack into KGB Chairman Kryuchkov. He rushed off, trying to avoid me, but I yelled after him, 'Vladimir Alexandrovich, do you know your guys have a tail on me?' Completely unembarrassed, he looked me straight in the eye, and without batting an eyelash, said, 'Galina Vasilyevna, what are you talking about? Our orders don't permit that. You're a people's deputy of Russia, a people's deputy of the Soviet Union, you have parliamentary immunity. We don't do such things.' "

"And now?" I asked Starovoitova.

"I recently asked Barannikov that same question," she said. "Thank God, I'm not a complete innocent; I can feel when I'm being bugged; I can hear them on the Kremlin *vertushka* and on my home phone. Barannikov and I were once seated next to each other at a meeting with Yeltsin. So I asked him, and he smiled, and said, 'Who knows? Maybe they *are* wiretapping you.' "[39]

Galina Starovoitova was the only one of Yeltsin's close aides who was not a member of the CPSU.

I've heard of many more cases of the shadowing that we "can't force anyone to do." In spring 1992, a man called me at the office. I didn't recognize his voice. "Is this Yevgenia Albats?" "Yes." "Can you go to another telephone, farther away from your office?" "Yes. But what's this all about?" "I'll explain when I call back."

He sounded like a military man. I gave him the telephone number of the reception desk.

"I'm a KGB officer," he said rather nervously when he called back. "I need to meet with you right away."

"First of all, explain why we can't talk on my telephone."

"Both your telephone and your office are under audio surveillance," he replied.

So we met. He turned out to be an officer of the Department to Combat Organized Crime. He wouldn't even enter my office; standing in the doorway, he pointed toward the "bugs"—the little microphones supposedly installed in various places. Apparently, they could even eavesdrop through the television set.

"Are you sure?" I asked.

He looked at me disdainfully. "I install these things myself. By the way, my bosses found out that I called you to arrange a meeting."

"What's the point of spending money on bugging my office when I put it all in the newspaper?"

"Your sources; they need to know your sources in the KGB. Barannikov even said at a meeting that the KGB is spawning too many traitors: unauthorized contacts with the press will be stopped, and traitors will be harshly punished."

I arranged immediately to tell my story on Central Television. On the air, I asked Minister Barannikov not to waste taxpayers' money on bugging my telephones. I report everything I learn about the KGB to my readers, I explained; I hide nothing. As for my sources, I protect them—I have a lot of experience in that, and the KGB can't hang a microphone on every tree.

But who am I kidding? What's my experience compared with the KGB's decades of training in political policing?

After my television appearance, the KGB's Public Liaison Center contacted the station, claiming that I was not under surveillance. Meanwhile, a colleague of mine was summoned to Lubyanka. A fresh-faced investigator spent several hours reciting what my colleague had done for the last two months, whom he had met, which women—besides his wife—he had slept with, and what he'd discussed with his fellow employees at the newspaper. The KGB guy had the details down cold: "as you said in Albats' office . . . what you reported to Gevorkyan . . ." My colleague, who wrote on business matters and had never done any stories on the KGB, was scared out of his wits. Since then, my office had become repugnant to me; I'm no exhibitionist.

More recently, in August 1993, my *Izvestia* colleague Irina D. received a telephone call from Lubyanka. The man calling was polite, even considerate. "I'm calling from the Ministry of Security of Russia; I'm sorry to disturb you. My name is Alexander Sergeyevich. I have something to discuss with you, preferably not over the telephone. Could you come in to our office for a talk?" Taken aback, she asked, "Why?" She'd never written about the KGB, never had anything to do with the Chekists, wasn't a member of any terrorist or unlawful organization, had never even entertained a journalistic interest in such organizations. Alexander Sergeyevich replied, "I think it will be interesting for both of us."

She could have refused to go; if the Chekists really wanted to see her, they were supposed to send an official summons. Nevertheless, she decided to go. What would happen to her if she *didn't* go, she wondered . . .

A pass was waiting for her; she was met at the door and escorted to an office.

Alexander Sergeyevich (he didn't give his last name, and she didn't ask) turned out to be a very nice young man. He asked after her parents and her child, and then began to talk about people she had met in recent months, prominent figures whom she had interviewed. He knew what she'd talked to them about, where they'd been . . . whether she'd spent the night with them. "You know, we all probably have things in our lives that we'd rather not have discussed," she said to me later. "That's the sort of stuff they knew about, that they talked about to me."

At first, she was curious whether they'd bugged only her office telephone, or perhaps her home phone as well. Then, she began to feel terrible.

What did the Chekists want from her? Nothing special; just access to information beyond what had appeared in the newspaper interviews or articles; to learn details of the lives, habits, weaknesses, or proclivities of public figures with whom she'd had contact. The Chekists wanted information, including compromising material, that would enable them to approach people in whom they were interested (including those whom they wanted to recruit); information they could use, if necessary, to intimidate people—what the political police, the KGB, has always wanted to know in our country.

Irina refused to give any information, but the Chekist refused to take no for an answer. "Take your time, think it over," Alexander Sergeyevich advised her, almost paternally. "We'll be in touch."

She emerged from Lubyanka feeling thoroughly besmirched. "I felt as if I didn't take a shower immediately, I would be sick," she told me.

A month later, Alexander Sergeyevich called her again. "Don't worry, we no longer have any interest in you," he assured her.

But what was it all for? Why was the KGB eavesdropping on journalists, even ones whose sources were of no interest? Why bug the conversations of Sergei Kovalyov, the prominent dissident and former political prisoner, and chairman of the parliamentary Committee on Human Rights?[40] Or bug the office of Konstantin Borovoy, director of the Russian Commodities Exchange? In the summer of 1993, the Exchange's security service discovered the devices in a routine sweep of the premises.[41]

Why shadow people when the clash between the Communists and democrats is over and newspapers are filled with stories that would have landed you in labor camp in the old days?

And why is it that in my country I can't simply gab on the phone as I could in Cambridge, Massachusetts? (It doesn't take long to get used to such luxuries.) As soon as the conversation leads to any subject except our children, people say, "Let's not get into that over the phone." It's just like the old days—and I don't mean the Gorbachev years, but the Brezhnev era.[42]

The answer to all of these rhetorical questions is the same: so long as there are political police in the country, they will always find work for themselves.

How will they keep busy? First, the government will always "request information" (that's the standard euphemism) about its political opponents. It wasn't necessarily the members of the Union of Communist Parties that the new government was interested in; maybe it was Mikhail Gorbachev.

Second, there is a power struggle going on, President vs. parliament, and vice versa; Rutskoi vs. Yeltsin, and vice versa; speaker of parliament vs. contentious parliamentary committee chairmen . . . Each side does whatever it can to gather *kompromat* by shamelessly tapping telephones or intercepting correspondence. Naturally, this information-gathering is done with the help of state security, regardless of the fact that this is absolutely illegal even in our country—only the KGB has technology capable of tapping into government communications lines.[43]

And so, the Chekists are unleashed. The government becomes dependent on them. This is bad enough in itself; but it also prompts the government to look the other way when the Chekists start bugging people at their own discretion. With all that's been written about the KGB, I still haven't heard of a single Chekist ever being punished for covert surveillance of any citizen.

Chekists occasionally do get burned. Viktor Barannikov, who for years had survived rumors of corruption, finally took a fall in August 1993. Apparently, Barannikov (who in his day had caught various other ministers red-handed) had been concealing the fact that nine fur coats, valued at $80,000, had been purchased abroad for his wife by the Canadian-Swiss firm Seabeco, which at the time was looking for advantageous contracts in Russia. (The KGB had

had a hand in founding this firm during the perestroika era.) Yet, according to information from well-placed sources, it was neither his Swiss bank account nor his wife's fondness for furs that led to his dismissal. Barannikov apparently had switched his loyalty from Yeltsin to Ruslan Khasbulatov, former speaker of parliament and a fierce opponent of Yeltsin. Barannikov's aides collected unfavorable material on people close to Yeltsin, as well as on Yeltsin himself, and sent it to the chairman of the Supreme Soviet. Some third party (name unknown, but clearly a member of the presidential team) learned of this, enlisted Chekist aid in getting a peek at the materials, and then reported to the President.[44]

Finally, the KGB shows no sign of giving up such routine information-gathering as the monitoring of public opinion "for a rainy day." Who knows, the government might change, and then these reports will come in handy . . . There may even be a market for them today . . .

In other words, abuse runs rampant. The Chekists consider themselves completely above the law. Worse, they tend to believe they are their homeland's salvation, the only voice of authority amidst the political and economic chaos that has engulfed the country. Nor is this far from the truth. It's no wonder that by July 1993, MB [Ministry of Security] directors were ordering provincial offices to shore up the faltering government by "encouraging advancement of the course of socioeconomic reforms," "neutralizing anticonstitutional attempts to overthrow the government," and keeping "political extremists" under surveillance."[45] (Just business as usual.) Vladimir Kryuchkov had issued a similar order expanding the KGB's constitutional rights. And it all ended with tanks, in August 1991.

The first sign that the KGB was regaining its strength came in the fall of 1992. At 7:00 a.m. on October 22, officers searched the apartments of two Moscow chemists, Lev Fyodorov and Vil Mirzoyanov. The Chekists themselves weren't entirely sure what they were looking for, so they went through everything—books, papers, scientific articles filled with indecipherable formulas, and letters. Both scientists were then taken to Lubyanka for questioning. Fyodorov, who was then released, later figured in the case as a witness. Mirzoyanov was held and charged under Art. 75 of the Penal Code, "divulging state secrets," and sent to Lefortovo Prison, where he spent eleven days. *Moscow News* was also searched on October 22, and science editor Leonard Nikishin was summoned to Lubyanka for questioning.

The reason for this operation was a *Moscow News* story by Fyodorov and Mirzoyanov entitled "Poisoned Politics," which revealed that despite agreements with the U.S. on chemical weapons disarmament, Russia had not suspended preparation for third-generation chemical warfare.[46] In violation of the Geneva Convention, work was continuing on production of internationally banned binary weapons. This work undermined Russia's international reputation; not only did the new Russia, like the old Soviet Union, violate its own agreements, but it was also taking money received from the West that was earmarked for defense conversion and investing it instead in the development of a chemical warfare facility. Furthermore, chemical weapons testing posed a serious environmental threat to Russia. Chemical factories were located in cities with large, dense populations (in Moscow alone, there were five). Moscow was also the site of the formerly top secret State Scientific Research Institute of Organic Chemistry and Technology (GOSNIIOKhT), which recent inspection had revealed to house an inadequately monitored store of extremely dangerous toxic substances.[47]

Predictably, the article provoked a furious reaction from generals in the military-industrial complex, especially the military-chemical facility's director, Gen. Kuntsevich. Particularly galling was the fact that the authors were prominent scientists; Mirzoyanov, in fact, was head of the technology counterintelligence department of the Institute of Organic Chemistry and Technology. After a lifetime spent keeping the secrets of Soviet chemical warfare, Mirzoyanov, checking to see if Western intelligence would be able to determine what toxins the Russians were manufacturing, had taken air and water samples near a chemical factory in Volgograd. To his horror, the levels were toxic for all living creatures, eighty times higher than the maximum safe concentration. Within a year, Mirzoyanov had quit the Party and joined the Democratic Russia movement.

Not one of the formulas or names of poisonous substances in the *Moscow News* article was new to the Soviet press, nor were locations of Soviet (now Russian) chemical weapons testing sites revealed. Expert testimony prepared for the KGB by three scientists who worked at the Institute of Chemistry under Gen. Kuntsevich contained a list of state secrets "exposed" by Fyodorov and Mirzoyanov; these included the existence of binary weapons and the testing grounds at Ust-Kut, which another Russian paper, *Trud* [Labor], had reported six months earlier. The real "state secret" revealed by Fyodorov and Mirzoyanov was that the generals had lied—and were still lying—to both the international community and their fellow citizens.

Furthermore, scientists had already published much of this information in another popular newspaper in September 1991, with no reaction from the authorities (precisely the reason the scientists had continued to sound the alarm).[48] Questioned why there had been no reaction, Capt. Viktor Shkarin, a KGB investigator, offered an astonishingly frank answer: "Yes, we knew about that article. But we didn't have our act together at the time; we didn't even know whether we'd continue to exist, whether or not we'd be dismantled."

They're not afraid any more.

Under pressure from the public and the press, Mirzoyanov was released from prison on his own recognizance after signing a statement that he would not leave town. The investigation dragged on for a year and a half, and five volumes of evidence were collected. In February 1994, the case was dropped with no judgment.

"The most frustrating thing," Fyodorov told me, "is that no one supported us—neither the parliament's Committee on Human Rights, nor political parties, nor the science and technology intelligentsia. It's just as it was before; they don't want to get involved with the military-industrial complex, which is as powerful as ever."

That's not quite true. Before, the KGB and MIC brought insubordinates into line through ideological means—if you said the wrong thing, you'd be accused of anti-Soviet activity and shipped off to labor camp. Now, punishment came in the form of financial blows: people fired from government work had no other way of making a living (including scientists who couldn't find a job in the West or who were barred from travel because of their knowledge of state secrets) and were reduced to utter poverty. With inflation rampant and the cost of living skyrocketing, they couldn't even feed their children.

As for parliament's hands-off stance, was that any surprise? Consider its record on security matters since the winter of 1992, when the Supreme Soviet announced that henceforth it would be monitoring the Ministry of Security. Scarcely had the announcement been made, when Sergei Stepashin, chairman of the parliamentary Committee on Defense and State Security, accepted the position of deputy minister of security and chairman of the St. Petersburg municipal KGB, while retaining his parliamentary post. Was he supposed to monitor himself? A year later, Stepashin left the St. Petersburg KGB and returned to Moscow. He was replaced by Col. Viktor Cherkesov, who even during the perestroika era had been notoriously fond of charging dissidents under the Penal Code's infamous Art. 70 ("anti-Soviet agitation and propaganda").

In March 1993, at the first in a series of international conferences on "The KGB: Yesterday, Today, and Tomorrow," Lt. Col. Nikolai Kuznetsov, then a member of the same Defense and State Security Committee, was asked to describe how he and his colleagues maintained oversight of state security. Kuznetsov's opening words—"As I am both a deputy and an officer of the Ministry of Security, assigned to work in the parliament"—were interrupted by hoots of laughter from an audience chock-full of dissidents who'd spent years in prisons and labor camps.

"So, is there oversight, or isn't there?" someone shouted from the back of the room. "There will be," replied Kuznetsov. "We're in the process of drafting a proposal for monitoring the organs of state security." Again, the audience roared. People at the conference knew very well that the Supreme Soviet was not allowed to oversee (or even to know) the KGB's budget, and thus lacked the most vital and effective means of supervising the secret service. It was the same story with the military-industrial complex: the parliament didn't know its budget either, and so could not monitor its expenditures.

The years since the August 1991 coup have proved that our victory at the walls of the Russian parliament lasted only a few days or, at best, months. The Party was defeated in that battle, but the other two structures of the oligarchy, the KGB and the MIC, regained their footing. And, to our misfortune, they are growing stronger every day.

On August 6, 1993, the parliament passed amendments to the Law on Organs of State Security, and Yeltsin signed them with unusual haste. These amendments granted the Chekists the right to conduct "operational investigative measures" (which usually include surveillance, wiretapping, and intercepting mail) without the warrant that previously was stipulated under criminal investigation law.

The KGB's hands had been untied.

Instead of the old "struggle against enemies of the people," or against "unlawful actions aimed at overthrowing the socialist state and social order," or "sabotage and profiteering," the KGB now commits its abuses in the name of the "struggle against corruption, drug dealing, and illegal weapons trade." The slogans may have changed, but the wholesale violation of human rights is sadly familiar.

In the months and years since August 1991 there have been regular predictions of another coup. We go to bed unsure what regime will be there when we wake up.

The country is in chaos. Government is paralyzed. Inflation is rampant: 5–7 percent per week or 20–30 percent per month. There are weeks when it jumps to 12 percent. One day you buy a loaf of bread for 75 rubles, and a week later it costs 130 rubles . . . or 300 rubles. Many predict that we haven't hit bottom yet. But how much worse can it get? Our buying power keeps diminishing, our falling wages mean less and less—if we even have a job—and unemployment is on the rise. Three-fourths of the country lives below the poverty line, and people are growing visibly poorer. Nevertheless, little more than half the electorate voted in favor of economic reforms in the April 1993 referendum.

It's true that our country now has some very rich people as well. There's probably no place in the world where one can make money so quickly—millions of dollars in a couple of years. But the new Russian capitalists prefer to send their families abroad while they're raking in the money—for fear of a coming social cataclysm?

Corruption has reached epic proportions: it's always been there, but never at these levels. Perhaps this is because the former oligarchy was sure that its power, if not infinite, was sufficient to guarantee a comfortable existence for the elite and their children and grandchildren—after all, they had the whole country at their disposal. But they were mistaken. Those who replaced them in the bureaucracy understood that the government was liable to change at any moment . . . so you'd better pick out your own reliable people and cut deals with them. Their system enabled two economies to operate simultaneously in our country: the distributive economy, that is, the socialist one; and the market economy. Now, as in the past, the country's chief natural resources—raw materials and the like—and sources of wealth are controlled by government bureaucrats; but today, that control is asserted by limiting the number of licenses for commercial enterprises, which are then "auctioned" in exchange for bribes. The payoffs must be made in hundred-dollar bills printed after 1991 (the country is flooded with counterfeits).

Top government bureaucrats have set up bank accounts abroad; their balances are in the hundreds of thousands of dollars. Practically every day, the newspapers carry new stories of people caught red-handed by the Procuracy's Interdepartmental Commission to Combat Government Corruption. The government's credibility takes one nosedive after another, as a deputy prime minister, a minister of security, a vice president, a deputy minister, go down.

Lenin said of revolutionary situations: "Those at the top, won't; those at the bottom, can't." He meant that the government won't solve the backlog of economic crises, and people can't endure their nightmarish existence any longer. I hope this doesn't describe our current situation, reminiscent as it is of the unforgettable summer of 1917, when the ruling structures of the tsarist government were in tatters and the Provisional Government's new structures were not yet in place. That was the wedge that admitted the Bolsheviks, with their promises of peace, bread, and equality.

Every day, I'm surprised to wake up and find the buses and trains still running, the gas and electricity still on at home. Perhaps it's just a matter of the law of inertia of large masses—a law that's not a bad description of Russia itself.

What will it take to push the country over the edge? I have no doubt that if it does explode, we'll find the old oligarchy at the heart of the cataclysm: the bureaucrats in the KGB and MIC who've managed to hang on, and the Party functionaries who were supposed to have left the scene.

It's not that I think that these people are about to announce that communism is being restored. No, they're more likely to install a Russian version, not necessarily extreme, of national socialism. Their ideology will be a mixture of Russian Orthodoxy and Russian nationalism. We've seen over the past couple of years how energetically the Orthodox Church has joined the secular political fray, gradually installing itself in the niche grudgingly abandoned by the Party.

Monopolistic state capitalism is likely to be the economic model for this regime. Private property and small business will be tolerated, but the economy will be dominated by large monopolies, which will operate under rigid state control and hand over 90 percent of their profits to the government. History has shown us that free enterprise is no guarantee of democracy; just think of the rise of national socialism in Weimar Germany.

But let's look at some facts, beginning with the Party. The Party bureaucrats did not face unemployment when they left their Central Committee and regional and city Party offices. A number found openings as administrators of state-owned enterprises, while others turned up in the executive and legislative branches of government. The leaders of two-thirds of the now-autonomous former republics of the Soviet Union came from the Party elite, and, in several cases, remained hard-line Party believers.

But, interestingly enough, the majority of Party apparatchiks chose instead to go into business, bringing to their efforts a rather substantial accumulation of investment capital. I've already mentioned some of the banks, holding companies, and firms in which the oligarchy has invested (at a conservative estimate) three billion rubles in raw materials, manufacturing, and real estate.[49] According to the Russian Procuracy, there are more than six hundred such companies in the country and three hundred abroad. All this is in line with an August 1990 secret memo entitled "Emergency Measures to Organize Commercial and Foreign Economic Activity for the Party":

Reasonable confidentiality will be required and in some cases anonymous firms will have to be used disguising the direct ties to the CPSU. Obviously the final goal will be to systematically create structures of an "invisible" Party economy along with commercializing available Party property. Only a small group of people may be involved in this work.[50]

The author of this memo, Nikolai Kruchin, the Party's administrative director, committed suicide under mysterious circumstances shortly after the failed coup. One of his trusted aides also ended his life, equally mysteriously. They took with them to the grave information about the foreign banks and companies where the oligarchy's funds had been transferred.

An example of the ways in which Party money apparently was shifted abroad is the firm Seabeco, which the Party had taken an active hand in establishing. Seabeco's president, Soviet émigré Boris Birshtein, was under the personal patronage of the author of the above-cited memo, Nikolai Kruchina, and former vice president, and coup-plotter, Gennady Yanayev. (It was a KGB colonel, Leonid Veselovsky, who had introduced Birshtein around in elite Party and government circles.) According to some sources, during the last years of perestroika, Seabeco was granted permission to export from the Soviet Union raw materials valued at 80 to 150 million dollars. These purchases were priced at 50 to 60 percent below world market rates, and there is reason to suspect that the difference was divided between Seabeco and the oligarchy's bank accounts.[51]

I'm sure that in Russia today, there are people in high government posts who know where—and how much—capital is invested in the West or stashed in bank accounts earning interest. Not expecting any of them to be very forthcoming, I've been making up my own list (far from complete) of Western firms that have been used to launder billions of dollars from the Soviet Communist Party. (Documents I've been able to obtain suggest that many of these companies are connected to foreign Communist parties—so-called friends.)[52]

Some of my informed sources believe that the billions of Party dollars (some cited a figure as high as 120 billion) now in the West may return to Russia and the other former Soviet republics sooner than one might think, as the current privatization program goes down in flames. With potential competition knocked out of the game, former Party bureaucrats and their KGB and MIC colleagues will buy up the most valuable real estate, petroleum products, uranium, gold, and controlling interests in factories and plants. They will form financial groups whose orientation will be anything but democratic. One can see a hint of this future in Kyrgyzstan, where Seabeco was the middleman in the sale of gold-prospecting rights to a Canadian firm, Cameco, at terms very unfavorable to Kyrgyzstan, and in Moldovia, where Seabeco acquired the best hotel in the capital, Chişinău.[53]

The army, too, has become entrepreneurial. In most regions of Russia, the army has been left without procurement funds and forced to earn its bread independently—for instance, by sending truckloads of soldiers to steal potatoes from collective farm fields. The former republics, already in a desperate plight, have no desire to feed thousands of soldiers (who, in many places, are perceived as an occupying army). In short, the country just doesn't have the cash to maintain an army, so the soldiers and officers earn it any way they can. The illegal arms trade is going full blast, with no attempt at concealment. There are terrible housing problems; about 200,000 families of officers and enlisted men are crammed into communal dwellings and barracks. The dreadful plight of these people is liable to become the kindling for a countrywide conflagration. According to a survey of the Russian military, more than two-thirds of the officers express disgust with the current government and its reforms.

In the spring of 1993, newspapers were full of reports of an All-Russian Congress of Officers, which took a public stance against the Yeltsin government. The ultraconservative newspaper *Den* reported that an underground officers' organization was already operating in the army, and reproduced a flier distributed among the regiments and units: "Comrade officers! The time has come to decide: are you with the people, or against them?" The appeal ended with the following passage:

> The strategic goal of uniting officers is active support of working-class denunciations of the pro-Zionist puppet Yeltsin regime and the formation of a government of national salvation. Officers of the state security organs and military counterintelligence! Join the struggle against traitors to the Fatherland![54]

Both state security and military counterintelligence officers have heeded the call. And while the flier was not *Den*'s creation, by publishing it, *Den* certainly gave it a boost.

As for the MIC, it is in even worse shape than the army. In 1992, the MIC's 1,100 plants were found to have lower average wages than any other branch of industry, owing to stringent government cutbacks (68 percent) in appropriations for purchases of military technology and arms.[55] Other countries' experience in defense conversion indicates that reductions should not exceed 5–7 percent per annum. The process itself is a positive one; the MIC was draining the country. (In the last sixty years of its existence, the MIC gobbled up 80–90 percent of all the country's raw materials and technical, financial, and intellectual resources.)[56] But the problem is that the former Soviet MIC employees and their families total 32 million people (approximately an eighth of the population), most of them residing in Russia.[57] Furthermore, since military production is often concentrated in "company towns" with no other industry, these people have nowhere to go for a new job. Thousands of Russian refugees from the former Soviet republics have flooded into other Russian cities, worsening the housing and job shortage and making nonsense of any thought of MIC workers relocating there. Funding for conversion is nil, many MIC factories have shut down entirely, and there's no money for wages or pensions. There's no need for me to belabor the point; it's obvious that the decline of the MIC means suffering and resentment for millions of people. For them, the restoration of the old order seems the only guarantee of a return to what was a reasonably normal and prosperous existence. The same is true of the directors of factories, design shops, and institutes, who are losing real power, along with everything else.

Analysts were warning the government as early as 1991: "The MIC, one of the main moving forces behind the August coup, has hardly been touched by personnel changes. Manufacturing processes are continuing to disintegrate and a powerful social explosion is building which, because of the extensive network and close ties among the branches of the MIC, could break out simultaneously in a number of regions and republics."[58]

Yeltsin, too, observed in 1992 that "the directors of the MIC factories are quite conservative."[59] In 1993, the military-industrial lobby in parliament forced the approval of 13.6 billion rubles in appropriations—money the government didn't have, but printed anyway, pushing the rate of inflation even higher. In 1994, the new parliament approved a new military budget under which every third ruble of Russian state income will go to the MIC.[60] The MIC held over the government's head the specter of a genuine social explosion; and the even more threatening fact that the MIC controlled the nation's nuclear program.

As for the KGB, the democrats seemed to be doing everything possible to earn the Chekists' utter disdain, what with the weakness they evinced in hesitating to do away with the Committee and the hypocrisy evident in their continuing need for the KGB they professed to despise. The Chekists will never forgive the democrats for the anxious autumn they endured in 1991, and they'll make every effort not to go through anything like it again.

Unlike the CPSU, the KGB had managed to preserve its vertical management structure (center, territory, region, city, district) by virtue of its militarized nature. Consequently, the KGB is essentially the only governmental institution in Russia able in the current conditions of political and economic chaos to give clear directions and to get people to follow its orders.

Furthermore, the KGB is the only institution from the previous regime to have preserved horizontal ties with the now-autonomous republics of the former Soviet Union. Most of these nations' state security ministers have signed agreements of cooperation with the KGB's successors in Russia. Ukraine, for example, sends its agents—in particular, those who specialize in obtaining scientific and technological secrets—to cities in Russia. Meanwhile, Russia is creating its own network of agents in the Ukraine, as elsewhere in the former Soviet republics. But despite this, in July 1993, the fifteen republics announced the creation of an integrated information system, headed by KGB Gen. Alexander Starovoitov, general director of the Federal Agency of Government Communications and Information, to coordinate the activities of all directorates of government communications and channels to protect information.[61]

Some of the 500,000 Chekists who had worked for the KGB were able to leave its ranks for new opportunities; these were, for the most part, specialists whose skills were in demand among commercial organizations, or who were able to create their own consulting firms and private security services. They constituted a pitifully small percentage of the total number of Chekists, a few thousand people at most. Tens of thousands of others had nowhere to go; they'd become superfluous. All they knew was how to be political police. Their chief task now became to prove to the government that they were necessary; that they'd more than earned their keep. And all the evidence suggests that they succeeded in their aim: there's been plenty of call for their expertise in bugging and spying, much of it on behalf of the new authorities.

Attempts by the government to monitor the Chekists more closely (let alone to eliminate them entirely) undoubtedly would meet with harsh resistance. For the Chekists, as for everyone else, it's come down to a question of survival, of bread for their families and a hint of a future for their children—things people are ready to do battle for.

Nothing else could have been expected. The KGB is not a secret service: it is a political institution of power, enormous in size, beautifully outfitted with both technology and armaments, and extremely conservative in mentality. It was inevitable that it would join the battle for power. There was no other way out for the Chekists.

According to Oleg Kalugin, whereas two-thirds of the army officers' corps holds extremely negative attitudes toward reform, the percentage is much higher in the KGB.[62] (This is an informed estimate; no official survey has been conducted.) But, unlike Party functionaries, whose principal has yet to earn interest, and the MIC, which remains a fairly insular institution because of its specific brief, the KGB possesses a wide range of opportunities to influence public opinion and government decisions. Here, we need to recall the role played by the KGB's shadow staff.

Lt. Col. Kichikhin (formerly of ideological counterintelligence) claims that he and his colleagues made special efforts in the last years and months of perestroika to search out informers among "socially active individuals," that is, the democrats. The Chekists were especially interested in the Russian Supreme Soviet. "Kryuchkov told us to concentrate on recruiting agents from the democratic faction in the Russian parliament." "What about the Communists?" I inquired. "Why bother?" replied Kichikhin. "Everything we wanted to know from them, we learned without any agents."[63] "I look at the members of parliament"—a KGB boss once confided in me—"and I see many of our people among them."[64]

(I should note that both of these sources were speaking of the "democratic" Russian parliament as it was up until September 1993 and the bloody events in Moscow.)

I understand the Chekists' delight when they see their agents and informers among the uncompromising orators of parliamentary skirmishes. But I'm afraid I can't share in their satisfaction.

We need only look at the experience of the former Czechoslovakia and East Germany to realize the leverage that secret police agents, even those who have been fired and lost their official access, can get out of the dossiers they hold on members of parliament, ministers, leaders of parties. The same thing began almost immediately in the crumbling Soviet Union. The first major case involved the publication in the Lithuanian press of the dossier of an agent called "Juozas," who turned out to be Vergilius Chepaitis, a critic and translator and former executive secretary of the council of Sajudis (the party campaigning for Lithuania's independence), chairman of the Commission on Civil Rights and International Affairs of the Lithuanian parliament, and friend and close adviser to the then-head of the republic.

Chepaitis had been a KGB agent for more than a decade. According to the Lithuanian press, he had supplied the KGB with information on forty people, including his comrades in the struggle for Lithuania's independence. After long soul-searching, Chepaitis publicly admitted his cooperation with the KGB. What's still not clear is how such documents ended up in the hands of reporters; the KGB claimed that it had taken all its agents' files with it back to Moscow after Lithuania declared independence.[65]

In Moscow, Yevgeny Kim, then a member of parliament, sent the KGB this statement: "I urge you to consider me released from cooperation with the organs of the KGB RSFSR and the KGB Directorate for Ulyanov Region and the signed statement concerning voluntary cooperation provided by me in 1972 (with the work name of 'Akimov'), and to consider my obligations to the said organization as no longer binding."[66] Again, it's unclear how this document made its way to the media; Kim himself claims that he had no intention of making public his involvement with the KGB.

In February 1993, a similar situation cropped up in the Ukrainian parliament, when the personal file of agent "Taras" was published: he turned out to be the writer Les Tanyuk, chairman of the parliamentary Committee on Cultural Affairs.[67]

Genrikh Altunyan, prominent dissident and former political

prisoner, and now a deputy of the Ukrainian parliament, sees the publication of these documents as no accident. The KGB is orchestrating "a series of well-planned provocations against the democratic segment of [Ukraine's] parliament." He believes that the KGB is being careful to expose only those agents who weren't much use to them and can be discredited in society's eyes. That way, he says, they can "protect their main helpers, the agents they need to express the 'aspirations of the people' and block democratic reform in the legislative and executive branches of government."[68]

There is no way of shielding ourselves from such Chekist provocations, except by opening the archives to public scrutiny. Otherwise, the dossiers will keep landing on the black market, allowing the KGB to keep any number of politicians on a short leash—and not just politicians, but members of all the professions and occupations riddled with "reliables," the informers, agents, and residents who constitute the KGB's chief force today.

But any hope of opening the archives has been definitely quashed. In the first days after the August coup, Yeltsin ordered all KGB files transferred to a specially created government archival agency. It didn't happen; the archives remained in the hands of the KGB. When some documents that exposed Russian Orthodox Church officials who had collaborated with the KGB were leaked, the government hastily passed a Law on Criminal Investigation (March 13, 1992) stipulating that information on persons "who cooperate or have cooperated with the organs . . . on a confidential basis is a state secret."

It's natural for security agencies to protect their agents; but the KGB, it must be recalled, is not a legitimate institution, but a political police whose informers engage in unconstitutional, political investigations. (No one has ever suggested exposing KGB agents among the police or within the criminal mafia.) Our citizens have no legal recourse against these informers.

In some cases, agents' files indeed may no longer exist; for, in September 1990, Kryuchkov ordered a sweeping purge of these documents. In September 1991, a special coded KGB telegram ordered the destruction of any outstanding files on the Church. But as historian Arseny Roginsky, a member of the Archives Commission of parliament, noted: "State security may have saved cases that in their view had 'special historical value.' "[69] The "work books" in which ideological counterintelligence agents recorded the real names and work names of their agents have also been preserved. And not only were lists kept of all the "secret helpers," but supervisors knew many of these helpers by sight—they habitually met with them to check whether their own subordinates had "allowed agents to be used for non-agency purposes." Agents whose personal files have been destroyed become "doubly covert," in the words of one counterintelligence agent—known only to specific Chekists. And an agent has no way of knowing whether the file on him has been kept. The 1993 Law on Archives stipulates that classified documents in the KGB's archives cannot be released any sooner than fifty years after the item's date, while files concerning specific individuals cannot be opened in anything less than seventy-five years. Once again, the history of at least half a century of our felonious government (as recorded in the KGB's files) has been made inaccessible. In passing this law, the government once again confirmed just how dependent it is on the KGB. And it gave the Chekists unlimited license to exploit people's fears of being exposed and publicly pilloried.

"When I realized I was in hot water, I tried to break off relations with the *komitetchiki*," a certain journalist told me. "They threatened to expose me as their agent. I'm afraid even to leave my magazine now, for fear that other people could be compromised."

There is only one thing to do, painful though it is. Those who have degraded themselves by informing, either by coercion or because of their weakness, should not await exposure and public condemnation. If they don't have the strength to speak of their misfortune, they should leave their government posts, turn in their parliamentary mandates, or leave their newspapers and journals. They should resist becoming Lubyanka's obedient tools.

They should; but they don't. The anxiety they felt in the autumn of 1991, when one after another came to me at the newspaper with their confessions, has disappeared; they've discovered that the KGB will protect them. It's a prison-camp mentality, and there's nothing to be done about it.

My five-year-old daughter, Lyolka, was given some parrots as a present. She tried to let them out of their cage so they could fly around the room. Frightened, they flew back into the cage. "Mama, they like it better in prison," she said to me, upset.

Yes, the KGB's informers do like it better behind the bars of their signed statements of cooperation: at least it's quiet there. But however painful and humiliating it may be to reveal such secrets, it's always better to have taken the initiative oneself. When agent "Juozas" Chepaitis was asked how he felt now that all of Lithuania knew that he was a KGB agent, he replied: "I am the first free man in Lithuania." And he was right.

But agents and informers in parliament and the executive branch are certainly not the only method of manipulation available to the KGB. No, they've found a way to go legal. For the last few years, a process has been under way in Russia, an effort to create the legal foundations for a civil society. This included a Law on Government Secrecy with provisions unknown in a Soviet Union ruled by thousands of extralegal institutional regulations that classified nearly everything, and concealed vital information from the public (for example, data on environmental disasters). But in January 1992, President Yeltsin was persuaded to sign a decree returning to the MB the role of chief preserver of state secrets—said secrets to be defined according to the old internal regulations. Worse, the Chekists were appointed the chief drafters of the legislation on state secrets. Entrepreneurs felt the impact immediately: information is their most valuable commodity, and if it isn't freely available, they have to buy it, with graft. The KGB used the law as a pretext to plant its people in factories, research institutes, and ministries, both to maintain secrecy and to regain control of the facts to be made available to the public and government. Once again, it had a monopoly on information. In a climate of total secrecy, the KGB could dole out information as it pleased, filtering it so as to distort its meaning and punishing those who attempted to resist such manipulation of public opinion.[70]

Today, it is just as hard as it was during the Brezhnev, Andropov, and Gorbachev years to obtain any information about the KGB's machinations and manipulations. Actually, in the perestroika era, there were people like Kalugin and Rubanov in the KGB who dared to criticize their bosses publicly (and subsequently were called "agents of Western special services and traitors" by the MB). But there's no one like them today. Fear of unemployment has put a damper on any dissent within the KGB.

"A corporate mentality has always been characteristic of the KGB; it has become even more severe now. Once again, they're circling the wagons," says my source at the GRU.

"Who's the enemy, now that the dissidents are gone?" I ask.

"Those who destroyed the Soviet Union, and who, they believe, are selling Russia to the foreigners. It can't be news to you that the KGB's always cultivated anti-Semitism."

It wasn't any news. On September 4, 1993, the Russian National Assembly and the Russian Party held one of their rallies in the center of Moscow. There were all the usual symbols, become commonplace now: the USSR's state insignia, the Russian Orthodox priest, the slogan "Save Russia, Beat a Yid," and a portrait of Jesus Christ.[71] The Russian National Assembly's current leader, and one of its founding fathers, is the retired KGB general and former counterintelligence agent Alexander Sterligov, whose programs and views are well known. Some samples:

Gorbachev's liberal and romantic "revolution from above," which emphasized Western values, individual freedom, and democracy—that is, everything that is historically least characteristic of our country and its people—quickly led to a profound crisis of national proportions.

We blame Yeltsin and his team for abusing the trust of the people using lies and treachery to destroy the Russian state and corrupt the Russian populace.

A number of organizations have conducted sociological surveys on the purchase and sale [of land]. The alien nature of the policy espoused by the government, and by Yeltsin himself, is particularly evident in this issue. The survey showed that 90 percent of ethnic Germans in Russia approve the purchase and sale of land; 76.4 percent of ethnic Jews; 21 percent of ethnic Russian peasants . . . Obviously, Germans and Jews will be the first to take an interest in purchasing Russian land.[72]

When I asked Sterligov at a press conference how his former colleagues felt about his views, he replied, "Ninety percent of KGB officers support me."

And in addition to his group, we have the Russian National Unity Party, the National Salvation Front, the infamous Pamyat, Zhirinovsky's Liberal Democratic Party, and no fewer than thirty-eight anti-Semitic and sometimes openly pro-fascist newspapers and magazines published in Moscow alone. Curiously, communists frequently join forces with the right-wing zealots. Gennady Zyuganov, chairman of today's Communist Party, is also one of the leaders of the Russian National Assembly. This confluence of communists and fascists is not unique to Russia; the same phenomenon is evident throughout the former East bloc and in other "postcommunist" societies.

Who finances the Russian nationalists and fascists? There are various vague explanations: "private entrepreneurs interested in establishing a Russian order"; "major banks and firms financed by funds from the CPSU and the KGB"; "the Central Bank of Russia, which transfers funds to the right through Soviet foreign banks abroad."[73] Whoever is doing it (and it would take a separate book to research this subject) has the blood of the ethnic clashes in Yugoslavia, Nagorno-Karabakh (the Armenian enclave in Azerbaijan), Georgia, Tadzhikistan, and Moldovia on his hands.

Aside from the parties and newspapers, there are also thousands of harried and harassed people who, by virtue of age, profession, or simple circumstance, have not found a place for themselves in the new market structures; my fellow citizens, educated to believe that enemies are responsible for all their troubles and misfortunes. Sometimes the enemy is external—American imperialism. Sometimes it's internal—"ethnics," i.e., non-Russians.

On August 23, 1991, the day Moscow buried three young people—two Russians and one Jew—killed by tanks during the terrible night of the coup, I overheard someone saying, "They should find out how that Yid ended up under a tank." I couldn't stand back and keep my mouth shut; my protest prompted more bile. "It's you Jews who are trying to kill Yeltsin; you staged the coup, now you'll answer for it."

In September 1993, a popular newspaper published an interview with a member of the radical right-wing Russian National Unity Party. "Kostya," a young man of about twenty wearing a swastika button, preferred not to give his name.

"What is the purpose of your party?" asked the reporter.

"Emancipation of the Russian people from the Communists, democrats, and Jews."

"How many of you are there?"

"It's hard to say exactly; we've got branches in 350 cities of the CIS [Commonwealth of Independent States] . . . We're gaining strength every day; the people are beginning to learn what we stand for."[74]

In retrospect, it seems a logical outcome of preceding events that a civil war in miniature should have broken out in the very center of Moscow. This happened in early October 1993, following President Yeltsin's Decree 1400, which dissolved the parliament headed by Ruslan Khasbulatov and scheduled new elections. The parliament refused to obey the illegal and unconstitutional decree. In a flash, barricades went up around the Russian parliament building, and people fed up with their miserable existence poured out to defend their "White House." Communists joined fascists as people's marshals. Hundreds of rifles were brought into the building. And the scenario unfolded . . . tanks firing on the White House . . . rooftop snipers from both sides shooting at unarmed civilians . . . Moscow's morgues filling with hundreds of bodies.

The thin veneer of faith in the ability of law to overrule force —barely nascent in Russia, where lawlessness had reigned for centuries—was destroyed.

And Yeltsin crossed the line: he saw no alternative but to shoot at his own people, the very same people who had come out to defend him in August 1991. On October 4, with black smoke engulfing the White House, I drove around the Moscow morgues and hospitals. Very few of the dead were members of the military; most appeared to be just ordinary folk. There were many young people, some in their early twenties, some teenagers. Although the official death toll was 147, estimates of the actual number of people killed run to several times that figure.

Gen. Viktor Barannikov, the former KGB head who had been dismissed by President Yeltsin the previous month on charges of corruption and negligence, was appointed security minister by the rebel parliament, and became one of the leaders of the uprising. He was carrying on a fine old Russian tradition: Vladimir Semichastny, chief of the KGB in the 1960s, had been among the organizers of the plot against Nikita Khrushchev in 1964, while Vladimir Kryuchkov, KGB chairman from 1988 to 1991, was the architect of the August 1991 coup against Mikhail Gorbachev. In 1993, it was Boris Yeltsin's turn to drink from the bitter cup as his former chief of secret police betrayed him.

The majority of the Chekists "sat on the fence and waited to see which side would win," according to Vladimir Rubanov, a former KGB colonel dismissed by Kryuchkov and currently serving as deputy secretary of the Security Council.[75] With accurate intelligence and an insider's understanding of how the last coup had gone, the Chekists waited to see which side the army would take. Meanwhile, the army was playing its own game of politics.

A presidential representative who paid a visit to the Tula Airborne Division to persuade these special assignment soldiers to come to Yeltsin's aid was simply chased out of the compound. So the Interior Ministry's elite Dzerzhinsky Division was brought to Moscow—and immediately, two hundred of its soldiers and officers vanished from their ranks, taking their weapons with them.

On the evening of October 3, rebels led by gunmen from the fascist Russian National Unity Party occupied the mayoralty building, and then crossed unimpeded to the state television building on the other side of town where they staged a massacre. Yegor Geidar, still vice prime minister of the government, delivered a radio address calling on unarmed Muscovites to defend their democracy against rampaging gangsters armed with assault rifles.

That evening, late into the night, I drove through Moscow; there wasn't a single policeman to be seen on the streets or squares. It seemed as if the city had been abandoned to the gunmen.

There was panic that night at the Kremlin. Muscovites—primarily the same impoverished members of the intelligentsia who continue to have illusions about democracy in Russia—put up barricades around the Kremlin and along Tverskaya, Moscow's main street: structures made of stones and garbage cans, to stop people who only a few hours before had seized the mayoralty building. None of us knew it at the time, but a helicopter was already waiting at President Yeltsin's residence, ready to spirit him away if things got any worse.[76]

That night, Yeltsin, despite his title of Supreme Commander in Chief, was reduced to paying a personal call, hat in hand, to the Defense Ministry in an effort to persuade his army generals (who had announced that they "would not become mixed up in politics") to bring their troops into Moscow.

The Chekists, who could have fought these armed gangsters and thereby secured their reputation in the arena of antiterrorism, instead officially declared their neutrality. Barannikov phoned Lubyanka repeatedly, urging his former subordinates to support the rebellion, but the Chekists were too smart for that; they wanted guarantees that the people they supported would really take power, that they wouldn't mess things up as the August 1991 plotters had done.

On October 4, President Yeltsin ordered the former KGB special assignment Vympel and Alpha units to clear the parliament building of rebels. The unit commanders refused to follow orders: "Don't get us mixed up in politics," was their reply to the President. (Alpha was later persuaded to approach the building.)

In short, on that black October day, the only thing that saved Russia from seeing gallows on its street corners, civil war in the provinces, and a Red-Brown coalition in the Kremlin, was the fact that, once again, rebellion was headed by people without sufficient authority over the army, the KGB, or the proletariat. (Of course, not everyone sees this in quite the same terms: according to the well-known filmmaker Stanislav Govorukhin, for example, "The parliament's trouble was that its leader, Ruslan Khasbulatov, wasn't a Russian, but a Chechen.")

On December 12, 1993, elections to the State Duma and the Federal Assembly (the lower and upper houses, respectively, of the new parliament) were finally held. It was for the sake of these elections that the country only weeks earlier had been brought to the very brink of a full-scale civil war.

Twenty-three percent of those who turned out to vote, eighteen million citizens of Russia, chose the Liberal Democratic Party of the ultranationalist Vladimir Zhirinovsky, who promised his constituents: "Russian solders will wash their boots in the Indian Ocean."

I see Russian soldiers gathering for this last southern campaign. I see Russian commanders in the headquarters of Russian divisions and armies, tracing the route of movement of troop formations and the final destinations of the routes. I see planes at air bases in the southern military districts of Russia. I see submarines surfacing at the shores of the Indian Ocean and aircraft carriers approaching the shores, where the soldiers of the Russian army are already marching, where armed assault vehicles are moving, and enormous masses of tanks are converging. At last, Russia is completing its final military campaign.

So Zhirinovsky ends his book *The Last Push to the South*.[77]

"We still don't realize that the postwar stage of world history is now ending, and the prewar stage is now beginning," said Andrei Grachev, a prominent political scientist and Gorbachev spokesman. Will he turn out to have been right?

December 21, 1993, was a red-letter day in my calendar: on that day, President Yeltsin decreed that the Ministry of Security of Russia—that is, the KGB—be dismantled, with the Federal Counterintelligence Service to be established in its place.

"The system of organs—the VChK-OGPU-NKVD-NKGB-KGB-MB—has turned out to be unreformable. The attempts to reorganize in recent years have been largely superficial and cosmetic in nature. At the present time, a strategic conception for establishing state security for the Russian Federation is lacking. Counterintelligence work has been weakened. The system of political police has been preserved, and could easily be resurrected," stated the decree's preamble.[78]

Five minutes after the decree was broadcast, my phone began to ring off the hook.

My friends congratulated me: "You see, the government listened after all!"

Chekists asked me: "Is it true you're the author of that Yeltsin decree?"

My colleagues clapped me on the back: "Well, you finally stuck it to them after all!"

I unplugged my phone and kept a low profile.

I hadn't drafted the decree, although the preamble was almost an exact quotation from a series of articles I'd published in *Izvestia* in early December 1993.[79]

I hadn't won, although by telling the truth for the first time, the government was confirming what I've been writing here.

I hadn't "stuck it" to anybody; indeed, as had been the case many times before, this grand proclamation of reform was followed almost immediately by a much less publicized retreat.

Moreover, the retreat apparently had begun while the decree was still being drafted. I say this because the second part of the decree didn't merely contradict the preamble, but undoes it altogether, proposing that the very same Chekist bosses use the very same KGB officers to create a new secret service. And this transformation was to be accomplished by Nikolai Golushko, director of the new Federal Counterintelligence Service, who had made his career in ideological counterintelligence. Under the decree, Golushko was given two weeks to design a charter for the new intelligence agency and submit it to the President for approval.

Golushko, a career KGB officer who had reached the rank of colonel general after thirty-one years of service, had been security minister at the time of the decree. Prior to 1991, he had been chairman of the Ukrainian KGB, and before that, for many years, an officer of the KGB's Fifth Directorate.

The second presidential decree came only two weeks later, and contained none of the radical fervor that had characterized the first one.[80] The charter of the Federal Counterintelligence Service was issued at the same time, and a commission was created to recertify 250 top KGB officials. Most passed the test: out of 250, 236 remained in place, while 14 retired. Like anyone else who elected to leave the service of state security, they were each paid about 10 million rubles, or $6,000 (for comparison's sake, the average monthly salary in Russia at the time was 75,000 rubles, or about 45 dollars a month).

So what, then, did change at Lubyanka, that Lubyanka the presidential decree had boldly declared "unreformable"?

Nothing to speak of. The Committee for Border Troops, which had become an independent agency in the fall of 1991 and had returned to the KGB in May 1992, was again declared an independent organization. It was also announced that the Federal Counterintelligence Service would no longer act as a law enforcement body; its power to conduct investigations was revoked, and its former Investigation Directorate was transferred to the Procurator General. (Actually, only the function was transferred; all five hundred KGB investigators remained just where they were in state security.)

Evidence for my assertions was given to me by Nikolai Golushko himself in a February 4, 1994, interview, from which I cite excerpts:[81]

YA: Nikolai Mikhailovich, in order to get a clear picture of the changes that have occurred in the structure (and, therefore, in the functions) of the ministry under your direction, I would like with your permission to go through the list of directorates in the old, pre-reform KGB.

In October 1991, the First Chief Directorate (intelligence) was separated from the KGB. The Second Chief Directorate (counterintelligence) obviously remained, correct?

NG: Yes.

YA: Seven departments of that directorate handled Soviet citizens' travel abroad. Does that function remain under your jurisdiction?

NG: Yes, only now it is not in the Second Chief; the Department of Registration and Records now takes care of that. Times have changed, of course; in previous years, any person who intended to go abroad had to run the gauntlet of the KGB. But internal regulations, including a government decree, still require the organs of state security to approve travel.

YA: What has happened to the former Third (military counterintelligence)?

NG: We still have it. Military counterintelligence includes more than six hundred components, which also control the central office, that is, the Minister of Defense, the General Staff, the GRU (military intelligence), troops, and regiment structures. Our job is to ensure the security of these structures from penetration by intelligence agencies of other countries.

YA: The Fourth Directorate, counterintelligence on transport?

NG: It has merged with the Directorate of Economic Security.

YA: And the Operations and Technology Directorate?

NG: We now have two such directorates. The scientific-technical directorate includes institutes for the design of special technology and intelligence equipment. The scientific-technological directorate, along with the designers and the institutes, numbers about ten thousand people. We also work for intelligence and help the Ministry of Internal Affairs. Through the second of these directorates, Operations and Technology, we carry out operational and technical activity with the sanction of the procurator—and, today, in compliance with the new Constitution and the courts.

YA: So the former department to bug telephones, the famous Twelfth Department, has now been merged with Operations and Technology?

NG: Yes. But you know, unlike before, the procurators can now maintain oversight of operational activity.

YA: What about the amendments to the legislation made on August 6, 1993, which in certain instances allow for the initiation of operational measures before a procurator's or court warrant has been obtained?

NG: That's for exceptional cases.

YA: Are those exceptional cases defined?

NG: No, they aren't. It's like a law. But I can tell you that we only make use of this right in isolated instances.

YA: To go on, what about the Directorate to Combat Terrorism, the former Fifth Directorate (ideological counter-intelligence)?

NG: Well, that is not the former Fifth, because in the Fifth there was only one department involved in terrorism. If you're thinking about political police, what foreign countries call the "struggle against the opposition," if we were to use the special services in the struggle against the opposition, that would be political police work—but the President has not charged us with such a task. But let's approach this question from another angle: we have fascists. Do we have to combat them? Of course.

YA: The Russian press has been writing for two years that activists from Russian National Unity—a pro-fascist party led by Alexander Barkashov—are arming themselves, and that these weapons are being delivered to them from various sources, including the KGB, which enabled them to become the chief fighting force of the October rebellion. Why didn't you take measures against them?

NG: We had them under surveillance. But in the summer of 1993, Barkashov's party was registered by the Ministry of Justice as a patriotic youth movement; therefore, it was legal, and we couldn't touch it. [That's an outright lie. Barkashov's gunmen were involved in activities that fell under the Penal Code's article regarding terrorism, which put them directly under Golushko's jurisdiction—Author.]

YA: What about the Sixth Directorate, economic counter-intelligence?

NG: Well, this is how it is: two directorates are now going to work in the economic field. One is the Directorate to Protect Strategic Installations, that is, military-industrial plants and nuclear power stations. The second is Economic Counterintelligence, whose mandate is foreign economic relations, monitoring joint ventures with the West, following some financial matters, some ministries and agencies. In addition, we are charged with combating drugs, and corruption among government officials—that's also economic counterintelligence.

YA: Has the Seventh Directorate, external surveillance (or the *toptuny*, as it was called) remained in place?

NG: Yes, it is now called the Operative Surveillance Directorate.

YA: The Eighth Chief Directorate, cryptography and protection of communication channels, was merged with the Directorate of Government Communications and the Sixteenth Directorate in the fall of 1991 to form the Federal Agency of Government Communications and Information (FAGCI).

NG: We reinstated the cryptography service. Now we are transferring it back to the FAGCI.

YA: The former KGB had eleven departments . . . The department to coordinate the activity of the special services of countries friendly to us;* has it been retained?

NG: That was called the international relations service. We eliminated it as a separate structure and attached it to the lawyers, to the contracts and law directorate.

YA: How about the Directorate to Combat Corruption and Contraband?

NG: It was dismantled, but some functions were transferred to economic counterintelligence—for example, stopping the shipment of contraband.

---

* Primarily the Warsaw Pact nations—Author.

YA: Where's the Fifteenth Directorate, the so-called bunker directorate, with the underground compounds?

NG: Under the new charter, it has been transferred entirely to the President's aegis. A special division has been created that will be in charge of ensuring the viability of chief government bodies in the event of emergency.

YA: Well, it seems that we now understand the Central Office. What about the territorial directorates? Are there still directorates of state security in the provinces, cities, and districts; that is, has the old top-down system been preserved?

NG: Yes. The components of the Russian Federation* have asked that these structures be preserved.

And so forth, and so on . . . This conversation lasted two hours, and it would be tedious to cite it in full. It would be simpler to just turn back to the first chapter and reread the whole book from the beginning.

In short, as we can see, some directorates changed their names, others merged, and still others separated. On the whole, everything returned to the status quo of the fall and winter of 1991, that is, to the reforms that in the President's famous decree of December 21, 1993, were called "cosmetic." There was a call for the number of officers of counterintelligence to be reduced to 75,000; but, as the presidential decree noted, that figure did not include "the number of workers in the scientific research and military medicine divisions and institutions, and the personnel in operations, security, and maintenance of official buildings and premises." The Chekists are in no hurry to reduce their numbers. And in any case, as all past reforms of the KGB, from Khrushchev to Yeltsin, have shown, the main thing is to preserve functions; then the "meat" of the KGB grows by itself.

In its new incarnation as the Federal Counterintelligence Service (FSK), the KGB has lost virtually none of its former functions. It

---

* The eighty-nine components of the Russian Federation (known as "subjects") include provinces and autonomous republics—Trans.

keeps a close watch on joint ventures with the West, still monitors every area that affects state interests. It still bugs whatever government lines it chooses. (Government ministers are quick to warn visitors to their offices to speak cautiously: "They're listening.") The KGB still has a monopoly on information. At one point after the August 1991 coup, the government dismantled the so-called first department in the state archives, the department where KGB officers decided what documents could be released. But I discovered recently at the Central Archives for Contemporary Documentation that the first department had been reinstated: according to Nikolai Shuster, director of the archives, the Chekists have again drawn up a list of documents that cannot be released to archive users. On what grounds, I asked. "On the grounds of the Law on State Secrecy, under which oversight of the government's secrets has once again passed to Lubyanka."[82] Under this law, passed a year ago, the KGB has become the *de jure* keeper of all state secrets; previously, it had enjoyed this privilege only *de facto*.

There is one change, however: before October 1993, the parliament had oversight of the various divisions of the KGB; now, they all report directly to the President. There is no public oversight. Just as before, the budget of KGB is kept secret.

All in all, it's a dreary and depressing tale I'm forced to write over and over again.

Perhaps the saddest aspect of the entire story of the reforms at the KGB is the change that has come over the attitudes of our once optimistic democrats. Two years ago, the democrats were united in public declarations of the need to dismantle the political police. Today, they're unanimous in saying that the secret police are vital to Russia. "Our society has not matured to the point where the political police can be eliminated," Gavriil Popov, prominent economist and well-known democrat, commented recently.

Well, I guess maturity is sobering. There was the August 1991 coup, the October 1993 rebellion . . . is it only good things, I wonder, that come in threes?

The answer to my question: Will there ever be an end to Lubyanka and the KGB? is clear now: *not in my lifetime.*

At the end of February 1994, the parliament passed an amnesty that freed both the organizers of the bloody October 1993 rebellion and the hapless plotters of the August 1991 coup. Vladimir Zhirinovsky was waiting with flowers at the prison gates to greet the released prisoners. Ruslan Khasbulatov, former speaker of parliament, announced that he was leaving politics and returned to Chechnya, his homeland. Former vice president Alexander Rutskoi, on the other hand, made no secret of his intention to pursue the presidency. The October tragedy turned into the usual farce . . .

On February 28, 1994, Nikolai Golushko, whom I had only recently interviewed, was forced to step down after he refused to obey President Yeltsin's request that he bar the parliament from granting amnesty to the coup-plotters and rebels. The new head of Lubyanka is Lt. Gen. Sergei Stepashin, forty-two, the same Stepashin who, in the fall of 1991, claimed in *Rossiyskaya gazeta* that "the KGB should be liquidated."

Today, Stepashin prefers to forget that quote.

On April 2, 1994, the Chekists sent me their latest present. *Trud* [Labor], the national trade union paper, with a circulation of more than 1.5 million, ran an article by retired KGB Maj. Gen. Boris Solomatin, the former KGB *rezident* in Washington, D.C., entitled "Mrs. Albats and Lubyanka." Aside from its snappy headline, it was almost a verbatim copy of the *Moscow News* article by Gen. Gurgenov with which I began this book. The reader will recall that Gen. Gurgenov wrote that the Chekists supported democracy along with the rest of the country (a month later, they organized the coup), and that we bad journalists were victimizing Chekists with our ruthless attacks. Solomatin wrote in the same vein: "The majority of KGB state security officers have reacted positively to the idea of democratic reform and are prepared to bow to progressive changes." He rued the fact that "through the efforts of some journalists and politicians, state security officers are being made outcasts in their own state." It was as if the three intervening years had never even passed!

Well, it was kind of the major general to provide me with such a satisfyingly symmetrical ending to my book. As a writer, I couldn't be anything but grateful to him and his ilk—but as a citizen of this country, I somehow cannot bring myself to utter any thanks.

So, what's in store for us? The time has probably come to draw some conclusions and turn the last pages of this book. Regrettably, they are not very optimistic.

Once again, the events of the last three years have demonstrated the KGB's fantastic capacity for regeneration and revival. Even my opponents have stopped claiming that the KGB was "nothing more than the combat division of the CPSU" or that the KGB "operated on Party orders."

The Communist Party and its regional and city committees were shut down in the fall of 1991, but the KGB still lives, regaining its lost positions, reclaiming the role of behind-the-scenes orchestrator. These past years have illustrated decisively that it is not so much the system of government that enables a structure like the KGB to rule the country; it's unimportant whether the chief executive is a president or a general secretary, whether the economy is tentatively headed toward the free market or remains a centrally planned one administered by the Communist Party. It's unimportant who runs local governments, whether they're first secretaries of Party regional committees, or governors and prefects like those installed by Yeltsin. The KGB, a special kind of organization nurtured by the totalitarian regime, is stronger, cleverer, and more versatile than any of these structures.

It doesn't matter who is in power—Yeltsin, Chernomyrdin, or

some third, as yet unknown person. The sad fact is, this book will not lose its currency until the KGB is destroyed.

Practically every day I get a phone call or a visit from someone asking me to help them because they are being persecuted by the KGB. Every week I receive letters containing similar pleas. In the majority of these cases, the people are not being persecuted by the KGB, but are hounded by fear of the political police instilled in them through the decades, handed down from generation to generation.

Some people claim that the KGB is zapping them with rays. And I explain that, although research is being conducted in this area (by the Defense Ministry, not the KGB), so far no one's been able to direct high-frequency shocks against individual citizens. Other people aren't crazy, but just afraid of sending a letter to a charitable foundation abroad, for example, and they wonder if Lubyanka can trace such things. One man called somebody a "CIA agent," and now he thinks the Chekists are following him. I've been particularly struck by the abundance of such anxieties in recent months. I try to tell these people that there is nothing to be afraid of, that they should fight their fear—that fear in itself is dangerous, because it grants additional power to the Chekists, more than they already have. But no one listens to me. And no one takes responsibility for these broken lives and broken minds. My God, I think, what has this country done to its citizens?

"The KGB is not an organization that can be improved or made worse," wrote noted dissident and former political prisoner Lev Timofeyev. "The KGB is a state of society, an illness of the public conscience. Society will heal only when the KGB is destroyed."

Afterword

An author always finds it hard to write the last sentence. I have tried to end this book several times—in December 1991, before the German edition was published; in August 1992, when the Russian version came out; in 1994, for the English edition, although I understand that, unfortunately, it is still too early to bid farewell to the KGB.

But the time has come for another farewell. Rika Berg-Razgon, to whom this book was dedicated, has passed away. Rika, if you can hear me: I did write this book after all. And I haven't forgotten the advice from your years of labor camp—what to take along when the Chekists come to arrest you, and how to maintain yourself in prison.

Rika, it is such a tragedy. The Lubyanka that killed your father, the Lubyanka that twice sent you to labor camp and stole fifteen years of your life—damn it, that Lubyanka is still alive.

Acknowledgments

Before any book reaches the reader, it must go through at least two equally difficult processes: first, the writing, and then the publishing. In these final pages I would like to express my gratitude to the people who helped me go through both.

First of all, I would like to express my gratitude to the sources in the KGB, named and unnamed, who helped me understand the Soviet political police, guided me through the labyrinth of its structure and departments, provided me with information, and helped me to obtain priceless documents.

I am also extremely grateful to the officers of the USSR's Chief Military Procuracy who gave me my first glimpses of files dealing with Stalinist genocide. I am especially grateful to those whom I am unable to name now, but whose help and contributions may, on some brighter day, be acknowledged.

Thanks are also due to former members of the Central Committee of the Communist Party, employees of the Ministry of Foreign Affairs of the USSR (and later, of Russia), the Supreme Court, the Constitutional Court, and the General Procuracy for the time they spent talking to me despite reservations and, in many cases, opposing political views.

I owe my greatest debt of gratitude to Yegor Yakovlev, former editor-in-chief of *Moscow News*, for the joy of having worked with him, for his tolerance of me and my investigations even though my articles sometimes drew unwanted attention of the KGB and the Central Committee of the CPSU. I hold dear the colleagues from *Moscow News* with whom I went through what was the high point of our professional lives—those years of perestroika.

And always, I must bow before those survivors of the Soviet jails, camps, and more than seventy years of totalitarian rule who not only gave me priceless information about these camps, but taught me about the art of survival. To them, I am personally grateful for their struggle against the regime: it is because of them that this book has come to be.

I want to express my very special thanks to a Russian poet and thinker of genius, Nobel Prize winner and prominent dissident Joseph Brodsky. It was Joseph Brodsky who, after reading my book in Russian, first presented it publicly in the United States, at Mount Holyoke College. He later recommended it to Roger Straus, president of Farrar, Straus and Giroux.

It is difficult to find words to convey my gratitude to Roger Straus, who decided to publish the book of an author unknown in the United States, and who has always treated me with warmth and friendship. My gratitude is especially great to Sara Bershtel, senior editor at Farrar, Straus and Giroux, who made the realities of Soviet life—not just that of a foreign country, but of a country from another planet, another mentality, and another level of civilization—comprehensible to American readers. As an author who endured years of censorship, I was definitely difficult to work with, and I am grateful to her for her tolerance and understanding. My thanks as well to Ariel Kaminer and Leslie Auerbach.

I am indebted to Professor Peter Reddaway of George Washington University, to Professor Edward L. Keenan of Harvard University; and to Amy Knight, American expert on the Russian political police, all of whom read the book in Russian and urged its publication in English.

I will never forget Alesandr Nekrich, Russian historian and co-author of *Utopia in Power: A History of the Soviet Union from 1917 to the Present*, who was forced to leave the Soviet Union, and whose books, published both in the Soviet Union and abroad, taught me my first lessons in the real history and tragedy of the Soviet Union. Alesandr Nekrich passed away a year ago, working to his last days as a Fellow of Harvard University's Russian Research Center.

My translator, Catherine Fitzpatrick, deserves much credit for taking my book very personally. Catherine is known in Russia not only as an excellent translator but also as a friend who helped us from overseas during the dark years of the regime as a member of the U.S. Helsinki Watch.

Lastly, I owe much to my family.

First and foremost, I have to thank my father, Mark Albats, even though it is too late to express my gratitude and appreciation to him personally. He passed away fourteen years ago. It was he who once who told me: "Nothing is more important than reputation." These words have been, and continue to be, my constant guide.

I have to thank my mother, Elena Izmailovskaya, and my sisters Tatyana and Asya, who never told me "Do not do this" even though my investigations of the KGB sometimes endangered their careers.

I am grateful also to my husband, Yaroslav Golovanov, who always was the first reader and editor of all I have ever written.

Above all, I must thank my lovely six-year-old daughter Lola. I began my investigation of the KGB before she was born and continued it as she was growing up. In a way she was a witness to and a participant in this undertaking. It was Lola who was the main impetus driving me to write this book—for the sake of her future.

YEVGENIA ALBATS

Notes

Titles of Russian books, articles, and reports are provided in transliteration of the Russian with the English translation. The author's descriptions of some documents or reports, or their informal titles (e.g., materials from parliamentary hearings) are also provided in Russian transliteration to assist researchers.

References to Russian archival sources contain Russian abbreviations as follows:

Arkhivnoye-ugolovnoye delo (AU) [archival-criminal file]
delo (d.) [file]
fond (f.) [fund or collection]
list dela (l.d.) [file page or folio]
opis (op.) [inventory]
Osobo sekretno [special secret]
Osoby inspektsii (OI) [Special Inspection]
poryadkovyy (por.) [order]
tom (t.) [volume]
stranitsa (s.) [page]
ugolovnoye delo (U) [criminal file]

Translation of Russian journals are as follows:

Argumenty i fakty [Arguments and facts]
Komsomolskaya pravda [Komsomol Truth]
Kuranty [Chimes]
Leningradskaya pravda [Leningrad Truth]

Literaturnaya gazeta [Literary Newspaper]
Moskovskiye novosti [Moscow News]
Nezavisimaya baltiyskaya gazeta [Independent Baltic Newspaper]
Nezavisimaya gazeta [Independent Newspaper]
Novoye vremya [New Times]
Ogonyok [Little Flame]
Pravda [Truth]
Rossiya [Russia]
Sobesednik [Interlocutor]
Sovershenno sekretno [Top Secret]
Sovetskaya kultura [Soviet Culture]
Sovetskaya Rossiya [Soviet Russia]
Stolitsa [Capital]
Trud [Labor]
Vek [Century]
Voprosy Leninizma [Problems of Leninism]

Introduction

1. *Stolitsa*, no. 16 (1991), pp. 3, 43.
2. *Literaturnaya gazeta*, no. 27, 10 July 1991.
3. Lev Razgon, *Nepridumannoye* [Unimaginable] (Moscow: Kniga, 1989).

Chapter 1 A State within a State

1. See Christopher Andrew and Oleg Gordievsky, *KGB: The Inside Story of Its Foreign Operations from Lenin to Gorbachev* (New York: Harper Collins, 1990) and Amy Knight, *KGB: Police and Politics in the Soviet Union* (Boston: Unwin Hyman, 1988).
2. Author's interview with then KGB Chairman Vadim Bakatin, October 1991.
3. Oleg Gordievsky in an interview with *Moskovskiye novosti* columnist Natalya (Natasha) Gevorkyan. See *Moskovskiye novosti*, no. 9, 3 March 1991, p. 15.
4. Yevgenia Albats, Natalya Gevorkyan, "The KGB We Don't Know," *Moskovskiye novosti*, no. 9, 3 March 1991, p. 15.
5. KGB Lt. Col. Valentin Korolyov, *Sekrety sekretnykh sluzhb* [Secrets of the Secret Services], *Ogonyok*, no. 43 (1990), p. 29.
6. KGB Maj. Gen. Oleg Kalugin, *Vzglyad s Lubyanki* [The View from Lubyanka], *Nezavisimaya Baltiyskaya gazeta*, March 1991, p. 16.

7. Instructions on the use of the USSR KGB SN troops [SN or specialnogo naznacheniya, special assignment] no. 21/1217 signed by KGB Col. V.V. Matveyev, senior inspector of the USSR KGB Inspectorate. Documents of KGB's internal investigation. Author's archive.
8. Army Gen. Filipp Bobkov in an interview with Andrei Karaulov, *Kuranty*, March 1, 1991, p. 6.
9. *Moskovskiye novosti*, no. 29, 21 July 1991, p. 15.
10. *Literaturnaya gazeta*, no. 27, 10 July 1991, p. 3.
11. *U.S. News & World Report*, 25 March 1991, p. 35.
12. *Moskovskiye novosti*, no. 29, 21 July 1991.
13. Albats and Gevorkyan, "The KGB We Don't Know."
14. Valentin Korolyov, *Sekrety sekretnykh sluzhb*.
15. Oleg Kalugin in an interview with Natalya Gevorkyan, *Moskovskiye novosti*, no. 17, 28 April 1991.
16. Oleg Kalugin, *Ne perekhodit na lichnosti* [Not Getting Personal], *Komsomolskaya pravda*, July 3, 1990.
17. Transcript of meeting of KGB Chairman Vladimir Kryuchkov with the international women journalists' press club. December 1990. Author's archive. Also, author's interview with then KGB chief Lt. Gen. Nikolai Golushko, February 4, 1994.
18. Valentin Korolyov, *Izrailskaya liniya* [The Israel Line], *Stolitsa*, no. 9 (1991), p. 24.
19. KGB Col. Mikhail Lyubimov, *Priznaniye nerasstrelyannogo shpiona* [Confession of an Unexecuted Spy], *Komsomolskaya pravda*, October 12, 1990.
20. *Moskovskiye novosti*, no. 6, 10 February 1991, p. 6.
21. KGB Lt. Col. Alexander Kichikhin, *KGB segodnya zashchishchayet konstitutsionny stroy i unichtozheniya arkhivov* [The KGB Today Defends the Constitutional Order and the Destruction of the Archives], *Stolitsa*, no. 1 (1991).
22. Author's interview with A. Kichikhin, October 1991.
23. Cited in V. Kisilyov, *Kak oni rabotali s nami* [How They Worked With Us], *Rossiya*, no. 4 (January 22–28, 1992), p. 5.
24. Ibid.
25. Vyacheslav Polosin, *Vechny RAB ChK* [Perpetual SLAVE of the Cheka], *Izvestia*, no. 18, 23 January 1992, p. 3.
26. Ibid.
27. USSR KGB f. 6, op. 10, por. no. 277, d. Ts.-175, t. 2, l.d. 111.
28. Ibid., f. 6, op. 6/16, por. no. 28, d. S-175, t. 6, l.d. 67.
29. Ibid., f. 6, op. 6/16, por. no. 24, d. T-175, t. 1, l.d. 291.
30. Ibid., f. 5, op. 27/16, por. no. 11, d. P-175, t. 2, l.d. 75.
31. Ibid., f. 6, op. 11, por. no. 150, d. Ch-175, t. 3, l.d. 217.
32. Ibid., f. 5, op. 27/16, por. no. 10, d. P-175, t. 1, l.d. 214.

33. Ibid., f. 6, op. 11, por. no. 148, d. Ch-175, t. 1, l.d. 209.

34. Author's interview with Fr. Gleb Yakunin, December 1991.

35. See for example KGB Archive, f. 6, op. 11, por. no. 148, d. Ch-175, t. 1, l.d. 163.

36. Author's interview with Fr. Georgy Edelshtein, November 1991.

37. KGB Archive, f. 6, op. 7/16, por. no. 25, d. U-175, t. 5, l.d. 285. See also *Izvestia*, no. 18 (January 23, 1992), p. 3.

38. KGB Archive, f. 6, op. 8/16, por. no. 21, d. F-175, t. 3, l.d. 284.

39. Ibid., f. 6, op. 9, por. no. 431, d. X-175, t. 3, l.d. 165

40. Ibid., f. 6, op. 6/16, por. no. 28, d. S-175, t. 6, l.d. 75.

41. *Moskovskiye novosti*, no. 23, 10 June 1990.

42. *Moskovskiye novosti*, no. 9, 3 March 1991, p. 15.

43. *Stolitsa*, no. 1 (1991), p. 26.

44. *Moskovskiye novosti*, no. 9, 3 March 1991, p. 15.

45. *U.S. News & World Report*, March 1991.

46. Author's interview with KGB Lt. Gen. Victor Ivanenko, October 1991.

47. *Rossiya*, no. 4 (January 22–28, 1992), p. 5.

48. Minutes of a meeting of the Organization Bureau of the Russian Communist Party (Bolshevik) Central Committee, no. 50, 2 September 1920, KGB Archive, f. 1, op. 4. por. no. 82.

49. KGB Archive, f. 1, op. 5, por. no. 651, d. *Shifrbyuro pri CO VChK* [Encryption Bureau of the All-Union Cheka Defense Bureau]. The document was given to the author by historian V.P. Kiselyov.

50. Ibid., por. no. 654, l.d. 74–74a.

51. Author's interview with KGB Lt. Gen. Viktor Ivanenko, October 1991.

52. Author's interview with KGB Capt. Viktor Orekhov, April 1991.

53. Yury Shchekhochikhin, *"Ya stukach, moya familiya Korchagin"* [I am an Informer, My Name is Korchagin], *Literaturnaya gazeta*, no. 7, 22 February 1991.

54. Author's interview with Viktor Orekhov.

55. *Rossiya*, no. 4 (1992).

56. Ye. Chernykh, *"Vsyo luchshee my shlyom na eksport"* [We Export All the Best Things], *Komsomolskaya pravda*, 30 April 1991. The archives of East Germany's Stasi revealed 180,000 secret helpers in a country with a population of 16.5 million. Czechoslovakia's StB had 140,000 informers—including twelve members of parliament and fourteen ministers and deputies of ministers—for a population of 15.5 million.

57. Author's interview with KGB Reserve Col. Yaroslav Karpovich, March 1991.

58. Author's interview with KGB Lt. Col. Kichikhin, December 1991.

59. Author's interview with Lt. Gen. V. Ivanenko, October 1991.

60. Author's archive.

61. Author's interview with col. Vladimir Rubanov, December 1990.

Chapter 2   Victims and Executioners

1. Memoirs of Elizabeta Shutser (in manuscript). Archive of the All-Union Institute of Horticulture, St. Petersburg.
2. The chief biographers of Academician Nikolai Vavilov are Mark Popovsky and Semyon Reznik, who were forced to emigrate in the late 1970s.
3. Armean Takhtadzhyan, *"Nenadetaya mantiya"* [The Mantle Not Worn], in *Vozvrashchennyye imena* [Names Restored], (Moscow: APN, 1989), pp. 101–02.
4. Yevgenia Albats, *"Proshcheniyu ne podlezhat"* [Forgiveness is not Warranted], *Moskovskiye novosti*, no. 19 (May 8, 1988), p. 13.
5. Ibid.
6. V.I. Lenin, *Polonoye sobraniye sochineny* [Complete Works] vol. 39, p. 62.
7. The Shakhty Trial of "wreckers" in the coal industry, actually members of the old intelligentsia, took place in 1928. The city of Shakhty is located in the Donbass, a rich coal region. See Boris Viktorov, *"Bez grifa 'Sekretno' "* [No "Secret" Stamp] in *Zapiski voyennogo prokurora* (Moscow: Yuridicheskaya literatura, 1990), pp. 148–152.
8. *Voprosy leninizma*, 2nd ed., p. 217.
9. Cited from *Sovetskoye gosudarstvo i pravo* [Soviet State and Law], no. 3 (1965), p. 24.
10. Cited from *Izvestia*, no. 160 (July 8, 1991).
11. *Nadzornoye proizvodstvo* [supervision file] no. 6628–37, Archive of the Chief Military Procuracy.
12. From Nikita Khrushchev's speech at the Twentieth Party Congress, February 25, 1956, from *Izvestiya TsK KPSS* [News of the CPSU Central Committee], no. 3 (1989), p. 145.
13. *Leningradskaya pravda*, 21–23 December 1954.
14. *Sb. postanovleniy, pazyasneniy i direktiv Verkhovnogo Suda SSSR* [Manual of Resolutions, Commentaries and Directives of the USSR Supreme Court], Moscow, 1935, p. 100.
15. Resolution of the Central Executive Committee and Soviet of People's Commissars of 5 November 1934.
16. Lt. Gen. Boris Viktorov, deputy Chief Military Procurator, 1955–67, *"Bez grifa 'sekretno',"* op. cit., pp. 192–193.
17. Cited from *Izvestia*, no. 160 (July 8, 1991).
18. Boris Viktorov, *"Bez grifa 'sekretno' "* [No "Secret" Stamp], pp. 192–93.
19. Ibid., p. 234.
20. Boris Viktorov, *Aktualnye voprosy teorii i praktiki primeneniya sovetskogo ugolovnogo zakonodatelstva ob osobo opasnykh gosudarstvennykh (kontrrevolyutsionnykh) prestupleniyakh*, classified dissertation for degree of candidate of historical sciences, Moscow, 1966, archive of B.V. Viktorov.
21. Boris Viktorov, *"Bez grifa 'sekretno'."*

22. Ibid.
23. *AU delo* No. 06–58, vol. 18, p. 15. Archive of the USSR Chief Military Procuracy.
24. *Krasnaya Kniga VChK* [The Cheka Red Book] (Moscow: Izdatelstvo politicheskoy literatury, 1989), vol. 1, p. 5.
25. V.I. Lenin, *Polnoye sobraniye sochineniy* [Complete Works], vol. 35, p. 286.
26. *Leninsky sbornik* [Lenin Anthology], XVIII, p. 189.
27. A. Latyshev, *"Genezis totalitarnoy systemy v SSSR"* [Genesis of the Totalitarian System in the USSR]; *Dokumenty Komissii VS Rossii po rassledovaniyu prichin i obstoyatelstva perevorota* [Documents on the Russian Supreme Soviet Commission to Investigate the Causes and Circumstances of the Coup]; *Leninsky sbornik* [Lenin Anthology], XXXIV, p. 65.
28. Cited in Sergei Melnik, *"Pervoistochnik* [Primary Source], *Stolitsa* [Capital], no. 20 (1991), p. 44.
29. *Yezhenedelnik VChK* [Cheka Weekly], no. 2.
30. Sergei Melgunov, *"Krasny terror v Rossii,"* (1918–1923) [Red Terror in Russia, 1918–1923] first edition, Berlin: Vataga, 1923. Cited from 4th ed., New York: Teleks, 1989, p. 21.
31. Ibid., p. 24.
32. Ibid.
33. *Kreml za reshetkoi* [Kremlin Behind Bars], Berlin, 1922, cited in *Stolitsa*, no. 20, p. 46.
34. S. Melgunov, *Krasny terror v Rossii*, p. 43.
35. Ibid., p. 6.
36. KGB Archive, f. 1, op. 2, d. 4, l.d. 64–65.
37. Melgunov, p. 6.
38. The documents are preserved at the Russian Supreme Soviet Commission.
39. Ibid.
40. V.I. Lenin, *Polnoye sobraniye sochineniy*, vol. 44, p. 261.
41. Melgunov, p. 87.
42. Ibid., p. 35.
43. *Stolitsa* [Capital], no. 20, p. 46.
44. V.I. Lenin, *Polnoye sobraniy sochineniy* [Complete Works], vol. 44, p. 328.
45. Vasily Grossman, *Zhizn i sudba* [Life and Fate] (Moscow: Knizhnaya palata, 1989), p. 304.
46. Otomar Karbauer, "Terrible Discovery in the Forest," *Berliner Zeitung*, cited from Russian translation (*"Strashnaya nakhodka v lesu"*) in *Za rubezhom* [Abroad], no. 17 (1990), p. 16.
47. *Komsomolskaya pravda*, October 28, 1990.
48. A. Latyshev, *"Genezis totalitarnoy systemy v SSR"* [The Genesis of the Totalitarian System in the USSR], author's archive.

49. Cited from *Izvestia*, no. 160 (July 8, 1991).

50. *Sbornik zadach po vneshkolnoy rabote bibliotek* [Anthology of Tasks for Extracurricular Work of Libraries]. Cited from Melgunov, *Krasny terror* [Red Terror], endnote to pp. 187–188.

51. *Moskovskiye novosti*, no. 44 (November 4, 1990).

52. Nikolai Mironov, *Ukrepleniye zakonnosti i pravoporyadka: programmnaya zadacha partii* [Strengthening Law and Order: The Party's Programmatic Task] (Moscow: Yurizdat, 1964), p. 12.

53. Russian translation of Guinness Book of Records [*Kniga rekordov Ginnesa*], *Sovetskaya Rossiya*, Moscow: 1989. Cited from *Literaturnaya gazeta*, no. 29 (July 24, 1991), p. 10.

54. B. Viktorov, *"Bez grifa 'sekretno' "* [Not Stamped Top Secret], p. 326.

55. Ibid., p. 268.

56. Ibid., p. 269.

57. V. Artyomov, *"Orden mechenostsev?"* [Order of the Sword-bearers?], *Moskovskiye novosti*, no. 25 Moscow (June 23, 1991), p. 15.

58. B. Viktorov, *"Bez grifa 'sekretno' "*, p. 270.

59. *Arkhivno-sledstvennoye delo Ushakova-Ushimirskogo Z.M.* [Archival Investigation File of Z.M. Ushakova-Ushimirsky], vol. 2, pp. 185–87. Archive of the USSR Chief Military Procuracy.

Chapter 3   Unnatural Selection

1. *Leningradskaya pravda*, 21–23 December 1954.

2. Author's conversation with Maj. Gen. Boris Viktorov, January 1988.

3. Viktorov.

4. B. Viktorov, *"Bez grifa 'sekretno' "* [No "Secret" Stamp].

5. *Izvestia CC CPSU* [News of the CPSU Central Committee], no. 3 (1989), pp. 128–166.

6. Author's conversations with Vladimir Semichastny, 6 July 1991 and September 1993.

7. *"KGB: na kogo natseleny bukvy?"* [KGB: Who are These Letters Targeting?], Oleg Moroz's interview with KGB Chairman Vladimir Kryuchkov, *Literaturnaya gazeta*, no. 3 (January 23, 1991), p. 7.

8. Author's conversation with B. Viktorov.

9. Decree of the USSR Supreme Soviet Presidium, 27 March 1953.

10. Art. 14 of the RSFSR Penal Code, 1941 edition.

11. Archive of B. Viktorov. Copy given to the author. First publication.

12. Lev Razgon, *"Net, ne raskayalis!"* [No, I Didn't Recant!], *Moskovskoye novosti*, no. 31, 5 August 1990.

13. *Literaturnaya gazeta*, no. 3, 1991.

14. Resolution of the Chief Military Procuracy, 24 February 1959.

15. Resolution of the Chief Military Procuracy, 3 August 1989.

16. V. Bilyak, *"Pravda ostalas pravdoy"* [Truth Remains Truth] (Moscow: Politizdat, 1972), pp. 73–74.
17. Person file of V.A. Boyarsky. OI-no. 4630. See also AU-No. 06-58, t. 3, ss. 247–248 on Boyarsky.
18. OI-No. 4630, p. 60.
19. Ibid., pp. 6–9.
20. AU-No. 06-58, t. 14, s. 11.
21. Ibid., s. 65.
22. *Lichnoye delo Boyarskogo V.A.* [V.A. Boyarsky's personal file]; AU-No. 06-58, t. 3, ss. 404–406; 407–421.
23. Ibid.
24. Ibid., t. 8, s. 11.
25. Ibid., t. 3, s. 262.
26. Memorandum from file No. 3612, *"Komprometiruyushchiye materialy na Boyarskogo Vladimira Ananyevich"* [Compromising Material on Vladimir Ananyevich Vladimir].
27. AU-No. 06-58, t. 13, ss. 204–06.
28. Ibid., s. 11.
29. Author's conversation with B. Viktorov.
30. Author's interview with Lt. Col. Dmitry Kashirin, March 9, 1988.
31. Ibid.
32. AU-No. 06-58, t. 8, s. 69.
33. Ibid., pp. 191–209.
34. Ibid., t. 3, ss. 161–66.
35. V.A. Boyarsky's dissertation file no. 108562, s. 73, from the USSR Academic Attestation Commission (VAK).
36. *Lichnoye delo Boyarskogo V.A.* [V.A. Boyarsky's personal file] at the Moscow Organization of the USSR Union of Journalists.
37. Author's interview with Maj. Zorma Volynsky, September 1988.
38. Testimony of Maklyarsky, NKVD-MGB screenwriter. OI-No. 4630.
39. Central Committee resolution of 14 July 1950.
40. OI-No. 4630, *Zaklyuchenkiye na Boyarskogo V.A. komissii MGB SSSR* [USSR MGB Commission Findings on V.A. Boyarsky].
41. Ibid.
42. Karel Kaplan, *"Sovetskiye eksperty v Chekhoslovakii v 1949–1956 gg."* [Soviet Experts in Czechoslovakia, 1949–1956]. *"Glava 1: Sovetskiye eksperty v Ministerstve gosbezopasnosti i razvedke"* [Chapter 1: Soviet Experts in the Ministry of State Security and Intelligence]. Here and elsewhere the author is citing an excerpted Russian translation of the Czech original prepared especially for the author.
43. OI-No. 4630.
44. Ibid.
45. Zorma Volynsky.

46. OI-No. 4630.

47. Ibid.

48. Karel Kaplan, *Sovetskiye eksperty v Chekhoslovakii.*

49. Karel Kaplan, *"Antigosudarstvennyy tsentr zagovorshchikov* [Anti-state Center of Plotters] in *Beskrovnaya revolyutsiya* [Bloodless Revolution], Canada, 1985.

50. Ibid.

51. Robert Conquest, *Bolshoy terror* [The Great Terror], translation from the English (Riga: Rakstnieks, 1991), t. 2, s. 204.

52. Karel Kaplan, *Sovetskiye eksperty v Chekhoslovakii.*

53. Ibid.

54. Ibid.

55. Ibid.

56. See for example, Meir Cotic, *The Prague Trial* (New York: Herzl Press/ Cornwall Books, 1987), p. 97; Karel Kaplan, *Sovetskiye eksperty v Chekhoslovakii.*

57. Andrew and Gordievsky, p. 415.

58. OI-No. 4630.

59. Ibid.

60. Ibid., t. 3.

61. *Stenogramma zasedaniya spetsializirovannogo soveta K-003, 11.03 pri Institute istorii estestvoznaniya i tekhniki* [transcript of a meeting of specialized council K-003, 11.03 of the Institute of the History of Natural Sciences and Technology], 1 March 1979.

62. AU-No. 06-58.

63. Ibid.

64. Ibid. *Iz pokazaniy zaklyuchennogo Bugakova L.M.* [from testimonies of prisoner L.M. Bugakov], t. 14, s. 136.

65. *Sovetskaya kultura* [Soviet Culture], 29 March 1988.

66. AU-No. 06-59, t. 2, ss. 302–03.

67. OI-No. 4630, t. 3.

68. *Iz spravki na ofitsera zapasa Boyarskogo V.A.* [from memorandum on V.A. Boyarsky, officer in the reserves].

69. Ibid.

70. In the early 1960s, the USSR Academic Attestation Commission (VAK) received an inquiry from the Scientific Research Institute of the Northern Ossetia ASSR Council of Ministers. Kh. Cherdzhiyev, director of the institute, requested information on the topic of Boyarsky's candidate's dissertation, and the date and place of his defense. He wrote: "It is quite likely that the defense was closed. The information cited is urgently needed in our work. The Lenin Library has neither the dissertation that is of interest to us nor any other information about it." *Delo Boyarskogo V.S.* [V.A. Boyarsky file], No. 108562, s. 23, archive of USSR VAK.

71. Ibid., s. 95.

72. Ibid. ss. 38–41.

73. Ibid., s. 32.

74. Ibid., ss. 19–20.

75. AU-No. 06-58, t. 14, s. 5.

76. Ibid., t. 3, s. 370.

77. Ibid.

78. VAK file No. 108562, s. 55.

79. AU-No. 06-58, t. 3, pp. 246–47.

80. *Ugolovnoye delo po obvineniyu Boyarskogo V.A.* [Criminal file on charges against V.A. Boyarsky] No. 11–88, USSR Chief Military Procuracy.

81. See for example, Boyarsky's certificate that he "had been subjected to a candidate's examination in the field of History of the USSR," in the Moscow Province Pedagogical Institute (MOP). The first signature, "Director MOP," is illegible. The second signature is "for Scientific Secretary of the Council, M. Ovsyannikov." *Delo* No. D 0379–0428/12, on the awarding of Boyarsky the decree of Doctor of Technical Sciences, s. 81, VAK archive.

82. VAK archive.

83. Ibid.

84. Here and ff., author's interview with M.G. Malkova, 15 September 1988.

85. From *Stenogramma obsuzhdeniya na zasedanii spetssoveta* [Transcript of discussion at session of special council], OI-No. 4630, 1 March 1979, VAK archive.

86. Ibid., s. 81.

87. Ibid., s. 90.

88. VAK archive transcript of discussion at specialized council meeting, page number not indicated.

89. Ibid.

90. *Postanovleniye Prezidiuma VAK SSSR* [Resolution of the USSR VAK Presidium] No. 5-1 of 21 April 1989: *"Priznat nedeystvitelnym diplom doktora tekhnicheskiykh nauk TN—No. 001842 and diploma kandidata istoricheskikh nauk MIT No. 001516* [To declare invalid technical sciences diploma No. 001842 and historical sciences diplomat No. 001516]; *Resheniye kolleqii Gosudarstvennogo komiteta po nauke i tekhnike SSSR* [Resolution of the Collegium of the USSR State Committee on Science and Technology] No. 2-1, 4 November 1989; *Resheniye Prezidiuma AN SSSR na osnovanii pisma VAK SSSR* [Decision of the Presidium of the USSR Academy of Sciences on the basis of USSR VAK letter] No. 3543/2, 22 June 1989; Author's information from the USSR Union of Journalists; *Postanovleniye Glavnoy voyennoy prokuratury SSSR o privilechenii Boyarskogo V.A. v kachestve obvinyayemogo* [Resolution of the USSR Chief Military Procuracy

on prosecution of V.A. Boyarsky], 3 August 1989, UD-No. 11-88. Author's archive.
91. AU-No. 06-58, t. 9, l.d. 196–97.

Chapter 4   Who Was Behind Perestroika?

1. Andrew and Gordievsky, p. 608.
2. Oleg Kalugin, *"KGB poka ne menyaet printsipov"* [The KGB Still Has Not Changed Its Principles], *Komsomolskaya pravda*, 20 April 1990.
3. Anatoly Golitsyn, *New Lies for Old* (New York: Dodd, Mead, 1984).
4. Sergei Georgiev, *"Perestroika-kulminatsiya strategicheskoy dezinformatsii Kremlya?"* [Perestroika: Culmination of the Kremlin's Strategic Disinformation?], *Chas pik* [Rush Hour], no. 32, 12 August 1991.
5. See for example, Fyodor Burlatsky, *Vozhdi i sovetniki* [Great Leaders and Advisors] (Moscow: Politicheskaya literatura, 1990), s. 275. Published in English as *Soviet Leaders*.
6. Secret Memorandum No. 2170-I of KGB Deputy Chaiman P. Ivashutin and USSR Procurator General R. Rudenko to the Central Committee, 23 August 1962. Copy of the original, author's archive.
7. Secret Memorandum No. 2343-S of KGB Chaiman V. Semichastny and USSR Procurator General R. Rudenko to the Central Committee, 23 December 1965. Copy of the original, author's archive.
8. Secret Memorandum No. 3468-S of Central Committee Department of Culture head V. Shauro, deputy Department of Agitation and Propaganda head A. Yakovlev, and deputy Administrative Organs Department head N. Salkikin, 3 February 1966. Copy of the original, author's archive.
9. Geoffrey Hosking, *A History of the Soviet Union* (London: Fontana, 1985), pp. 423–24. Citation from Andrew and Gordievsky, pp. 480–81.
10. Author's interview with Alexander Shelepin, September 1993.
11. *Materialy Komissii VS Rossii po rassledovaniyu prichin i obstoyatelstv perevorota* [Materials from the Russian Supreme Soviet Commission to Investigate the Causes and Circumstances of the Coup]. See also I. Sichka, *"Tayny Lubyanskogo dvora"*, *Komsomolskaya pravda*, 11 January 1992.
12. Top Secret Memorandum No. 123-A (Politbureau Special Folder) of KGB Chaiman Y. Andropov and USSR Procurator General R. Rudenko, *O merakh po presecheniyu prestupnoi deyatelnosti Orlova, Ginsburga, Rudenko, i Venclova* [Measures to terminate the criminal activity of Orlov, Ginsburg, Rudenko, and Venclova], 2 January 1977.
13. Copy of the original, author's archive. Memorandum no. 2278-f, of KGB Chairman V. Fyodorchuk to the Central Committee, *O brakakh deytateley sovetskoy kultury s inostrantsami iz kapitalisticheskhikh gosudarstv* [On marriages of Soviet cultural figures with foreigners from capitalist counties], 22 November 1982. Copy of the original, author's archive. Secret Mem-

orandum No. 1479-f of KGB Chaiman V. Fyodorchuk to the Central Committee, *O negativnykh proyavleniyakh v povedenii otdelnykh kategory zritelei v khode vystupleniya zarubezhnykh artistov i prosmotrov proizvedeny zapadnogo iskusstva.* [Negative expressions in the behavior of the certain categories of spectators during performances by foreign artists and screenings of Western movie productions], 19 July 1982. Copy of the original, author's archive.

14. Top Secret Minutes of the Secretariat of the Central Committee No. St-101/62gs, *O sozdany Antisionistskogo komiteta sovetskoi obshchestvennosti* [About the creation of the Anti-Zionist Committee of the Soviet Public], 29 March 1983. Copy of the original, author's archive.

15. *Izvestia TsK KPSU* [Central Committee News], No. 1 (1989), s. 24.

16. *Trud* [Labor], 28 December 1990.

17. *Komsomolskaya pravda*, June 20, 1990.

18. *Moskovskiye novosti*, no. 25 (June 24, 1990).

19. Fyodor Burlatsky, *Vozhdi i Sovetniki* [Great Leaders and Advisors], p. 363.

20. Author's interview with Alexander Yakovlev, February 1992.

21. Information from the military-political department of the Institute of the U.S. and Canada Institute of the USSR Academy of Sciences, December 1991; *Krasnaya Zvezda* [Red Star], 8 April 1989; *Pravda*, December 16, 1989.

22. *Komsomolskaya pravda*, 19 January 1991.

23. Author's interview with Sergei Rogov, director of the military and political department, Institute of U.S. and Canada of the USSR Academy of Sciences, October 1991.

24. *Izvestia*, 12 January 1991.

25. *Komsomolskaya pravda*, 19 January 1991.

26. Sergei Rogov.

27. Ibid.

28. Ibid.

29. Author's interview with KGB Col. Vladimir Rubanov, September 1991.

30. Information from the Congress of the Council of Labor Collectives of the USSR, October 1991.

31. *Izvestia*, 6 February 1991.

32. Oleg Moroz, *"Zheleznaya maska"* [Iron Mask], *Literaturnaya gazeta*, no. 42 (October 17, 1990).

33. *Sovershenno sekretno*, no. 1 (1993), pp. 26–27.

34. *Moskovskiye novosti*, no. 9, 3 March 1991, p. 15.

35. *Nezavisimaya gazeta*, no. 55, 12 May 1991.

36. Central Television broadcast, *"Na sluzhbe Otechestva"* [In Service of the Fatherland], 14 April 1991.

37. *Komsomolskaya pravda*, 20 July 1991, p. 4.

38. I. Cicha's interview with Col. V. Rubanov, *"Gostayna vyshe zakona?"* [State Secrets Above the Law?], *Komsomolskaya pravda*, 30 August 1990.

39. *Moskovskiye novosti*, no. 16, 21 April 1991.

40. Author's discussion with Tatyana Koryagina, August 1991.

41. *Nezavisimaya gazeta* [Independent Newspaper], 28 December 1990.

42. *Literaturnaya gazeta*, no. 3, 23 January 1991.

43. *Znamya*, no. 10 (1990), s. 210.

44. Academician Nikolai Petrakov, *"Litsom k litsu"* [Face to Face], *Literaturnaya gazeta*, 31 July 1985.

45. *Nedelya* [Week], no. 36 (1990), pp. 6–7.

46. Vadim Pechenev, *Gorbachev: k vershinam vlasti* [Gorbachev: To the Summits of Power], (Moscow: Gospodin Narod, 1991), pp. 90–91; 94.

47. Mikhail Gorbachev, *Izbrannye rechi i statyi* [Selected Speeches and Articles] (Moscow: Politizdat, 1986), p. 241.

48. *Materialy XXVII cyezda KPSS* [Materials of the XXVII Party Congress] (Moscow: Politizdat, 1986), p. 241.

49. Konstantin Simonov, *Glazami cheloveka moego pokoleniya* [Through the Eyes of a Person of My Generation] (Moscow: APN, 1988), p. 134.

50. Andrew and Gordievsky, pp. 606–608.

51. *Izvestia*, 29 March 1990; also Andrew and Gordievsky, pp. 534–536.

Chapter 5 Realities of the Glasnost Era

1. Nikolai Popkov, *"Petlya"* [Noose], *Literaturnaya gazeta*, no. 52, 27 December 1989.

2. A. Karaulov's interview with V. Semichastny, *Teatralnaya zhizn* [Theater Life], no. 10 (May 1989), p. 32.

3. *Komsomolskaya pravda*, 26 June 1990.

4. Here and following cited from *Stenogramma vstrechi Predsedatelya KGB Vladimira Kryuchkova s chlenami Mezhdunarodnogo press-kluba zhenshchin-zhurnalistok* [Transcript of Meeting of KGB Chairman Vladimir Kryuchkov with Members of the International Women Journalists' Press Club], December 1989. Author's archive.

5. KGB Secretariat archives, f. 6, op. 10, por. no. 45, d. 132, l.d. 104–106.

6. *Ukaz Prezidiuma Verkhovnogo Soveta SSSR o prinyatii Zakona o poryadke organizatsii i provedenii sobraniy, mitingov, ulichnykh shestviy i demonstratsiy v SSSR* [Decree of the Presidium of the USSR Supreme Soviet on the Passing of the Law on Procedures for Organizing and Conducting Meetings, Rallies, Street Processions, and Demonstrations in the USSR], 28 July 1988.

7. Author's interview with a KGB officer who wished to remain anonymous.

8. Valentin Korolyov, *"Sekrety sekretnykh sluzhb"* [Secrets of the Secret Service].

9. Ibid.

10. *Materialy Komissii VS SSSR po rassledovaniyu obstoyatelstv avgustovskogo perevorota* [Materials of the USSR Supreme Soviet Commission to Investigate the Circumstances of the August Coup], d. no. 4, t. 5, l.d. 331.

11. *Rossiyskaya gazeta*, 29 November 1991.

12. *Ekspress-khronika*, no. 14, 2 April 1991.

13. Igor Gamayunov, *"Kak izmenyayut KGB"* [How the KGB is Being Changed], *Yunost* [Youth], no. 6 (1991), p. 90.

14. *Moskovskiye novosti*, no. 24, 24 June 1990, p. 11.

15. Alexander Kichikhin, *Stolitsa* [Capital], no. 1 (1991), p. 25.

16. KGB Col. Mikhail Lyubimov (Reserves), *"Razzhalovan bez dokazatelstv"* [Demoted Without Proof], *Moskovskiye novosti*, No. 27, 8 July 1990, p. 4.

17. *Moskovskiye novosti*, no. 24, 1990.

18. *Moskovskiye novosti*, no. 44, November 3, 1991.

19. Unpublished interview by Natalya Gevorkyan with Jan Ruml in Prague, July 1990. Printed with permission of Gevorkyan.

20. *Stenogramma parlamentskiy slushaniy po rassledovaniyu finansovoy deyatelnosti KPSS* [Transcript of parliamentary hearings investigating the financial activity of the CPSU], 10 February 1992; author's interview with Alexei Pushkev, former employee of the International Department of the Central Committee of the CPSU, March 1992.

21. KGB Archive, f. 4-OS, op. 11, por. no. 7, d. OP-3, t. 4, l.d. 253.

22. KGB Archive, f. 4-OS, op. 11, d. OP-1, t. 8, l.d. 41.

23. Central Committee Special File. Copy of original, author's archive.

24. Central Committee Special File. Copy of original, author's archive.

25. KGB Archive, f. 5, op. 6, por. no. 12, d. 131, t. 1, l.d. 103–104.

26. Yevgenia Albats and Natalya Gevorkyan, *"Denqi dlya prizraka"* [Money for a Ghost], *Moskovskiye novosti* [Moscow News], no. 49, 8 December 1991, pp. 1, 5; also *Vypiska iz spetsialnoy kniqi uchyota Sekretariata Mezhdunarodnogo Otdela TsK KPSS* [Excerpt from special records book of the Central Committee International Department Secretariat], copy of original, author's archive.

27. Marat Zubko, *"Khelsinskiy filial KGB pri svete dnya"* [The KGB's Helsinki Branch in the Light of Day], *Izvestia*, no. 87, 11 April 1992.

28. *Stennogramma parlamentskiy slushaniy po rassledovaniyu finansovoy deyatelnosti KPSS* [Transcript of parliamentary hearings investigating the financial activity of the Communist Party of the Soviet Union], 10 February 1992.

29. From a letter from V. Falin, head of the Central Committee's International Department and V. Vlasov, head of the Central Committee's Socioeconomic Policy Department to the Central Committee leadership, dated 19 February 1991. Copy of original in author's archive.

30. Copy of original in author's archive.

31. Top Secret Memorandum of the KGB to the Central Committee, No. 3240-A, 31 December 1975. Copy of original in author's archive.
32. Top Secret Memorandum from Vladimir Kryuchkov to Mikhail Gorbachev, No. 405-K/OV, KGB archive, f. 6, op. 12, d. 13, t. 1, l.d. 304–305.
33. Copy of original in author's archive.
34. Memorandum from the KGB to Leonid Brezhnev, 16 May 1975, No. 1218-A/OV. Copy of the original from author's archive.
35. Copy from original in author's archive.
36. Copy from original in author's archive.
37. See 28.
38. *Komsomolskaya pravda*, June 20, 1990.
39. R. Lynev interview with Boris Yeltsin, *Izvestia*, 23 May 1991.
40. *Otchyot Pyatogo upravleniya KGB SSSR "Ob itogakh organizatsionnoy i agenturno-operativnoy deyatelnosti za 1982"* [Report of the Fifth Directorate of the USSR KGB "On the Results of Organizational and Agent-Operative Activity for 1982"] KGB archives, f. 6, op. 6/16, por. no. 28, d. S-175, t. 6, l.d. 68.
41. *Sovetskaya Rossiya*, November 4, 1990.
42. Copy from original in author's archive.
43. *Materialy Komissii VS SSSR po rassledovaniyu obstoyatelstv gosudarstvennogo perevorot v SSSR* [Materials from the USSR Supreme Soviet Commission to Investigate the Circumstances of the Coup d'Etat in the USSR], d. no. 4, t. 5, l.d. 60.
44. *Spravka po materialam, obnaruzhennym v seyfe Boldina V.I.* [Memorandum on materials discovered in the safe of V.I. Boldin] signed by Lt. Col. A.P. Pronin, senior inspector of the KGB Inspectorate. Copy of original in author's archive.
45. *Rossiya*, no. 4 (1992).
46. KGB Archive, f. 6, op. 12, por. no. 110, d. Sh-175, t. 1, l.d. 115.
47. *Stolitsa*, no. 1 (1991), p. 26.
48. *Rossiya*, no. 4 (1992).
49. The document was first published by Yury Shchekhochikhin in *Literaturnaya gazeta*, no. 15 (April 17, 1991), p. 2.
50. KGB Maj. Alexander Mavrin, *"Yavka v kurlike"* [Secret Rendezvous in the Smoking Room], *Komsomolskaya pravda*, 20 March 1991, p. 2.
51. Speech by Anatoly Sobchak at the IV Congress of People's Deputies, December 1990.
52. Interview of Army Gen. Filipp Bobkov by A. Karaulov, *Nezavisimaya gazeta*, 28 December 1990, p. 5.
53. V. Sergeyev, *"Ubiystvo po zakazu KGB"* [Murder on KGB Orders], *Nezavisimaya gazeta*, 5 October 1991.
54. *Stolitsa*, no. 1 (1991), p. 24.

55. Author's converstaion with KGB Lt. Col. Alexander Kichikhin, March 1991.

56. Lt. Col. A. Kichikhin, *"KGB vsyo znal i deystvoval"* [The KGB Knew Everything and Acted], *Novoye vremya*, no. 35 (1991), p. 16.

57. Valentin Korolyov, *Sekrety sekretnykh sluzhb.*

58. Lt. Col. A. Kichikhin, *"KGB vsyo znal i deystvoval"* [The KGB Knew Everything and Acted].

59. Author's interview with Maj. Sergei Petruchik of motorized rifle division special department of the KGB Third Chief Directorate, Vladikavkaz, October 1991.

60. *Stenogramma vstrechi V. Kryuchkova s press-klubom zhenshchin-zhurnalistok* [Transcript of Meeting of V. Kryuchkov with Women Journalists' Press Club].

61. S. Sokolov, S. Pluzhnikov, *"Kak KGB svodil schyoty s KPSS"* [How the KGB Settled Scores with the Communist Party], *Komsomolskaya pravda*, 22 January 1992.

62. *Komsomolskaya pravda*, 22 January 1992.

63. *Megapolis-Ekspress*, no. 40 (October 1991).

64. Nikolai Andreyev, *"Delo ANTa"* [The ANT Affair], *Izvestia*, nos. 261, 263, 264, 268, 272, 277, November 1991. Citation from no. 263, 4 November 1991.

65. Author's interview with Yevgeny Lisov, Deputy Procurator General of Russia, 10 February 1992; *Nezavisimaya gazeta*, 5 October 1991; Author's interview with Yevgeny Savostyanov, chief of the Russian State Security [MBR] Directorate for Moscow and Moscow Province, November 1991.

66. KGB Archive, f. 6-OS, op. 8, por. no. 2, d. 131, t. 1, l.d. 269–270.

67. KGB Archive, f. 6-OS, op. 1, por. no. 3, d. OV-1, l.d. 159–160.

68. See for example *"Nadyozhna li zashchita? Intervyu s nachalnikom Shestogo Upravleniya KGB general-leytennatom N. Savenkovym"* [Is the Protection Reliable? Interview with Lt. Gen. N. Savenkov, Head of KGB Sixth Directorate], *Pravda*, 12 March 1991; *"Tri rublya za korobok spichek"* [Three Rubles for a Box of Matches], *Sovetskaya Rossiya*, 5 December 1990.

69. Sociological analysis by Prof. Yury Levada, *Moskovskiye novosti*, no. 1, 6 January 1991.

70. S. Shpilko, *"Poryadok no ne rezhim"* [Order But Not Regimen], *Izvestia*, no. 15, 17 January 1990.

71. Yury Levada, *Moskovskiye novosti*, no. 1, 6 January 1991.

72. *Dannyye sotsiologicheskogo oprosa, "Obshchestvennoye meneniye o reytinge gosudarstvennykh struktur, obshchestvennykh is politicheskikh organizatsiy"* [Data from a sociological survey, "Public Opinion on the Rating of Government Agencies, Public and Political Organizations"], *Sotsiologicheskaya sluzhba Verkhovnogo Soveta RSFSR* [RSFSR Supreme Soviet Sociological Service], March 1991. Author's archive.

73. Olga Kryshtanovskaya, *"Smena vsekh ili smena stilya"* [Change of Everything or Change of Style?], *Moskovskiye novosti*, no. 16, 21 April 1991.
74. Ibid.
75. Copy from the original, author's archive.
76. *Opros sotsiologisheckoy sluzhby VS RSFSR* [Survey of the RSFSR Supreme Soviet Sociological Service] (see note 81).
77. *Izvestia*, no. 15, 17 January 1990.
78. Copy from the original, author's archive.
79. Alexander Mavrin, *"Yavka v kurilke"* [Secret Rendezvous in the Smoking Room].
80. Top Secret Memo No. 359-K. Copy of original, author's archive.
81. Statistics from the RSFSR Foreign Ministry.
82. *Intervyu Ministra inostrannykh del SSSR s sentybrya po noyabr 1991 goda Borisa Pankina A. Afanasyevu* [Interviews of USSR Foreign Minister Boris Pankin with A. Afanasyev], September-November 1991, *Komsomolskaya pravda*, 23 November 1991, p. 4.
83. Boris Yeltsin, *Ispoved na zadannuyu temu* [Confession on an Assigned Theme], Spektr Tsentr, Naverezhnyye Chelny, 1990, pp. 147–148. (Published in English as *Against the Grain I*, New York: Summit Books, 1990).
84. *Komsomolskaya pravda*, 26 September 1990.
85. *Pravda*, 12 September 1990.
86. Boris Pinsker, *"Kazhdyy dvadtsaty—vrag?"* [Every twentieth—an enemy?] *Moskovskiye novosti*, no. 42, 21 October 1990.
87. Ibid.
88. Author's archive.
89. *Moskovskiye novosti*, no. 41, 11 November 1990.
90. *Sovetskaya Rossiya*, 13 December 1990.
91. *Pravda*, 23 December 1990.
92. Dmitry Pushkar, *Suzhyonnoye zasedaniye obyavlyaetsya otkrytym* [A Closed Meeting is Declared Open], *Moskovskiye novosti*, no. 27, 7 July 1991.
93. *Moskovskiye novosti*, no. 10, 10 March 1991, p. 3.
94. Copy of the original, author's archive.
95. *Trud*, 12 February 1991.
96. *Kuranty*, 23 April 1991; *Izvestia*, 22 April 1991.
97. *Moskovskiye novosti*, 24 March 1991.
98. The 103rd Division of the VDV [military–air special forces] and the 75th Motorized Rifle Division were transferred to the KGB by Order No. 314 of the USSR Security Council.
99. Author's interview with Alexander Yakovlev, September 1993.
100. Author's archive.
101. *Komsomolskaya pravda*, 5 July 1991.
102. *Komsomolskaya pravda*, 17 August 1991.

Chapter 6 The Coup

1. From *Obrashcheniya GKChP k narodu* [Appeal of the State Committee for the State of Emergency (GKChP) to the People], 19 August 1991. Author's archive.

2. Main sources of information: *Otchyot Gosudarstvennoy Komissii po rassledovaniyu deyatelnosti KGB SSSR vo vremya putscha* [Report of the State Commission to Investigate the Activity of the USSR KGB during the Coup]; Col. Sergei Stepashin, commission chairman and chairman of the RSFSR Supreme Soviet Committee on Security; after November 1991, chairman of the MBR [Ministry of Security and Intelligence] Leningrad and Leningrad Province Directorate, now Director of the Federal Counterintelligence Service; *Materialy sluzhebnogo rassledovaniyu KGB SSSR* [Materials from USSR KGB Internal Investigation]; *dokumenty Komissii VS SSSR po rassledovaniyu obstoyatelstv qosudarstvennoqo perevorota v SSSR* [Documents of the USSR Supreme Soviet Commission to Investigate the Circumstances of the Coup d'Etat in the USSR]; the USSR Supreme Soviet Commission, chaired by A. Obolensky; Lt. Gen. Vadim Bakatin, KGB Chairman, then chairman of the Inter-Republican Security Service; KGB Maj. Gen. Viktor Ivanenko, director of the Federal Security Agency (RSFSR KGB) at the time of my interview with him; and sources who asked to remain anonymous.

3. *Obyasnitelnaya zapiska* [Explanatory memo] by KGB Lt. Gen. V.I. Zhizhin, head of Kruchkov's Secretariat till 21 August 1991. From *Materialy Komissii VS SSSR* [Materials of the USSR Supreme Soviet Commission], d. no. 4, t. 1, l.d. 287.

4. *Obyasnitelnaya zapiska* [Explanatory memo] by KGB Col. A.I. Yegorov, then assistant to the chief of counterintelligence. Ibid., l.d. 37–48. Copy of the original in author's archive.

5. A. Kichikhin, *"KGB vsyo znal i deystvoval"* [The KGB Knew Everything and Acted].

6. *Obyasnitelnaya zapiska* [Explanatory memo] by A.I. Yegorov.

7. *"Allo, my vas podslushivayem!"* [Hi, We're Bugging You!] *Argumenty i fakty*, no. 38.

8. *Otchyot Gosudarstvennoy komissii po rassledovaniyu deyatelnosti KGB* [Report of the State Commission to Investigate the KGB's Activity].

9. *Obyasnitelnaya zapiska* [Explanatory memo] by Col. V.I. Vedenin, then deputy chief of the First section of the 12th Department, 11 September 1991. Copy from original author's archive.

10. Report of V. V. Nechayev. *Materialy Komissii VS SSSR* [Materials of the USSR Supreme Soviet Commission], d. no. 4, t. 1, l.d. 331.

11. Author's interview with Alexander Yakovlev, September 1993.

12. Here and following from *Obyasnitelnaya zapiska* [Explanatory memo] from A.I. Yegorov.

13. Ibid., l.d. 39.

14. Ibid., l.d. 40.

sm 15. From testimony of Lt. Gen. Prilukov, former chief of the KGB Moscow Directorate, to the State Commission to Investigate KGB Activities During the Coup.

16. *Obyasnitelnaya zapiska* [Explanatory memo] by A.I. Yegorov.

17. Ibid., l.d. 42.

18. Ibid., l.d. 43.

19. *Pravda*, 6 November 1991

20. *Izvestia*, 20 September 1991.

21. *Komsomolskaya pravda*, 5 September 1991.

22. A. Kichikhin, *"KGB vsyo znal i deystvoval"* [The KGB Knew Everything and Acted].

23. *Izvestia*, 27 August 1991.

24. *Izvestia*, no. 202, 26 August 1991.

25. Testimony of Prilukov.

26. *Materialy Komissii VS SSSR* [Materials of the USSR Supreme Soviet Commission].

27. *Komsomolskaya pravda*, 29 August 1991.

28. A. Kichikhin, *"KGB vsyo znal i deystvoval"* [KGB Knew Everything and Acted].

29. Interview of KGB Maj. Gen. Viktor Karpukhin by D. Belovetsky and S. Boguslavsky, *Zerkalo* [Mirror] newsletter, 12 October 1991.

30. *Dokumenty Komissii VS SSSR* [Documents of the USSR Supreme Soviet Commission].

31. Author's interview with Leonid Shebarshin, 15 October 1991.

32. A. Kichikhin, *"KGB vsyo znal i deystvoval"* [The KGB Knew Everything and Acted].

33. *Literaturnaya gazeta*, 11 September 1991.

34. *Rossiyskaya gazeta*, 28 August 1991.

35. *Literaturnaya gazeta*, 11 September 1991.

Chapter 7 Lyubanka: Now and Forever

1. *Rossiyskaya gazeta*, no. 177, 27 August 1991.

2. Author's interview with Gen. Vadim Bakatin, then USSR KGB Chairman, September 1991.

3. Author's interview with KGB Lt. Gen. Viktor Ivanenko, September 1991.

4. Author's interview with KGB Gen. Oleg Kalugin, 27 August 1991.

5. Author's interview with KGB Lt. Gen. Viktor Ivanenko.

6. Author's interview with KGB Lt. Col. Alexander Kichikhin, September 1991.

7. Author's interview with KGB Lt. Vladimir Rubanov, September 1991.

8. Author's archive.

9. Author's interview with KGB Lt. Gen. Viktor Ivanenko, September 1991.

10. Yevgenia Albats, *"Lubyanka v shoke"* [Lubyanka in Shock], *Moskovskiye novosti*, no. 38, 22 September 1991.

11. David Wise, "Closing Down the KGB," *The New York Times Magazine*, 24 November 1991, p. 30.

12. Author's interview with then KGB Chairman Vadim Bakatin. December 1991.

13. Author's interview with then KGB Chairman Vadim Bakatin, February 1992.

14. Author's interview with KGB Lt. Gen. Viktor Ivanenko, November 1991.

15. *Russkiy monitor* 1: 2 (10 November 1991).

16. Author's information from confidential sources at the KGB First Chief Directorate (intelligence), September 1991.

17. *Kommersant*, 7 October 1991.

18. Author's interview with then KGB Chairman Vadim Bakatin, 13 December 1991.

19. Author's interview with KGB Gen. Oleg Kalugin, October 1992.

20. Author's interview with (Ret.) KGB Lt. Yaroslav Karpovich, February 1993. Also: Boris Zolotukhin, RSFSR people's deputy, member *Komissii Verkhovnogo Soveta RSFSR po rassledovaniyu prichin is obstoyatelstv gosudarstvennogo perevorota* [RSFSR Supreme Soviet Commission to Investigate the Causes and Circumstances of the Coup d'Etat], in the publication *Gosudarstvennaya bezopasnot i demokratiya* [State Security and Democracy], no. 3 (May 1993), Glasnost Foundation, Moscow, 1993.

21. *Izvestia*, December 19, 1991.

22. *Argumenty i fakty* no. 39 (1991); no. 45, 1991.

23. Andrei Oligov, *"Politicheskiy ssysk budyet vsegda"* [There Will Always be Political Police], *Sovetskiy sport*, 13 November 1991.

24. Author's interview with then KGB Chairman Vadim Bakatin, 13 December 1991.

25. Interview of Yury Fedoseyev by A. Barinov, *Nezavisimaya gazeta*, 12 December 1991.

26. *Izvestia*, 17 December 1991.

27. Information cited by the author from the following sources: a colonel of the GRU's [Military Intelligence] scientific and technical intelligence office, under conditions of anonymity; KGB Gen. Oleg Kalugin; then KGB Chairman Vadim Bakatin. See also: Yevgenia Albats, *"Otkuda rasut ushi?"* [How Do the Ears Grow?], *Moskovskiye novosti*, no. 52, 29 December 1991.

28. Author's interview with then KGB Chairman Vadim Bakatin, 27 December 1991.

29. Decoding of the text of the speech of Gen. Viktor Barannikov at a KGB meeting, 27 December 1991, author's archive.

30. Author's interview with Deputy Prime Minister Sergei Shakhrai, August 1992.

31. Interview with Deputy Prime Minister Sergei Shakhrai and Galina Starovoitova, then adviser to President Yeltsin on international affairs, November 1992.

32. From interview with *Moscow News* columnist Nella Loginovaya with K. Ilyumzhinov, April 1993, cited with permission of Loginovaya.

33. A. Oligov, *"Politicheskiy ssysk budyet vsegda"*.

34. Here and following, author's interview with Yevgeny Savostyanov, November 1991. See also *Mostovskiye novosti*, no. 47, 24 November 1991.

35. Author's interview with Yevgeny Savostyanov, April 1992.

36. Yegor Ligachev in interview with VID television company, 7 September 1993.

37. Author's interview with then KGB Chairman Vadim Bakatin, March 1992.

38. See note 35.

39. Galina Starovoitova in film by Yevgenia Albats and Tatyana Mitkovaya, *Strana pod kolpakom* [A Country Under a Bell Jar], 1992. Interview conducted in April 1992. Broadcast August 21, 1992, over WDR in Germany.

40. Speech by Sergei Kovalyov at the first international conference "KGB: Yesterday, Today, and Tomorrow," 19 February 1993. Author's tape.

41. Author's interview with Konstantin Borovoy, President of the Russian Commodities and Raw Materials Exchange, August 1993.

42. I was a Nieman Fellow at Harvard University in 1993 and returned to Russia in July 1993.

43. Author's information from a confidential source.

44. Author's information from anonymous source close to President Yeltsin.

45. Information obtained by the author from the Ministry of Security's Center for Public Liaison, August 1993.

46. V. Mirzoyanov, L. Fyodorov, *Moskovskiye novosti*, 20 September 1992.

47. Here and following, author's conversation with V. Mirzoyanov and L. Fyodorov, February 1993.

48. *Sovershenno Sekretno*, September 1991.

49. *Materialy rassledovaniya parlamentskoi komissii Rossii* [Materials from Investigation by Russian Parliamentary Commission]. See also: S. Pluzhnikov, S. Sokolov, K. Bayalinov, *"Zolotoy sovetnik Prezidenta"* [Golden Advisor of the President], *Komsomolskaya pravda*, 4 February 1993.

50. Excerpt from copy of original, author's archive.

51. See note 49. See also Alexander Fyodorov, *"Brilliantovyye zvyozdy 'siabeko' "* [The Brilliant Stars of Siabeko], *Moskovskiye novosti*, no. 35, 29 August 1993.

52. The 50-odd companies in my list include 9 in Malta, 8 in Portugal, 6 in Italy, 5 in Greece, 4 in Cyprus, engaged in a wide variety of activities, from oil sales to publishing. Of the 3 American firms, 2 appear to be closely

connected to the U.S. Communist Party. Top European detective agencies' efforts to locate the lost Communist Party finds have thus far proved fruitless.

53. See note 51.
54. *Den*, 21–22 February 1993.
55. *Komsomolskaya pravda*, 14 April 1993.
56. Yaroslav Golovanov, *"Mech i molot"* [The Sword and the Hammer], *Vek*, nos. 2, 3, 5, 10, 12, 17 in 1992; nos. 12, 15 in 1993.
57. Ibid.
58. Analytical report by (Ret.) KGB Col. Vladimir Rubanov, former head of the KGB's Analytical Directorate, to the country's leadership, December 1991. Author's archive.
59. See note 56.
60. Ibid.
61. *Komsomolskaya pravda*, 28 August 1993, p. 2.
62. From a speech by Gen. Oleg Kalugin at the conference *"KGB: Vchera, Segodnya, Zavtra"* [KGB: Yesterday, Today and Tomorrow], 19 February 1993.
63. Author's interview with KGB Lt. Col. A. Kichikhin, October 1991.
64. Author's interview with KGB Lt. Gen. V. Ivanenko, October 1991.
65. *Komsomolskaya pravda*, 19 November 1991.
66. *Argumenty i fakty*, no. 47, 1991.
67. Author's interview with the Ukrainian parliament member Genrikh Altunyan, February 1993.
68. Ibid.
69. Arseny Roginskiy, Nikita Okhotin, members of the Government commission on archives *"Archivi KGB: god posle putscha"* [KGB archives: a year after a coup (1991)], manuscript copy, author's archive.
70. KGB Col. Peter Groza, former head of the KGB Research Institute on Security. In the collection: "State security and democracy", no. 3, May 1993, published by Glasnost Foundation.
71. *Argumenty i fakty*, no. 36, 1993.
72. *Pravda*, 16 June 1992.
73. From a well-informed anonymous source.
74. *Argumenti i fakty*, no. 36, 1993.
75. Author's interview with (Ret.) KGB Col. Vladimir Rubanov, 6 October 1993.
76. Special issue of *Komsomolskaya pravda*, 5 October 1993.
77. Vladimir Zhirinovsky, *Posledniy brosok na yug* [The Last Push to the South] (Moscow: TOO Pisatel, 1993), pp. 142–143.
78. Decree of President Boris Yeltsin, 21 December 1993, cited from copy of original.

79. Yevgenia Albats, *"Lubyanka: Budyet li etomu konets?"* [Lubyanka: Will There Ever Be an End?], *Izvestia*, 3, 4, 6 December 1993.
80. Decree of President Boris Yeltsin, no. 19, 5 January 1994.
81. Author's interview of KGB Lt. Gen. Nikolai Golushko, 4 February 1994.
82. Author's interview of the director of the Central Archives for Contemporary Documentation, Nikolai Shuster, March 1994.

Index

	Первая категория	Вторая категория	ВСЕГО
1. Азербайджанская ССР	1500	3750	5250
2. Армянская ССР	500	1000	1500
3. Белорусская ССР	2000	10000	12000
4. Грузинская ССР	2000	3000	5000
5. Киргизская ССР	250	500	750
6. Таджикская ССР	500	1300	1800
7. Туркменская ССР	500	1500	2000
8. Узбекская ССР	750	4000	4750
9. Башкирская АССР	500	1500	2000
10. Бурято-Монгольская АССР	350	1500	1850
11. Дагестанская АССР	500	2500	3000
12. Карельская АССР	300	700	1000
13. Кабардино-Балкарская АССР	300	700	1000
14. Крымская АССР	300	1200	1500
15. Коми АССР	100	300	400
16. Калмыцкая АССР	100	300	400
17. Марийская АССР	300	1500	1800
18. Мордовская АССР	300	1500	1800
19. Немцев Поволжья АССР	200	700	900
20. Северо-Осетинская АССР	200	500	700
21. Татарская АССР	500	1500	2000
22. Удмурдская АССР	200	500	700
23. Чечено-Ингушская АССР	500	1500	2000
24. Чувашская АССР	300	1500	1800